Bill Hefley and Wendy Murphy (Eds.)

Service Science, Management and Engineering
Education for the 21st Century

Service Science: Research and Innovations in the Service Economy

Series Editors

IT Services Qualification Center (ITSqc)
Carnegie Mellon University
5000 Forbes Avenue
Pittsburgh, PA 15213 USA
hefley@cmu.edu

Wendy Murphy
IBM c/o
1954 Rocky Cove Lane
Denton, NC 27239
wendym@us.ibm.com

Selected titles from this series:

Bill Hefley and Wendy Murphy
Service Science, Management, and Engineering Education for the 21ˢᵗ Century,
2008
ISBN 978-0-387-76577-8

For a complete listing of books in this series, go to http://www.springer.com

Bill Hefley
Wendy Murphy
(Eds.)

Service Science, Management and Engineering

Education for the 21st Century

Springer

Bill Hefley
IT Services Qualification Center (ITSqc)
Carnegie Mellon University
5000 Forbes Ave
Pittsburgh, PA 15213 USA
hefley@cmu.edu

Wendy Murphy
IBM c/o
1954 Rocky Cove Lane
Denton, NC 27239 USA
wendym@us.ibm.com

Series Editors:

Bill Hefley
IT Services Qualification Center (ITSqc)
Carnegie Mellon University
5000 Forbes Ave
Pittsburgh, PA 15213 USA
hefley@cmu.edu

Wendy Murphy
IBM c/o
1954 Rocky Cove Lane
Denton, NC 27239 USA
wendym@us.ibm.com

ISBN-13: 978-0-387-76577-8   e-ISBN-13: 978-0-387-76578-5

Library of Congress Control Number: 2007938346

Printed on acid-free paper.

9 8 7 6 5 4 3 2 1

springer.com

SSME RESEARCH

CONCLUSION

Preface

If you look at IBM's business last year, services revenues were roughly over 50%, while systems (hardware) and software revenues were around 25% and 20% respectively. But services constituted around one-third of the company's profit, for a very simple reason. Systems and software products leverage technology assets and apply engineering principles to improve quality, scale-up capacity, and achieve higher productivity and profit margins. Services, on the other hand, have historically been significantly more labor-based, less prone to economies of scale, subject to higher quality variations, and generally less productive and profitable.

The picture is similar across most businesses around the world. Services are an increasing portion of their revenues, but they are more labor-intensive than their product-based revenues and therefore not as profitable.

Another way to appreciate the increased importance of services is to look at the three main sectors into which economies are usually grouped - the service, industrial and agriculture sectors. The service sector already accounts for more than 75% of the labor force in the US and UK, with the industrial sector being around 20% and agriculture in low single digits. In other developed countries like Japan, Germany and France, services are more than two thirds of the labor force, and in Brazil, Russia and South Korea they are well over fifty percent. While huge progress has been made in the productivity of the industrial and agricultural sectors, the service sector has lagged far behind.

A few years ago we started a major initiative across IBM's technical community to better understand the nature of services, with particular focus on how to improve their productivity at IBM and in our clients' businesses around the world. We wanted to bring to bear on services the kinds of engineering, scientific and management disciplines that have been so successful in systems and software in the IT industry, as well as in the industrial and agricultural sectors of the economy. We therefore gave our initiative the somewhat unwieldy though academically inclusive name of Services Sciences, Management and Engineering, or SSME. Over time we decide to use the term Services Sciences.

What are services – anyway? It is very interesting that while services are increasingly important to so many companies as well as the dominant sector of the economy, its nature is not well understood. A while back The Economist defined a service as anything sold in trade that cannot be dropped on your foot[1].

Beyond something that you cannot drop on your foot, we can all agree that services is all about people and organizations performing tasks for each other, such as providing medical treatment, selling products and solutions and making sure customers are satisfied. As we

---

1 Lane, P. World Trade Survey: The wired trade organization. *The Economist, v 349*, Issue 8088, pg. S16, October 3, 1998.

continue to standardize and automate back-office operations, it is not surprising that the front-office, market-facing activities involving people, - i.e., services – have become the largest and fastest growing components of any business, not just businesses in the service sector, but also those in the industrial and agricultural sectors. Every business has markets and deals with people as employees, customers and partners. Thus, to a greater of lesser degree, every business is in services.

There is a very serious economic imperative for addressing the productivity of services. It is practically impossible to improve the profit margins of a business or the standard of living of a country or region without significantly improving the productivity of services. But beyond the economic imperative, why do we think that the time is ripe to establish the new discipline of Services Sciences? Let's address this question by looking at the evolution of information technology (IT) over the last forty years or so.

At first, IT was primarily applied to automate back office, highly repetitive and fairly standardized tasks, such as financial transactions, payroll, and inventory management. The *machine-like* nature of these tasks made it possible to develop *data processing* applications that no longer required a human in the loop unless there was a problem.

As time went on, IT was increasingly applied to interactive applications that enabled people to do for themselves tasks that previously required human assistance. For example, the advent of ATMs in the '70s, allowed people to get money on their own without having to go to the bank and queue up in front of a teller. Word processing applications in the 1980s enabled people to type or at least edit their own documents without requiring the services of a professional secretary.

Customer self-service was arguably the commercial killer-app of the Web in the '90s. It seemed almost magical how easy it was to now do for yourself so many activities that previously required a trip to a store or office, or at least a phone call during office hours. All of a sudden you could track the status of your packages, access tax information, check the weather of any city in the world or buy a book with nothing more than a browser and an Internet connection.

Beyond back-office automation, personal productivity and customer self-service, I believe that recent advances in IT are now enabling us to apply technology to significantly improve the productivity of services, and is thus ushering us into the next major phase in the evolution of work.

Many services essentially involve people interacting with each other - e.g., health care providers and patients, teachers and students, financial advisors and clients. It has been very difficult to apply IT to these activities because the human interactions are an essential part of the work, and the unstructured, highly variable nature of these interactions defies automation, no matter how powerful the computers are.

But the emergence of social networks, Web-based collaborative platforms, wireless communications, mobile devices and Internet-enabled sensors of all sorts over the last few years has enabled us to apply IT to these people-oriented social systems. The aim is not to get people out of the loop, but to make the overall service experience more productive and of higher quality – that is, more satisfying for both clients and providers.

This first volume in the book series *Service Science: Research and Innovations in the Service Economy* is a compilation of position papers collected for IBM's 2006 conference "Service Science, Management, and Engineering – Education for the 21st Century". The conference was organized to collect and share current thinking about Service Science, and to promote the advancement and development of the discipline. You will find this text organized around three areas of thought: creation of a new discipline, status of educational offerings and services research planned or in progress.

Irving Wladawsky-Berger
Vice President, Technology and Strategy
IBM
September 2007

Executive Summary

Service Science, Management, and Engineering (SSME) has come a long way in a short time. Just three years ago, no one had heard of SSME. And now here is a volume that collects papers prepared for an SSME conference held at the IBM Palisades Conference Center in October, 2006, which contains more than 55 papers from 56 institutions and 14 countries aiming to define the discipline, describe the education, and discuss the research relevant to SSME. How did we get here?

We first heard the term *service science* from Professor Henry Chesbrough of UC Berkeley in early 2004 [3, 4]. He reminded us that IBM had been instrumental in helping to establish the field of computer science sixty years earlier, when IBM found its business dependent on computers after World War II [1]. Chesbrough suggested now IBM ought to pay the same kind of scientific attention to our service business (see also [2]). In 2004, three public events began the journey. First in April, IBM Research held the Almaden Institute in San Jose, California, on "Work in the Era of the Global Extensible Enterprise" where Chesbrough conducted a breakout session to discuss the idea of creating a service science with some of the assembled academics.[1] Most were skeptical. Second in May, IBM Research held a conference on the "Architecture of On Demand Business" in Yorktown Heights, New York, where the head of IBM Research, Paul Horn, and the head of IBM Business Consulting Services, Ginni Rometty, opened the conference by describing the need for a science of service. This meeting resulted in a white paper on the topic ([11]; see also [10]). Third in November, IBM Research held a conference on "Service Innovations for the 21st Century" in San Jose, California, where specific research and educational agendas for service innovation were discussed by academics from many related areas.[2] Eventually, the scope of service science came to include engineering discipline and management discipline as well, and we started referring to the idea broadly as SSME.[3]

Despite all this talk of a new science of service, there were already deep academic literatures on specific aspects of service – angling in on it from disciplines such as marketing, operations, management, engineering, and computing, among others. For instance, since even before Shostack's seminal paper on service marketing [14], there had been much thinking, research, and teaching on service from a marketing perspective (see [7] for a review). There is also a long tradition of focusing on service in the operations and management areas, for instance, connecting operational factors that affect quality to customer loyalty and service orientation [8]. More recently, there has been some focus on service engineering from the industrial engineering perspective [17], and there has been some focus on service computing from the computer science perspective [13]. And of course, there is a much longer tradition of service thinking in economics as well (see [5]). We will not review any

---

1   http://www.almaden.ibm.com/institute/2004
2   http://www.almaden.ibm.com/asr/events/serviceinnovation
3   http://www.ibm.com/university/ssme

of this – or other disciplinary work on service – here. The point is that efforts in each area proceeded independently (for the most part).

At IBM, we saw the need for new skills and for on-going innovation in our service businesses. And we didn't see the issues breaking along standard disciplinary lines. Knowledge-intensive service activities depend critically on people working together (organizations) and with technology (tools) to create value, and so service innovation means creating efficient, effective, and sustainable configurations of people and technology that create value both *for* clients (back stage activities) and *with* clients (front stage activities). One can invest to improve service activities by improving the people through increased education or through organizational or incentive changes. One can invest to improve service activities by improving the technology that workers and customers use or that provides back stage service activities, making systems faster or adding more features. One can invest to improve service activities by enhancing the value propositions between clients, providers, partners, and employees, changing the risk-reward profile to encourage better relationships and more long-term value However, no one can achieve continuous and sustainable improvements – or effective and lasting innovation – without doing all of these. Recently, we've come to view *service systems* – value-co-creation configurations of people, technology, and organizations connected internally and externally by value propositions and shared information – as the basic unit of analysis for understanding knowledge-intensive service activities [15]. We have to break down disciplinary barriers to create an integrated understanding of service systems and service innovation.

Recognizing the growth of knowledge-intensive service activities in national economies and corporate revenues, SSME began as a call to action for industry, academics, and governments to focus squarely on service system innovation. For instance, following the idea that service systems depend on people, technology, and business value, it seemed to us that service education has to be interdisciplinary education [12], combining aspects of social and cognitive science, technology and engineering, and business and management. An effective service innovation professional easily speaks the languages of organization, technology, and business value together. A number of others began to take SSME's call to action seriously and have begun to describe opportunities for cross-disciplinary research and education in service (e.g., [6, 9, 16]). The IT service industry has begun to take it seriously too, with the formation of the Service Research and Innovation Initiative, an industry and academic consortium aimed at raising the profile of service research.[4] A growing number of nations have also established programs to study and advance service system innovation, or have approved legislation that specifically calls out the emerging study of service science.[5]

---

4   http://www.thesrii.org/
5   See the America Competes Act, US HR 2272, Section 1106.

In the end, we're all just students of service. Service systems are evolving rapidly driven by information technology advances, new business models, globalization, and demographic trends. We can point to some issues and some problems, and we can help sound the call to action. But answers and a solid scientific foundation will take time to emerge. We think this volume marks another important step along the way toward understanding service systems and service innovation. So SSME has come a long way in a short time, but it's only just begun. What will it be like in twenty years? Let's find out!

Jim Spohrer and Paul Maglio
IBM Almaden Research Center

References

[1]   Aspray, W., B. O. Williams. 1994. Arming American scientists: NSF and the provision of scientific computing facilities for universities, 1950-1973. *IEEE Annals of the History of Computing, 16* (4), 60-74.

[2]   Baba, M. L. (2006). Industry-university relationships and the context of intellectual property dynamics: The case of IBM. In F. Yammarin & F. Dansereau (Eds.), *Multi-level Issues in Social Systems.* New York, NY: Elsevier.

[3]   Chesbrough, H. (2004). A failing grade for the innovation academy. *Financial Times,* Sept 4, 2004.

[4]   Chesbrough, H. (2005). Toward a science of services. *Harvard Business Review, 83,* 16-17.

[5]   Delaunay, J. & Gadrey, J. (1992). *Services in economic thought.* Boston: Kluwer.

[6]   Dietrich, B. & Harrison, T. (2006). Serving the services: The emerging science of service management opens opportunities for operations research and management science. *ORMS Today,* June 2006.

[7]   Fisk, R. P., Brown, S. W., & Bitner, M. (1993). Tracking the evolution of the services marketing literature. *Journal of Retailing, 69,* 61 – 103.

[8]   Heskett, J. L., Jones, T. O., Loveman, G. W. , Sasser, W. E. J., & Schlesinger, L. A. (1994). Putting the Service-Profit Chain to Work. *Harvard Business Review, 72*(2), 164-174.

[9]   Hidaka, K. (2006). Trends in services sciences in Japan and abroad. *Science and Technology Trends, Quarterly Review, 19,* 35 – 47.

[10] Horn, P. (2006). The new discipline of services science. *Business Week,* Jan 21, 2006.

[11] IBM Research, (2004). Services Sciences: A new academic discipline? Report on the Architecture of On Demand Business Summit, Yorktown Heights, NY. Available at http://www.almaden.ibm.com/asr/SSME/facsummit.pdf

[12] Maglio, P. P., Srinivasan, S., Kreulen, J. T., & Spohrer, J., (2006). Service Systems, Service Scientists, SSME, and Innovation. *Communications of the ACM, 49*(7), 81-85.

[13] Papazoglu M. (2003). Service-oriented computing: Concepts, characteristics and directions. In *Proceedings of the Fourth International Conference on Web Information Systems Engineering.*

[14] Shostack, G. L. (1977). Breaking free from product marketing. *Journal of Marketing, 41,* 73 – 80.

[15] Spohrer, J., Maglio, P. P., Bailey, J., & Gruhl, D. (2007). Steps toward a science of service systems. *Computer, 40,* 71-77.

[16] Spohrer, J. & Riecken, D. (2006). Special Issue on Services Science, *Communications of the ACM, 49*(7).

[17] Tien, J. M. & Berg, D. (2003). A case for service systems engineering. *Journal of Systems Science and Systems Engineering, 12,* 13 – 38.

Conference Summary: A View from Palisades

Wendy Murphy, Cheryl A. Kieliszewski, Paul Maglio, Bill Hefley, Nirmal Pal, and Ioannis Viniotis

Overview

The IBM conference on Service Science, Management, and Engineering – Education for the 21st Century was announced in April 2006. Through email and a website, we invited interested academics and others to submit position papers.

With IBM Global Services being the largest IT services organization in the world, IBM has taken the lead in recognizing that college graduates need new skills to address business and technical issues in a service business environment. Because services depend critically on people working together and with technology to provide value for others, these new skills include the ability to integrate across traditional disciplinary areas to obtain globally effective solutions (rather than merely locally effective solutions). Service Science, Management and Engineering (SSME)[1] is one approach to integrating a variety of disciplines, including areas in engineering, social sciences and management, to properly focus education and research on services.

Many universities around the world are developing new services-oriented courses and curricula; others are expanding their existing focus on services. But a significant effort is still needed to develop a truly cross-disciplinary approach to SSME. This conference was planned in order to share information and learn about the current status of SSME and to foster its advancement and development.

The conference goals were to:

— Demonstrate substantive results in the formation of multi-disciplinary Services Sciences, Management and Engineering by presenting ways SSME has been introduced into curricula to date and learning about services research underway or planned.

— Outline a roadmap for establishing SSME as a legitimate discipline within the academic community by identifying how practitioners can join with faculty and administrators to focus efforts on cross-functional, service-oriented courses and research, recommended actions for academia and governments, and roadblocks and challenges.

Interested faculty from around the world were invited to submit position papers related to any aspect of SSME, such as:

---

1   http://www.research.ibm.com/ssme/

— How do science, management and engineering play in services? Where, why and how are they needed?

— What is the current state of SSME either globally or at your institution?

— How do you see SSME evolving? What would you like SSME to be?

— What are your main services research questions and how do you address them?

— What SSME courses have you created or do you plan to create?

— What are your top three topics or concerns related to SSME?

— What are your collaborations around services research and education?

— What role might industry play in developing SSME at your institution?

— What is the role of government in developing SSME?

— How do you envision society benefiting from the development of interdisciplinary SSME?

From October 5 through 7, 2006, two-hundred and fifty-four people, representing 21 countries and many areas of government, industry, and academia, gathered at the IBM Palisades Conference Center in New York to discuss Service Science, Management, and Engineering (SSME). Sponsored by IBM Research, IBM University Relations, and IBM Government Programs, the conference aimed to demonstrate results in the formation of multi-disciplinary SSME, including ways SSME has been introduced into curricula, services research that is underway or is planned, and also to outline a roadmap for establishing SSME as its own discipline, including how practitioners can join with faculty and administrators to focus efforts on cross-functional, service-oriented courses and research, and recommended actions for academia and governments. In addition to presenters, the audience included leadership outside academia and IBM, including representation from foundation agencies, government agencies, agencies for advanced studies and industries.

A welcome reception was held the evening of October 5 with an opening talk by Gina Poole, IBM Vice President, Innovation and IBM University Relations.

On the morning of October 6, the meeting was kicked off by Robert Morris, IBM Vice President, Services Research, who set the context and expectations for the two days. The keynote address by Nick Donofrio, IBM Executive Vice President, Innovation and Technology, focused on the need for a national post-secondary educational strategy and activities to create it. There were talks from multiple university representatives and a government panel session that addressed new funding initiatives. Carl Schramm, President and CEO, Kauffman Foundation,[2] gave an address on the changing economy and new roles of individuals, government, industry, and education. He highlighted many themes in his recent books [1,5]. Val Rahmani, IBM General Manager, Infrastructure Management Services, shared her views on the practical application of service science. Irving Wladawsky-Berger, IBM Vice President, Technical Strategy and Innovation, provided a wrap-up for the day, focusing on the relation between service systems and complex engineering systems.[3] The day ended with a poster reception that further highlighted service education and research at more than 30 universities world-wide.

The second day's opening talk was given by Debra Stewart, President, Council of Graduate Schools,[4] on the mobilization of training and research around compelling areas that will drive the economy of the future. The day included additional talks from university representatives. A business partner panel that discussed the need for experiential learning, acquisition of skill, and the need for implementation and application of services thinking in the marketplace completed the sessions.

The conference closed with a summary given by Stuart Feldman, (former) IBM Vice President, Computer Science Research, who articulated the need for pi-shaped people — not just T-shaped people — that is, those with depth in multiple areas along with breadth in even more areas.

Insights and Outcomes

There seemed to be much excitement at the meeting, perhaps generated because, for the first time, the study and understanding of service had come together as unique, distinguishable topic. Of course, not everyone agreed on how to approach the topic, but a common language is starting to develop, drawing government, industry, and education together and generating new questions, intellectual excitement, and ultimately economic value.

A community is coming together with at least five clusters of intellectual impetus.

1. operations research / mathematics / optimization,

2. industrial engineering / systems engineering,

3. computer science / information technology / information management,

4. process formalization / physics / complexity, and

5. business / organizational sciences / social sciences.

2   http://www.kauffman.org/
3   http://irvingwb.typepad.com/blog/2006/10/peopleoriented_.html
4   http://www.cgsnet.org/

As Stu Feldman stated, "anything really exciting will happen with a crossing at the clusters."

Many university faculty demonstrated substantive results in the formation of multidisciplinary Service Science, Management and Engineering initiatives. They presented ways SSME has been introduced into curricula to date and about services research underway or planned. Several outlined suggested steps for establishing SSME as a legitimate discipline within the academic community. A few identified how practitioners can join with faculty and administrators to focus efforts on cross-functional, service-oriented courses and research. Others identified recommended actions for academia and governments.

At a Tipping Point

Presentations ranged from detailed descriptions of service program development and implementation to granting and funding to economic impact and imperatives. Some key factors driving the need for service science and education that we identified include:

— Innovation is a culture, not a department

  — Service innovation is a test of leadership for the academy, government, and industry.

  — Need for service innovation because services are not seen as being innovative; foreseen imperatives include:

    — Integration of technological and social research domains

    — Education and training of college graduates

    — Understanding how service innovation is captured, as intellectual property or through other avenues?

— Need for government and institutional advocacy and support as catalyst.

— The global economy is at a tipping point.

  — Technological advances that fuel the tipping point include network ubiquity and a new state of openness, from sharing of personal information to sharing of technological and transactional specifications.

  — Business design advances through horizontally-integrated operations that allow for dynamic transformation with limited disruption to the organization.

  — A new view of revenue expansion and customer equity as key corporate metrics.

— Continued need for domain experts and new demand for people who have focused knowledge in one or two domains and spectral knowledge about related domains. Demand for people skilled at fusing their technical competency with industry-specific knowledge and business-process expertise.

— Evolution of new institutional forms. A restructuring of the economic landscape through the creation and propagation of entrepreneurial capitalism. Effects have been struggles in corporate restructuring and new institutional forms such as venture capitalism, foundations and research institutions.

— The state of services curriculum and research, demonstrated through a surge of services programs at the masters level and samples of program development and evolution.

— Need for an integrated research program that generates a more coherent and standard definition and language around services and builds on a sample of research that is underway; overcoming the tendency for productivity- and efficiency-focused work.

— Need for trained and hirable people

    — There is an urgent need for graduate education in service.

    — Service has not been viewed as a business function, but instead as a personal matter or skill. Service has not been documented, so innovation is difficult.

Themes

We also identified several themes that cut across many presentations and hallway discussions.

— Aspects of service
Social interaction and relationship management are at the core of service. We need increased attention to the role and contribution of social sciences to fuel service innovation. The commonly understood definition of SSME is too narrowly focused. There is need for public funding of social science research. For example, in the United States, there is substantial NSF funding of basic sciences like physics, biology and engineering, but far less not in psychology, sociology, design, and business.

There is recognition that traditional management and engineering frameworks have problems defining service and service management. Most systems in services are still too rigid; there is a need to identify and examine the exceptions or variability in service systems to determine if they should become the rule and feedback into the system design. Optimizing the system in one way will not work.

We need to use different levels of examination in our research. For example: the microscopic level and operation level. A microscopic level examination could be to determine how service networks are the same / different from other networks. How are they formed and how can we predict their formation? And, is this connected to the innovation process? Can the innovation spaces then be characterized? An operation level examination could be to determine the options to cost cutting in business models to understand how to generate revenue and profit from a service.

— Multidisciplinarity
  The interdisciplinary nature of service science is essential, but not necessarily a random activity. How will accountability and credibility across disciplines be created and sustained? There is a need for new expertise that can bridge among science, engineering, social science, management, and ethics.

— Challenges for higher education

  — Changing the structure of higher education: silos and tenure process. The common path for recognition is to gain tenure within a single discipline. Now, where do we publish, how can we reach an appropriate audience? There may be interdisciplinary research and publication problems or issues with the research being accepted and published considering most publications focus on depth, not breadth today. The old reward and incentive, funding, and resource structures need to evolve or be replaced by new frameworks that support inter-disciplinary activities.

  — Migration of courses across all degree levels. The primary focus for SSME initiatives have been at the graduate level with most progress being made in master's level programs. How should service education be included across degree levels, particularly into undergraduate learning?

  — Teaching through experience and teaching around real problems. Some faculty have small companies so there is practical experience and cases for use of methods. However, this is not the norm at all universities. There needs to be an experimental component to learning to be able to process the content from the curricula allowing people to have experiences that solidify their abilities to network, distilling insights, and extrapolate to identify value. The notions of creating spaces to think and implementation of the journeyman model of learning were recommended.

— Acceleration factors for higher education
  Already there are established centers of study and development of new programs.

The redefinition of the American university has begun. Industry is working with universities to meet their unmet needs. Service research and application are beginning to progress in parallel.

Significant Progress in a Short Time

There is a tendency to take what you have and rework it. Undoubtedly much of the focus of SSME has been the result of reworking or re-labeling. What follows are some more innovative approaches and challenges for service education and research.

— Designing a discipline and designing a curriculum, where design of a discipline is the creation of a principled model of a coherent body of research and practice, and design of a curriculum is the creation of a program of study leading to a degree or certificate.

— Key issues need to be addressed during these design processes, including

  — Identifying the key issues (for a discipline) and key topics (for a curriculum) that need to be addressed and start from there.

  — Determining the goals; then determining what must be included to support the program. It cannot be taken for granted that you can start with what you already have.

  — Focus on being right to market, not necessarily first to market.

— Employ a back-to-the-basics research paradigm to create simple useful models of the complex realities of service. Note that the creation of simple will probably require deep analysis to yield scientifically-based principles.

— Creating competency models

  — Cross-industry for a foundation in domains such as business processes, information engineering, information architecture and technologies.

  — Industry-specific for a foundation in project work, case study, and knowledge of industry-specific models.

  — Development of new kinds of interactional expertise that combines science, engineering, social science, management and ethics towards evolution and agreement on a language that reflect core concepts.

  — Leading to a commons of services.

There needs to be consideration for the long cycle of research, the short cycle of practice, and the intersection at dissemination. We should consider reinventing part of our past to examine the applicability of current models to what we think is a new problem. For example, review history of wholesaling to understand how it spread around the world and its evolution and impact on current thinking. Or, the study of cluster evolution to determine the stickiness of service and service innovation through socio-geographical examination on a global scale.

Your Turn

Many attendees took away action plans. Some examples are

— Moving forward with SSME-related curriculum development, program planning and implementation.

— Writing grant proposals

— Collaborating with others on material development for education in services

— Starting special SSME interest groups

— Meeting with others to discuss new electives for undergraduate and graduate students

— Forming a group of companies, academics and national economic development agencies to establish an SSME development center

This Book

This book captures many of the results of this vibrant meeting. As interest in service science increases, several conference presentations have already been presented or published elsewhere and are not included in this volume [2, 3, 4, 6]. The papers in this book are presented in groupings around the development and maturation of the SSME discipline, SSME educational offerings and curriculum advances, and SSME research activities. These groupings are just a way of organizing this content, as many papers could easily be classified in multiple categories; for example, as research informs education.

Development and maturation of the SSME discipline is the focus of the first set of papers in this volume. These papers address developing a common understanding of SSME or what constitutes SSME as a discipline. Several of these directly show how various existing disciplines, as divergent as operations research and design, can contribute to service science. Several papers address the need and approaches for maturing the SSME discipline.

SSME educational activities and curriculum advances are the topics of the second section of this volume. Existing courses and curricula, especially as service marketing courses and programs, particularly at the undergraduate level, have been around for many years. These have been offered mainly by business or management schools; sample courses include topics in customer service, call centers, service quality, and organizational integration. Some universities have long-established research centers that aim to enhance and add to knowledge of service marketing and related areas. Today, service marketing courses and programs are appearing at the master's level, along with related courses and programs in service management and service engineering. Almost all are designed as multidisciplinary, incorporating faculty and content from management, business, engineering, and computer science, among other fields. Some expand existing programs, for instance, programs in production and operations management may begin to incorporate both goods and services as two aspects of the production and operations process. Others bring in cognitive science, economics, or innovation and entrepreneurship in a multidisciplinary approach to creating courses for service science. In any event, the need for graduate level education in services is urgent, and many universities are either extending existing programs into services, or designing brand new multidisciplinary programs from scratch.

SSME research activities are the third focus of this volume. Though diverse, most existing research in service (in the sample of papers in this volume) relies on established methods, such as queuing theory, graphs, network flow, Petri nets, Markov processes, and event simulations, and typically focuses narrowly on increasing productivity and efficiency. Most future research focuses on specific problems rather than on high-level, grand challenges. Some suggest that new methods are needed to study service. Some outline research questions and approaches, and others aim create models and tools. Many discuss the need to broaden service engineering research to include management and social sciences. The consensus is that integrated research will improve the utility of any future results.

In summary, we see clear progress toward broad and deep education and research focused on service. Many education and research programs already exist, but have most often incorporated a single perspective, such as marketing or management. Yet, now we see a shift, as many aim to incorporate a variety of perspectives at once, including several of management, business, social science, computer science, and engineering. There is little doubt of the need for an interdisciplinary study of service and that many are seeing this need and are taking up the charge.

References

[1]   Baumol, W. J., Lithan, R. E., & Schramm, C. J. *Good Capitalism, Bad Capitalism, and the Economics of Growth and Prosperity*. New Haven: Yale University Press, 2007.
[2]   Rafiq Dossani and Martin Kenney. The Next Wave of Globalization: Relocating Service Provision to India. *World Development*, Vol. 35, No. 5, pp. 772-791, 2007.

[3]   Marjatta Maula. Managerial and Research Perspective on Knowledge-Intensive Services. Paper presented at *The European Conference on Knowledge Management (ECKM)*, Barcelona, 6-7 September 2007.

[4]   Javier Reynoso. The Evolution Of Services Management In Latin America: Building A New Academic Field. In Christopher Lovelock (ed.). *Services Marketing, , 4th edition*, 2001, Prentice Hall, USA.

[5]   Carl J. Schramm, *The Entrepreneurial Imperative: How America's Economic Miracle Will Reshape the World (and change your life)*. New York: Collins, 2006.

[6]   James M. Tien and Daniel Berg. On Services Research and Education. *J. Systems Science and Systems Engineering*, Vol.15, No.3, pp. 257-283, September 2006.

SSME DISCIPLINE

Legitimizing SSME in Academia: Critical Considerations and Essential Actions

Jane Siegel, Ph.D.
Director, IT Services Qualification Center
Carnegie Mellon University
Pittsburgh, PA 15213, USA
jals@cs.cmu.edu
+(412) 268-6764

Bill Hefley, Ph.D.
Associate Teaching Professor
Institute for Software Research and
IT Services Qualification Center
Carnegie Mellon University
Pittsburgh, PA 15213, USA
hefley@cmu.edu
+(412) 268-4576

Shelley Evenson
Associate Professor
School of Design
Carnegie Mellon University
Pittsburgh, PA 15213, USA
evenson@cmu.edu
+(412) 268-4638

Sandra Slaughter, Ph.D.
Professor of IT Management and Costley Chair
Georgia Institute of Technology
Atlanta, GA 30309, USA
sandra.slaughter@mgt.gatech.edu
+(404) 385-3115

ABSTRACT

Legitimizing Services Sciences, Management, and Engineering (SSME) in the global academic community necessitates delineation of the critical considerations and professional actions associated with spawning any new field. For Services Science, the broad set of academic disciplines that may be involved are identified in this paper. A set of seven major actions needed to bring clarity and credibility to those engaged in Services Science are described along with examples from Information Systems, Design, and Strategic Services Management and Sourcing. Academics who are pioneering in this highly inter-disciplinary field may use this paper to plan a course of action that will rapidly advance Services Science both within their specific disciplines and in building the global Services Science academic base.

Introduction

SSME is gaining visibility and attracting the attention of leading university researchers, teaching faculty, industry and government officials. Several top U.S. universities are formulating and offering professional Masters-level concentrations or degree programs containing courses related to this field [1]. The authors start with the assumption that the field of Services Science should be fostered and accepted as a scientific discipline. There are previous experiences, e.g., the evolution of Computer Science or Human-Computer Interaction that help to inform the approach needed to realize the goal of legitimizing SSME. This paper builds upon past experience and begins with an enumeration of several major challenges facing the SSME community working to legitimize this field. Critical considerations include:

1. defining and agreeing on the set of academic disciplines to be represented/associated with SSME curriculum and research;

2. establishing research agendas and funding sources to advance both theoretical and empirical SSME research;

3. investing in development, delivery, and evaluation of courses and degree programs from undergraduate through Ph.D.-levels to foster rapid growth of competent and creative professionals who can contribute to SSME efforts in both Academe and industry;

4. developing publication opportunities in reputable, juried journals and books, both within related disciplines and in newer SSME-focused publications;

5. identifying and establishing Special Interest Groups (SIGs), Chapters, or other appropriate entities in key professional societies, e.g., ACM and IEEE;

6. creating endowed chairs in SSME to attract the best and brightest academic talent and to provide visibility and stature for faculty working in this field within and across universities throughout the world; and

7. growing this field so that in the long-term a globally recognized profession of "Services Scientists and Engineers" is established.

Each of the critical considerations and needed actions is delineated below.

Defining Fields in SSME

SSME may include a large set of existing disciplines as well as spawning new areas of academic inquiry and educational focus. Current SSME programs generally involve:

1. Behavioral and Social Sciences, e.g., Anthropology, Economics, Marketing, Industrial and Organizational Psychology,

2. Computer Science and Engineering,

3. Design, e.g., Industrial and Service Design,

4. Information Systems,

5. Knowledge discovery/Data Mining,

6. Operations Research and Operations Management,

7. Security (of Information and Technology), and

8. Systems Engineering and Software Engineering.

More recent trans-disciplinary or inter-disciplinary fields are developing in support of the educational requirements for the Services sector. Several examples of these emerging fields are described in [2]. Carnegie Mellon has a very successful history of creating or contributing significantly to the growth of highly respected and accepted interdisciplinary professional fields including:

— Computation, Organizations, and Society,

— Electronic Business Technology,

— Engineering and Public Policy,

— Human-Computer Interaction,

— Information Networking,

— Information Security,

— Knowledge Discovery & Data Mining,

— Software Engineering, and

— Very Large Information Systems.

There is a leadership void that must be filled to bring qualified representatives of the disciplines noted above together with industry and government representatives to establish initial boundaries and define the academic disciplines that will be actively involved in legitimizing SSME.

In parallel with efforts to bound and define the disciplines associated with SSME, there is an urgent need to establish interdisciplinary research agendas to:

— Understand fundamental changes at the global, national, and enterprise levels [3],

— Measure the economic impact and growth of the Services sector,

— Determine the impact of the Services sector on individuals, organizations, communities,

— Foster innovation and societal advances to improve the quality of life, and

— Contribute to basic understanding of opportunities to leverage Information and Communication Technologies (ICT).

Establishing Research Programs

There are two key aspects to consider. First is building a research agenda that has broad industry and government support and second is developing the strategy and actions to secure significant, sustaining research support.

Several of the fields listed in the previous section are relevant to Services Science. Examples of research topics that may be addressed by faculty in these fields include:

— Applied Studies in International Management,

— Automation to support on-demand services delivery,

— Better understanding of stakeholder needs and issues,

— Impacts of globalization and standardization,

— Organizational learning and innovation (including research on effective teams),

— Learning from history,

— Privacy and Security,

— Process Management and Enablement,

— Process and Performance Modeling,

— Software as a Service,

— Service as Systems of Systems with emergent behavior, and

— Studies of Information Technology and Society

To launch significant research efforts on any of these or other key topics related to Services Science will require a significant multi-year funding commitment (5 to 10 years) from government, foundation, and industry sources. For Computer Science it was NSF funding that helped to truly launch rigorous research in that field. Other examples of significant funding to foster legitimate, academically based research programs have come from DARPA, NASA, NIH, and Foundations, e.g., Ford and Rockefeller. Given the importance of Services Science to the global economy, it would seem appropriate to approach not only NSF, but also major foundations, e.g. Gates as well as IT industry leaders to supply the resources needed to support the research agendas in this field.

Curriculum Development

The July 2006 *Communications of the ACM* issue about Services Science documented the state of many inter-disciplinary and innovative SSME curricular initiatives. At Carnegie Mellon, during the past year, we launched the first graduate-level IT service management program with a six course concentration in our Masters of Information Systems Management. Course topics cover Service Operations and Management, Capability and Process Improvement in Service Organizations, Sourcing Management, IT Program Management, Contracts, and Negotiations. The School of Design has developed a course and is currently considering an undergraduate track in service design. Work is underway to launch a Masters Degree in Service Management as shown in figure 1 below.

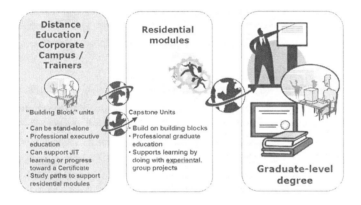

Fig. 1 Proposed Carnegie Mellon Masters Degree in Service Management

Development of the needed globally available curriculum to support all aspects of SSME is a huge undertaking for any one institution of higher education. Carnegie Mellon faculty recently proposed serving in a leadership role to foster collaborative efforts with global university, industry and government thought leaders to create graduate-level curriculum in Services Science [4]. Several first-tier universities need to join together to rapidly address this need.

Publication Opportunities

Perhaps the most critical factor in establishing a legitimate field in the academic world is the publication of knowledge gained through use of scientific methods in journals where submissions are peer reviewed. The range of publication venues for Services Science literature is extensive, but diffuse. Examples of relevant and reputable academic journals include: *Academy of Management Journal, Administrative Science Quarterly, Communications of ACM, Decision Sciences, Design Issues, European Journal of Information Systems, IBM Systems Journal, IEEE Transactions, Interactions, Information Research, Journal of Information*

Technology, Management Science, Manufacturing and Service Operations Management and *Sloan Management Review*.

The Services Science community needs to determine whether to found a new journal or establish a book series[1] to focus attention on results of rigorous SSME research and/or to target a set of well-established, highly reputed journals and publishers as venues for their work.

Professional Society Presence

Three options that need to be considered and pursued are: (1) whether to establish a special interest group (SIG) , chapter, or other clearly designated organization to foster professional dialogue and visibility; (2) which conference(s) or seminars to target for dissemination of research results or to encourage academic research outlets; and (3) how to create honors and awards programs to recognize outstanding academic achievements in the Services Science field.

There are numerous organizations with academic credibility where fields contributing to SSME already have conferences and award programs established. Examples include IEEE's International Conference on Service-Oriented Computing and Applications or the Annual Meeting of the Institute for Operations Research and Management Sciences (INFORMS). There also are some recently developed conferences, e.g., the Computer Human Interaction for the Management of Information Technology 2006, the International Conference on Service Oriented Computing 2006, Carnegie Mellon's service design conference[2] and the Art and Science of Service Conferences.

Awards and special recognition for accomplishments in fields that contribute to SSME may already exist, but there is nothing equivalent to the Turing award or other prestigious awards that would confer rapid credibility on university faculty engaged in SSME research.

An analysis of the relative advantages of creating an organizational identity, coupled with conferences, seminars, and an award program needs to be conducted. Based on the results of this analysis, academic leaders from the SSME fields need to develop plans and identify resources to support implementation of plans to attain global, professional visibility for SSME professionals.

---

1   This paper appears in the first volume in a new Springer book series on Service Science: Research and Innovations in the Service Economy, which has been founded since this paper was first written.
2   http://www.design.cmu.edu/emergence/index.htm

Endowments and Chairs

Almost as important as robust and rigorous research and publications based on that research is the attention and value that academic communities place on significant charitable contributions and endowments to support Chaired faculty positions in any given discipline. The establishment of these types of resources, designated for faculty in the SSME field, will enable these academicians to concentrate on and accelerate their educational and research efforts. Efforts to identify and attract potential industry contributors from the global IT and Services arena should be pursued actively by leaders of the SSME community.

Conclusions: Summary of Essential Actions

To rapidly evolve and gain serious academic credibility for SSME, the following actions are essential:

1. Define and engage the academic disciplines needing to be actively involved in legitimizing SSME.

2. Build a research agenda with broad academic, industry, and government support and develop the strategy and actions to secure significant, sustaining research support.

3. Create a global university group to build on and develop a globally available curriculum to support all aspects of SSME.

4. Determine the best academically credible publication venues to focus attention on results of rigorous SSME research and gain representation on their editorial boards.

5. Analyze options and develop plans to attain global, professional visibility for SSME academics.

6. Identify and attract potential private sector contributors to fund endowed chairs and endowments ear-marked for SSME.

7. Attract top academics in SSME to join in the actions called for in this paper.

References

[1] Maglio, P.P., Srinivasan, S., Kreulen, J.T., and Spohrer, J., Services Systems, Service Scientists, SSME, and Innovation, *Communications of ACM*, V.49, No. 7: 81-85, ACM, July, 2006.

[2] Bitner, M.J. and Brown, S.W., The Evolution and Discovery of Services Science in Business Schools, *Communications of ACM*, V.49, No. 7: 73-78, ACM, July, 2006.

[3] Rouse, W.B. and Baba, M.L., Enterprise Transformation, *Communications of ACM*, V.49, No. 7: 66-72, ACM, July, 2006.

[4] Hefley, B. Educating an Innovative Services Science Workforce. Position paper for *Workshop on Education for Service Innovation,* National Science Foundation, US Department of Commerce, and IBM Research, Washington, D.C., April 18, 2006.

Holistic Trinity of Services Sciences:
Management, Social, and Engineering Sciences

Richard C. Larson
Massachusetts Institute of Technology
Cambridge, Massachusetts 02139
rclarson@mit.edu
617 253 3604

ABSTRACT

Services industries comprise about 75% of the economy of developed nations. To design and operate services systems for today and tomorrow, we need to educate a new type of engineer who focuses not on manufacturing but on services. Such an engineer must be able to integrate 3 sciences -management, social and engineering – into her analysis of services systems. Within the context of a new research center at MIT – CESF (Center for Engineering Systems Fundamentals) – we show how newly emerging services systems require such a 3-way holistic analysis. We deliberately select some non-standard services, as many business services such as supply chains have been studied extensively.

Introduction

CESF was created on September 1, 2005, by then-Director of MIT's Engineering Systems Division (ESD), Prof. Dan Hastings. ESD is a crosscutting new entity in the School of Engineering that includes faculty from all 7 departments in the school as well as faculty from the Sloan School of Management and the School of Humanities, Arts and Social Sciences. ESD focuses on complex 'messy' systems involving people and technology. Our research and teaching are at the intersection of a 'Venn diagram' whose overlapping circles represent traditional engineering, management and social sciences.

CESF is to advance 'fundamentals' of this new field called *Engineering Systems*. 'Engineering' in this phrase could be viewed as an adjective or a verb. Our preference is to consider both interpretations simultaneously.

Services system design and operation require attention to all three circles of the Venn diagram. Narrow, purely technocratic solutions are not adequate for services systems. Since we are applying the full range of scientific methods to the analysis and synthesis of services systems, we choose to label as *science* not only *social science* but also *management science* and *engineering science*. Truly transformative in nature, engineering science is a fundamental approach first brought to undergraduate engineering education by MIT in the 1960's.

Among ESD faculty members there has been an active discussion as to whether Fundamentals for Engineering Systems could be derived in a context-free environment or as a result of generalizing results discovered doing contextually motivated research. CESF has been emphasizing research on real systems, with the hypothesis that generalized Fundamentals may be extracted from contextually motivated results. This has been the dominant history of fundamentals discovery in related fields such as Operations Research and Optimal Control.

We now briefly review several of the services sector research initiatives started by CESF in its first year. A continuing theme is the need to work at the intersection of an ESD 'Venn diagram' whose three circles are respectively labeled engineering, management and social sciences.

CESF Research Initiatives in Services

Demand Management for Critical Infrastructures

We start with 'rush hours' in infrastructure systems. Infrastructure systems are connected networks delivering services and/or products from point to point along the network. They include transportation networks, telecommunication networks, and utilities. Each is a fixed capacity system having marked time-of-day and day-of-week demand patterns. Usually, the statistics of demand, including hourly patterns, are well known and often correlated with outside factors such as weather (short term) and the general economy (longer term).

An infrastructure system is difficult and expensive to design and construct. Once built, it can have a mean lifetime of 20 years (telecommunications) to over 100 years (water). As populations grow and the economy improves, increasingly large demands are being placed on infrastructure systems. Eventually they must be upgraded with additional capacity. However, if capacity upgrades can be delayed, huge cost savings are possible. One attempts to do this by 'managing demands' for service away from peak periods, in essence by 'shaving the peaks' and 'filling in the valleys' of demand. That is the focus of this research.

Some current examples include time-of-day congestion pricing for vehicles to go into city centers in Singapore and London; for-profit 'toll-ways' adjacent to freeways; time-of-day pricing for electricity; time-of-day pricing for long distance telephone calls; use of revenue management in airlines to balance travel demands over the course of a week and over the year; auction type bidding for some infrastructure services, with higher prices paid for congestion periods.

The research aims to create a uniform framing of the topic Strategies To Overcome Network Congestion In Infrastructure Systems. We seek to identify new, exciting and previously unexplored strategies that show promise for one or more of the types of infrastructure systems mentioned above.

About the holistic trinity: Traditional engineering can be found everywhere in the design and operation of critical networked infrastructure. Where is the social science? It is in understanding the cost/benefit relationships that would make users willing to defer services consumption at times of peak demands. These are often life style issues – when to travel or when to do the laundry. Where is the management? It is in the planning and managing of large infrastructure capital investment projects and in the management of dynamic pricing and related strategies for shaving peak demands and deferring them to off-peak times[1].

Voting in U.S. Presidential Elections

Perhaps unusual among services systems, voting systems in democracies are services systems, very important systems indeed. Voters go to voting facilities and – if all voting machines are busy when they arrive —may have to stand in queue and wait their turn to vote. In the USA these queueing times in Presidential Elections range from zero minutes to over 8 hours! There are no accepted standards. There are many who argue that *potential* voters were discouraged from voting in both the 2000 and 2004 Presidential Elections due to long lines, caused by too few voting machines and support personnel in certain voting places[2]. As there are no "exit polls" of queue discouraged voters to raise the red flag, we have the possibility of a *stealth disenfranchisement*.

About the holistic trinity: Traditional engineering here is in the industrial engineering or operations research of the *physics* of queues. There is a need to create a deployment algorithm to distribute voting machines ('queue servers') across voting precincts. Social science is in the psychology of queues: what makes potential voters balk at joining long lines or renege (i.e., leave the queue) in slow moving lines? Is it life style constraints, impatience, frustration at queue wait disparity, …? Management becomes involved with the supervision of implementing a voting machine deployment system and in responding to unanticipated long queues during Election Day.

---

1   These ideas are expanded in a CESF White Paper, *The 3 R's of Critical Energy Networks: Reliability, Robustness and Resiliency* (to MIT Energy Research Council, 10/30/05).
2   To Queue or Not To Queue? In a U.S. Presidential Election, that should NOT be a question!, June 2006 *OR/MS Today* (http://www.lionhrtpub.com/orms/orms-6-06/frqueues.html)

Social Distancing in an Influenza Pandemic

Health care services comprise over 15% of the US GDP, making health care the largest single services system in the US. A major threat to human health today is the possible emergence of a deadly influenza virus that could be efficiently transmitted from human to human, as was the virus responsible for the 1918-1919 'Spanish Flu'. That influenza pandemic killed more Americans in one year than all the wars of the 20th Century combined.

CESF has arranged a team to examine preparedness and response to a potential influenza pandemic. Our focus is on 'social distancing' as a control strategy for containing the spread of the influenza virus. Our students and faculty have drafted preliminary research papers on this topic, often examining social distancing historically used in 1918, and later in 2003 to combat the SARS epidemic.

We view this as a topic of extreme national and international importance, as hundreds of millions of lives could be at stake – depending on how we individually and collectively respond to a pandemic should one occur.

About the holistic trinity: Traditional engineering here is really engineering science, using operations research and related fields to create ever more accurate and insightful mathematical models of flu progression under alternative assumptions. Management is extremely complex, as if one imagines 100 "Hurricane Katrina's" occurring simultaneously across the country. Each town and city will be responsible for its local public response as will individuals, families and businesses. Laterally aligning the objectives of all stakeholders will be difficult but important. Psychology is one branch of social sciences that will be key: under what circumstances will families decide to withdraw from unusual social interactions in an attempt to isolate themselves from the virus? How do we collectively avoid panic responses to the threat of the illness and the shortage of supplies that may be created by supply chain breakdowns?

Hurricane Preparedness & Response

Disaster preparedness and response requires the design of service systems to confront likely disasters, be they acts of nature, industrial accidents or terrorist attacks. Some of these are now called High Consequence, Low Probability (HCLP) events.

We are developing a planning model to formulate rational policies for preparedness and response to hurricanes. Given a hurricane off the coast with a certain location, intensity and movement vector, we are examining important decision questions such as when to mobilize response personnel, to pre-position supplies and equipment, and eventually to evacuate residents. One analytical framework we are employing is *stochastic dynamic programming*.

About the holistic trinity: Engineering science is again operations research, married to meteorology to develop the probabilistic inclinations of the approaching hurricane. A social science component involves a local population's propensity to evacuate, given an evacuation order. There is a 'boy-who-cried-wolf' syndrome here. If a recent hurricane evacuation order elsewhere proved to be unnecessary (in retrospect), then the people currently threatened are less prone to follow a new evacuation order. If on the other hand, as with Hurricane Katrina, an order is given and people do not evacuate and as a result there are numerous deaths, then the currently threatened population is more likely to follow an evacuation order. This latter propensity was shown in Houston, Texas with Hurricane Rita, when the entire city was eager to evacuate. These tendencies can be quantified and incorporated into the model. Social science often provides equation-based relationships that are just as critical as Newtonian physics. Management requires the proper execution of recommendations from the model, tempered with all-important human discretion.

Water Systems

Water distribution systems for drinking, irrigation and cleaning are services systems. CESF hopes to bring together a multi-disciplinary team to examine water systems within an international perspective.

> *"We plan to embark on a major, multi-year research effort that examines water systems in all-important aspects, with special emphasis on applications in Asian countries. Our interests are water distribution systems… in poor rural regions without modern support networks, use of water in the design and operations of homes and other buildings, and more… rural Asia is a special focus of this work.*
>
> *Our work must be contextualized within constraints and traditions of Asian culture. Asian countries have well-developed traditional cultures that are, for various reasons, not always compatible with 21st century Western approaches to decision-making. The institutional issues are tied up with the local culture, and westerners often have relatively little credibility in this area. Naïve application of western 'scientific methods' can backfire…"* [3]

About the holistic trinity: Traditional civil and environmental engineering are everywhere in design and operation of water distribution systems. The social science lies in understanding how water and its use are embedded in local culture, traditions and history of the country or region being studied. Management again is in the planning and execution of large capital investment projects and in operating the created systems.

---

3   *Water: East Meets West, The Need for Appropriate Technologies and Systems*, 3/19/06, a joint effort: CESF & the Department of Civil & Environmental Engineering. At the time of this writing, this CESF White Paper is under review by a committee creating the Singapore Research Initiative.

MIT LINC Teaching Initiative in the Middle East

Provision of education to a populace is a service. Education is the 2nd largest services sector in the USA, comprising about 10% of the GDP. Needless to say, education is important in all parts of the world.

MIT LINC is the Learning International Networks Consortium. http://linc.mit.edu LINC, a volunteer effort housed in CESF, is a quasi-professional society of leaders world-wide who believe in the following transformative nature of technology as it pertains to education: *With today's computer & telecommunications technologies, every young person can have a quality education regardless of his or her place of birth.* Until recently, the assets of a country lay buried underground, such as oil, gas, gold, silver and diamonds. Today, the key assets of a country lie *'buried between the ears of its citizens!'* Investing in the mind – that is the key to a better tomorrow for all.

LINC is concerned with design and implementation of technology-enabled education systems in developing regions of the world. This might be the exemplary messy and complex Engineering Systems problem! As an example of LINC's activities, LINC has submitted a proposal to USAID: *Blended Learning for High School Math Classes: A Partnership Between MIT and Arab Universities to Foster Creative Critical Thinking in High School Math Classes.* The extended abstract starts with this overview:

> *"Our focus will be on high school teachers of mathematics, with the idea of inspiring high school students to study math-oriented careers in engineering and science. ... we propose to create a set of short 'Learning Modules,' offered by volunteer professors from MIT and from participating... universities in the Middle East. Each learning module will be available either on line... or on CD, DVD or videotape. Each will be configured to be compatible with any given curriculum as an interesting, informative and insightful addition to the usual mathematics program. A learning module might... be a short video lecture followed in class by some exercise, building from the usual curriculum content plus the new 'challenge content' of the module. The usual in-class teacher would... direct the in-class activity. This type of learning is an example of 'Blended Learning,' a new and growing pedagogical model in which the content expert enlightens the class with... new ideas and mind-extending challenges, and the class with its regular teacher follows up, climbing new exciting learning heights. ..."*

About the holistic trinity: All three parts of the ESD Venn diagram are vital to understanding and improving education in the emerging world. Engineering sciences involve distributed learning ICT technologies & operations research for system design. Social sciences here include economics, history, and country culture especially related to learning and the effectiveness of alternative pedagogical models. Management relates to the supervision of the entire educational system.

Summary Table

A summary of the major research initiatives of CESF are shown in Table 1, with examples of how each of the Venn diagram components – engineering, management and social sciences – is important in undertaking that research.

Research Topic Area	Engineering	Management	Social Sciences
Critical Energy Infrastructures	Electrical & Systems Engineering	Planning large capital investment projects; maintaining systems	Understanding cost/benefit relationships for users in order to shave peak demands
Election Queues	Operations Research of Queueing Physics	Managing the pre-election day deployment and real time re-deployment of resources	Understanding voters' choices to balk or renege from voting lines
Flu Pandemic	Modeling the physics of disease progression	Planning Responses of Government, Businesses and Families	Understanding and Managing Human Behavior in the presence of a pandemic
Hurricane Response	Modeling the physics of hurricane progression	Managing evacuations and related responses	Understanding people's propensity to follow evacuation orders
Water Systems	Traditional Civil Engineering plus Operations Research	Planning large capital investment projects; maintaining systems	Understanding people's culture in their need for and use of water
e-Learning in Developing Countries	Computer Science, Electrical Engineering & Operations Research	Managing the deployment of technology and human assets and maintaining the system	Understanding learners' responses to pedagogy by culture, gender, age and related measures

Table 1. CESF Research Initiatives: Components of Engineering, Management & Social Sciences

Summary Reflections

Engineering Systems is different from Systems Engineering because the former explores complex systems using the three components of the Venn diagram intersection: traditional engineering, management and social sciences. Systems Engineering does not. Each of the research initiatives described here involves all three components. The social sciences component is sometimes the most difficult from a research perspective. While the social science and/or the management component may be difficult and interesting research, we must also recall that Engineering Systems *is* engineering. So, of the three components, engineering must be the dominant paradigm in the sense that ultimately we want to design and create a system. We want to build and operate something, in the finest tradition of engineering.

We will be *engineering* systems. We include social sciences and management in order to design, build and operate systems intelligently, with full awareness of all essential aspects of the problem. Our students must become expert in the integrated analysis of systems, incorporating social, management and engineering science. If we are successful, Engineering Systems may indeed become a transformative multidiscipline for approaching design and operation of complex systems.

SSME, Operations Research and Education

Giovanni Righini
Dipartimento di Tecnologie dell'Informazione
Università degli Studi di Milano Via Bramante 65
26013 Crema, Italy
righini@dti.unimi.it

ABSTRACT

In this paper I express my personal views about SSME and its development. In particular I will discuss its relations with Operations Research/Management Science (OR/MS) and the opportunities to introduce SSME in the educational program of the universities. I will also cite some personal experiences as an OR academic.

Introduction

My point of view on SSME is that of an academic professor of Operations Research, who belongs to a Faculty of Sciences in a Department of Information Technologies in Italy. My research activities related to services mainly concern optimization techniques in logistics and transportation as well as in space science for security and other applications. Since I am heavily involved in academic teaching, here I will pay special attention to the possible role that SSME can play in university-level education.

SSME and Operations Research

Quoting the call for papers of this workshop, "services depend critically on people working together and with technology to provide value". Starting from this statement I would like to stress the importance of Operations Research (OR) in SSME. The role of OR is (at least) twofold, for its use of mathematical models and for its strong links with Information and Communication Technology (ICT).

To make people working together

To "make people working together" a common language is needed and this is mathematics. Young generations *must* be educated to communicate using mathematics as a language to describe systems and problems. Teaching mathematics not as a tool to execute (boring) computations but as a universal language to allow people working together has a much deeper cultural impact than the trivial interpretation of "working together" as "using the same ICT tools." My experience with students, colleagues and industrial companies suggests that working together is not only a matter of technology, but of culture.

This kind of education to the use of mathematical models is exactly what we OR teachers try to achieve when we give our introductory courses. We do not put the accent on sophisticated algorithms but rather on the representation of complex systems and complex decision problems in mathematical terms, defining data, variables, contraints and objective functions. The expressive power of this approach cannot be overestimated. This is a first reason for which I consider OR education crucial to the success of SSME and SSME as a wonderful educational opportunity.

To make people working with technology
To "make people working with technology" is the goal of many academics whose efforts are devoted at enlarging the access to ICT tools as much as possible, including users without any scientific or technological education.

In the past years usability has been a weak point for OR: in spite of wonderful scientific achievements in optimization algorithms and mathematical programming, for a long time OR has been confined into the ivory tower and it is still unknown to many outside the academic environment. Two clear reasons to explain the difficulty in using the products of OR research are the following: (a) they were too sophisticated to be used by non-experts; (b) there was no ICT infrastructure providing necessary input data.

Today, owing to the great development of ICT, OR techniques have enormous potential to become a common tool of work in everyday life even for non-experts, provided that the scientific communities of OR and ICT are willing to make an effort towards *integration*.

Just to give an example, the integration of optimization algorithms into geographical information systems (GIS) is becoming compulsory to cope with huge territory planning problems or with the optimization of distribution networks providing services both in the private and in the public sector, since this requires the solution of complex network design problems or large-scale location and routing problems. However, in spite of this evident need, it is still quite uncommon (at least in Italy) to find courses on GIS and courses in OR in the same degree course. The two scientific communities are still separated, and this is only an example out of many. The result is that we are not educating young generations at making the best of ICT and OR by integrating them. An *interdisciplinary* initiative like SSME, coming from outside the academy, may be of great impact in promoting interdisciplinary education and integration.

To provide value

When I hear sentences like "Information is power" or "Information is money" they recall me a parallel with oil, engines and energy. Without engines transforming it into energy, oil will have little or no value. Analogously digital information (here I am not referring to "information" from TV or newspapers that still make use of modern technologies, but to information stored in databases, GIS, web resources and so on) would be useless if we would not be able to transform it into effective, efficient, robust, timely, rational *decisions*. The value of information depends on our ability to transform it into decisions. For this reason I claim that the next step of Information and Communication Technology is Decision Technology, which is nothing but another name of OR. Decision Technology (DT) is OR properly integrated with ICT as mentioned above. Hence SSME will "provide value"as much as it will promote the step forward from ICT to DT.

SSME and Education: The Present

The above considerations lead me to a very synthetic SWOT analysis of the current situation, to put in evidence strengths, weaknesses, opportunities and threats.

Strengths

The main points of strength for SSME in my view are the following:

— SSME is supported by IBM, which is a credible company, with a long history of excellent collaboration with the academy;

— SSME is the right thing at the right moment: today economy *is* shifting from production to services, independently of any academic initiative. It is a phenomenon, not an opinion.

— European economy is also influenced by the integration process in the EU and the adoption of a common currency together with common rules that every country must adhere to: this is an increasing *demand for efficiency* coming from public administrations providing *public services*.

Weaknesses

Even if services are certainly mentioned in different contexts in several courses in science, engineering and business faculties, SSME as such is currently unknown in my academic environment: I could not hear of any colleague of mine dealing with it. I discovered SSME when I got in contact with IBM-Italy.

Opportunities

The list of the opportunities is longer than the others. This is mainly because many elements of weakness can be interpreted as opportunities.

Interdisciplinary education

This is the right moment to promote innovative ideas in university-level education, especially in Italy, where we have had a deep reformation seven years ago, introducing the distinction between undergraduate and postgraduate degree courses and a successive reformation aimed at correcting some bad effects observed on the quality of several curricula. Today interdisciplinarity is definitely a keyword that is often invoked; however there are not many successful examples of its implementation yet.

Promoting scientific studies in a changing economy

Another opportunity comes from the need to promote the study of scientific and technological disciplines. The percentage of Italian students pursuing scientific studies is decreasing with obvious negative effects on the innovation potential of the society and its economical system.

At the same time the Italian productive system, mainly relying upon SMEs, suffers from the competition with low-cost producers in India and China and economy clearly shows a shift from production to services. This is exactly the key idea of SSME, which can open up a lot of new possibilities of employment to the young. If we can spread this message, we can educate new generations of students to be competent actors in a services-based economy, where a scientific background and technological competencies can have even more value than in a production-based economy.

A personal experience

My department, an ICT department, currently offers among others an undergraduate 3-years degree course, named "Techonologies for the Information Society", where computer science and information technology courses are mixed with many others ranging from Economics to Psychology, from Finance to Logistics, from Communications Sociology to Marketing. This non-traditional degree course is now perceived as too dispersive and unable to offer a clear cultural identity to the students. Therefore an effort is being made to re-design it, though maintaining its interdisciplinary character: my proposal is to transform it into a degree course in "Information and Decision Technology", where existing ICT courses will be complemented by OR/MS (Operations Research/Management Science) courses. SSME can find its place in this non-traditional and interdisciplinary degree course much more easily than in traditional degree courses. The involvement of a well-reputed industrial partner such as IBM in re-shaping this degree course would be certainly appreciated.

Some similar opportunities may well exist in other universities.

Lack of OR courses

I am convinced that SSME can also play a very important role in education at postgraduate level, where the links between teaching and research are much stronger. Also in this case ad hoc non-traditional and interdisciplinary postgraduate courses should be preferred and the most effective "weapon" to achieve this, at least in Europe, is OR. At the best of my knowledge there are currently no examples of degree courses (at either level) in OR — or with equivalent denominations such as Decision Science or Management Science — not only in Italy but in the whole Mediterranean Europe. A list of such degree courses can be found on the website of INFORMS – the INstitute For Operations Research and the Management Sciences (www.informs.org). After eliminating spurious entries related to research laboratories or to single courses, one is left with not more than a dozen such degree courses in Europe, half of which in the U.K., one in Denmark, one in France, three in Germany. In the U.S. nearly one hundred are listed.

Besides being an obvious reason of concern, this tremendous gap represents at the same time a fantastic opportunity. OR is interdisciplinary in itself and OR academics are spread into different kinds of faculties, mainly science (in both math departments and ICT departments), engineering and management. A postgraduate course in OR could attract students and teachers from all these areas and it could be the ideal cradle to promote SSME in a sound scientific way and without the cultural limitations that are typical of other disciplines.

In addition, OR academics, being spread in different types of faculties and departments, will not react to SSME like those who want to "defend their territory" but more likely they will make their best to exploit the commonalities between OR and SSME to promote both at the same time.

Not surprisingly the reason that put me in contact with IBM-Italy, when I discovered SSME, was to investigate the feasibility of a proposal I was preparing for a new interdisciplinary postgraduate 2-years course focussed on optimization and OR in integration with ICT.

Threats
Negative academic reactions

If an objective of the IBM initiative is "to establish SSME as a legitimate discipline within the academic community," this may easily sound as a "threat to the territory" to some academics, above all in countries like Italy, characterized by a rigid fragmentation of the academy into disciplines whose representatives compete against each other for very scarce resources and academic careers strongly depend on the affiliation to a "disciplinary sector." In such an environment, where interdisciplinarity in general and OR in particular are heavily penalized, a new legitimate discipline is likely to be regarded as "yet another competitor," in spite of its cultural importance. To achieve the above goal a strong cooperation between IBM and a scientific community already acting inside the academy is absolutely needed. I have already listed a number of cultural reasons for which I am convinced that the main collaborators for IBM to achieve this goal should be searched within the OR community. I add to them this "political" reason.

Reducing SSME to ICT

A common trend I have observed when working on practical problems with industrial companies is that of emphasizing the use of ICT tools instead of the achievement of provably good results. What should be a mean often becomes the goal. There is a lot of rumour around ICT and ICT attracts many investments today. However the optimization of systems and services is not pursued as it could be. For project leaders the target is often "It must work" rather than "It must work well".

In the academy there is a similar threat. Working in an ICT department, I have direct experience of the difficulties of promoting the passage from ICT to Decision Technology within traditional degree courses. Today ICT academics are in a position of strength and most of them have no interest about promoting disciplines such as OR or DT which are out of their area of competency.

The threat is to reduce SSME to ICT: it would be a lost opportunity to go beyond ICT.

Conclusions

In this paper I have tried to summarize my personal views about SSME and its development with special attention to its relations with Operations Research and with education.

I am convinced that the best success can be obtained from a strict collaboration between research people involved in SSME and OR academics, who are spread in science, management and engineering faculties and departments.

I identify one of the main targets of this collaboration in the joint design and development of undergraduate and postgraduate courses with interdisciplinary character, where ICT and OR/MS are integrated, breaking the academic disciplinary borders and barriers between science, management and engineering.

A Designer's View of SSME

Shelley Evenson
Carnegie Mellon University
School of Design MMC 110
Pittsburgh, PA 15232
evenson@cmu.edu
412.268.4638

ABSTRACT

A designer's view of the interplay, challenges and opportunities for innovation and research across disciplines is presented. A case is made for the inclusion of design as a discipline that can forge and leverage the required lateral linkages across multiple communities. Examples of some of the opportunities and challenges that arise at the intersection of the disciplines are described.

Introduction

Services Sciences, Management and Engineering (SSME) brings together people from a variety of disciplines in support of service innovation, design, delivery, and management. For the past three years we at Carnegie Mellon University have been concentrating on service innovation and design, via activities in curriculum design, undergraduate and graduate education, and collaboration with the international Service Design Network (SDN) [1,2].

In establishing this new direction at Carnegie Mellon we wanted to explore how we could design to deliver new forms of interactions spanning machine to machine (m2m), person to machine (p2m), and person to person (p2p) modalities, to provide higher quality service with more powerful connections between service providers and the people using those services in their everyday lives. Our goal has been to develop an approach to the design of services that simultaneously builds value, utility, and delight.

What is Service Design?

A key issue is the definition of service inclusive enough to deal with the entire m2m, p2m, and p2p service system interaction continuum. We define services as activities or events that form a *product* through an interaction with designed elements of the service organization, the customer, and any mediating technology. We view services as *performances*: choreographed interactions manufactured at the point of delivery that form a process and co-produce value, utility, satisfaction, and delight in response to human needs.

Correspondingly, we view the design of these services as the act of conceiving, planning, and, constructing (often iteratively) a framework and its elements into a functional entity which we conventionally label a communication, product, or service, any of which can be subsets of larger systems of products, service environments, or integrated customer experiences.

As shown in Figure 1, the service design process we have adopted addresses the context of the service by investigating issues such as social, economic (management) and technical (engineering) (SET) factors[3]. At the setting or servicescape level the impact of the setting or environment is explored. The activities or customer journey is documented, and touchpoints that enable the journey are described. Touchpoints are made up of elements that mediate the interaction. As a person or machine performs in the journey they move through various stages in the cycle of experience (similar to Bitner's Customer Trial of Technology Service Innovation [4]). When properly executed, the outcome is an experience with meaning and value.

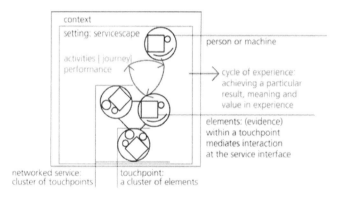

Figure 1. Experience model of service systems

We see service design as a *process* based on a deep understanding of people, context, service provider, market strategies, and social practices. We approach service design as a *systems challenge* driven by an understanding of human experience. As such, the service design process is driven by: 1) human-centered research that is exploratory, generative, and evaluative; and 2) design methods and tools that result in evidence (or combined elements into touchpoints) and results in stakeholder-oriented service systems interaction.

Who's Involved in SSME?

Business, the social and cognitive sciences, and engineering each bring different and valuable perspectives to service science, management and engineering. But these are merely components of a potential SSME "solution", without the holistic perspective that the design community brings to the table. Designers today are particularly skilled not only in understanding and navigating the longitudinal process that runs from concept generation to prototype evaluation, but also in forging and leveraging the required lateral linkages across multiple communities, particularly business strategists, social scientists, and engineers[5,6]. Designers also bring the ability to build tangible artifacts that crystallize the issues at these intersections. We briefly outline some of these issues in the following sections.

A View of the Issues at the Intersections of SSME

Figure 2 illustrates the role that design plays in support of SSME and highlight many of the opportunities and issues that lie at the intersections of the disciplines and are outlined below.

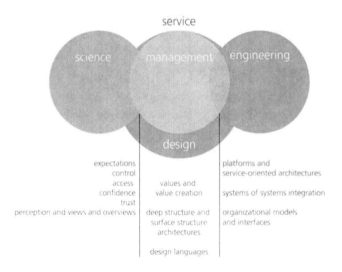

Figure 2. SSME and Design

Science

Work in the social and cognitive sciences has begun to define service quality, [9] but there is a strong need for service designers to collaborate more closely with social scientists to understand the role of *expectations* and *expectation setting* at the service encounter if we are to deliver maximum value in the service experience. There is also an opportunity to explore how expectations for a particular service type may vary across global cultures and sub-cultures. Similar needs exist for elaborating on issues surrounding *user control, access, confidence* and *trust*. Finally, another fruitful area for designer/scientist collaboration is in how everyday people perceive and understand views and overviews—or dynamic information at the point of need. For example, imagine travelers being able to access views of their airline ticket purchases and being able to trade and barter with the airlines, and other travelers, as their demands change. What are the business dynamics, the issues of cognitive load, the dynamics of the social networks that will form and re-form, and, most importantly, what are the implications of all these factors on the design of an effective service interaction that builds service provider value while providing the traveler a satisfying—and perhaps even delightful—user experience?

Engineering

One of the greatest challenges at the intersection of engineering and business is in the development of service platforms and service-oriented architectures (SOA) [7] Not only are standards required, but if they are to be adopted and used effectively, it is crucial that the SSME community build a knowledge-base of how people understand specific activities. Design contributes by developing appropriate ways for the activities to be represented that will fuel adoption and use. This will require a design level understanding of how deep structures (such as SOAs) and surface structures (service elements at the interface and across touchpoints) can be reflected and updated seamlessly.

Views into the activity of the organization are also an area of interest for design, from challenges such as tracking activity across a supply chain or value web, to views into an entire business ecosystem. Can we produce models of organizations that enable people to see and better predict the impact of a new service concept? Can we produce prototypes of organizations that enable people to explore the implications of a change in organizational design? In either case— there is a challenge in the representation of the information that touches all the disciplines that make up SSME.

Picture a situation where network agents report changing end-customer needs. The report is validated with purchase history data and product development notified and a project design team is formed. As the team models possible futures, they also produce prototypes of elements of the service that are "seeded" into the customer collaboration environment. The results from the co-lab are incorporated into sets of working field probes for sales and marketing to validate with key customers. The probes are quickly 'reformed' as products as they are validated and the information, design specs and available to marketing and customer support

Management

Some of the issues in the overlap between management and design are in the area of value creation and brand management. How will people perceive value if they are the producers of their own services? With so much personalization will brands as they are perceived today still exist? Will the boundaries between organizations blur and will organizations only be known for their roles in a greater ecosystem? Another challenge will be in managing for emergent behavior. As people participate in the design of their own services, knowing when, if, and how to capitalize on the innovations will be critical to management success.

Design and SSME

Design can and should respond to the issues at the intersection, but there are also challenges that it must address in SSME. As noted above there is a real need to explore the relationships between surface structures and the types of deep structures offered by service platforms. Research into the quality and nature of service design languages will contribute to the speed and effectiveness with which new services can be adopted by business or consumer populations.

An approach to service design and innovation needs to grow up in the same way that product development has established itself with industry. In product development it took years to adopt a human-centered process, but we've now learned the benefits from this approach. Service design should also benefit, by *starting* with this viewpoint, and bringing together the SSME components—our scientific knowledge of people and organizations, our engineering capabilities, and our business management skills—and unifying them in a user-centric design-guided service development process.

Conclusions

The stage has been set for the collaboration of disciplines in SSME. The challenge in bringing such a diverse workgroup together is that they may not share common references, language, or tools. Our work in the design community— which, by its very nature is transdisciplinary—has made it abundantly clear that how critical it is to first establish common ground for seeing and experiencing the opportunities at the intersections. We believe this is particularly true for this new SSME initiative, and it is critical that there be collaboration among all the disciplines from the beginning. With that power it is likely we will be able to develop new and innovative models of service that can continue to accelerate the service economy.

References

[1]   Mager, B. *Service Design, a review*. Köln International School of Design Fachhochschule Köln Service Design Network, 2004

[2]   Service Design Network. *Service design network manifesto*. Unpublished, 2005.

[3]   Cagan, J., Vogel, C. *Creating Breakthrough Products: Innovation from Product Planning to Program Approval*. Upper Saddle River , NJ Prentice Hall; PTR, 2002.

[4]   Zeithaml, Valarie, Mary Jo Bitner, and Dwayne Gremler, *Services Marketing: Integrating Customer Focus Across the Firm, 4th edition*, New York: McGraw-Hill, 2006.

[5]   Evenson, S. Designing for Service. *Proceedings of DPPI 2005*, Eindhoven.

[6]   Evenson, S. *Designing design: Establishing a new common ground for collaboration*. HCII Session on Interaction Design Education and Research: Current and Future Trends, 2005.

[7]   Chesbrough H., Spohrer, J. A Research Manifesto for Services Sceince. *Comm. ACM 49*, 7 (July 2005) 35-40.

[8]   Edvardsson, B. Gustafsson, A. Johnson, M. and Sanden, B. *New Service Development and Innovation in the New Economy*. Studentlitteratur AB, 2000.

[9]   Zeithaml, V., Parasuraman, A. *Service Quality*. Cambridge, MA, Marketing Science Institute, 2004

[10] Shostack, G. Lynn Designing Services that Deliver *Harvard Business Review*, 133-139, 1984.

[11] Bitner, M. Servicescapes: The Impact of Physical Surroundings on Customers and Employees. *Journal of Marketing 55* (Jan): 10-25, 1992.

SSME—Let's Not Forget About Customers and Revenue

Roland T. Rust
University of Maryland
Robert H. Smith School of Business
rrust@rhsmith.umd.edu
301-405-4300

ABSTRACT

The SSME movement, as currently defined, seems to be primarily focused on engineering/systems/operations approaches to service. This viewpoint is too limited, in that there is more to service than efficiency and productivity. In particular the customer side of service seems to be largely neglected. For SSME to achieve its potential, the topic of how to attract and grow revenue from customers needs to be a central element.

Introduction

At the SSME meetings to date, almost all of the participants from academia have come from one particular point of view—that of engineering, systems science, and operations. This is strange, given that by far the largest and best-established academic literature in service has emerged from service marketing. While the engineering/systems/operations viewpoint is a valuable one, and is an integral part of what SSME should be, its present dominance in the discussion threatens to make SSME much narrower than it ought to be.

What About The Customer?

It is axiomatic in business that profit is equal to revenue minus cost. The cost side is addressed well by the engineering/systems/operations approach, but the revenue side is not. The revenue side of service is addressed primarily by the marketing point of view, supported by such fields as human resources, economics, psychology, sociology, and information technology. Work in the revenue side of service can involve quantitative models [5] or behavioral (e.g., [2]). The perspective, in either case, is firmly rooted in the social sciences. Thus, it is essential that the social science viewpoint, as typified by marketing, be included as a key part of SSME.

Tradeoffs

Too much emphasis on the productivity and efficiency side of service can be counter-productive. Unlike the manufacturing environment, the service environment involves important tradeoffs between productivity and customer satisfaction. While the quality movement of such gurus as Deming and Juran saw efficiency and productivity as the road to customer satisfaction and revenues, their theories were developed in a manufacturing context. More recent research shows that their ideas do not hold as confidently in the service context.

Specifically, uncritical attention to productivity and efficiency in service can result in a downward spiral of customer satisfaction and revenues [4]. Research also shows that firms should focus on either high productivity or high customer satisfaction, but not both simultaneously [1], and that firms that try to emphasize both cost reduction and revenue expansion simultaneously (or cost reduction alone) may be less profitable than those that place more emphasis on revenue expansion [7]. Collectively, the research tends to indicate that focus on revenue expansion is a key element of service profitability.

Understanding Customers

While the engineering viewpoint toward service tends to look internally toward the systems and procedures by which service is supplied, the marketing/social science viewpoint tends to look externally toward customers. Understanding customers is critical for any service business, because customers and their decisions are the source of all revenue. Research to understand customers is generally based on the social sciences. We need to understand how individuals (psychology), groups (sociology) and cultures (anthropology) choose to buy and to form relationships with the firm (marketing). We also need to understand how groups within the company work with each other to provide service teams that serve customers effectively (human resources), and how such teams can be effectively managed (management).

Customers Over Time

One of the most important characteristics of service is that it often involves relationships with customers that unfold over time. In other words, the dynamics of the customer relationship dictate how the firm should look at revenues and profits. This means that current snapshots such as market share, revenues, and profits, are less important than long-term measures such as the discounted cash flows of future profits and customer equity share. Customer lifetime value is the most important customer measure. Aggregating this across all of the firm's current and future customers yields the firm's customer equity [8], which has been shown to be a reasonable proxy for the value of the firm [8, 3].

Making Service Revenue Improvement Financially Accountable

The customer equity perspective makes managerial actions designed to increase service revenues financially accountable. By relating the increase in customer equity to the investment required to produce that increase, a return on investment (ROI) can be obtained [6]. Being able to do this is essential, because it creates a way to evaluate the financial impact of service improvements. Thus, while the financial impact of cost cutting efforts is often very easily evaluated, the financial impact of revenue expansion efforts requires more effort and more sophisticated models. Nevertheless this is an essential task for any company that seeks to build its service profitability.

Grant Funding

A serious continuing problem with the service research agenda is that the largest funding source, the National Science Foundation, shares the very narrow view of the scope of fundable service research as being engineering/systems/operations. If this narrow viewpoint persists, it will greatly hinder the advancement of the field. Reasons for not funding revenue/marketing-related service research include that such work is "not science," but that objection is patently ridiculous. Social sciences are sciences, too. What's more, much of what is currently funded is really technology and not science. That is legitimate (technology is valuable, too) but there are also social technologies (e.g., models for providing better service to customers) as well as engineering-based models (e.g., how to build more efficient service systems).

Conclusions

In summary, SSME should expand its horizons. Currently the people and topics involved are too narrowly defined. In particular the revenue expansion wing (the customer side) of service research is almost completely overlooked. This points to the need to expand SSME's inclusion of service marketing and the social science point of view in general. This is also important in terms of providing grant support. The most interesting developments in service research will occur when different ways of thinking collide, and currently that is not happening enough.

References

[1]   Anderson, Eugene W., Claes Fornell, and Roland T. Rust (1997), "Customer Satisfaction, Productivity, and Profitability: Differences Between Goods and Services," *Marketing Science, 16* (2), 129-145.

[2]   Finn, Adam (2005), "Reassessing the Foundations of Customer Delight," *Journal of Service Research, 8* (2), 103-116.

[3]   Gupta, Sunil, Donald R. Lehmann and J. A. Stuart (2004), "Valuing Customers," *Journal of Marketing Research, 41* (1), 7-18.

[4] Oliva, Rogelio and John Sterman (2001), "Cutting Corners and Working Overtime: Quality Erosion in the Service Industry," *Management Science, 47* (7), 894-914.

[5] Rust, Roland T. and Tuck Siong Chung (2006), "Marketing Models of Service and Relationships," *Marketing Science*, forthcoming.

[6] Rust, Roland T., Katherine N. Lemon, and Valarie A. Zeithaml (2004), "Return on Marketing: Using Customer Equity to Focus Marketing Strategy," *Journal of Marketing, 68* (1), 109-127.

[7] Rust, Roland T., Christine Moorman, and Peter R. Dickson (2002), "Getting Return on Quality: Revenue Expansion, Cost Reduction, or Both?" *Journal of Marketing, 66* (October), 7-24.

[8] Rust, Roland T., Valarie A. Zeithaml and Katherine N. Lemon (2000), *Driving Customer Equity*, New York: Free Press.

Psychology of the Experience:
The Missing Link in Service Science

Richard B. Chase
Marshall School of Business
University of Southern California
rchase@marshall.usc.edu
(213) 740-0184

Sriram Dasu
Marshall School of Business
University of Southern California
rchase@marshall.usc.edu
(213) 740-4837

ABSTRACT

For service science to be a complete discipline it must address how customers experience services with the same depth of analysis as it studies the analytics of information and physical flow processes that deliver the service. In this paper we identify topics and insights drawn from the behavioral sciences that can be used to provide the initial underpinnings of the psychological side of service science. We also propose an agenda for research and education in the area.

Introduction

The heart of a service is the encounter between the server and the customer. It is here where emotions meet economics in real time and where most people judge the quality of service. As currently conceived, service science treats customer satisfaction with an encounter predominantly as a function of engineering measures of throughput and output quality. Thus if a service is performed efficiently and process output variability is low, it is assumed that the service process has been optimized. Our view is that this misses critical psychological variables that lie at the subconscious level, and which, if understood by management could be managed in such a way as to enhance customer satisfaction.

Psychological Underpinnings

Figure 1 illustrates our conception of the service encounter as a core task surrounded by the customer's psychological experience during the transaction. Over the past five years we have engaged in an extensive review of the behavioral literature to see what if any concepts and research findings seem promising to apply to service encounters. We contend that while the impact of psychology is no doubt highest in face-to-face and phone interactions, many of the concepts and research findings are very applicable to internet and email interactions as well.

Figure 1. Service encounter.

Though a complete listing of articles is beyond the scope of this paper, the work of Daniel Khaneman [1] and his colleagues provided a the initial source of our research. In Chase and Dasu [2] we presented some initial applications, and in the process of developing these ideas for a book, the following categories were determined to be useful enough, extensive enough, and cohesive enough to stand as separate chapters:

— Understanding emotions

— Sequence effects

— Duration effects

— Shaping attributions

— Perceived control

Understanding Emotions

Emotions are both an input and an output of an encounter. Creating a good experience requires understanding what triggers different types of positive and negative emotions. This allows managers at an aggregate level to develop an emotional platform and at a tactical or process level to identify stages of the systems that are likely to engender strong emotions and to proactively manage them. A useful way of classifying emotional responses is through appraisal theory which specifies the conditions that result in different emotions as a result of change from a neutral emotional state. According to this theory, the type of emotion (positive or negative) we experience depends on whether the outcome:

— improves our situation or makes it worse,

— is associated with a penalty or a reward,

— is certain or just a possibility,

— is a significant / powerful event that is difficult to cope with or it's not a very significant event and we can easily cope with the change, and

— is caused by the individual or an outside agency

A modification of the standard I.E. process map called an "experience print" can be used to analyze the variation in emotions throughout a service encounter. We can do this either through surveys or anticipate them by applying appraisal theory. Once we have a sense for potential emotions, we can introduce in to the process appropriate responses. The expectation is that we build in emotional intelligence in to the system.

Sequence Effects

Most service experiences consist of a series of events that occur over time. Lay tendency is to focus on a strong start and assume things will take care of themselves as the service encounter unfolds. At the other extreme we have service folklore that maintains every minute is significant. We now know that neither belief is accurate. According to numerous studies, people focus on the peak event, the ending event, and the trend of a sequence. The implications of this for design are profound: in the way we present information, for example, in a call center (get the bad news out of the way first) to the way we conduct a class (end on a high note, or "stick the dismount").

Duration Effects

We all know that an hour is not an hour. How quickly it passes depends on a number of factors such as whether we are involved in pleasant or unpleasant activities, whether we are paying attention to the passage of time, how many segments the experience is divided into, etc. A big question is how do we make positive events seem longer and negative events shorter in retrospect? There is some evidence that the greater the number of discrete segments that are perceived to the customer, the longer the process appears. Thus for an amusement park visit, several shorter rides make the day seem longer and more enjoyable than a few longer rides, even though the time spent actually riding was the same. In a call center, more steps and options create the perception of the interaction being longer than it actually is. In general we find that perceived duration of a wait, or equivalently the level of dissatisfaction with a wait depends on (i) emotions and moods, (ii) rate of goal progress and evidence of goal progress, (iii) degree of perceived control, and (iv) attention paid to passage of time. Existing techniques for handling the psychology of waiting can be inferred from these four variables. These variables also suggest other techniques for improving the waiting experience. For instance, a call back option in call centers affords greater control to the customers.

Shaping Attributions

Every service outcome contains the potential for placing blame or claiming credit. Attribution theory provides insights into how people make these judgments. One such insight is that we are predisposed to accept responsibility for success and reject responsibility for failure. (Protecting one's self-esteem is a dominate reason for such attributions.) For service encounter design, we want to find ways of conveying up front what is the customers' responsibility without damaging their self-esteem. Another insight is that we overestimate our ability to cause an outcome that is actually determined by chance. (We engage in counterfactual thinking—mental simulations—as to what might have been.) Often this is seen as the last step in an extended process and leads to the practical guideline that servers should avoid communicating near misses when dealing with a customer in situations when a constellation of factors resulted in the undesired final outcome.

Perceived Control

In virtually every service encounter, customers must relinquish some control to the service firm to get the job done, yet customers like situations where they perceive they have some control. Research in many service settings has shown there is a relationship between perceptions of control and satisfaction. For example, studies in health care management have consistently shown that when patients have reasonable control over their treatment regimens, they are more satisfied than when doctors are in total control. In simple options such as allowing a patient to choose which arm from to draw blood from results in less feeling of pain than when ordered to draw blood from a specific arm. Even in intensive care situations, patients who are allowed to choose when they received visitors, when they eat and the level of exercise they could undertake, exhibit lower levels of stress and get well faster. Another form, and often a substitute for actual control is *cognitive control* where the customer feels she/he can rely on the system to work fairly. For example, calls will be answered in order of arrival in a call center; or paychecks will be issued on the 15th of the month. When viewed this way, the concept of control can be approached in a more sophisticated way in planning service encounters.

Research and Education Agenda

This new way of looking at service encounters presents exciting opportunities for interdisciplinary research and educational initiatives. We also see an important role for IBM to play in these initiatives.

Interdisciplinary Research Conference on Service Psychology

We propose an interdisciplinary conference on service psychology. The conference would invite leading researchers from psychology, consumer behavior, and sociology to provide overview sessions on the basics and recent developments in their fields of specialization.

The audience would be researchers from business schools, engineering schools, and practitioners who are interested in SSME. We also propose that representatives from IBM, Oracle, and other high tech firms in the SSME group provide profiles of their customer touch points. This has the advantage of not only identifying where encounters occur but also uncovering subsets of encounters that may call for creating different and unanticipated applications of service psychology. This would also provide the basis for developing serviceware that incorporates psychological protocols. For example, automatically adjusting information event sequences to generate an upward trend in an internet encounter. We are particularly interested in new developments in applied computer science so we can incorporate service psychology into the design of 21st century electronic encounters.

Service Psychology Clearinghouse
In addition to offering a kick-off conference to study the service psychology, we would also propose the establishment of a service psychology clearinghouse which would focus on applications that focus on high tech organizations. The goal would be to provide occasional newsletters on service psychology research and industrial applications. This information could be used to enrich service courses of virtually all types.

Curriculum Development
Service system design has relied on mathematical models to carefully match supply and demand. Queuing models have been used to anticipate queue lengths and work force requirements. In the last decade we have observed the emergence of dynamic pricing models that allow firms to manage demand. Dynamic pricing models can increase social welfare not just firm profitability.

While we have developed rigorous approaches for managing supply and demand, the psychological dimensions of service encounters have not been approached with equal rigor. Focus has largely been on satisfaction and its antecedents. Our exploration of the social psychology literature suggests that there is now an opportunity to develop scientifically well grounded principles for design of service systems. Training the next generation of service "engineers" in these principles will add considerable value to the progress of service system design.

Conclusions
Our ability to manage the psychological side of service encounters has lagged our ability to create the means by which encounters occur. Given the ubiquity of service encounters throughout all of industry, even just modest success in enhancing the practice of service psychology can have a huge impact on society.

References

[1]   Kahneman, Daniel and Amos Tversky, *Choices, Values and Frames*, Cambridge University Press, Cambridge, England, 2000.

[2]   Chase, Richard B. and Sriram Dasu, Want to Perfect Your Company's Service? Use Behavioral Science," *Harvard Business Review*, vol. 79, no. 6, June 2001, pp 78-85.

Challenges of Industrial Service Business Development

Vesa Salminen
Lappeenranta University of Technology
Technology Laboratory Nihtisillankuja 3A,
02630 ESPOO, Finland
Vesa.Salminen@lut.fi
+358 40 5441577

Petri Kalliokoski
VTT Technical Research Centre of Finland
P.O.Box 1000, 02044 VTT Finland
Petri.Kalliokoski@vtt.fi

ABSTRACT

Industrial Service business is a fast-growing business area in engineering and manufacturing industry. Many companies have tried to develop Industrial Services to create new business with customers but many of them have failed. In many cases, customers have not valued the proposed service models because of the lack of added value to current cooperation between supplier and customer. This article presents the findings of a BestServ Forum which is a collaborative consortium of 35 Finnish Enterprises on Manufacturing Industry. The objective of this consortium is to benchmark best practises, recognise the current status, development needs and future challenges of Industrial Service business in Finnish manufacturing industry. One of the most challenging objectives of the Forum has been to give guidance from industry to future research and development directions. This article introduces the directions of industrial research challenges which are now under accomplishment in national technology development programme SERVE coordinated and partially funded by Technology development centre, TEKES.

Introduction

The business environment is influenced by variety of economic and dynamic trends according to which companies have to consolidate on a global scale. Companies can at the same time be driven by technological and business innovations, all kinds of deregulation, customer requirements and other factors. All these factors and trends add to the complexity of solutions development and make fast new product and service introductions even more important and challenging [2].

The engineering industry is currently undergoing a transition from being the product provider to being the provider of customer value and product-related value-added services [1]. Enterprises have proclaimed and tried to undergo this transition but have failed in reality in several respects. Some of the product-related services are partly implemented with technological solutions, but most of the Industrial Services are only pilot schemes.

The challenge is to identify customer's critical processes and develop services to support these processes.

This transition from "ownership" to "access" and the potential sustainable growth of the business lies with the creation and capture of these services. Business related to Industrial Services tends to grow out of a commodity trap. This transition can be termed the "framework of value transition". This framework covers the complete transition of the industry from "parts supplier" to "value provider" (Figure 1). It points out the main elements that an enterprise or value network of enterprises needs to become an integrated product-service provider [6].

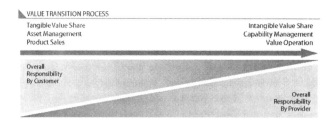

Figure 1. The framework of value transition.

This value transition means that traditional products are changing into solutions covering both products and services. Typically, customers have no capability to use these solutions without solution-provider services. The transition from products to solutions creates the basis for new kind of business and co-operation models between networked companies.

There is a great need for most of businesses to develop their product and service management in open system architecture. Business concepts are changing towards a knowledge-intensive and value-critical approach over the product life cycle. Value networks of companies are responsible for solution offerings consisting of service and product elements produced by various enterprises. Management of offering structure and further innovation needs a semantic structure [4].

State Of The Art Of Industrial Services In Finland

During recent years, there have been feasibility studies on the state of Industrial Services in Finnish industry. The studies were done by several research groups under one project, called BestServ. According to the feasibility studies, a common understanding has been created about what an Industrial Service is and how it interrelates with normal product businesses [3]. Manufacturing companies position themselves differently in terms of customer intimacy through their industrial service offerings and operations. For practical reasons, in the beginning of the study, five different supplier positions or "roles" (Figure 2), relative to the customer, were defined:

— **Machine supplier.** The focus of the business relationship is on delivering a piece of machinery or equipment that fits the customer's technical specification.

— **Solution provider.** The focus of business is on delivery of a system, e.g. a production line, which is usually designed for the specific customer's process and comprises a wider scope of supply than just one piece of equipment.

— **Maintenance partner.** The focus of business expands to also include continued supplier involvement during the continuing life cycle of the delivery. This role adds contractual after-market elements, such as spares and consumables agreements, to the supplier-customer relationship.

— **Performance partner.** In this role the supplier is closely involved in operating the customer's technical process by taking partial responsibility for the performance of the system, e.g. through availability warranties. This role requires the supplier to maintain at least a minimum of continuous on-site presence. The focus of the customer relationship is on securing the effective operation of the unit or production line.

— **Value partner.** The supplier is directly involved in the customer's business, e.g. through 'operate and maintain' agreements, where the customer pays a pre-determined price for the actual output of the system. Both parties focus on profitable daily operations, and the supplier is responsible for the day-to-day operation of the plant or line.

Each of these five supplier business models has its own "mindset." When a supplier aims to progress from one model to the next, it faces tough challenges, mostly in terms of getting the customer involved in this and developing its own technical and business competencies in order to advance. The strategic positioning decision between supplier and customer is important and has to be prepared as thoroughly as any other strategic decision.

The first two models focus the supplier's activities on the customer's investment decision and do not concentrate too much on supporting the life cycle of the customer's process. A solution supplier needs the ability to understand and interpret the customer's actual operations in its offering. A maintenance partner concentrates on professional maintenance management as a continuous process. As a performance partner, the supplier can have a responsibility for the actual daily performance of the customer process. When the supplier is a value partner, it is involved in the customer's value generation, e.g. producing optical cable in a cable factory at a given quality and price exactly according market need estimated. The supplier has to have competence in the customer's business. The level of knowledge and experience is increasing and creates competence for productive communication between partners of a value network.

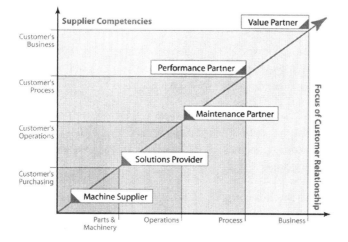

Figure 2: Business model analysis according to customer intimacy

The BestServ feasibility study showed that Industrial Services have been seen as a strategic intent to manage global competition and the evolution of current business models. This approach leads to the overall management of the customer offering through life cycles, from both a solution and a customer viewpoint. The main long-term development areas identified were:

— It is difficult to recognize the benefits of Industrial Services for customers and for all suppliers. The main challenge in this may be the lack of a shared value model of Industrial Services. The shared value model enables discussion about the potential benefits and values to be captured by the services.

— Industrial Services are usually built like extended products based on current product architectures and not on management of customer requirements and values. We need a customer-oriented solution architecture that integrates both product and service offering and enables efficient market segment management.

— It is difficult to determine an interoperable structure for Industrial Services to be integrated with product structure. This complicates the creation of new and innovative business models. Enterprises should have overall reference business models based on the integrated structure of product and Industrial Services (earnings logic, business strategy, organizational models etc.). The efficient development and use of reference models enables the continuous innovation of an integrated offering over the life cycle of the customer process and own business model.

— At the moment, many Industrial Services are traditionally oriented, while the need is for knowledge-intensive services (e.g. proactive maintenance, all kind of business consultation). The development of knowledge-intensive services requires a deep understanding of customer processes as well as the development of one's own competence. These require the reinventing of the customer offering and the related business model.

Technological solutions (e.g. telecom, automation, operative systems) are mainly developed to support separate operations and processes. There is a development challenge to manage the integration of separate technological solution. Continuous Industrial Service development requires parallel development of both business architecture and information as well as communication technology architecture

Industrial Service Business Research Topics

During the survey we recognized that most of the companies need to adapt their business according the paradigm shift from ownership to access and that potential sustainable growth of business lies in services created and captured. The framework of value transition means a transition from parts or machine supplier to value provider including services. There will be a continuous change in business models, which can be run according to the analysis of the rough value and evolving business models. It is difficult to manage this transition without system understanding and a well structured, customer-value based, and process for business transition.

The research topics should be understood as a system, with subsystems and individual R&D topics dependent on each other. It is only possible to concentrate on a few topics at the same time in any given business network and individual enterprise. Prioritizing according to changing system requirements is essential. It should be remembered that everything is changing as the move towards service-oriented business is made. Results in one development area have an influence on requirements that develop another. Business system understanding should support continuous prioritizing.

The main long-term focus areas when developing Industrial Service business were analyzed after the industrial survey. Figure 3 illustrates the R&D topics from a system point of view. The basic idea is that various development areas are dependent on each other.

Figure3.Main research areas based on BestsServ feasibility study.

The main research areas identified by BestServ can be summarized as following:

Value network management over the solution life cycle

There is a great need for a new approach to life-cycle management. This will be based on a value model supported by all stakeholders. Because the main partners in a value network are at some level responsible for customer business, customer value management becomes even more important. Organizational culture becomes more networked and value-oriented. Value has to be created, evaluated, captured and finally maximized and delivered over the life cycle of a customer application. This cannot be achieved without excellent collaboration network management over the product and service life-cycle.

Business models and architecture supporting the business transition process

The business transition process with suitable metrics is the one of the most essential development areas. Continuous Industrial Service development requires parallel development of both business architecture and ICT architecture. A well understood and structured business model supporting business architecture is a very important strategic tool when business is evolving according to market requirements. Life-cycle innovation needs new approaches and leads to business-concept management. In future, it will be possible and essential to sell business models based on the available architectural structure of a company. The main problem is that a reference business model and mechanism for the creation of new business model schemas are missing.

Solution architectures, platforms and configurations

Solution architecture is at the heart of business alignment. Solutions consist of service and product elements. When there are reusable elements in the architecture it is easier to build up new ones. Customer and functional requirements, features, modules, components and interfaces build the core structure of an enterprise solution structure. It is important to have an integrated service and product development process to create new offerings according both requirements. Service and product platforms supported by the solution architecture are used in the solution and in the customer configuration. The main challenges are the development and implementation of relevant solution architecture and platform knowledge that enables efficient customer and market management.

Solution life-cycle management and the supporting business intelligence system

A life-cycle business intelligence system is important when the competitiveness of a customer application has been secured. A life-cycle business intelligence concept needs to be created to combine application knowledge and organizational knowledge in the value network for life-cycle information management. An intelligent decision management system will also be needed to support new product and service element development. This is a parallel activity to development competence, service and the product as a whole. Development and other operational processes such as Industrial Service delivery, business logistics and communication will alter due to the changes in offerings and targeted market segmentation.

Organization culture and service competence

Many companies refer to "developing a new mindset" in the organization, as the main challenge in establishing a new Industrial Service role [5]. It is essential when developing business according the related architecture that also information and communication systems are developed at the same time to support the business evolution, organization culture and service competence are most important areas to develop at the same time. It is difficult to manage the evolutionary process without changing the organization and competence structure at the same time.

Enabling technologies and infrastructures

Finally it is essential to develop methodologies, solutions and customs in information and communication management in a value network. Research and development of enabling technologies and infrastructures is a parallel activity alongside the others presented above. We need new integration technologies to get intelligent control systems and intelligent operational systems as well as intelligent telecom systems and open system architecture to fully support the operational Industrial Service. There will be a need for new types of remote diagnostics and wireless systems. New types of business hub systems will be developed to support fluent collaboration in a value network. Common semantics management is essential and should be developed for Industrial Service-oriented, knowledge-intensive business.

Conclusions

35 Finnish companies, all of them operating in the global market, and several universities and research institutes have been participating on a project and round table work called BestServ[1]. It has been an interest group and knowledge community for companies, research organizations and financiers to activate and guide Industrial Service development. The purpose of this analysis work has been to find out the state of Industrial Service business globally, in various business sectors and also in individual enterprises. During the round table work, several generic frameworks have been created to help enterprises to face future challenges. BestServ work has given also guidance and alignment for future research and development challenges.

Industrial Service development activities should be both collaborative, enterprise-driven development and long-term cross-scientific research that combines the various sectors of the relevant research traditions and themes (management, technology, psychology, etc.).

This article introduced the directions of industrial research challenges which are now under accomplishment in national technology development programme SERVE coordinated and partially funded by Technology development centre, TEKES.

References

[1]   Clarke, T., Clegg, S., *Changing Paradigms-The Transformation of Management Knowledge for the 21st Century*, Harper Collins Publishers, London,1998.
[2]   Grönroos, C., *Service management and marketing*. West Sussex: John Wiley& Sons,2000.
[3]   Kalliokoski, P, Salminen, V, Andersson, G, Hemilä, J., *BestServ. Feasibility Study, Final Report*. Teknologiateollisuus, Kerava: Savion Kirjapaino Oy, 2003.
[4]   Pallot, M., Salminen, V., Pillai, B., Kulvant, P., Business Semantics: The Magic Instrument Enabling Plug & Play Collaboration?, *ICE 2004, International Conference on Concurrent Engineering*, ICE, Sevilla, June14-16, 2004.
[5]   Prahalad,C.K., Ramaswamy, V., *The future of competition. Co-creating unique value with customers*. Boston: Harvard Business School Press, 2004.
[6]   Tushman, M., Anderson, P., *Managing strategic innovation and change*. New York: Oxford University Press, 1997.

---

1   For more information, see BestServ web-site www.bestserv.fi.

A Research Based Educational Initiative: The Institute for International Services Innovation at Trinity College Dublin

John Murray
Professor of Business Studies, Director of Research
School of Business
Trinity College
University of Dublin
jmurray@tcd.ie
http://www.business.tcd.ie/research/faculty/murjoh.php

ABSTRACT

This paper takes the importance to economic and social development of the scale, scope, growth rate and global pervasiveness of the 'service economy' as given. In that context, it describes the Institute for International Services Innovation initiative at Trinity, noting its rationale, design, interdependencies and key challenges. It also notes the conjoined roles of industry, organizations more generally, Government and IBM, and makes some suggestions for progress in the emerging SSME and related knowledge creation communities.

Introduction

Given the importance to economic and social development of the scale, scope, growth rate and global pervasiveness of the 'service economy', this paper describes the *Institute for International Services Innovation* initiative at Trinity College, University of Dublin. It addresses the rationale, design, interdependencies and key challenges facing this initiative.

Origins and rationale

The origins of the Institute in 2005 were fourfold. First was the recognition of the extent of services sector growth. This growth and its attendant scope reflects the size and value-creating importance of embedded services within traditional manufacturing sector; the growth of the 'pure' services' arena driven by the traditional (e.g. distribution), newer (e.g. financial, information and professional) and emergent (e.g. digital service) businesses; the challenge of reform in public and voluntary services sectors; and the lack of specialized knowledge of their structure, dynamics and evolutionary trajectories.

Second was the recognition of significant global aspects of service sector evolution, especially the international mobility of service management, operations and delivery and the associated issues of service cluster phenomena on a worldwide scale. This concern has particular resonance in Ireland as one of the world's most open economies (largest services exporter in world in per-capita terms in 2003; 14th largest in absolute terms & 2.2% share of world service exports in 2004; population of 4m) with a front seat view of the manufacturing – service transition and daily locational competition for globally mobile high-value service enterprise.

A third stimulus came from government, in the form of Ireland's Industrial Development Authority (IDA), and its policy-driven desire to understand the evolving dynamics of the global services sector in order to attract appropriately targeted foreign direct investment (FDI) in services to an Irish location and to help create a services oriented research capability that would provide part of the supporting knowledge infrastructure for a new generation of global service firms located in Ireland. The focal emphasis on *internationally traded services* and *innovation* were, in particular, supported by interactions with IDA as these confirmed the existence of a policy based urgency; the role of innovation in the success of "advanced services work"; and its role in the global competition for mobile or potentially mobile high-value service activity location.

A fourth spur was the SSME initiative of IBM, accessed directly at Almaden and via parallel access to IBM Ireland (with a 50 year service, sales and manufacturing history in Ireland). These interactions were solely knowledge and information-exchange based, and were important to motivation, to validating judgements about the services imperative and to legitimating the initiative as 'business relevant'.

Finally, a process of strategic reform and renewal in the university generated opportunities around programmatic research capable of creating new knowledge of global relevance, linked to support from government and industry and built through global research networks. In parallel, the business school was seen as contributing an enabling research and education role across a series of central and large-scale strategic research programmes. These central university-wide research programmes include International Integration, Communications Technology & Value Chain Research, Nano-Technology, Neuroscience, and Molecular Medicine. The business school's enabling role is to provide a 'Business & Innovation' contribution across all these. At one level, this involves a teaching and learning input to stimulate and support commercialisation of the research output of these major institutional programmes. At another it is to conduct research that joins the business school's research activity to the science, engineering and technology focus of colleagues working on the programmes. This is being initiated on the basis of a focus on business system / value chain implications of the new technologies and their application, and on their novel service implications.

These five different but convergent forces form the origins of the initiative and came together more-or-less simultaneously within a period of 18 months. Serendipity and emergence, without doubt, play a major role in the Institute's provenance!

Design Concept

The design of the Institute embodies some features that may be of interest more generally. These are the commitment to research driven education, a multidisciplinary – multi-level - multimodal approach, engagement with leading edge new technology research, and the intention to use Ireland as 'a laboratory' of special interest because of its extreme 'globalisation', its position in the global market for high-value services FDI, and its small and compact scale.

The commitment to research-led education is simple to explain. The guiding philosophy is to lead with research, to engage students, practitioners and policy makers in that research and to drive education and learning from that base either through direct involvement or through research derived learning materials and research active faculty. The philosophy fits well within the context of a research driven university and the policy and professional managerial demand for new knowledge rooted in contemporary practice and dilemmas.

The multidisciplinary – multilevel - multimodal approach is based on conceptualizing services research as posing questions, and demanding understanding and explanation, at the interlocking levels of global, national, community, industry, firm and individual, each with a related set of disciplinary research traditions and lenses. The multi-modal aspect allows inductive research (case research, for example) to discover patterns and generate hypotheses that may then be tested by, for example, statistical or econometric analysis while deductive methods may be deployed for quantitative data gathering and analysis or for simulation modeling of aspects of services as complex adaptive systems. The multidisciplinary, multilevel, multimodal design philosophy attempts to match the variety of the services 'problematique' with matching variety in research strategy. It seeks to embrace and integrate a group of researchers whose training and interest is diverse[1] and it seeks to draw managers and policy makers into the research process through action research and action learning modalities.

---

1 The core Trinity group comprises Louis Brennan, Paul Coughlan, Mairead Brady, David Coghlan, Brian Lucey, Mary Lee Rhodes, all at http://www.business.tcd.ie/research/faculty/index.php#aca

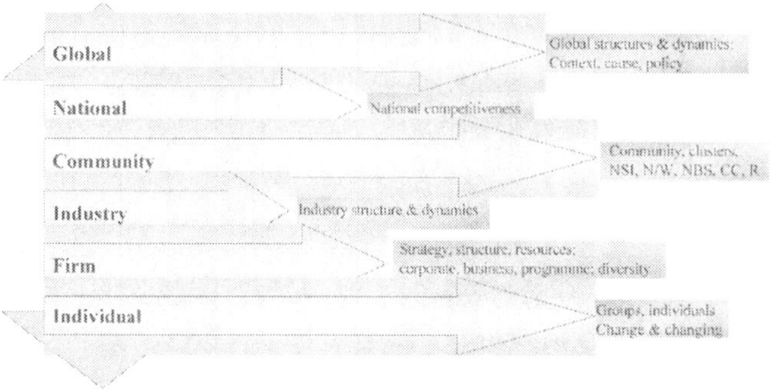

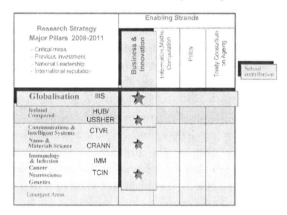

Figure 1. Multilevel, multidisciplinary, multimodal approach

The engagement with leading-edge new technology research is directly driven by a mandate within the university and adopts the twin conceptual foci of a) global business system / value chain implications and b) novel services implications of the new technology. This focus provides a means of developing a coherent knowledge base with depth and focus that is relevant to a diverse set of science, engineering and technology research programmes.

Figure 2. University New-Tech & Services

The 'Ireland as a laboratory' feature may be seen as exploiting a gift of location. A natural advantage of the Institute's location lies in its interconnectedness with a tiny (by global standards) population of 4 millions that combines to produce one of the most dynamic, highly globalised economies in the world, that is well advanced in the manufacturing-services transition, that lives by its ability to compete for the locational decisions of domestic and internationally mobile high-value service enterprises, that is 'home' to many domestic international services as well as most of the world's best known global corporations in selected sectors, that is pursuing a programme of public sector reform, and that, critically, is characterized by a significant established degree of working interconnectedness between industry, policy makers and universities. In this context, it is possible to realistically conceive of a truly multi-level approach to research that lies within the bounds of feasible scale.

Interdependencies

Interdependencies are central to the design concept, rendering the Institute something of a network organization. The central interdependencies are with colleagues in other faculties and schools in the university, with policy agents, with practicing managers and with an international network of researchers pursuing similar disciplinary and applied goals.

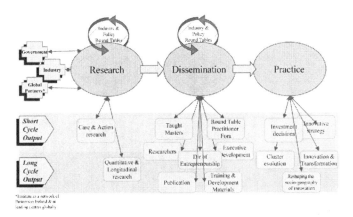

Figure 3. Institute for International Services Innovation

Conferences such as this are vital to building and developing the network on which the Institute's ambitions rest. It is impossible in an emerging discipline, such as envisaged for SSME by IMB, to hope to build capability across the full range of disciplinary areas and research methods necessary to command an integrated understanding of the field. While that is a real institutional and intellectual limitation the extent of the knowledge base involved also makes it impossible from a resourcing perspective for most research groups. The need to build a community with 'dense ties' is therefore urgent and pivotal to continuing development.

With this in mind, it is suggested that an 'open source' approach to community building and knowledge creation is the appropriate direction for collective development.

Suggestion: An 'Open Source' SSME Enterprise

It is suggested that the emergent 'community' involved in the SSME and related initiatives consider committing to an 'open source' approach to the creation and development of services knowledge. This involves working with what some call the 'economics of the commons' rather than the historically more recent focus on markets or hierarchies as governance frameworks. The SSME enterprise seems ideally suited to this approach. Peer production - production systems that depend on individual action that is self-selected and decentralised, rather than hierarchically assigned and that is not locked up by market based IP - is an approach suited to the endeavour and to the university tradition of many of the researchers likely to be involved, or needing inducement to join in.

In this context it seems possible for an Institute like ours to contribute as a node with its particular specialised focus (internationally traded services, service innovation, business system and value chain structures and dynamics, the service opportunities of selected new technologies, multidisciplinary/level/modal methodology) and to draw on other specialised nodes in a manner that could lead to a celebration of the commons rather than a tragedy of the commons.

Defining the Research Agenda: Technology Management as a Contributor to Service Sciences, Management and Engineering

Dundar F Kocaoglu, Tugrul U. Daim, Antonie J. Jetter
Department of Engineering and Technology Management
Portland State University
Portland, OR 97207-0751

ABSTRACT

Technology Management is a dynamically evolving discipline that integrates the technology-dominated world of the engineer with management. The field is distinguishable from its neighbor disciplines through characteristic research questions, specialized Production, and more than 200 educational programs. Currently, the field changes its face and increasingly focuses on the service industry. It thus reflects the blur-ring boundaries between services and goods companies and the service sector's growing dependency on (information) technology. This paper describes these changes and presents contributions of Technology Management to SSME. Based on these findings and a survey of industry needs in the "Silicon Forest", it outlines an agenda for education and research.

Technology Management Defined

Technology Management (TM), also referred to as "Engineering Management" has been characterized as the link among "engineering, science and management disciplines to plan, develop and implement technological capabilities to shape and accomplish the strategic and operational objectives of an organization" [12]. It thus encompasses two sets of activities (see fig. 1): (1) activities related to the *innovation process*, leading to new technologies (research, product and process development and commercialization), and (2) the activities that define a company's "strategic make up" – the *strategic integration* of its technology strategy (definition of the technologies to engage in, including timing and resource commitment), its business strategy (markets to serve, and needed resources and organizational structures), and its financial strategies. Modern technologies are usually developed in industry, but the under-lying scientific research is predominantly per-formed in universities. TM therefore researches efficient means for transferring technology from the research into the development domain (see (1) in fig. 1) that range from the design of educational programs to the creation of strategic re-search alliances.

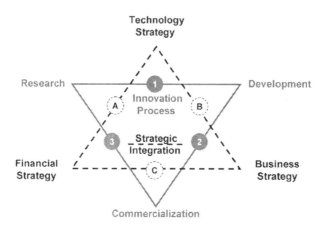

Figure 1: The scope of Technology Management

Companies employ science-based technologies to develop and commercialize new technology products (see (2) in fig. 1) that can range from materials (e.g. nano-technology-based surface coatings), over systems (e.g. computers) to services (e.g. technical consulting). TM researches how the new product/service development process should be organized effectively and efficiently. These decisions are closely linked to decision of technology assessment and acquisition (see (3) in fig. 2): companies have to assess evolving technologies with regard to their present and future potential so that they choose technologies that deliver competitive advantages. They furthermore need to decide on acquisition strategies that can range from investing in in-house research to buying IP, services, or physical goods that embody the technology that is to be acquired. The innovation process is thus closely linked to a company's overall technology strategy, which determines its present product and process technologies, as well as a roadmap for the future. TM researches the process of technology integration – the way in which technology strategy and business strategies are aligned (see B in fig. 1) to make sure that the organization is ready for new technologies (e.g. availability of technical infrastructure, skilled personnel, innovation-friendly company culture) and that the markets and product offerings are in line with the technology potentials. It furthermore looks at how the business strategy creates value for the customer throughout the extended value chain. Since this value is translated into financial returns, business strategy and financial strategy are closely linked (see C in fig. 1). Also, technology and financial strategies have to be aligned. TM therefore deals with the selection of R&D project portfolios that balance risk and opportunities and long- and short term expenditures and financial returns (see A in fig. 1).

TM, in summary, is a discipline that does not focus on the development of specific technologies, but on means to efficiently and effectively organize innovation and strategic integration in any organization that uses or develops technologies, be it governments, manufacturing firms, high-tech spin offs, or service providers. The management solutions offered in TM are new methods for forecasting, planning, coordinating and decision-making, sometimes software-based, that are targeted at "real-world" people. Consequently, they commonly take "noise" factors, such as lack of information, bounded rationality, micro-motives, and group effects into account. TM thus integrates science, engineering, management and public policy.

TM In The Service Industry – A Brief Review Of Past Research

TM as a discipline dates back to the 1940s, when first educational programs were established, and has seen an accelerated growth since the 1970s. By the mid-1990s more than 200 educational programs in engineering and technology management existed worldwide, many of them on the graduate level in engineering colleges and business schools [6]. In the same time frame, several high-quality journals dedicate to TM issues have evolved, namely the *IEEE Transactions in Engineering Management* (established 1954), *Technological Forecasting and Social Change* (established 1969), *Technovation* (established 1981), *R&D Management* (established 1986), *The Journal of Product Innovation Management* (established 1986), *Engineering Management Journal* (established 1989), and others. They increasingly cover topics of interest for the service industry, as a content analysis of two of the above mentioned TM journals (*IEEE Transactions* and *EMT* from 1993-2000), which was conducted by Kern, uncovered "The largest growing area of interest is in the services economy. The finance, insurance, real estate, wholesale, and trade industries are underrepresented and therefore may represent opportunities for expansion of the engineering management field interest and research" [8]. This expansion is visible in TM publications for several years now. In 1999, the *IEEE Transactions* dedicated a special issue to the health care sector, followed by a special cluster on TM in the service industries in 2001. Furthermore a large number of publications with relevance for the service industry are scattered in the TM literature, covering a wide range of topics from strategy development to project management. Despite the diversity of topics, most of these publications have a few common themes. Many authors investigate the differences between services and physical goods and attempt to translate existing TM findings to the service sector. Their research covers the question if innovation success in both areas depends on the same factors [5], [16], if "traditional" TM practices known from goods industries, such as technology roadmapping [17], platform planning [11], integrated process mapping and failure mode effect analysis [9], and concurrent product development [7] can be applied to services, and if strategy recommendations for manufacturing firms, for example the pursuit of pioneering ad-vantages, are also suitable for service development [15].

Other authors focus on present TM practices in the service sector, such as R&D strategies [14] and emerging technologies [13] in the health care sector, IP strategies in the knowledge and entertainment industry [2], and technology transfer efficiency. Also, changes in service industries, such as the evolution of product development services and consulting engineering firms and their impact on innovation in goods industry are researched [1, 4]. Finally, the growing interest in services within the TM community has let to first attempts to come up with a framework and systematic research agenda for "TM in the service industry" [10] or "Service Engineering"[3]. The many research activities have provided an already strong and dynamically growing research base for the young field of TM for services. However, industry practitioners frequently express the need for further efforts, as will be discussed in the following section.

Industry Needs: TM for Services in the "Silicon Forest"

The "Silicon Forest," located in the Portland, Oregon metropolitan area, is home to high-tech companies in semi-conductor, computer, and software industry, such as Intel, Novellus, Hewlett Packard, Tektronix, InFocus, and Mentor Graphics. Many of these companies deliver value to their customers through extended value chains that consist of components, hardware systems, different layers of software and different services, thus forcing even manufacturing-oriented companies to focus in on service issues. Intel, for example, recently reorganized the company across plat-forms, such as "Health Care", "Digital Home" and "Mobility", and works with the service providers that impact each platform. We surveyed the executives of the "Silicon Forest's" key players and asked about their most pressing TM concerns. The three leading issues were:

— Efficient identification and evaluation of technologies that will be important in the future, either as a disruptor, a source of competitive advantage or a competitive threat. How can this analysis be supported for multiple technologies across multiple product lines? How can adoption rates of new technologies be forecasted correctly?

— Coping with the complexity of the value creation process through improved decision-support tools that capture the multitude of aspects, rather than over-simplifying them.

— Means to capture and use knowledge about the usage environment and the business, cultural, and legal ecosystem of a planned new product in order to provide value. (An illustrative example for these thoughts is Apple i-pod – the hardware in itself does not create value to the customer, but requires software, fast internet infrastruc-ture, legal download sites, and attractive music content). How can the knowledge captured from multiple sources be systematically used? How can value creation be modeled?

As can be seen by these topics, industry needs in the "Silicon Forest" cut across the increasingly artificial division of "goods" and "services" and require an integrative research approach.

Conclusion – A Research Agenda

In a technology-driven world, service companies' success depends on the ability to in-novate, and to strategically integrate technology into their over-all business strategy. TM addresses these topics and thus provides a natural home for efforts in SSME, particularly as TM presently shifts its focus from traditional manufacturing to service is-sues. It should continue to do so at an accelerated pace, making sure that the increased service orien-tation of the field is not only reflected through sporadic conference presentations and special journal issues, but through a steady streams of high-quality proposals to NSF's "Service Enterprise Engineering Program (SEE)", through industry-sponsored research, and through the curricula of TM programs which already today pro-vide many gradu-ates for the service sector. High tech products and services are often created in "value networks" with partners that differ in age (entrepreneurial start-ups, as well as established companies), size, and main industry affiliation. TM research should therefore be orga-nized in centers that span across industry boundaries and foster cross-industry and mul-tidisciplinary cooperation. NSF programs that can be avenues for such activities include "Partnership for Innovation" and "Industry University Cooperative Re-search Centers (I/UCRC)". Industry support should be targeted at sponsoring the research in such centers, at communicating the industry needs to the TM community, and at endorsing important curricula changes. Colleges, departments and programs in the TM field should em-brace those changes and reflect them in their funding, research, teaching and publication strate-gies. The Department of Engineering and Technology Management (ETM) at Portland State University, for example, developed the following action plan:

— Increased focus on a service-oriented research agenda with proposals for industrial partners and research funding agencies. Topics include models for the diffusion of new health care services as a result of emerging technologies and models for IT-based health services.

— Increased visibility for service-related research in the 2007 PICMET through a special track on *TM for the Service Industry* with workshops, tutorials and panels. PICMET (www.picmet.org) is an international conference on technology and engi-neering management that is organized by ETM. It is now in its 15th year.

— Proposal of an collaborative Industry-University Research Center on TM that will make SSME a research priority. The center, which is named "Technology Management Research Center" (TMRC), is supported through industry in the "Silicon Forest" and is presently seeking NSF funding through the I/UCRC and the SEE program.

Similar efforts in other institutions and a strong network of researchers engaged in SSME in the TM community will help to further define the field and provide the needed research base for service engineering.

References

[1]   Alam, I. Commercial Innovations from Consulting Engineer-ing Firms: An Empirical Exploration of a Novel Source of New Product Ideas. *Journal of Product Innovation Management*, Vol. 20, Issue 4, Jul2003.

[2]   Arnold Reisman. Technology Management: A Brief Review of the Last 40 Years and Some Thoughts on Its Future. *IEEE Transactions on Engineering Management*, Vol. 41, No. 4, 1994.

[3]   Bullinger, H.-J; Scheer, A.-W, *Service Engineering*, Berlin: Springer, 2003.

[4]   Chiesa, V, Manzini, R, Pizzurno, E. The externalization of R&D activities and the growing market of product development services. *R&D Management*, Vol. 34, Issue 1, Jan. 2004.

[5]   de Brentani, U. Innovative versus Incremental New Business Services: Different Keys for Achieving Success. *Journal of Product Innovation Management*, Vol. 18, Issue 3, May 2001.

[6]   Dundar, F. Kocaoglu. Technology Mangement: Educational Trends. *IEEE Transactions on Engineering Management*, Vol. 41, No. 4, 1994.

[7]   Hull, F.M. A Composite Model of Product Development Effec-tiveness: Application to Services. *IEEE Transactions on Engineering Management*, Vol. 51, Issue 4, May 004.

[8]   Kern, D. Content and Trends in Engineering Management Literature. *Engineering Management Journal*, Vol. 14, No. 1, March 2002.

[9]   Linton, J.D. Facing the Challenges of Service Automation: An Enabler for E-Commerce and Productivity Gain in Traditional Services. *IEEE Transactions on Engineering Management*, Vol. 50, Issue 4, Nov. 2003.

[10] McDermott, C., Kang, H., Walsh, S. A Framework for Technology Management in Services. *IEEE Transactions on Engineering Management*, Vol. 48, Issue 3, Aug. 2001.

[11] Meyer, M.C., DeTore, A. Perspective: Creating a Platform-based Approach for Developing New Services. *Journal of Product Innovation Management*, Vol. 18, Issue 3, May 2001.

[12] National Research Council. *Management of Technology: The Hidden Competitive Advantage*. National Academy Press, 1987.

[13] Rostagi A., T Daim, Exploring Emerging Technologies in Health Care Services. *INFORMS Fall National Meeting*, November 2006, Pittsburgh, PA.

[14] Rogers, D. The Evolution of a local R&D strategy: the Experience of a Service in the UK National Health Service (NHS). *R&D Management*, Vol. 34, Issue 1, Jan 2004.

[15] Song, X.M, di Benedetto, C.A., Song, L. Pioneering Advantage in New Service Development: A Multi-Country Study of Managerial Perceptions. *Journal of Product Innovation Management*, Vol. 17, Issue 5, Sep 2000.

[16] Van Riel, Alan C.R., Lemmink J., Ouwersloot H. High-Technology Service Innovation Success: A Decision-Making Perspective. *Journal of Product Innovation Management*, Vol. 21, Issue 5, Sep 2004.

[17] Wells, R., Phaal, R., Farrukh, C., Probert D., Technology Roadmapping for a Service Organization. *Research Technology Management*, Vol. 47, Issue 2, March/April 2004.

Actionable Process Theories: A Unique Selling Proposition for a Science of Services

Nick V. Flor
Marketing, Info. Systems & Decision Sciences Group
Anderson Schools of Management
University of New Mexico
nickflor@unm.edu
505-277-6471

ABSTRACT

A key objective for a science of services should be to produce *actionable process theories*. Doing so will distinguish a science of services from competing fields like management information systems, and allow a science of services to have more immediate real-world impact.

Introduction

The academic side of management information systems (MIS) has a serious problem that a science of services can solve—MIS research lacks real-world impact. To see this, answer this question: When do you think was the last time a manager in a top technology organization picked up *MIS Quarterly* or *Information Systems Research* (two of the top journals in MIS) to get ideas for improving his or her organization?

The answer: Probably never. And this is strange considering that we are currently in the midst of a revolution in both information technology and networking.

MIS researchers should be driving this revolution. Instead, they are reacting to it by merely analyzing *existing* information system—using statistical methods to finding relationships between variables.

The problem with statistical studies of existing information systems is that the systems are complex and constantly changing. Therefore, today's findings may not be statistically valid tomorrow.

I can think of no better example of this problem than the famous study by Kraut et al [9], who initially reported that spending time on the internet was positively correlated with depression, loneliness, and stress: However, several years later, Kraut reported that his follow-up studies showed that most of the bad effects had disappeared! [8] According to Kraut: "Either the Internet has changed, or people have learned to use it more constructively, or both." [3]

When studying complex, socio-technical systems, that are constantly changing, it is not sufficient to identify correlations between an independent X and some dependent variable Y. It is also important to understand the causal chain of structures and processes by which some variable X produces an observable outcome Y. The former is known as a variable theory, and the latter a process theory [10].

Classic examples of process theory in the natural world include, how malaria is spread from mosquitoes to humans, and Mendel's theory of inheritance.

Knowledge of process in the natural world allows people to develop treatments, e.g., methods for preventing malaria, or to produce novel kinds of plants and animals, e.g., hybrids and cross breeds. Similarly, knowledge of process in the "artificial" world allows researchers and developers to create technologies that improve existing information systems, or to develop new kinds of information systems.

The need for process theories in the organization sciences is well known. Mackenzie [11] wrote:

> "We have reached the point in the organization sciences where our traditional methods of positing variables, gathering data across groups and organizations, and then linking variables by linear models using standard statistical methods is breaking down... We are left with a proliferation of competing paradigms..., little understanding of how things work in actual organizations, and generally inconclusive (or unconvincing) results from these labors. It is possible that this state of affairs is a direct consequence of how research is being done." (p. 123)

Unfortunately, in the field of MIS this is unlikely to change. MIS is dominated by variable theories, especially in the top journals. Moreover, the tenure and promotion process is intricately linked to publishing in these top journals. Thus, MIS researchers do not have any incentive to produce process theories.

This is where a science of services (SOS) can make an impact. It can focus on creating process theories for information systems or, more generally, service systems. If the theories could somehow be written up so that they were understandable, not only to academics, but managers and other practitioners, they would be *actionable process theories*.

The remainder of this paper describes what students would need to know in order to create actionable process theories, and provides a possible example of how an actionable process theory could be used to improve an existing service system.

Actionable Process Theories in Education

What would an undergraduate or graduate student in MIS have to know in order to create actionable process theories for service systems? Recall that a process theory describes the causal chain of structures and processes by which some variable X produces an outcome Y, and that a service system consists of both people and technology. Therefore, to create an actionable process theory of an existing service system, one needs:

1. Methods for mapping the observable structure and process of socio-technological systems. Examples of such methods include *physical* (versus logical) data flow diagrams [2] and information activity maps [6].

2. Methods for mapping the structure and process within technological systems. Examples of such methods include Unified Modeling Language [7] and Object-Oriented Analysis and Design [1].

3. Methods for mapping structure and processes within people—within mental systems. The only example of such a method that I know of, that is also actionable, is the mental-space mapping technique used by conceptual blending [4] researchers.

It would be a great help to universities if there were a single methodology that combined all three kinds of methods—a kind of UML, but for socio-technological systems instead of software systems, e.g. STML.

An Example of an Actionable Process Theory

An distance organization has a problem with excessive mailing costs which are currently at $100,000 / year (actual case based on Flor [5]).

The task of a service scientist is to first represent the people, technology, information, and physical goods in the mailing process. Figure 1 depicts one way of representing this information using information activity maps [6].

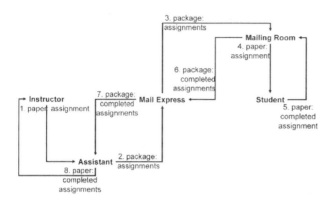

Figure 1. Information Activity Map: Step 1, Representing the Current Process

These maps are actionable. A researcher, manager, or practitioner can understand them with minimal explanation. Furthermore, the maps allow one to visually explore possible problem areas. For example, each individual agent could be driving up costs (see Figure 2).

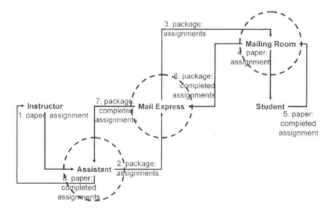

Figure 2. Information Activity Map: Step 2, Examining Possible Problem Areas

Or pairs of agents may be driving up costs (see Figure 3). Or all the intermediate agents could be driving up costs (not shown).

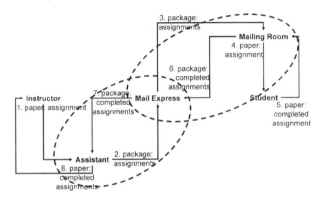

Figure 3. Information Activity Map: Step 2 (cont.), Examining Possible Problem Areas

Suppose a service scientist has a hypothesis about what agents are driving up costs. To support this hypothesis the service scientist can build a cost model in (e.g.) Microsoft Excel that assigns a cost to each arrow in the model. The costs represent media, production, and distribution costs for each information transaction (see Figure 4)

INTERACTION MATRIX:				
FROM/TO	I	A	M	S
I		$ 5.85		
A	$ 2.75		$ 123.30	
M		$ 1.25		
S				$ 120.00

SUMMARY:				
SINGLE	WEEKLY	MINI	MINI-ALL	YEARLY
$ 253.15	$ 506.31	$ 3,544.15	$ 14,176.59	$ 85,059.52
			ORIGINAL	$ 85,059.52
			REDUCTION	0.00%

CONTROL PANEL:	units	comment	50%
IWAGE	$ 50.00	per hour	1.15%
AWAGE	$ 15.00	per hour	1.28%
PTIME	0.03 hours	2 minutes	0.33%
DTIME	0.08 hours	5 minutes	0.82%
CTIME	0.08 hours	5 minutes	0.25%
MTIME	0.08 hours	5 minutes	0.25%
STIME	0.08 hours	5 minutes	0.25%
RTIME	0.02 hours	1 minute	0.30%
WTIME	0.08 hours	5 minutes	0.25%
CPAGE	$ 0.01 per page	1 penny	0.16%
NPAGES	2 pages		0.16%
NSTUD	40 students		0.16%
NSITES	6 locations		47.70%
MAILXFEE	$ 20.00	overnight	47.40%
TFREQ	2	per week	50.00%
NINST	4	instructors	50.00%
WMINI	7 weeks	per mini	50.00%
NMINI	6	per year	50.00%

Figure 4. Information Activity Map: Step 3. Diagnosing Problem Areas (Cost Drivers) By Modeling Information Transaction Costs

By manipulating the variables in the control panel for this model, the service scientist can discover the cost driver. In this case, the variable is the mailing fee (see Figure 5).

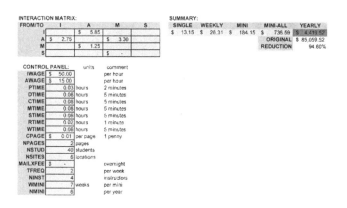

Figure 5. Information Activity Map: Step 3. Diagnosing Problem Areas (Cost Drivers) By Modeling Information Transaction Costs

This cost driver corresponds to the Mail Express agent in the information activity map. Thus, the service scientist knows that to drive down costs he or she must create a solution that eliminates the Mail Express agent (see Figure 6).

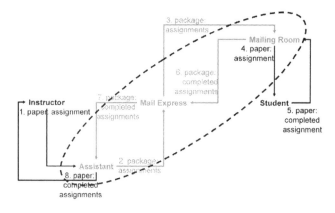

Figure 6. Information Activity Map: Step 4. Developing a treatment

A common solution is to use the web for electronic mailings. However, using the information activity map, the service scientist can find alternative solutions. Note that the arrows into and out of the Mail Express agent—the agent that is driving up costs and that must be eliminated—form a kind of functional specification for the technology (see Figure 7).

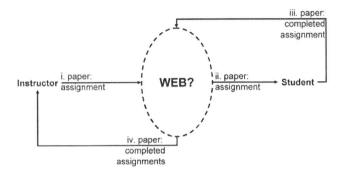

Figure 7. Information Activity Map: Step 4 (cont.). Developing a treatment through analysis of the information activity map

Given this functional specification, a "low-tech" solution like a FAX would be just as effective in driving down costs as the Web (see Figure 8), and no bridging technologies need to be purchased to convert the paper assignments to electronic form.

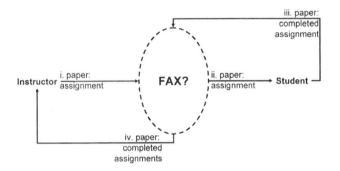

Figure 8. Information Activity Map: Step 4 (cont.). Developing a treatment through analysis of the information activity map

Summary

A science of services is a science of the artificial [12]. The systems studied are complex socio-technical systems that are constantly changing. The dynamic nature of these systems limits the value of variable theories. Instead, using process theories one can better design treatments and develop new service systems.

References

[1]   Booch, G. (1994). *Object Oriented Analysis and Design*. Redwood City, CA: Benjamin Cummings Publishing.

[2]   Demarco, T. (1979). *Structured Analysis and System Specification*. Englewood Cliffs, NJ: Yourdon Press.

[3]   Elias, M. (2001). Study: Net use doesn't increase depression, after all. *USA Today*, July 23, 2001. http://www.usatoday.com/tech/news/2001-07-23-web-depression-study.htm.

[4]   Fauconnier, G., & Turner, M. (2002). *The Way We Think*. New York, NY: Basic Books.

[5]   Flor, N. (2000). *Web Business Engineering*. Reading, MA: Addison-Wesley.

[6]   Flor, N., & Maglio, P. (2004). Modeling Business Representational Activity Online: A Case Study of a Customer-Centered Business. *Knowledge-Based Systems, 17*, 39-56.

[7]   Fowler, M. (2003). *UML Distilled*. Reading, MA: Addison-Wesley.

[8]   Kraut, R., Kiesler, S., Boneva, B., Cummings, J., Helgeson, V., Crawford, A. (2002). Internet Paradox Revisited, *Journal of Social Issues, 58*, 49-74.

[9]   Kraut, R. Patterson, M., Lundmark, V., Kiesler, S, Mukophadhyay, T. & Scherlis, W. (1998). Internet paradox: A social technology that reduces social involvement and psychological well-being? *American Psychologist, 53*, 10171-031.

[10] Mohr, L. (1982). *Explaining Organizational Behavior*. San Francisco, CA: Jossey-Bass.

[11] Mackenzie, K. D. (2000). Processes and their Frameworks. *Management Science, 46*, 110-125.

[12] Simon, H. (1981). *The Sciences of the Artificial (2nd Edition)*. Cambridge, MA: MIT Press.

Quality System Management and Education in Service Environments

Richard R. Perdue
Hospitality and Tourism Management
Pamplin College of Business
Virginia Polytechnic Institute and State
University
Blacksburg, VA 24060
rick.perdue@vt.edu
540-231-4373

Steven D. Sheetz
Director, Center for Global e-Commerce
Pamplin College of Business
Virginia Polytechnic Institute and State
University
Blacksburg, VA 24060
sheetz@vt.edu
540- 231-6096

ABSTRACT

Service quality is widely recognized as a core construct of services management. Effective service quality management, however, requires integration both across organizational units and the functional areas of a corporation. Using the Gaps Model of Service Quality, this paper articulates numerous quality challenges of large, multi-unit organizations, including measurement, service design, service delivery, and marketing communications. Meeting these challenges requires effective integration of various business disciplines, particularly marketing, human resource management, accounting, and information systems management. The paper concludes by relaying the challenges experienced in teaching this integration in service operations and marketing courses.

Introduction

Quality is widely recognized as a critical services management challenge, due to three separate, but converging trends. First, there is an increasing emphasis on customer loyalty, personal referrals, and relationship marketing throughout the service industry [5]. Service quality and customer satisfaction are recognized as primary determinants of both loyalty and personal referrals [7]. Second, service consumers expect higher and higher levels of quality, not only in service design, but also in the quality and personalization of services received [1]. Third, for a variety of reasons, service businesses are finding it increasingly difficult to attract and retain quality employees [3, 8]. Yet, quality employees have historically been considered the *raison d'etre* of service quality.

Facing these challenges, it is essential that service businesses identify ways of increasing employee productivity, defined as increasing the quality of service provided to consumers while, at the same time, reducing the necessary number of employees [8]. Further, to be competitive for employees, service businesses must identify ways of improving the quality of jobs; making them both easier and more enjoyable [2]. Effective integration of traditional functional areas of business, particularly marketing, human resource and operations management, accounting, and information systems management is widely recognized as the key means by which these divergent goals may be attained [2,4]. The purpose of this paper is to examine this integration. The implications to services management education are then discussed.

Service Quality Challenges

The Gaps Model of Service Quality [6] will be used to organize the following discussion of key service quality challenges impacting this integration (Figure 1). Consistent with the service quality literature, the Gaps Model conceptualizes quality as the congruence between a customer's service expectations and the perceived quality of service received. Four potential gaps or problem sources are identified.

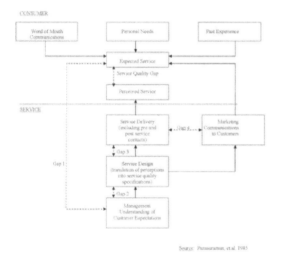

Figure 1. The GAPS Model of Service Quality

First, in order to design and provide quality services, management must understand customer expectations both overall and by an ever increasing variety of market segments, particularly given the dramatic growth in customer relationship management and service customization. Much of the existing services research has focused on developing diagnostic measures of service quality and assessing their relationship with customer satisfaction, repeat consumption and referral propensity. While this work certainly continues, the management challenge now is to develop the capacity to integrate various quality measures, make the results easily and quickly available to managers, and train managers in the effective interpretation and use of these data. If expectations change or quality problems occur, managers and employees must quickly identify these changes and respond with appropriate service recovery and improvements. This is further complicated for service categories which experience cyclical changes in customer segments and demand.

Second, management must design products and services that satisfy those expectations. Mass customization seems to be the focus of virtually every service category. Customer relationship systems are creating massive amounts of data which theoretically enhance both service improvements and innovations. Along with data provided by competitive benchmarking and quality monitoring systems, the options are virtually unlimited. Given the human resource challenges of service delivery, however, the key question seems to be how much of the service design and delivery process can be effectively shifted to the consumer through technology-enhanced self service systems. Further, since entire service categories are sharing essentially the same technologies, the issues of product commodification and shorter cycles for both development and competitive advantage put ever greater pressure on service design and process improvement teams. Traditional market research and product development methodologies such as conjoint analysis, process blueprinting and fishbone analyses are increasingly challenged by these pressures.

Third, even if expectations are well understood and appropriate products and services have been designed, it is still critical to effectively deliver those services. Determining the best investments is to improve, facilitate, and speed up the actual delivery of services is perhaps the key challenge. For a variety of reasons, providing customer services can be both physically and emotionally difficult. Employee burnout is a serious problem impacting service quality both directly through discourteous employees and indirectly through employee turnover. Consequently, given the difficulty of recruiting and retaining a quality workforce, employee satisfaction is equally or even more important than customer satisfaction.

Three major trends reflect current practices. First, and by far most important, improving employee training systems is essential. Creating more flexible, technology-based systems is enhancing both initial and, particularly, on-going training systems. Second, many businesses are significantly investing in technology to improve both service processes and the ability of employees to answer customer questions. As examples, customer history and membership databases are being used to reduce the service delivery times and improve process accuracy. Third, information technology can also reduce number-of-employee needs, particularly for repetitive services which have highly cyclical demand. For example, customer relationship management and loyalty systems are being used in some cases to greatly reduce customer service.

Fourth, customer expectations are a function not only of the customer's background and experience, but also of effective and appropriate marketing communications. Much of the excitement surrounding services marketing communications focuses on e-commerce. As an example, recent travel industry data indicate that 78 percent of U.S. adults are now using the Internet for travel planning, as compared to 38 percent in 1998. Beyond traditional advertising, travel industry companies are using the Internet for advertising fulfillment, e-club management and direct marketing, on-line reservation systems, ancillary product sales, and, in some cases, for customer blogs. As with any marketing communication, the key service quality issue is effectively delivering on promotional promises, including not only making realistic promises, but also keeping customers and intermediaries informed of service availability and changes in schedules and offerings. Further, as service businesses increasingly shift to self-service systems, customer education must be an element of the marketing communications strategy.

Service Education Implications

The preceding discussion reflects the complexities and challenges of one key service construct, service quality. It is largely based on the author's research experience focusing on the travel industry, specifically the resort industry. The following reflects the author's experiences concerning the design and implementation of corresponding service education systems. These experiences are based on eight years of teaching a course entitled "Services Marketing" within a more traditional undergraduate marketing curriculum at a major AACSB accredited institution.

Constraints

The obvious conclusion of the preceding discussion is the need for services management education to integrate across the traditional functional areas of business education, particularly marketing, human resource and operations management, and information systems management. There are a number of constraints, both bureaucratic and faculty based, to such integration.

It is important to recognize that specialized coursework in service marketing and management is a relatively new phenomena. As recently as the mid 1990's, it was difficult to get approval of such courses. Effectively arguing that services were fundamentally different from other product categories and, consequently, deserving of special treatment in the form of "services marketing or management" courses required both persistence and perseverance. Even today most business schools offer a limited array of such courses and very few require services coursework as a core curricula component. Specific treatment of services concepts is sporadic in core curricula courses, such as Introduction to Marketing, Management, etc.

True integration of multiple functional areas within a given course or even a series of courses is also difficult. Rarely does an individual faculty member have the necessary range of experience and expertise. While team teaching is a possible solution, it is difficult to implement within the personnel accounting systems of most universities, particularly at the undergraduate level. In most cases, team teaching is reserved for capstone strategy and policy courses, which again tend not to focus heavily on services.

As always, budget issues are also a concern. Most universities have in some shape or another an accounting system based on credit hour production, again particularly at the undergraduate level. Such systems are an impediment both to team teaching and to teaching relatively small classes. Additionally, over the past decade, a combination of student and budget pressures has reduced the range of coursework available in many business schools. Many business schools face enrollment pressures that exceed faculty capacities. Yet, business school budgets have not kept pace, often resulting in fewer "non-traditional" and "non-core" courses being offered as schools attempt to just meet core course demand.

As already noted, rarely does an individual faculty member have the range of experience and expertise to teach a truly integrated services management course. Importantly, most university reward systems do not encourage such a range of expertise, particularly for research activities. Over the past two decades, there has been an enormous proliferation of research journals, leading business schools to increasingly encourage and reward faculty for publishing in a limited set of "top tier" outlets. While it is certainly possible to publish services research in these outlets, most require research which adheres to the traditional functional areas of business. For example, in marketing most schools recognize the *Journal of Marketing*, *Journal of Marketing Research*, *Journal of Consumer Research*, and the *Academy of Marketing Sciences* as the premier journals. All of these journals publish services research, but require a fairly focused emphasis on marketing theory and practices.

Innovative Solutions

The "cluster hire" as recently implemented at Virginia Tech is a possible solution to these problems. Essentially, the purpose of a cluster hire is to bring together a multi-disciplinary group focused on a core topic. While developed primarily in the biological and physical sciences, this same concept could be applied to services sciences. Bringing together a concentrated group of faculty from various business and engineering disciplines with common interest in services management and operation would effectively address the identified integration issues.

References

[1]   Bolton, R.N. and J.H. Drew. Linking Customer Satisfaction to Service Operations and Outcomes. Pp 173 – 200. In R.T. Rust and R.L. Oliver (eds.), *Service Quality: New Directions in Theory and Practice.* Thousand Oaks: Sage Publications.
[2]   Gronroos, C. 2000. Service Reflections: Service Marketing Comes of Age. Pp 13 – 21. In Swartz, T. A. and D. Iacobucci (eds.), *Handbook of Services Marketing and Management.* Thousand Oaks: Sage Publications.
[3]   Heskett. J.L. 1986. *Managing in the Service Economy.* Boston: Harvard Business School Press.

[4]   Lovelock, C. and E. Gummesson. 2004. Whither Services Marketing? In Search of a New Paradigm and Fresh Perspectives. *Journal of Services Research, 7*(1): 20-41.

[5]   Oliver, R.L. 1996. *Satisfaction: A Behavioral Perspective on the Consumer.* New York: McGraw Hill.

[6]   Parasuraman, A., V. Zeithaml, and L.L. Berry. 1985. A Conceptual Model of Service Quality and Its Implications for Future Research. *Journal of Marketing, 49*(Fall): 41-50.

[7]   Rust, R.T. and R.L. Oliver. 1994. Service Quality: Insights and Implications from the Frontier. Pp 1 – 20. In R.T. Rust and R.L. Oliver (eds.), *Service Quality: New Directions in Theory and Practice.* Thousand Oaks: Sage Publications.

[8]   Zeithaml, V.A. and M.J. Bitner. 2003. *Services Marketing: Integrating Customer Focus Across the Firm 3ed.* Boston, McGraw-Hill.

Art of Service: Drawing the Arts to Inform Service Design and Specification

Birgit Mager
Professor of Service Design
Köln International School of Design
mager@service-design.de

Shelley Evenson
Carnegie Mellon University
School of Design MMC 110
Pittsburgh, Pennsylvania 15232
evenson@cmu.edu
412.268.4638

ABSTRACT

Services are complex and specifying them is challenging. This paper suggests that service design and specification could be informed by a systematic study of notation and specification systems from other arts to create an approach to service scoring that would enable service designers to write and stakeholders to enact service performances with value and beauty.

Introduction

Services are complex. Specifying service encounters can be challenging because interactions in service are a "dynamic dance" between people and people, people and machines, and machines and machines. The choreography of different processes, among humans and machines often requires seemingly individual responses. In some sense, services may need to always be under determined, which is what makes the specification and documentation so challenging.

The reciprocal effect of these different dimensions in service organization and development is challenged by linear thinking and representational forms. Blueprinting, introduced by Lynn Shostack is one of the tools available in analysis and design that really attempts to address the multiplicity of dimensions [1]. Though an excellent tool, there is a need for more and better notation systems to capture the "soul" of the service, and communicate the facilitation of the experience, which is connected with the consumption of a service.

Learning From The Arts

Many expressive arts (music, dance, theater) have a long tradition of documentation with unique forms (and design languages) for authors to express their intents of performance and at the same time enable others to "read" and express the performance without being over determined and with some relation to the author's intent.

In the past 10 years some isolated attempts in Service Marketing and Service Design have drawn from art-similar models to further discussion, innovation, and tools generation in support of services [2]. Basic investigation into the possible use of the concept of genres and the application of style analyses and style charts [3], film-similar methods such as film scripts [4], descriptions of role, service acting and stage setting [5] have drawn from theory and have been tested in facets of practice. Concepts such as service production and service dramaturgy also reference front stage and back stage—terms that are found again and again in the description of services [6, 1].

These terms rise from equivalent art movements, in which the participants are orchestrating experience as the experience happens over time. It seems that many art worlds parallel services in their dynamics and complexity—the multilayeredness, interactivity, and animation or life of service systems, yet there is little collaboration between the arts and service design and development.

Conclusions

A systematic analysis of the art-similar thinking, representational forms, and notation systems as applied to the development and communication of service systems is needed. The origins, methods, and representational forms from different arts (such as theatre and film, dance and ballet, music and literature) should be explored, documented and analyzed in order to describe the way it functions in the context of the art. Special attention should be paid to the attributes or qualities of "good form" for authors and performers. This is similar to the notation of design and object languages referenced in product design [7,8]. The results from this type of research, we believe, could provide the foundation for the development an approach to service scoring—a way for service designers to write and stakeholders to perform services that deliver both value and beauty.

References

[1]   Shostack, G. Lynn. Designing Services that Deliver. *Harvard Business Review*, 133-139, 1984.
[2]   Mager/von der Auwera: Genrestudien, Köln 2005, unveröffentlichte Untersuchung.
[3]   Mager: Stilübungen, Köln 2005, unveröffentlichte Untersuchung.
[4]   Moeritz, Markus: unveröffentlichte Studienarbeit, 2003.
[5]   Fisk: The Theater Metaphor, in Lovelock, *Services Marketing*, 2004 und Mager: Service Methoden, in: Erlhoff, Mager, Manzini, *Dienstleistung braucht Design*, Luchterhand 1997.
[6]   Moritz, Stefan: *Service Design*, Masterarbeit, 2005.
[7]   Evenson S., Rheinfrank J., The design of experiences and languages of interaction. *Interact American Center for Design Journal ACD* (1994), 112-117.
[8]   Bitner, M. Servicescapes: The Impact of Physical Surroundings on Customers and Employees. *Journal of Marketing 55* (Jan):10-25, 1992.

Service Science, Management And Engineering: A Way of Managing Sociotechnical Systems

Michael E. Gorman
STS
University of Virginia

ABSTRACT

This paper discusses an expanded notion of services, ones that can lead to the transformation of systems in ways that are beneficial for business, engineering and society—because all of these are parts of a larger system. But what I say here also applies, on a reduced level, to systems problems that are apparently more local, like modeling and responding to a changing business environment in a specific market and area.

Introduction

I would like to discuss an expanded notion of services, ones that can lead to the transformation of systems in ways that are beneficial for business, engineering and society—because all of these are parts of a larger system. But what I say here also applies, on a reduced level, to systems problems that are apparently more local, like modeling and responding to a changing business environment in a specific market and area. The smaller problem is a sub-set of the larger one. I will use a framework for interdisciplinary collaboration highlighted at a recent workshop on "Trading Zones and Interactional Expertise".[1]

Earth Systems Engineering Management

To begin, let us consider an example from environmental systems management.

Brad Allenby has called for an Earth Systems Engineering and Management (ESEM) capability to manage the global eco-system where human beings, nature and technology are closely coupled in a complex, dynamic network [1]. Every part of the globe is now affected by human activity; therefore, our species has a responsibility to monitor and manage our interactions. Because the global ecosystem is complex and dynamic, new technologies and policies will have unintended consequences. Therefore, continuous monitoring and adaptive management are required. Furthermore, perturbations in this system will affect a wide range of stakeholders; therefore, constant dialogue is also required.

---

1   http://bart.tcc.virginia.edu/Tradzoneworkshop/index.htm

Smaller, apparently more local environmental problems can no longer be considered in isolation. Management of the Everglades, for example, will be affected by global warming, which could bury much of this delicately-balanced system under salt water. Furthermore, optimizing management at the local level may have unintended global consequences. Prohibiting logging in one part of the planet may simply increase logging in others— unless the prohibition is accompanied by measures to reduce global demand or develop appropriate substitutes.

The growing service sector of the global economy [16] poses a similar set of problems. Changes in one part of this growing global network may have unanticipated ripple effects in others. Allenby proposes developing an ESEM expertise to facilitate management of the global ecosystem. Similarly, managing the service economy requires a new kind of expertise.

SSME, like ESEM, involves combining multiple disciplines to form a new specialty that increases our ability to manage the way in which we are transforming the sociotechnical systems we inhabit. Interdisciplinary efforts lead to generalists that after some time become specialists in a new domain [16]. Computer science, for example, combined software and algorithm complexity theory, as well as hardware and logic design, into a new specialty that increases our understanding of computation in technological systems. Ultimately, this deeper understanding of service system evolution could lead to more systematic approaches to service innovation. Service innovations have the potential to impact service productivity, service quality, and rates of growth and return for service systems.

The service scientist as an interactional expert

Two sociologists of science [5] have described three levels of shared expertise in socio-technical networks:

None: Here experts in different disciplines 'throw solutions over the wall' to each other. There is no effort to share knowledge, or understand the other experts' mental model. For example, designers of a technological system can make no effort to understand the user's mental models [11]. In other cases, the user community may have no readily identifiable formal expertise, but still possess important knowledge. Consider those suffering from AIDs who did not want to be in the placebo groups for testing new AIDs treatments. Members of this community decided to learn as much as they could about research protocols, so they could modify them.

Interactional: These AIDS activists gradually acquired enough expertise to be able to discuss research strategies with members of the medical research communities. Eventually, they were able to make contributions to the design of research studies, based in part of their knowledge of how their community would get around protocols by buying street versions of the drugs being tested. [6]. Collins and Evans use the term 'interactional' to refer to the ability to interact intelligibly with members of more than one expertise community, facilitating knowledge exchanges [5].

Contributory: This kind of shared expertise involves experts who learn enough about other disciplines to make original contributions. The physicist Luis Alvarez, working with his son Walter, a geologist, was able to make a significant contribution to paleontology by discovering a geological level corresponding to the Cretaceous that contained thirty times more iridium than the layers above and below it. Based on this and other evidence, the Alvarezes proposed that a meteor collision with Earth accounted for the extinction of the dinosaurs [2, 17].

The service scientist will have an expertise of her or his own, but may also have to become an interactional expert. The service scientist cannot master all domains of knowledge relevant to a societal and/or client problem; instead, she or he needs to be able to interact intelligently with expertise communities whose knowledge bears on a pressing problem. The challenge of getting a diverse population of scientists to speak a common language around "service innovation" will also require training at least some of them to be able to converse across disciplinary cultures. Such training will be facilitated by exposure to case-studies from the cutting edge of services business. As the number of different disciplines required for state-of-the-art service innovation expands, so will the need for interactional experts who can bridge the disciplinary cultures.

To be successful, the SSME expert, other experts, clients and other stakeholders involved in a problem or opportunity will have to create an effective trading zone.

Trading Zones

Peter Galison used the metaphor of a trading zone to explain how scientists and engineers from distinct disciplinary cultures manage to collaborate on the design of new technologies [7]. He studied the development of radar and particle accelerators and found that different expertise communities had to develop first jargons, then pidgins, and finally full-scale creoles to get around linguistic and conceptual barriers. The key to Galison's approach is that it is possible for communication to take place locally even when they disagree about "global" meanings: "They can come to a consensus about the procedure of exchange, about the mechanisms to determine when goods are 'equal' to one another. They can even both understand that the continuation of the exchange is a prerequisite to the survival of the larger community of which they are part" (p. 803).

In NSF workshops developing new interdisciplinary initiatives, "One of the most striking features of the workshop process is the amount of reciprocal adjustment required to get all participants, from within NSF and without, talking about the same topics in a mutually comprehensible language" [10, p. 254]. These workshops are trading zones, where the participants are funded to work together but need to adopt at least a common pidgin, and also the development of metaphors that can " help groups of people from disparate backgrounds think about a problem in the same way" [13, p. 12.]

For example, in a workshop Gorman conducted on scientific and technological thinking [9], spanning disciplines such as psychology, cognitive science, philosophy, history and sociology, the pidgin consisted of agreeing on meaning for certain terms like problem space and mental model, The workshop also adopted two primary metaphors: shared toothbrushes and spherical horses. The former referred to the perception that most scholars liked to share frameworks about as much as they liked to share toothbrushes. The latter referred to a joke about a physicist who said he could predict the winner of any horse race to multiple decimal points—provided it was a spherical horse moving through a vacuum. These metaphors emerged early in the workshop and kept the participants aware of the importance of developing a shared framework (not a toothbrush) and conducting research that was relevant to science and engineering practice (not just spherical horses). By the end of the meeting, all a participant had to say was 'shared toothbrush' or 'spherical horse' and everyone else in the room knew what was implied.

Service scientists as agents in trading zones

Early in the development of MRI, surgeons interpreted as a lesion what an engineer would have recognized as an artifact of the way the device was being used, This breakdown in the creole between these communities was recognized and solved by an interactional expert who had a background in both physics and medicine [3]. This case study suggests that interactional experts can serve a function similar to agents or brokers, mastering enough of the language and metaphors of different communities of practice to facilitate trades. For example, agents of the Hudson's Bay Company worked the interface between two kinds of civilization, European and Native American [12]; similarly, service scientists will work on the boundaries between multiple communities of practice [4].

The service scientist could serve as this kind of interactional agent in trading zones, facilitating exchanges of knowledge and resources across different communities of practice. The service scientist might work for a company, offering adaptive solutions to a variety of problems. Or she might be a consultant, working with clients. The service scientist would be capable of visualizing and monitoring the impacts of solutions on the socio-technical system, at both local and global levels.

Consider telework: a suite of technologies for facilitating trading zones over a distance, cutting-down on the need for commuting and flying, saving hours and reducing greenhouse gases. But face-to-face contact is still important in gaining trust, including the ritual aspects of 'breaking bread together' and sharing experiences outside of work. To adopt telework, human practices have to change along with the technology. A service scientist attempting to implement such a solution would have to look at the impact on the local system, in terms of work patterns, distributed physical space, what activities and persons require face-to-face communications, synchronous and/or asynchronous. She would also have to consider environmental benefits and potential harms, as seen from the perspective of multiple stakeholders. What would happen if multiple organizations adopted a similar telework strategy? Would this undermine existing communities? Create new ones?

SSME as Transformative

The word service implies that SSME will serve the needs of clients, giving them what they want. In fact, SSME requires what Systems Engineers refer to as outscoping, or determining what a client really needs—which may be different from what they say they want [8]. Service Scientists need to be looking ahead, imagining the way in which techno-social coevolution will transform systems on a variety of levels [16]. At least some Service Scientists should be outscoping on a global level, facilitating the development of systems that will raise the standard of affluence, enable increased transparency, and improve the environment.

Every service scientists will end up being a reflective practitioner [14], seeing not just the system but also her part in it. Cognitive diaries are a good tool for this kind of reflection [15]. Service scientists will need training in a core discipline, like computer science, or cognitive science, or environmental science or medicine, or law, depending on the type of systems they intend to specialize in—though the boundaries between systems are fuzzy at best, and do not correspond to traditional disciplines. The interactional component will require every service scientist to gain skills in facilitating and managing trading zones, a new kind of competence that will draw on disciplines like anthropology and social psychology, but move beyond what is currently known. Inevitably, such training will have an experiential component, in which service scientists serve as apprentices to those more experienced, learning and reflecting.

References

[1]   Allenby, B. (2005). Technology at the global scale: Integrative cognitivism and Earth Systems Engineering Management. In M. E. Gorman, R. D. Tweney, D. C. Gooding & A. Kincannon (Eds.), *Scientific and technological thinking* (pp. 303-344). Mahwah, NJ: Lawrence Erlbaum Associates.

[2]   Alvarez, W. (1997). *T.rex and the crater of doom*. Princeton, NJ: Princeton University Press.

[3]   Baird, D., & Cohen, M. (1999). Why trade? *Perspectives on science*, 7(2), 231-254.

[4]   Brown, J. S., & Duguid, P. (1991). Organizational learning and communities of practice: Toward a unified view of working, learning, and innovation. *Organizational Science, 2*(1), 40-57.

[5]   Collins, H. M., & Evans, R. (2002). The third wave of science studies. *Social Studies of Science, 32*(2), 235-296.

[6]   Epstein, S. (1996). *Impure science: AIDs, activism, and the politics of knowledge*. Berkeley: University of California Press.

[7]   Galison, P. (1997). *Image & logic: A material culture of microphysics*. Chicago: The University of Chicago Press.

[8]   Gibson, J., & Scherer, W. T. (2006). *How to Do Systems Analysis*. Indianapolis: Wiley.

[9] Gorman, M. E., Kincannon, A., & Mehalik, M. M. (2001). *Spherical Horses and Shared Toothbrushes: Lessons learned from a workshop on scientific and technological thinking.* Paper presented at the Discovery Science 2001, Washington, D.C.

[10] Hackett, E. (2000). Interdisciplinary research initiatives at the U.S. National Science Foundation. In P. Weingart & N. Stehr (Eds.), *Practising interdisciplinarity* (pp. 248-259). Toronto: University of Toronto Press.

[11] Norman, D. A. (1993). *Things That Make Us Smart: Defending Human Attributes in the Age of the Machine.* New York: Addison Wesley.

[12] O'Leary, M., Orikowski, W., & Yates, J. (2002). Distributed work over the centuries: Trust and control in the Hudson's Bay Company, 1670-1826. In P. Hinds & S. Kiesler (Eds.), *Distributed work.* Cambridge, MA: MIT Press.

[13] Palmer, C. L. (2001). *Work at the boundaries of science: Information and the interdisciplinary research process.* Dordrecht: Kluwer Academic Publishers.

[14] Schon, D. A. (1987). *Educating the reflective practitioner: Toward a new design for teaching and learning in the professions.* San Francisco: Jossey-Bass.

[15] Shrager, J. (2005). Diary of an insane cell mechanic. In M. E. Gorman, R. D. Tweney, D. C. Gooding & A. Kincannon (Eds.), *Scientific and technological thinking* (pp. 119-136). Mahwah, NJ: Lawrence Erlbaum Associates.

[16] Spohrer, J. C., McDavid, D., Maglio, P. P., & Cortada, J. W. (2006). NBIC Convergence and Technology-Business Coevolution: Towards a Services Science to Increase Productivity Capacity. In B. Bainbridge & M. C. Roco (Eds.), *Managing Nano-Bio-Info-Cogno Innovations: Converging Technologies in Society* (pp. 227-253). Dordrecht, The Netherlands: Springer.

[17] Thagard, P. (1988). *Computational Philosophy of Science.* Cambridge: MIT Press.

A Service Logic for Service Science

Stephen L. Vargo
College of Business Administration
University of Hawaii at Manoa
2404 Maile Way
Honolulu, HI 96822
svargo@hawaii.edu

Robert F. Lusch
Eller College of Management
Department of Marketing
University of Arizona
Tucson, AZ 85721
rlusch@eller.arizona.edu

ABSTRACT

There are two distinct logics that could be used in the development of a service(s) science. One, goods-dominant logic, is based on the idea that services are special forms of intangible goods and therefore points toward a model concerned with the production of intangible units of output. The other is based on a concept of service as a process of the co-creation of reciprocal value, where the output of an entity is viewed as an input into a continuing process of resource integration. We argue that a service science built on the latter, service-dominant logic is more likely to result in a science that makes significant strides in the knowledge base than is a services science based on a goods logic. We then point toward additional foundational shifts that are indicated by the adoption of this service logic.

Introduction

The purpose of "service science, management and engineering" (Service Science) is to develop a "new academic discipline" to support application of "more scientific rigor to the practice of services." The need is predicated on the observation that both companies and economies are migrating toward services and "historically, most scientific research has been geared to supporting and assisting manufacturing, which was once a dominant force in the world economy." [11]

The intent is groundbreaking and forward thinking. But this statement of purpose and its justification also raise questions about the foundation on which a service science should be built. They appear to reflect, at least partially, a traditional underlying logic of economic exchange in which (1) services are a special type of good and, thus, (2) the "scientific" principles of goods manufacturing can, with some modification necessitated by the differences between goods and services, be applied to these services. However, this is neither the only nor perhaps the best foundation.

The purpose of this paper is to explore this traditional logical foundation and to propose an alternative logic, one grounded in a revised understanding of the meaning of service and its central role in economic exchange and society. We argue that this more service-centric logic not only amplifies the necessity for the development of service science but it also provides a stronger foundation for its development, growth, and maturation as a true science.

Alternative Logics

Broadly speaking, there are two perspectives for the conceptualization of service(s). One views *goods as the primary focus of economic exchange* and services as either (1) a restricted type of (intangible) goods or (2) an add-on that enhances the value of a good. We call this logic *goods-dominant (G-D) logic* [6, 9]. Others have referred to it as the "neoclassical economics research tradition" [5], "manufacturing logic" [7] and, "old enterprise logic" [13]. This G-D logic points toward using principles developed for goods to understand and manage services—both the "production" and the "delivery" of this service output to customers.

The second logic considers service in its own right, without reference to goods and regards *service as the primary focus of exchange activity*. We call this logic *service-dominant (S-D) logic*. In S-D logic goods continue to play an important, service-delivery role, at least in a subset of economic exchange. This S-D logic points toward using principles centered on processes and interactions to manage the co-creation of value with customers and other value-network members. Rather than implying that goods models should provide the foundation for service science, as does G-D logic, S-D logic points to the development of service-driven principles as the foundation of service science [6, 9, 10].

Goods-Dominant Logic

As the label implies, G-D logic is centered on the good—or more generally, the "product," to include both tangible (goods) and intangible (services) units of output—as prototypic of exchange. The essence of G-D logic is that economic exchange is fundamentally concerned with units of output (products) that are embedded with value during the manufacturing (or agricultural, or extraction) process. For efficiency, this production ideally takes place in isolation from the customer and results in standardized goods that can be inventoried.

The roots of G-D are found in the work of Smith [8]. It became solidified in the context of the Industrial Revolution during the quest for a science of economics at a time when "science" meant Newtonian mechanics, a paradigm for which the idea of goods embedded with value was particularly amenable. Management and marketing, as well as society in general, inherited this logic from economics.

According to G-D logic, intangible units of output—that is, services—since they cannot be standardized and inventoried, represent somewhat inferior goods. They can, however, be used to add value to (the preferred) tangible goods (e.g., sales service, after sale service, and other forms of customer service). The challenge then is to design systems for the production of these otherwise inefficiently produced, intangible products through the adaptation and refinement of goods-production principles. It follows, at least in the logic of G-D logic, that this need for better service design and production has become particularly critical, since many world economies are transitioning from a manufacturing (goods) economy to a "services economy."

Service-Dominant Logic

The most critical distinction between G-D logic and S-D logic is found in the conceptualization of service. In S-D logic, *service* is defined as the application of competences (skills and knowledge) for the benefit of another party (or for oneself). The use of the singular "service," as opposed to the plural *"services,"* as traditionally employed in G-D logic, is intentional and non-trivial. That is, whereas G-D logic sees services as (somewhat inferior to goods) *units of output*, S-D logic sees service as a *process*—doing something for (and in conjunction with) another party, sometimes with the aid of goods.

In S-D logic, this process of providing service to another party in order to obtain reciprocal service is the purpose of economic exchange. Some combination of money, organizations, and goods are almost always involved in the process but they are merely intermediaries. That is, goods, in their role as *appliances* for service provision, are conveyors of competences; organizations represent macro competences, created by the integration of micro-specialized resources (competences); and money is an option on the future, applied competences (service) of other entities. In all cases—service provided directly or through a good, organization and/or money—it is the knowledge and skills (competences) of the providers that represent the essential source of value creation, not the goods, which are only sometimes used to convey them. Thus, in S-D logic, goods are still important; but service is superordinate.

Importantly, S-D logic represents a fundamental shift in logic of exchange, not just a shift in type of product (unit of output) that is under investigation. Arguably, this shift to a process-driven, service-centric logic provides a more solid foundation for a true science of service than a logic that considers services to be inferior goods. This shift to a process of mutual service provision also points to several additional foundational shifts and the associated superordination of additional S-D logic concepts to their G-D logic counterparts.

Superodination of Operant Resources to Operand Resources

G-D logic has focused primarily on operand resources. Operant resources are static, usually tangible resources that require something be done to them to be useful. In contrast, operant resources are dynamic, largely intangible resources that can produce effects [9]. In service-dominant logic, operant resources, particularly the knowledge and skills of both parties to exchange, are the source of value creation. Thus, in S-D logic, operant resources are considered superodinate to operand resources.

This, in turn, implies that value cannot be an embedded property, even when a good is part of the service-provision process. In fact, S-D logic points toward value creation as an interactive process, occurring at the intersection of the provider's and the beneficiary's operant resources. That is, no value is created until benefit is realized; in S-D logic, value-in-use is superodinate to value-in-exchange, the traditional focus of G-D logic.

Relational Models of Exchange

As noted, G-D logic is grounded in classical and neoclassical economic thought. Consequently, at its heart is the notion of a discrete transaction taking place between a creator of value (producer) and a destroyer of value (consumer). But this producer/consumer dichotomy is inconsistent with the service-for service basis of exchange and the co-creation-of-value tenet of S-D logic. The idea that service is exchanged for service implies reciprocal exchange—that is, all parties are simultaneously both "producers" and "consumers, " and coequal in value creation

This is actually very close to Smith's [8] original, foundational logic of the reasons and nature of, as well as the individual and collective well being afforded by, the division of labor (specialization) and exchange. But it is a logic he abandoned, simply because it was not essential to his normative theory of national wealth based on exportable production—surplus goods output. However, it is a logic that contemporary economists are attempting to reclaim under the rubric of inframarginal analysis [12]. It is also an essential foundation for understanding the "customer" as a value-co-creator.

Reciprocal, service-for-service exchange also implies relationship. But the relationship of S-D logic is more than the repeat patronage notion of relationship that has been popularized in the marketing literature, particularly in the U.S. In fact, we argue that the repeat patronage interpretation, centered on transactions and value-in-exchange, of "relationship" is more of a G-D logic interpretation than an essential S-D logic concept. The S-D logic meaning of relationship as co-creation is closer to the "interactivity" and "many-to-many" relational concept found in the Nordic school of service marketing [2, 3].

Superordination of Dynamic, Process Models to Newtonian Mechanics

As noted, G-D logic is built on a deterministic, equilibrium-based, Newtonian model of science [1]. But, the service-for-service, interactive model of S-D logic implies dynamic, non-equilibrium, and non-deterministic relationships and models. Thus, just as Newtonian models of science have been subordinated to more dynamic, relational, and emergent models like relativity, quantum theory, and complexity theory, so too should a service-based science of service. Fortunately, much of the groundwork for this development of more dynamic non-linear models can be found in a variety of economic, physical science, and social science literatures [10].

Research Methods

If the foundation of a science of service is a service-centered logic of exchange, based on humans using their knowledge and skills for mutual benefit, and it models are dynamic and process driven, then the bounds of traditional research methods will be challenged. Co-creation involves the processes and interactions that unfold over time and requires methods that can deal with emergent properties, fractal patterns, non-linear patterns, and surprise. This suggests two related research reorientations: adoption of diverse and divergent methods and increased attention toward discovery.

The traditional practice of the scientific method in business, and the social sciences in general, is based heavily on a logic of justification [4], which has usually been considered superordinate to the logic of discovery. Thus, the methods of science, at least until recently, have been almost entirely reliant on classical statistics and the general linear model. However, a science of service based on a logic that considers service to be an emergent, uniquely determined, interactive process will benefit from a diversity of methods, especially those amenable to discovery. Thus, it needs to embrace interpretive research methods such as ethnography, historical and literary interpretation, and semiotics, as well as dynamical methods such as simulations and agent-based modeling.

This does not obviate the need for traditional methods typically employed, primarily in justification, such as experimental and survey methodologies. However, even when used they will often need to be longitudinal and the analyses of independent and dependent variables non- linear. Traditional approaches, including the logic of justification, remain essential, but confirmation needs be subordinated to discovery, especially in the development of a new science of a dynamic and non-linear process, such as service.

Conclusion

The foundational logic with which we approach scientific inquiry and through which we enhance intellectual enlightenment can also be confining. This constraint does not just affect how we formulate answers to our inquiries; more significantly, it affects how we frame the questions. The question of how to build a foundation for the production of better and more efficient services is fundamentally different from the question of how to build a foundation for more effective co-creation of service processes. Clearly, the answers will be even more strikingly different. We argue that service science built on service logic is more likely to provide a more fertile knowledge base than is a services science built on the logic of a good.

References

[1]   Giarini, O. and W. R. Stahel (1989), *The Limits of Certainty: Facing Risks in the New Service Economy*, Dordrecht, Netherlands: Kluwer.

[2]   Gronroos, C. (2006), "What Can a Service Logic Offer Marketing Theory?" in R.F. Lusch and S.L. Vargo (eds.) *The Service-Dominant Logic of Marketing: Dialog, Debate, and Directions*, Armonk, NY: M.E. Sharpe. 354-364.

[3]   Gummesson, E. (2006), "Many-to-Many Marketing as Grand Theory: A Nordic School Contribution," in R.F. Lusch and S.L. Vargo (eds.) *The Service-Dominant Logic of Marketing: Dialog, Debate, and Directions*, Armonk, NY: M.E. Sharpe. 339-353.

[4]   Hunt, S. (1991), *Modern Marketing Theory: Critical Issues in the Philosophy of Marketing Science*, Cincinnati: Southwestern Publishing.

[5]   Hunt, S. (2000), *A General Theory of Competition: Resources, Competences, Productivity, and Growth*, Thousand Oaks, CA: Sage.

[6]   Lusch, R.F. and S.L. Vargo Eds. (2006), *The Service-Dominant Logic of Marketing: Dialog, Debate, and Directions*. Armonk, NY: M.E. Sharpe.

[7]   Normann, R. (2001), *Reframing Business*, Chichester: Wiley.

[8]   Smith, Adam, *An Inquiry into the Nature and Causes of the Wealth of Nations*, (1776), Reprint, London: Printed for W. Strahan and T. Cadell.

[9]   Vargo, S.L. and R. F. Lusch (2004), "Evolving to a New Dominant Logic for Marketing," *Journal of Marketing, 68*(January): 1-17.

[10] Vargo, S.L. and F.W. Morgan (2005), "Services in Society and Academic Thought," *Journal of Macromarketing, 25*(1): 42-53.

[11] Service Science Management and Engineering (IBM). (http://www.research.ibm.com/ssme/

[12] Yang, X (2003), "A Review of the Literature of Inframarginal Analysis of Networks and Division of Labor," in Y. Ng, H. Shi, and G. Sun (eds.), *The Economics of E-Commerce and Networking Decisions*, New York: Palgrave, 69-100.

[13] Zuboff, S. and J. Maxmin (2004), *The Support Economy*, New York: Penguin

The Service-Dominant Mindset[1]

Robert F. Lusch
University of Arizona
rlusch@eller.arizona.edu

Stephen L. Vargo
University of Hawaii
svargo@hawaii.edu

ABSTRACT

We argue that the universal role of service in the economy and firm can provide a frame of reference to help guide a management philosophy that is more effective and better contributes to competing in the future than a frame of reference based on tangible goods. We call this revised philosophy service-dominant logic (S-D logic) and suggest eight key behaviors that characterize its effective implementation.

Introduction

As the world becomes more globally interconnected and turbulent the words of Peter F. Drucker are especially poignant, "The greatest danger in times of turbulence is not the turbulence; it is to act with yesterday's logic." Yesterday's logic, which continues to linger, focused on separating the producer from the consumer. This was done for maximum production control, efficiency and profit maximization and usually accomplished by standardizing the product and producing it away from the market [2]. In contrast, the emerging service-dominant logic is focused on the interaction of the producer and the consumer and other supply and value network partners as they co-create value through collaborative processes. This new logic is being referred to as service-dominant (S-D) logic [3,6,7].

S-D logic is driven by an innate purpose of doing something for and with another party, and is thus customer-centric and customer responsive. In fact, it defines service as the application of competences through deeds, processes and performances for the benefit of another entity or the entity itself [6]. It leverages the strengths of the firm to satisfy customer needs and achieve organizational and societal objectives. The unique matching of firm capabilities with customer needs, guided by an on-going conversation between them generates long-term customer loyalty and competitive advantage.

---

1 This essay draws substantial material from [4].

A New Mindset

A dramatic new mindset is required for S-D logic to be effective. This shift can be captured in eight areas: (1) a shift to the process of serving rather than the creation of goods, (2) a shift to the primacy of intangibles rather than tangibles, (3) a shift to the creation and use of dynamic operant resources as opposed to the consumption and depletion of static operand resources, (4) a recognition of the strategic advantage of symmetric rather than asymmetric information, (5) a shift to conversation and dialog as opposed to propaganda, (6) an understanding that the firm can only make and follow through on value propositions rather than create or add value, (7) a shift in focus to relational rather than transactional exchange, and (8) a shift to an emphasis on financial performance for information feedback rather than a goal of profit maximization (Table 1) [4].

Table 1. Contrasting G-D and S-D Logics

Goods Dominant Logic	Service-Dominant Logic
Goods	Service(s)
Tangible	Intangible
Operand Resources	Operant Resources
Asymmetric Information	Symmetric Information
Propaganda	Conversation
Value Added	Value Proposition
Transactional	Relational
Profit Maximization	Financial Feedback

Goods to Service

When a firm sees itself primarily as a manufacturer with an implied purpose of selling what it makes, it sees the key to making more money as selling more goods. There is little or no logic in selling fewer goods—why should Volkswagen want to sell fewer cars or Dow to sell fewer chemicals? In contrast, the service-dominant logic suggests that since these goods are actually mechanisms for service provision, the customer is always buying a service flow rather than a tangible thing, and thus the firm should focus on selling a flow of service. This would encourage it to determine the optimal configuration of goods, if any, for a level of service, the optimal organization or network configuration to maintain the service, and the optimal payment mechanism in exchange for providing the service. That is, the organization is encouraged to think about the service system. Tangible resources that are part of our ecosystem can also be viewed in terms of service provision. For example, natural pollination of crops by insects or trees that help prevent erosion and protect the watershed are examples of service provision, as are trees planted around houses to provide shade in summer but sunlight and warmth during winter. These service flows can be a substitute for industrial products. For instance, sediment and nutrients flow into the Panama Canal due to deforestation along the canal. The sediments clog the canal while the nutrients do so indirectly by stimulating growth of waterweeds. The government can purchase equipment and hire workers to continuously dredge the canal to keep it clean or, alternatively, replant trees. The trees would trap sediments and nutrients and also help regulate the supply of fresh water. The forests would serve as a replacement for building vast reservoirs and filtration beds [1].

Tangibles to Intangibles

MasterCard has developed a global marketing campaign around the theme of "priceless." A typical advertisement shows consumers purchasing tangible goods such as food, wine, furniture, apparel, or jewelry. The advertisement then displays the price (value-in-exchange) of each of the items. However, each advertisement ends with a statement emphasizing that the goods were only the means to provide a "priceless" experience (value-in-use)—for instance, spending time with your loved one at a special dinner or watching your children win a soccer game. In a service-dominant world, it is central to understanding: exchange is fundamentally, primarily about the intangible rather than the tangible.

The shift from the tangible to the intangible also focuses the organization on the solution that the customer is seeking. It is the old adage that people don't buy drills they buy quarter inch holes. In business-to-business marketing it is called solution selling. But in all firms and industries, the increasing mantra is about providing solutions [5]. DuPont and Dow providing solutions that use chemistry to improve life and global sustainability, Cargill providing solutions to improve yields for farmers or enhance the nutritional value of foods, British Petroleum providing solutions to help industry and consumers meet their energy needs. When the focus becomes the solution and the intangible, what firms learn is that the tangible content cost of their product becomes smaller and smaller and the brand rises in value and importance. Adidas, Apple, Benetton, Coca Cola, Rolex, Starbucks all are about the intangible experience; the tangible content is only the appliance used for the more important and more enduring experience [7].

Operand to Operant Resources

A static operand resource is usually tangible and requires something be done to it to be useful, whereas a dynamic operant resource is largely intangible and can produce an effect [6]. In service-dominant logic, knowledge an intangible resource is the primal source of wealth and the only sustainable source of competitive advantage. The global companies (and countries) that will be able to adapt in a rapidly changing technological world are those that invest heavily in knowledge development. Even firms (or countries) that move labor to lower-cost areas of the world, such as China or India, need to recognize that it is in their interest to develop the knowledge and skills of their new work force.

Service-dominant logic suggests that all participants in the value-creation process be viewed as dynamic operant resources. Accordingly, they should be viewed as the primary source of firm and national innovation and value creation.

Asymmetric to Symmetric

Service-dominant logic suggests that all exchanges should be symmetric. A focus on symmetric information and treatment implies: (1) one does not mislead customers, employees or partners by not sharing relevant information that could enable them to make better and more informed choices, and (2) all exchange or trading partners are treated equitably. The first implication is largely at the firm level, however, the second provides major guidance for countries.

In a globally networked economy, information symmetry becomes essential because the system will drive out those organizations that are not trustworthy. Organizations must promote the symmetric flow of information both across firms and customers and within the firm where different departments and divisions can be internal customers and suppliers of one another. In brief, this argues for truth telling as a globally pervasive norm in business.

A second type of symmetry advocated by service-dominant logic relates to the treatment of trading partners. This has national and global, in addition to inter-firm, implications. Essentially the symmetric treatment of trading partners means treating others the way you would want to be treated. It means removing barriers that are artificially created to give differential advantage to one partner over others.

Propaganda to Conversation

Advertising, at least as normally practiced, has tended to be propagandistic. Since its purpose is to sell the advertiser's products, it typically advocates the views and perspective of that advertiser, the seller, and thus, is one-sided and favorably biased. While this is not necessarily bad, buyers now have access to more and more information, causing them to turn away from communications that appear to be inaccurate, abusive, intrusive or overly one-sided.

Service-dominant logic argues that communication should be characterized by conversation and dialog. This approach should include not only customers, but also employees and other relevant stakeholders that may be affected by service exchange. All stakeholders need to be part of the market dialog.

In service-dominant logic, firms are encouraged to emphasize listening as much, if not more than, talking. It suggests that marketers should focus on hearing the voice of the market and the signals that arise from the market. In this regard, more and more people that are not part of a direct economic exchange are voicing their views about the economic exchanges of global entities. For instance, the voicing of views about the practices of firms or their suppliers in employing child labor or the marketing practices that spread global brands that influence local cultures. The service-dominant logic enterprise will not only listen to all of these voices, but will also participate in the conversations.

Value Added to Value Proposition

In the goods-dominant logic, value was viewed as a property (utility) of a good that was added in the manufacturing process, equivalent to value-in-exchange. Thus, if a customer paid a price for an offering, then the exchange of money was assumed to reflect the value in the transaction. This logic implied that as firms accumulated costs in manufacturing and distribution (they exchanged money for capital and labor), they should set prices based on these added costs. Traders adopted a "cost-plus" mindset, believing that any cost could be pushed onto the next party in the supply chain and eventually onto consumers and society.

This idea that value is something determined by the customer implies that the firm can only make an offer of value creation through the application of its resources to some need of the customer—that is, through service. Thus, the firm can only make a value proposition and then, if it is accepted, value is co-created in concert with the customer. Value-in-exchange, as reflected in price paid, is just an indication of the customer's perceived probability that at least some minimum desired value results from acceptance of the value proposition.

Transactional to Relational

Whenever there is specialization and division of labor, specialists become interdependent for well-being, if not survival. As specialization increases, as it is presently on a global basis, so does this interdependence. As entities become more interdependent their potential for collective action increases.

One way this collective action is fostered is through the development of relational, or social, contracts. These relational contracts allow the entities (individually and collectively) to relate to the environment. Organizations have been moving toward recapturing and elaborating this relational (as opposed to transactional) orientation for the last 25 years. This is not surprising; since, as specialization and exchange increase over time, so do relationships. In fact, society in general, and the emergence of a global society specifically, are relational phenomena. Service-dominant logic is inherently relational, partly because it implies that parties co-create value. Firms guided by service-dominant logic cannot be indifferent to customers or society.

Profits to Financial Feedback

Profit maximization is not in the vocabulary of service-dominant logic. Service-dominant logic views business and marketing as an on-going stream of social and economic processes in which firms continually generate and test hypotheses. Firms learn from financial outcomes as they attempt to better serve customers and obtain cash flows for the firm. Service-dominant logic embraces market and customer orientation and a learning orientation. Therefore, financial success is not just an end in itself but an important form of marketplace feedback about the fulfillment of value propositions.

Thus, price paid, profits and cash flow are important signals (though not the only signals) to the firm regarding the extent to which it is serving and meeting customer needs. The "price" that firms receive for their offerings (value-in-exchange) is essentially a co-produced signal. It represents supply (seller) and demand (buyer) factors coming together to agree upon the minimum potential value of resources in use. These prices are a much better signal or instruction on consumer wants and needs than those that are mandated from top down by a government or other planning organization.

Executing On Service-Dominant Logic

Executing on service-dominant logic in a globally hyper-competitive marketplace will be challenging for many organizations. Old ways of doing things and entrenched habits die slowly. When this involves not only ways of doing things in the firm but also across the firms, in today's large global supply and value-creation networks, the challenge is even more daunting.

Don't be surprised if your biggest barrier or resistance comes from your marketing staff. They are used to thinking of their job as built around traditional concepts of product, price, promotion and place (the magical "4 P's" of marketing). In many respects, marketing has failed in the past because marketing actually had little control over these 4 P's even though they thought they did. Much of product development was housed in the engineering department, price and terms of trade was pretty much the responsibility of the finance department, promotion was usually split between advertising, public relations and sales management but often not reporting through a singular chain of command, and place was often controlled by a transportation and logistics department or the real estate department. This high division of labor and specialization grew out of the classic industrial organization where specialists were separated and unified through a centralized strategic and tactical plan. This simply won't work in the future because in a hyper-competitive global environment change is both rapid, turbulent and surprising and thus a model of separation is giving way to a model of interaction which S-D logic embraces.

There are two meta-competences we have found to be pivotal to adopting service-dominant logic. *Collaborative capability* represents the ability of the organization to work with other parties in an open, truthful and symmetric manner. To do so the organization must also have internal specialized capabilities and knowledge because otherwise no other organization would benefit from working with the organization. *Absorptive capability* is the ability of the organization to absorb new information from the environment, including your collaborative partners. Importantly, both of these are organizational capabilities that are part of the organization's culture. We all know cultures change slowly; so if your firm does not have these two meta-competences you need to first work at improving these to provide a platform for more successful service-dominant logic implementation.

Concluding Comments

At least since the days of Adam Smith's study of what contributes to national well-being, we have been taught to think of the value of resources in terms of their tangibility and to view the economic world in terms of the exchange of tangible goods. Service-dominant logic takes a broader, more comprehensive view of exchange. It focuses on the intangible, often information that can now be transmitted across national boundaries instantly, as well as higher-order skills that can be exported in addition to, or increasingly in lieu of, tangible goods. Thus, it is a logic focused primarily on the application of dynamic operant resources—service. This logic points both firms and nations toward policies and approaches to the market that is somewhat contrary to their existing prevailing logic. It implies that just as the well-being of the individual and firm are tied to societal well-being, national wealth is tied to global wealth. The inverse of these well-being and wealth relationships is also true.

References

[1]   Economist (2005) "Are you being Served?" *The Economist* (April 23): 76-78.
[2]   Haeckel, S. (1999). *Creating and Leading Sense-and-Respond Organizations*. Boston: Harvard Business School Press.
[3]   Lusch, R.F. and S.L. Vargo, Eds. (2006). *The Service-Dominant Logic of Marketing*. Armonk, New York: M.E. Sharpe.
[4]   Lusch, R.F., S.L. Vargo, A. Malter (2006). "Marketing as Service-Exchange: Taking a Leadership Role in Global Marketing Management," *Organizational Dynamics* (forthcoming).
[5]   Sawhney, M., S. Balasubramanian, and V. Krishnan (2004). "Creating Growth with Services," *MIT Sloan Management Review*, 45 (Winter): 34-43.

[6]   Vargo, S.L. and R.F. Lusch (2004). "Evolving to a New Dominant Logic for Marketing," *Journal of Marketing 68* (January): 1-17.

[7]   Vargo, S. L. and R.F. Lusch (2004). "The Four Services Marketing Myths: Remnants from a Manufacturing Model," *Journal of Service Research* (May): 324-335.

An Integrated Approach to Service Innovation

Greg Oxton
Consortium for Service Innovation[1]
751 Laurel St, Ste 533,
San Carlos, CA 94070 USA
goxton@serviceinnovation.org
+1.650.596.0772

ABSTRACT

Can we approach service innovation in the same way we have approached product innovation? Will the traditional engineering approach and R&D investments yield services that are feasible and relevant to the customer?

The Consortium for Service Innovation has observed that innovation in services cannot happen in R&D labs nor be engineered in ways we have engineered products. We feel this is true for two reasons. First, the customer is not sufficiently present in the R&D and product engineering process. Second, the traditional approach is based on a manufacturing model that is good at producing tangible products, but not well suited to intangible, value-based services. We believe business has to develop organizational models or systems where customer involvement and innovation is both persistent and inherent in the system.

This paper articulates an Adaptive Organization model that enables sustained innovation in a dynamic environment based on persistent learning, relevant knowledge, fluid roles, and value-based metrics.

The Adaptive Organization

The Adaptive Organization is a business strategy developed by the members of the Consortium for Service Innovation. It has evolved from a process of collective thinking and collective experiences. The "Project Betty team" has developed the initial principles of the organizational model described in this paper [1]. The Consortium members are currently working on developing and operationally validating the emerging practices.

The Adaptive Organization model seeks to integrate the customer perspective, learning, and innovation into the entire life cycle of the services business. It also seeks to improve innovation and service delivery processes by connecting people with people and people with content with continuously increasing levels of relevance.

---

1 The Consortium For Service Innovation is a non-profit alliance of high tech customer support organizations. For more information about the Consortium, please visit the web site at www.serviceinnovation.org.

Introduction

Why an Adaptive Organization? In developing and implementing the Knowledge-Centered Support (KCS[sm]) methodology, the Consortium members encountered numerous obstacles. While the principles of KCS are quite simple, the adoption proved to be extremely challenging. Exploring these challenges exposed the dysfunction of our traditional business model. The conversations centered on the issues of people, knowledge and the relevance of interactions. From this discussion emerged the realization that relationship is the core building block of a healthy services organization. It became clear from the experience of the members that traditional manufacturing-based business principles and practices were at odds with a relationship-based model. Three key issues have emerged that justify a new approach:

— **Intangibles represent the greatest source of value** – for most companies the source of value has shifted from tangible assets - physical goods, products - to intangible assets - services, information, relationships, reputation, and influence.

— **Our business practices are optimized for tangible outcomes** – our traditional hierarchical organizational structures and command and control practices reflect a linear, manufacturing process model evolved over the past hundred years with the objective of efficiently producing tangible assets (physical products). While the source of value has shifted to intangible assets, we have not changed our management and measurement practices.

— **The power of one** – The growth of internet and open source communities have changed reputation and influence dynamics such that a single individual can affect an institution, from inside or outside. By sharing their experience through blogs or wikis an individual customer can have more impact on a company's reputation than the millions of marketing dollars spent by the company in creating a market image. The "Dell Hell" blog about a frustrating service experience has over 5 million hits on Google and has been referenced in *The New York Times* and *Business Week*. Companies need to give up the illusion of control and learn to engage with employees and customers in ways that build evangelists, not terrorists.

If the current practices are inadequate and we need to consider a new organizational model, what does that look like? A team at the Consortium has been exploring and developing the answer in a concept called the Adaptive Organization.

A Knowledge-Enabled Network

The Adaptive Organization is a knowledge-enabled network of people and interactions. Rather than the static, predictable capability and capacity of traditional product manufacturing, it is optimized for the creation and evolution of a dynamic capability and capacity for producing intangible, flexible results. The difference is an ever increasing level of *relevance* between people and people, and people and knowledge.

The Adaptive Organization model represents a shift in focus, shown in Table 1.

Table 1. Shift in focus in the Adaptive Organization model.

Traditional Focus	New Focus
Products	Services
Activity	Creation of value
Transaction	Interaction
Satisfaction	Loyalty

The new focus seeks to enable long-term, sustained value creation. Most organizations become so entrenched in past successes that they lack the ability to see beyond the events in which they are engaged. They do not engage the fringe and fail to recognize the patterns and insights that enable learning and innovation beyond what has made them successful.

Rethinking Roles and Boundaries

Rather than emphasizing compartmentalized roles and decision-making that sub-optimizes productivity and results, the Adaptive Organization enables greater productivity through flexible contributions. Its focus is to improve the relevance of interactions between people, regardless of role. In the old model, people are treated as 1-dimensional resources tightly bounded by their role or position in the organization, and innovation is confined to those participants who are explicitly designated as "innovators" – such as an R&D lab or a product team. In contrast, the Adaptive Organization recognizes people as multidimensional and therefore eligible to contribute across a wide range of areas. Their opportunity to contribute is a function of the complete range of their capabilities and reputation, not their job description. Their reputation is developed over time based on the full range of capabilities they demonstrate. The roles people play in the organization are based on the combination of their capabilities and the situation. The Adaptive Organization enables unanticipated but legitimate contributions from customers, partners, and service and support delivery staff.

Interactions between people are based on need, context, and legitimacy. Integrating the customer *into* the process, as opposed to being the target of the process, enables the organization to continuously align its strategies and products to the customer's needs. In fact, the customer becomes integral to the organization to the point that the distinction between customers and employees becomes blurred. The Adaptive Organization network transcends traditional organizational boundaries.

The Principles

Adaptive Organizations are less like hierarchies and more like networks. They are based on applying relationship-oriented organizational principles:

— Alignment

— Transparency

— Identity

— Networks

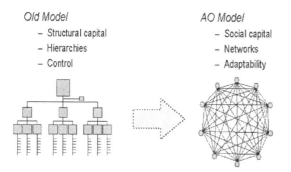

Figure 1. A Shift from Static Hierarchies to Dynamic Networks

Alignment

It is critical that the players in the network be able to make decisions that align with the purpose and values of the organization. The purpose or goals identify the organization's intent: what it seeks to accomplish. The values are the criteria by which they assess acceptable behavior in achieving the purpose. Alignment to the organization's purpose and values must occur at all levels across the organization.

Alignment starts with leadership. The leader(s) must create a higher-level purpose that people can relate to and a set of meaningful values. The purpose reflects a vision; ideally it is a simple, compelling value proposition that enlists a positive emotional response from those in the organization.

At an operational and more detailed level, alignment takes on the form of a strategic framework that links the purpose and vision with goals and objectives that cascade through the organization. The balanced score card is an effective methodology for this.

The principle of alignment enables the organization to move from a focus on task level direction -how things should be done -to a focus on what we are trying to accomplish -the desired outcome. This shift from how to what enables the people doing the work to figure out how best to get it done, thereby enabling a level of creativity and innovation that does not exist in the traditional, compartmentalized organizational structures.

People in the Adaptive Organization (all the people) need to understand the big picture (purpose and values) and their role in that picture.

Transparency – Removing Boundaries

A network approach establishes point-to-point connections between key players. The overall effectiveness of the relationship between the vendor and the customer depends on the ability to map offerings into the understanding of the customer. So, the customer engagement and experience starts before the point of sale and before the service interaction.

Unfortunately, the traditional hierarchical and linear model creates silos of interactions and organizational layers that buffer the customer from decision makers (i.e. the people at the vision layers would be at opposite ends of the chain). This linear approach to the market does not facilitate interactions at common points of interest and even worse, each transaction is like the first transaction over and over again, since there is no organizational learning taking place.

In contrast, the network model engages vendor Vice Presidents with customer Vice Presidents and developers with developers. These interactions are not managed or directed. They are invited, stimulated and nurtured. As a result, perceptions, decisions, and directions are influenced by a company's most valuable asset -its customers. The relevance of products and services is greatly enhanced because vendors and customers know much more about each other.

If we use open source as an example, often the customer is the user. Unlike the traditional business model where the customer is not present in the R&D lab or in the development of corporate strategies or services, the customer puts the emphasis on the really useful capabilities, rather than the "bells and whistles" frequently designed in drive-by requirements capture and ivory tower engineering.

To be effective then, interactions that connect these customer expectations with results need to happen at a strategic level. Strategies start to converge into common actions when customers participate in strategic level discussions and vendors integrate customer requirements for success into their requirements for success.

This network-based interaction model aligns people with common purposes (e.g. market and business strategy, development with the customer's solution architecture, or support with the customer situation) so they can interact and develop common perspectives and understanding. The customer becomes integral to the vendor's business processes through the entire services life cycle.

The principle of transparency is critical to optimizing the relevance of the connections. It is also fundamental to the integrity or trustworthiness of the network. If the players have visibility to the nature of the interactions and the value being created, it provides them with a way to assess the credibility and legitimacy of others in the network. The integrity factor in a self-managing network is the combination of identity and transparency.

Identity – Profiles and Reputation
In the Adaptive Organization, people engage with content and with other people according to their interests and needs.

Identity and reputation become the critical enablers. Both people and content in the network have an identity. Reputation as part of identity is developed over time and based on the patterns of behavior in the network. It is through reputation that content and players in the network gain or lose legitimacy.

Identity in the network is enabled through rich profiles that include static and dynamic information about content and people. The goal of the profile is to be rich enough to enable relevant connections and a sense of trust.

Security and privacy are challenging issues that must be considered in the requirements for the profiles. Just as we do in our social interactions, we want to manage the level of detail we share with others based on how well we know them.

Enabling the right interactions through visibility and awareness creates a value for the network that is quite different from the hierarchical, linear processes of the traditional business model. Through the network, people will:

— *Engage resources* (e.g. people or content) based on what is relevant to them in the moment (not predefined, fixed processes)

— *Contribute value* because it aligns with their values and interests and builds their legitimacy (not because they have to)

— *Perceive others* based on their unique identity and reputation because it reflects their capability through realized value (not based on compartmentalized job descriptions)

— *Establish legitimacy* in the community through their own identity and reputation, which is based on their pattern of participation and contribution (not based on title or hierarchical position)

Networks – Relevant Interactions

The traditional organizations measure their business with event level, activity-based metrics. This is a transaction-or manufacturing-based view of the world where activity has a strong correlation to outcome. In a value-based model, activity has a weak correlation to outcome. In the Adaptive Organization we engage in interactions, not transactions, the distinction being that interaction implies learning.

Interactions over time create a relationship. Each interaction is an opportunity to learn about each other, which becomes the basis to improve the value of future interactions. Persistent learning is a fundamental characteristic of an Adaptive Organization.

The "health and value" of relationships is determined from the patterns that emerge from interactions over time and the learning that occurs. For example, Microsoft MVPs (most valued professionals) emerge as a function of an individual's behavior in a community. Rather than being an explicit process, it is implicit [Marc A. Smith, personal communication]. From an appreciation of the implicit patterns of behavior and learning, we can identify the drivers of results. These drivers help us determine who is creating value in the network and how to improve the relevance of the interactions. We can gauge the health of the network as a function of the relevance, richness and diversity of the interactions, the value that is created, and the organization's ability to learn from its collective experience.

The Service Network

The qualitative aspect of a "service" business introduces performance dimensions that can only be understood by studying the interactions over time – not through isolated events or explicit feedback. While measures about interactions in the environment are being monitored, they are used for studying the dynamics and identifying patterns - not for creating goals and incentives at the activity level.

The network health is directly related to the profitability of the services business. In the traditional hierarchical structure, profit margins on value-added services are often problematic. In an Adaptive Organization, the ability of the network structure to provide just-in-time learning based on the collective experience reduces the reinvention factor of capability and improves the efficiency of the organization.

The Approach – A Matter Of Finesse

The Adaptive Organization requires nurturing, not directing. Connections are made and knowledge and value are created and shared because the players feel a sense of common purpose, connectedness, and belonging.

Knowledge is personal. While the unenlightened business may feel they own their employees' knowledge, the employees know otherwise. Our knowledge is a huge part of who we are as individuals: our identity, our value. There has to be an emotional connection and a positive consequence for us to offer it up to others. That connection is about alignment to a common purpose and confidence that others' commitment to that purpose is sincere.

Conclusion

Imagine if every interaction in the course of our day were highly relevant to something we cared about, and we were recognized for our unique and diverse capabilities. What would happen to our productivity, our sense of value, our level of job satisfaction? Would the source of exhaustion shift from a basis of frustration to a basis of excitement and overwhelming opportunity?

The Adaptive Organization enables:

— Increased capacity, capability and agility

— Persistent learning

— Inspired innovation and creativity

— Increased relevance between

— The creation of economic value

Shift happens – It is not new news that we have shifted to a services economy. For most businesses the source of value, especially profit, has shifted from tangible, physical things – products – to intangible, abstract things – relationships and loyalty. The source of differentiation for business has shifted from feature, functionality, and price-performance to the customer experience.

The source of value for business has shifted, while our structures and practices have not. The manufacturing approach of a production line, with compartmentalized responsibilities, linear processes, activity-based metrics, and discreet outcomes targeted at large collections of customers, is not optimal for a services business. A new set of business practices is required, moving organizations from the traditional command and control, hierarchical, linear processes to a nurturing, unbounded network of people and knowledge.

This new model embraces non-linear processes and diversity to create a dynamic system of persistent learning. Knowledge creation and dissemination as well as innovation are inherent; it is an integrated approach.

References

[1]   The Adaptive Organization Operational Model
http://www.serviceinnovation.org/included/docs/library/programs/ao_opmodel_v1.4.pdf

The following work has been instrumental in our thinking:
[1]   Allee, Verna. *The Future of Knowledge*. Butterworth-Heinemann, 2002.
[2]   Christensen, Clayton M. *The Innovator's Dilemma*. Harvard Business School Press, 1997.
[3]   Collins, Jim. *Good to Great*. Random House Business Books, 2001.
[4]   Cross, Rob, and Parker, Andrew. *The Hidden Power of Social Networks*. Harvard Business School Press, 2004.
[5]   Hagel, III, John, and Brown, John Seely. *The Only Sustainable Edge*. Harvard Business School Press, 2005.
[6]   Reichheld, Frederick F. *Loyalty Rules*. Harvard Business School Press, 2003.
[7]   Snowden, David, Complex Acts of Knowing, *Journal of Knowledge Management*, v. 6 (May 2002), p. 100-111.
[8]   Wheatley, Margaret, *Leadership and the New Science*. Berrett-Koehler Publishers, 1992.
[9]   Zuboff, Shoshana, and Maxmin, James, *The Support Economy*. Penguin Books, 2002.

SSME EDUCATION

Moving the Service Science Concept to Curricular Reality

Eleanor L. Babco
ebabco@cgs.nche.edu
Carol B. Lynch
clynch@cgs.nche.edu
Patricia McAllister
pmcallister@cgs.nche.edu

Council of Graduate Schools
One Dupont Circle
NW, Suite 430
Washington, DC 20036
(202) 223-3791

ABSTRACT

As the focus of the U.S. economy changes from manufacturing to services, as the participants in higher education diversify, and as global market pressures induce educational institutions to create new programs and practices, there is increasing need for comprehensive knowledge about how graduate education responds to these new circumstances. Two matters need attention: What is the fundamental knowledge base underpinning a service science field? What are the appropriate curricular responses at the post baccalaureate level across fields of study? The Council of Graduate Schools (CGS), the leading national organization devoted to advancing graduate education, is uniquely positioned to lead such a discussion. This presentation will highlight some intellectual questions being addressed by service science curricula and provide a preliminary outline of relevant programs at CGS member institutions. It will also form the background paper for a 2007 meeting organized by CGS to discuss next steps in curricular development in services sciences globally.

Introduction

The Council of Graduate Schools (CGS) is the only organization dedicated solely to advancing and representing the interests of graduate education. Its membership currently includes over 470 universities in the United States and Canada, and 13 universities outside North America. Collectively, these member institutions award over 95 percent of all U.S. doctorates and approximately 85 percent of all U.S. master's degrees.

To ensure the continued success of its mission to advance graduate education, CGS serves as a forum for ideas exchange on the major issues of the day. Its unique relationship with the graduate community allows it to promote the role of graduate deans as agents of change within their institutions. It does so by encouraging them to play a leadership role among faculty in developing new programs and among academic administrators in supporting and approving new programs to carry out that change.

An example of this strategy is the Preparing Future Faculty (PFF) program, which was launched by CGS in conjunction with the Association of American Colleges and

Universities to change the "culture" of research-oriented departments with the intent of training doctoral students for the careers in teaching that they are likely to encounter, emphasizing teaching careers in institutions other than research-oriented universities. Today, PFF programs are active in more than 45 doctoral degree-granting institutions and nearly 300 partner institutions in the U.S. The CGS PFF project has become a well-recognized national movement.

Another example is its current effort to institutionalize Professional Science Masters (PSM) programs by working with the graduate deans to promote, support, and grow the PSM initiative. CGS views the PSM as the most important new development in graduate education at the master's level. The "PSM" was introduced as a formal concept in 1997 by two major private foundations: The Alfred P. Sloan Foundation and the William M. Keck Foundation. It is based on standard curriculum elements requiring two academic years to complete. It includes four basic components: 1) advanced science/math courses (approximately two-thirds of requirements); 2) "plus" courses in business principles and other professional skills, such as written and oral communication, intellectual property and entrepreneurship; 3) an internship (usually paid and in the summer between academic years) in the employment sector which that particular PSM targets; and capstone project often done in the interdisciplinary teams in lieu of a thesis.

The development of individual PSM programs can be considered an "R&D" project, especially in the mode of a "start-up" company. A sustainable business plan, often including differential tuition, is required as part of the "research" (planning) phase, but in "development" (implementation) it must be recognized that the program will be "burning capitol" initially (investment in new staff positions and faculty buy-outs), but that successful programs that meet the needs of employers and capture the interest of students will produce "products" (enrollments) that sustain the programs.

The degrees are particularly well suited to respond to the national innovation and competitiveness agenda. The Goldman Sachs Foundation has succinctly stated the challenge: "Today's global economy requires sophisticated, well educated workers adept at utilizing rapidly changing technologies, processing complex information, and communicating across multiple languages and cultures" [1]. Although as yet PSM degrees do not typically include language training (increasingly English is accepted as the language of science), they are designed to meet the needs of non-academic employers with explicit input from advisory boards representing the targeted sector. The combination of advanced science/math, interdisciplinary exposure and professional business skills creates highly adaptable graduates interested in innovation. As such, the PSM with its combination of advanced study and professional and interdisciplinary training, can serve as a model for professional stand-alone master's degrees across the curriculum.

The intent is to have the term "PSM" become as familiar to graduate deans, science faculty, policy makers and others as the term "PFF" has become, and to produce an expanded and more capable "knowledge workforce." The multidisciplinary, employer-oriented PSM curriculum could serve as a model for the development of service science programs.

We believe, therefore, that CGS is uniquely positioned to lead a national discussion on the most promising practices to advance understanding of the intellectual foundation and the curricular potential of a field of inquiry and training around the services sector, and that the graduate deans will be key players in institutionalization of services sciences.

The Services Economy

The U.S. Department of Labor, Bureau of Labor Statistics projects that the service-providing sector will be responsible for all of the growth in nonagricultural wage and salary employment, accounting for four out of every five jobs in the U.S. economy by 2014. Due to this overwhelming dominance and the challenges the U.S. faces competing globally in this sector, it is imperative to conceptualize a framework and to develop methods that lead to services efficiency and services innovation. To create a cadre of workers who not only deliver a service, but also add "value" to that service, it is necessary to integrate new paradigms and practices into preparing these professionals to work in the service science sector.

A five-year study by the National Academy of Engineering [2] reported that despite the dominance of the services sector, the academic research community has not focused or been organized to meet the needs of services businesses. They cite three challenges faced by services industries that universities could address: 1) "the adoption and application of systems and industrial engineering concepts, methodologies, and quality-control processes to serve functions and businesses; 2) the integration of technological research and social science, management and policy research; and the 3) the education and training of engineering and science graduates prepared to deal with management, policy, and social issues."

A number of efforts to address these challenges and create a curriculum in services sciences has begun, all with the goal to produce graduates for the services sector. One such example is the Service Science, Management and Engineering (SSME) curriculum development work at the University of California, Berkeley that will form the basis for a new SSME discipline. It is cross-disciplinary, involving the college of engineering, the school of information and management, the school of business, and the Center for Information Technology Research in the Interest of Society (CITRIS). The plan is to begin a certificate program at the master's level in Fall 2006 for students in each of the participating schools.

Other examples include:

1. The service management program concentration in the graduate information systems programs developed by the IT Services Qualification Center (ITSqc) at Carnegie Mellon University. This program is offered as a service management concentration in their graduate information systems programs.

2. At North Carolina State University, there will be two degrees dealing with services: the MBA and the Master's of Science in Computer Networking (MSCN). The MBA program with a services management concentration will start in Fall 2006. It will have two tracks–one emphasizing the management of relationships between services providers and their clients and the other emphasizing service innovation. The MSCN will begin a new concentration in services engineering which will include a course on services management and engineering as well as courses on services technology.

3. At Rensselaer Polytechnic Institute, the Department of Decision Sciences and Engineering Systems (DSES) has been involved in multidisciplinary education and research through its integration of the disciplines of statistics, operations research, systems engineering, industrial and management engineering, and information systems into a synergistic interdiscipline that underpins real-time, information-based decision making.

Other higher education institutions are also recognizing the need to develop programs to prepare graduates who will be employed in the services sector. All have the goal to create curriculum and programs that address the problems, challenges, and issues of developing and deploying a workforce capable of innovating and providing leadership for the evolving and growing services economy. Our challenge is to build on the experiences of these pioneering programs and to develop a research base that provides intellectual underpinnings, in order to strengthen the depth and breadth of curricular offerings.

Developing Innovations In Graduate Education

CGS has been at the forefront of identifying issues and developing initiatives at the intersection of graduate education and the national interest, and then working toward institutionalizing those initiatives so that they become regular features of graduate education. This approach was employed during the development of the Preparing Future Faculty, the Professional Science Masters, the PhD Completion Project, and the Responsible Conduct of Research initiatives. The fruits of all these projects will result in identification of "best practices" of each individual initiative for consideration by all academic institutions, the government, and the private sector as appropriate.

When CGS identifies an issue deemed in need of further study, a background white paper to ascertain what is currently known about the issue is prepared. The CGS presentation at this conference highlights some of what we currently know about the questions to be addressed by a service science curriculum, and provides a very preliminary outline of the range of relevant programs available in CGS member institutions. It will form the background paper for a future convening in 2007 of a group of leading scholars/researchers, graduate deans, and corporate partners who will discuss the issue in depth and, if appropriate, formulate best next steps. Among their recommendations will be identifying ways to spotlight the initiative not only to the graduate community, but to the other stakeholders as well, and identifying the initiative as a key element in the nation's effort to maintain its global competitive edge in science and technology.

Throughout this process, the CGS membership of graduate deans will play a leadership role in helping identify appropriate practitioners who can join with their faculty and academic administrators to develop cross-college, multidisciplinary programs, curriculum and research. Because graduate deans have a multidisciplinary perspective and agenda, and work collaboratively across schools and colleges, they are key players in the institutionalization of any new feature of graduate education. They will play an important role as we move the services sciences deliberations from the "concept" mode to the "operational mode." We also recognize that other stakeholders are necessary to work toward this goal, including other academic institutional administrators, the corporate partners whose employees increasingly require this training and the federal government who will ultimately need to support the research underlying service science and engineering.

Some of the intellectual questions that must be addressed include, but are not limited to:

— How can graduate education create an integrated curriculum that produces graduates able to create and add value to the delivery of services? This is imperative since the services sector has traditionally been a low-margin, labor-intensive sector.

— How can graduates be produced that can operate between two worlds–the technology world and the business world? The PSM has been particularly successful at this combination.

The field also requires graduates that can compete both technically and economically in a global environment and that are flexible enough to change when economic and technological demands dictate.

Summary
CGS has sufficient experience and influence to bring about the institutionalization of the services sciences as a regular feature of U.S. graduate education. By conducting special plenary and concurrent sessions at its national meetings, CGS can keep the services sciences concept in the foreground of the priorities of graduate deans.

At present, significant opportunities exist for university-academic interaction with the services sector to create the new knowledge necessary to both develop academic programs and to influence national policy in order to produce the workforce for the services sector, and the Council of Graduate Schools is uniquely situated to lead this effort. We believe that working in conjunction with the IBM Corporation, the industry leader in the services sciences arena, that a new field can be created that will provide the skills and training that students need as they enter the services workforce to compete globally.

References

[1]   Goldman Sachs Foundation, University Access Program Proposal, 2006.
[2]   National Academy of Engineering. *Impact of Academic Research on Industrial Performance.* The National Academies Press, Washington, DC, USA, 2003.

Defining a Curriculum for Service Systems Engineering

Sheryl A. Sorby, Leonard J. Bohmann, Tom Drummer, Jim Frendewey,
Dana Johnson, Kris Mattila, John Sutherland, & Robert Warrington
Michigan Technological University

ABSTRACT

The U.S. economy has gradually changed from one based in agriculture, to one focused on manufacturing, to one now that relies heavily on the service sector. The service sector, including governmental agencies, retail stores, the entertainment business, public utilities, and providers of similar services, now makes up more than 80% of the total U.S. economy. Engineering programs, which typically have their roots in the era of manufacturing, have a focus on the design and fabrication of "products" rather than the design and creation of service systems. While curricula such as engineering management and industrial engineering provide some support to service systems engineering, their legacies are tied to the manufacturing sector, and as a result, they are not optimized to support the service sector. With this in mind, a Delphi Study was performed to identify the features, characteristics, and topics relevant to a service systems engineering curriculum. This paper describes the planning, conduct, and results of the service systems Delphi Study and how this information is being used to establish a new engineering degree program at Michigan Tech.[1]

Delphi Study

In September 2003, Michigan Tech received a planning grant from the Department-Level Reform program of the National Science Foundation (NSF) to define a Service Systems Engineering (SSE) curriculum with the help of industry leaders. Using our recently completed Delphi study we have identified several components of a curriculum for this new discipline that are presented here.

Panel of Experts

A key to conducting a Delphi Study for curricular design is to identify and recruit an appropriate panel of experts. For our planning grant activities, we contacted program officers at NSF, attended an NSF-sponsored conference on engineering the service sector, met with individuals from various industrial advisory boards associated with Michigan Tech,

1   The authors gratefully acknowledge the support of the National Science Foundation for the conduct of this project through grant EEC-0343187.

and networked with others identified through our efforts. We sent a letter to potential panel members asking for their assistance in defining the curriculum.

Approximately 21 leaders from a range of service industries agreed to participate as members of our panel of experts. The major service sectors represented were: 1) universities, 2) health care services, 3) banking, insurance, and legal services, 4) technology and engineering services, 5) shipping and transport, 6) consumer and retail services, 7) utilities and communications, and 8) community services. It should be noted that not all panelists returned all survey rounds, so the sample size (n-values) differed slightly from one survey round to the next. The years of experience for the panelists ranged from 6 to 43 years with a mean of 22 years. Consultant was the most frequently checked occupation category (n = 4).

Brainstorming Session

In December 2003, we conducted a brainstorming session with several industry leaders on the campus of Michigan Tech to help identify topics that might be important for the curriculum. The authors of this paper also participated in the day-long session.

Round 1 – Delphi Study

After establishing our panel of experts and identifying potential curricular topics through our brainstorming session, we began the Delphi Study. For the first round of the study, we developed a survey instrument that was based on examples from previously successful curricular Delphi studies. This instrument contained several categories and characteristics that might be relevant to a Service Systems Engineering curriculum. In the first round, experts were asked to accept, modify, delete, or add to the list of categories and characteristics on the instrument. Panel members then had several options: 1) they could state that an entire category should be deleted, 2) they could select individual characteristics from each list for deletion, 3) they could add to the list of characteristics within a category, or 4) they could rename individual characteristics. Panel members were also allowed to move characteristics from one category to another if necessary. In developing our instrument for round one, we took care to ensure that all categories and characteristics were listed randomly.

The survey for Round 1 consisted of 9 major curriculum sectors/categories, each containing multiple characteristics. A total of 50 characteristics were available across the 9 categories. We asked survey respondents to Accept or Reject each characteristic and to provide specific comments about other items that needed to be included, or general comments. We obtained a variety of demographic data: gender, years of experience, terminal degree, and occupation. The Round 1 survey was distributed by regular mail, and responses were returned either by mail or facsimile. Nine of the 50 items were rejected by greater than 50% of the respondents and we received many valuable comments and suggestions for characteristics to add.

Round 2 – Delphi Study

Based on the Round 1 survey data we added and deleted items and reorganized the curricular topics into 6 major categories: Analysis Skills, Interpersonal Issues, Business Management and Finance, Service Processes and Systems, Management and Operation of Service Systems, and Public Policy and Law. We asked respondents to rate each item on a 5 point Likert scale with "1" denoting "Not Important" and 5 "Important." To compare mean scores of items we performed an analysis of variance, treating respondents as blocks and items as treatments. We conducted this analysis for each major category. If we found a significant difference among item mean scores ($p < 0.05$) we then compared items using Bonferronni pairwise comparisons. We also asked each respondent to rate the 6 main categories.

We received n = 20 completed surveys in Round 2. Of the 6 main categories, the "Public Policy and Law" category received the lowest overall score (mean = 3.4), with "Analysis Skills" and "Interpersonal Issues" receiving the highest mean scores of 4.5. Five of the 6 categories had significant differences among item mean scores, the exception being "Public Policy and Law" in which all items received uniformly low scores with means ranging from 3.1 to 3.7. Within the category "Analysis Skills", computer programming and database design received significantly lower mean scores. The mean scores for the other items were not significantly different. In "Interpersonal Issues", public relations and dispute resolution received low scores. In "Business Management and Finance" marketing had the lowest mean and project costing and change management the highest scores. Other characteristics receiving significantly lower scores within their categories were simulation (Service Processes and Systems) and human resources (Management and Operation of Service Systems). Items with mean scores significantly lower than the other items within a category were eliminated for subsequent Delphi rounds.

Round 3 – Delphi Study

In Round 3, each respondent was requested to rank order the items within each major category. The six categories each contained approximately 6 items of interest, and therefore, an item rank ordered as 1 was the most important, and an item rank ordered as 6 was the least important. The major topic categories were also rank ordered based on their importance. Treating each respondent as a block and the 6 items as the treatments, we employed Friedman's test to check for significant differences ($p < 0.05$) between mean rankings. If significant differences were found we conducted pair-wise comparisons among the mean rankings to further test for differences.

We also requested each respondent to identify 10 of 36 characteristic items that they thought should be included in a service systems curriculum. We calculated the fraction of respondents who checked each item and compared the calculated proportions using an analysis of means for proportions.

We received n = 19 responses for Round 3. Considering the 6 major categories, we found that there were significant differences among the mean rankings (p = 0.019). The lowest mean rankings were associated with interpersonal skills and analytical skills (Table 1). It should be remembered that a lower value for the mean rank indicates greater importance.

Table 1. Mean Rankings for 6 major categories.

Category	Mean Rank
Interpersonal Skills	2.08
Analysis Skills	2.58
Business Management	3.25
Service Processes	3.42
Operation of Service Systems	4.25
Management of Service Systems	4.92

In considering the rank order means associated with the items within the six major categories, the statistical analysis revealed several conclusions, as shown in Table 2. Within the category "Analysis Skills", there were significant differences among the mean rankings (p = 0.021). The highest mean rank (least important item) was received by simulation (mean = 4.63) and the lowest mean (most important item) was received by probability and statistics (mean = 2.79). For the category "Interpersonal Issues" there were no significant differences among the mean rankings (p = 0.11), as means ranged from 3.1 for verbal skills to 4.6 for facilitator skills. For "Business Management", the differences in means were borderline significant (p = 0.06). The lowest mean rank was 2.8 for project costing and budgeting and the highest mean rank was 4.5 for cost accounting. In the category "Service Processes" the mean ranks were significantly different (p = 0.01). The performance measurement item had the lowest mean rank (2.3) and lean concepts the highest mean rank (4.6). For "Operation of Service Systems" the mean ranks were significantly different (p = 0.002). Process evaluation and improvement received the lowest mean rank (2.2) and safety the highest (4.8). In "Management of Service Systems" the item mean ranks were significantly different (p = 0.017) ranging from 2.6 for scheduling to 4.7 for liability.

Table 2 Categories and Characteristics of Service Systems Curriculum

Category	Characteristics
Analysis Skills	Problem Solving Economic Decision Analysis Risk Analysis Cost Estimating Probability & Statistics
Interpersonal Issues	Professional Responsibility Verbal Skills Leadership Technical Writing Facilitator Skills Team Building
Business Management	Project Costing Business Planning Change Management
Service Processes	Performance Measurement Flowcharting Work Task Breakdown
Operation of Service Systems	Process Evaluation & Improvement Quality Improvement Customer Relations Risk Management
Management of Service Systems	Scheduling Budgeting MIS

In considering the proportion response (fraction of respondents checking an item as being one of the ten most important items in the survey), three of the 36 items evaluated received significantly more selections than the other characteristic items. These items were Problem Solving (13 of 19), Economic Decision Analysis (11 of 19), and Technical Writing (11 of 19).

We then examined in detail the combined results of Rounds 2 and 3. This examination included assessing the relationship between the item mean scores from Round 2 (large value indicates greater importance) and item mean rank order from Round 3 (small value indicates greater importance). The relative importance of a characteristic item was judged by comparing its mean Round 2 score to the overall mean of Round 2 and its mean rank from Round 3 to the overall mean rank from Round 3. High priority items were considered to be those characteristic items with mean ranks below the average and above average mean scores, whereas an above average Round 3 mean rank and below average Round 2 mean score indicated a low priority characteristic item and a candidate for elimination. We also conducted a principal components analysis to produce a composite score for each characteristic to facilitate prioritization of characteristics.

Thirteen characteristics had below average Round 3 mean ranks and above average Round 2 mean scores. Figure 1 shows the results from this analysis; in this figure, items in the lower right corner of this were deemed more important (higher than average on the Likert scale, lower than average on the ranking). The best composite scores were attained by the characteristics of process performance measurement and of process evaluation and improvement. The remaining characteristics with below average Round 3 ranks and above average Round 2 mean scores were task breakdown, change management, technical writing, professional responsibility, quality improvement, leadership, verbal skills, risk analysis, project costing, and flowcharting (see Figure 1). These characteristics received among the best composite scores from our principal components analysis as well. Other characteristics that received high composite scores that are not shown in Figure 1 were scheduling, customer relations, planning, and probability and statistics.

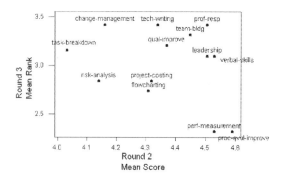

Figure 1. Results from Rounds 2 and 3

Round 4 – Delphi Study

A new survey instrument was developed based on the results from Rounds 2 & 3. For this round, surviving categories and characteristics were presented to the panelists who were asked to rate them as "Yes" (the topic must be included in the service systems curriculum) or "No" (the topic need not be included in the curriculum). Items were selected for inclusion when at least 75% of the panelists agreed that they must be a part of the service systems curriculum. Table 2 gives the results from this final round of the Delphi Study. The results from the Delphi Study are now being used to design the specific courses that will make up the service systems engineering curricula. The challenge will be in making sure that the curriculum we design is viewed as an "engineering" curriculum in the eyes of external constituencies. One of the possibilities that we are considering is to include enough "traditional" topics (statics, mechanics of materials, thermodynamics, etc.) in the program to: a) fully develop students problem-solving skills, b) satisfy external constituencies (including ABET) that this really is an engineering degree program, and c) enable our graduates to pass the Fundamentals of Engineering exam to obtain eventual licensure. We will be working in the coming year to fully develop the courses in this innovative new program.

Curriculum Implementation

In August 2006, a 2-day workshop will be held on Michigan Tech's campus to distill the information gleaned from our Delphi Study into a series of courses and a structure for the curriculum. Participants in the workshop will consist of 8-10 industry and academic leaders who served on our panel of experts as well as project leaders. The results from this workshop were presented at the SSME workshop.

The proposed service systems engineering program will be established using the structure of Michigan Tech's ABET-accredited Bachelor of Science in Engineering program. The BSE curriculum has been used to introduce several other degree programs at MTU, e.g., environmental and biomedical engineering. The 2-day workshop focused on defining the engineering emphasis associated with service systems engineering. Based on the findings from our planning grant, we anticipate that the Workshop will identify approximately 7-9 courses for the engineering emphasis area. The workshop will also seek to pinpoint technical electives for the curriculum.

Accreditation Issues

We plan to initially launch our program through our existing BSE program, ensuring that our students graduate from an ABET-accredited program. As the program becomes more firmly established, we anticipate that it will evolve into a discipline in its own right. It should be noted that in the early 1980s, our environmental engineering program was started through the BSE and has now evolved into a separate discipline. As more universities establish SSE programs, ABET will likely respond by recognizing SSE as a discipline, similar to the evolution of environmental engineering. Based on our past experiences, as ABET begins to recognize the emerging discipline, they will appoint a committee to determine discipline-specific outcomes and a parent professional society for SSE. In forming this committee, ABET will likely rely heavily on universities who have already worked to establish programs on their respective campuses. At Michigan Tech, we are committed to being involved in this exciting curricular development and will work through our established contacts within ABET to gain national acceptance for Service Systems Engineering. One of the authors is currently the VP for Education for ASME and is ASME's representative on an ABET task force to look into Service Systems Engineering. Results from this activity will also be presented.

Summary and Conclusions

The Delphi technique for consensus-building was successfully employed in this study to define the characteristics of an emerging engineering discipline – Service Systems Engineering. Through input from a panel of experts, elements of the curriculum were identified to meet the needs of service sector industries. Through these planning activities we are now poised to begin the development of a curriculum aimed at service systems engineering.

Educating The Service Manager in Europe— Assessing Gaps And Opportunities

Paolo Pasini
SDA Bocconi
School of Management
Via Bocconi, 8 – 20136
Milan, Italy
Paolo.pasini@unibocconi.it

ABSTRACT

The objective of this paper is to outline the initiatives related to service science at SDA Bocconi School of Management, particularly in the field of executive education. Over the last decade it has become more evident that the ideal curricula of managers in European companies go beyond excellent competencies in a single functional area. Over and over the market requires managers, both of manufacturing and service industry, to cross functional expertise and gain, instead, more developed knowledge of the interdependencies between traditional functions, as well as about the various options that companies have to related with the external environment (e.g. outsourcing, network of alliances, etc.). Based on that, we are starting delineating specific initiatives for executive education of service managers in Europe.

Introduction

SDA Bocconi School of Management considers Service Science as a promising field for educational offering. As Service Science-related contents are not fully covered in current graduate and executive curricula, there are opportunities to offer Service Science-related knowledge both to enterprises and to graduate students.

Based on this understanding, SDA Bocconi is starting a research initiative meant to achieve the following objectives:

— Understand and address the skill gap among professionals dealing with ICT Services, Business Processes, Change Management, Business Strategy, People Management, and Innovation Management. We want to understand in which terms these actors would benefit from a more comprehensive understanding of service-related peculiarities and from an inter-functional perspective.

— Elaborate on the existing literature considering service management and develop a solid knowledge base that integrates precedent studies and the more recent knowledge developed about Service Science.

— Support and improve managerial skills in three different clusters of companies where services are relevant: 1. Service companies, especially those where IT represents the core "manufacturing system" (e.g. insurance, banking, financial services, international carriers, telecommunications, etc.), which are reinventing their internal and external processes and core services; 2. Manufacturing companies which are using peripheral services to differentiate themselves from competitors (e.g. home appliances, motorcycles, vending machines, …); 3. Manufacturing companies which are transforming their products into services (e.g. software as a service, pay per use hardware, fleet management, pay per hour machine tools). This last cluster is the one that is more represented among Italian companies and the one we want to leverage more in the development of teaching material for the educational program.

— Based on the result of the research, situated in the Italian and European markets, we plan to foster the development of reliable competencies regarding general management and multidisciplinary foundations for the above cited professionals (or other interested), set on a valid m ix of knowledge areas. Specific contents will need to be corroborated by the research results, but we may hypothesize they will pertain to six discipline areas: Business and Marketing Strategy, Organization Design and People Management, IT Management, Innovation Management and Service Management. We believe that the integration between these competencies and a cross-cultural approach are foundational for the ideal profile of a Service Manager.

The Contribution of Service Science Studies to Management Problems

In the past, there have been various studies about Service Management. Most of them have been developed in the '80s and are a foundational component for Service Science. On the other hand, no matter the precise theoretical belonging of Service Science management, we recognize that today enterprises need new manager profiles to govern higher level of business complexity and to ride new opportunities that evolving ICTs offer to all businesses. Current market opportunities regarding Open Innovation, self-service models and consumer prosumership, as well the last perspectives as SOA models and the role of web in service-design and service-delivery, require specific vision and capabilities that seem to be different form the ones that are traditionally addressed by academic knowledge.

A New "Service Manager" Professional Profile?

The Service Manager will ideally constitute the missing expertise among those managerial positions that are currently in charge of discovering and implementing real business changes and opportunities in strategic, organizational and IT contexts, for the following reasons:

— Managers often exploit narrow functional competencies (R&D, IS, Organization, HR, Business strategy, etc.) and apply established managerial tools and techniques grounded in a functional bounded perspective;

— Rarely managers have a process-oriented approach, even when facing business changes that impact over the entire input/output value chain (crossing the boundaries between functions or divisions). These comprehensive business changes are the ones that lead to real process innovation (internal or external process in terms of rationalization, efficiency, time to market, customer or supplier relationship, new process owner roles, new HR management systems, and so on);

— Rarely functional managers possess all the necessary managerial tools for analyzing, evaluating and rethinking business and service processes, taking into account also "make or buy" choices (in-sourcing, outsourcing, off-shoring, delocalization, etc.), customer and supplier collaboration opportunities (ex. co-R&D, co-design, co-makership, co-marketing, self-service systems, etc.), and, finally, industry boundaries re-configuration;

— Rarely functional managers are able to exploit opportunities emerging from ICTs, from content "convergence" that often modify industry sector boundaries, create innovative businesses (e.g. wireless based or self-service oriented) and modify fundamentally competitive rules in existing industries.

Structure and Content of an Executive Program for Service Managers

The objective of the executive program is to train new service manager professional, based on training needs evidenced from the related research projects and from SDA and IBM knowledge on Service Science. The executive program could be designed for a mix of traditional classroom, distance learning and field projects with tutorship. Educational contents will be designed carefully, especially in order to define the best ways to integrate disciplines and knowledge domains together with diverse professional backgrounds (see figure 1).

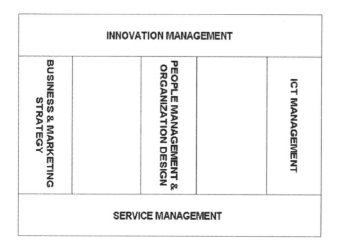

Figure 1

Multidisciplinary integration must be the first factor of strength of the program: teaching must be held always with a right mix of experts coming from the different disciplines, interacting always between each others and with participants. There is a real risk that a "silos-like" mindset of the teacher (focused only on its experienced background) might end being the same of the practitioners and managers we want to educate: that's why we believe that there is a strong need of active and "real-time" interdisciplinary teaching, and that only new pedagogical materials are not enough to break down the barriers existing between the above knowledge areas and mindsets (see figure 2 for some examples).

Figure 2

The program's contents and modules will be related to the following knowledge domains:

1. Service management and Innovation Management, as the two wide layers and consolidated disciplines to integrate with solid knowledge coming from the following four disciplines or knowledge domains;

2. Business and Marketing Strategy, crafting its methods and techniques to take into due account the progressive shift from product to service in a high variety of businesses;

3. People management, to cover the need to reinvent new skills, competencies and new ways of working in a more collaborative, global and dematerialized environments;

4. IT/IS management, that faces new challenges to survive and to demonstrate its contribution to business value and performances with new concepts of IT governance and with new way to manage implementation of new ICTs and their life cycle in a company (not in the IT market).

Design of contents will be based upon:

1. Active team work between IBM experts (BCS, IBM Research, etc.), SDA Bocconi professors, researchers and opinion-leaders coming from different fields of knowledge and business managers coming from different industries;

2. Knowledge exchange between SDA and the other institutions involved in developing Service Science contents;

3. Analysis of international bibliographic materials, both managerial and scientific, and similar educational curricula;

4. The results of the Italian/European study previously mentioned.

Conclusions

In our effort to develop an executive initiative expressively targeted to service manager we are willing to take a situated perspective, which will first consider the characteristics of executives and managers that are currently in charge of service-related activities in European markets. We recognize that peculiarities linked to the different educational curricula may affect the learning needs of European service science managers, as compared to American and Asian ones. Starting from an understanding of the current training needs of service science managers, as compared to best practices identified in the literature and in service-related research, we believe it would be possible to design educational offers target to executives and to graduate students, that will allow the development of enhanced service science competencies among European managers.

Service Science, Management and Engineering Curricula and Research at NC State University

Steven Allen
Associate Dean, College of Management
NC State University, Raleigh, NC 27695-7229
steve_allen@ncsu.edu
(919) 515-6941

Harry Perros
Professor, Department of Computer Science,
NC State University, Raleigh, NC 27695-8206
hp@csc.ncsu.edu
(919) 515-2041

Ioannis Viniotis
Professor, Department of Electrical and
Computer Engineering
NC State University, Raleigh, NC 27695-7911
candice@ncsu.edu
(919) 515-7357

Michael Devetsikiotis
Professor, Department of Electrical and
Computer Engineering
NC State University, Raleigh, NC 27695-7911
mdevets@ncsu.edu
(919) 515-5253

Andrew Rindos
Head, RTP Center for Advanced Studies
(CAS) and Coordinator, IBM Research/
AIM Joint Program, Research Triangle Park,
NC 27709
rindos@us.ibm.com
(919) 486-2016

Craig Nygard
Senior Technical Staff Member and Manager,
South Service Delivery, Executive Briefing
Center, IBM Global Services
Research Triangle Park, NC 27709
nygard@us.ibm.com
(919) 254-7754

Lynda Aiman-Smith
Associate Professor, Department of Business
Management
NC State University, Raleigh NC 27695-7229
Lynda_Aiman-Smith@ncsu.edu
(919) 515-8699

John McCreery
Associate Professor, Department of Business
Management
NC State University, Raleigh NC 27695-7229
John_McCreery@ncsu.edu
(919) 515-4093

Mitzi Montoya-Weiss
Professor, Department of Business Management
NC State University, Raleigh NC 27695-7229
Mitzi_Montoya-Weiss@ncsu.edu
(919) 515-8080

ABSTRACT

With the support of IBM, NC State's Colleges of Engineering and Management will begin offering masters-level curricula in Service Sciences, Management and Engineering (SSME) in fall 2006. This paper reports the rationale for these new programs, describes their content, summarizes some SSME research that is underway, and notes future directions.

Introduction

The term "service sector" once was associated with unskilled, labor-intensive activities in industries such as wholesale and retail trade, personal services, and restaurants. Now services dominate our economy (three-fourths of all jobs), and a rising share of service jobs are highly skilled and technology-intensive, including such activities such as outsourcing, consulting, and process re-engineering. Large corporations in the service sector, including IBM, Hewlett Packard, Accenture, Oracle, and EDS, are asking universities to re-evaluate degree programs in light of these changes. The key drivers are

— Fear of outsourcing: Many young people today, especially those in IT-related disciplines, have seen what has happened to jobs where the skills are purely technical. They are looking for a blend of managerial and technical skills that creates greater value.

— Need for customer focus: Hiring managers bemoan the failure of recent graduates to grasp the customer's perspective and how it relates to technology and business processes. A quote from a manager in a highly visible IT firm: "We would rather hire someone from Starbucks who understands customers than someone from MIT who only knows technology."

— Baby-boomer exodus: This generation obtained an integrated perspective about customer wants, business processes, and technology through informal and lengthy on-the-job experiences. They will soon be retiring – in droves. Companies need the next generation to hit the ground running.

The standard programs offered by universities in technology and management are not set up to meet these challenges. Leading-edge corporations in the new service sector are now asking universities to respond. This article summarizes the experience at NC State University, reporting recent innovations in its curricula and research.

NC State's Competitive Advantage

NC State is in an excellent position to form a service science partnership with IBM because

— IBM and NC State have a strong relationship: IBM hires more graduates from NC State than from any other university. Also, IBM has been a long time supporter of research at NC State.

— NC State works collaboratively: NC State's Colleges of Engineering (COE) and Management (COM) have a history of successful collaboration in high-tech entrepreneurship, product innovation and management, electronic commerce, and computer networking

— NC State moves fast: NC State was able to plan a program in summer and fall of 2005 to launch in fall 2006. We did this because we already had a platform of courses in place in the MBA and MS in Computer Networking programs

— NC State is a leader in innovation research: NC State's motto is "Innovation in Action." NC State is ranked 6th in technology strength of patents, 7th among national research universities in industry-funded research, and 12th among national research universities in non-federally funded research. NC State also is home to a virtual research organization, the Center for Innovation Management Studies (CIMS), with a network of over 100 researchers in varied disciplines from many universities and a solid track record in research on innovation.

The Curriculum Initiative

New Courses at NC State

NC State will begin admitting students in fall 2006 to new service science concentrations in two degree programs that are designed to bridge technical and management education. The College of Engineering will add a Services Engineering concentration to its Masters of Computer Networking (MSCN) program. The College of Management will add a Services Management concentration to its MBA program.

With IBM's support, five new courses will be developed that will be combined with existing courses to launch these new concentrations:

1. Services Management (team-taught by MBA and MSCN faculty) – The course will provide an overview of service management from an integrated viewpoint with a focus on customer satisfaction. The material will integrate operations, marketing, strategy, information technology and organizational issues with examples and case studies.

2. Process Analysis and Design – Business processes cut across traditional functional and organizational boundaries to create value and satisfy customer needs. This course will develop a process-centric view of the organization and provide students will knowledge and skills in business process management.

3. Organizational Culture – This course is intended as an overview of different aspects, artifacts, rituals and languages of different organizational cultures. The course will provide students with tools, knowledge, and first-hand experience in understanding the cultural values of a services-oriented organization.

4. Architecture and Design of IT Service Systems – The course will survey the state-of-the-art in the area of overall system design for efficient Web services. Customer service requirements in terms of throughput, availability, power, and cost will be included in the course.

5. Design and Performance Evaluation of Network Services and Systems – The course will provide an introduction to advanced topics in providing services based on modern high-speed telecommunication networks and in the related quantitative design and performance evaluation methods for the design of service-driven network systems.

Services Management in the MBA

The services management concentration in the MBA will teach service management from an integrated viewpoint — including operations, marketing, strategy, information technology and organizational issues — with a focus on customer satisfaction. Students will have the opportunity to choose between a Relationship Management track or an Innovation Management track within the services management curriculum.

The Relationship Management track focuses on the coproduction relationship that is critical in the services context. Service engagements must be designed and managed to meet the client's and provider's expectations, to achieve satisfactory returns and performance. The relationship management curriculum will provide essential tools and frameworks for effective customer analysis and engagement management. Students who select the Relationship Management track would take courses in Business Relationship Management, Consulting, and Services Management as well as an additional elective from the following: Organizational Culture, Market Analytics, Marketing Research, Marketing Strategy, Project Management, Service Modeling, or Supplier Relations.

The Innovation Management track focuses on the analysis and optimization of business processes and value chains or networks. One of the major challenges in managing new service development is the need for integration between management skills, technical & design capability, and market analysis. The service innovation curriculum will provide essential tools and frameworks for successful service innovation. Students who select the Innovation Management track would take courses in Consulting, Process Analysis and Design, and Services Management and then select an elective from the following: Organizational Culture, New Service Development, Project Management, Marketing Strategy, Service Modeling, or the IT Practicum.

Networking and IT Services Curriculum

The Computer Networking program is a joint effort between the Colleges of Engineering and Management to deliver a unique educational program that addresses the needs of

North Carolina's computer networking industry. By working together, the colleges deliver a curriculum that allows students the flexibility to pursue studies that emphasize the technical and management aspects of computer networking.

The program is intended for students with electrical and computer engineering or computer science undergraduate degrees who wish to pursue careers in research, development, operations, and information technology management in the computer networking and IT industry. It is designed to address a specific need in the computer networking industry in North Carolina, and, as such, is consistent with the land-grant mission of the university. The program is unique in the UNC system (and nationally) in blending the technical and management aspects of computer networking to offer students a truly unique educational opportunity.

Evolving in a direction consistent with the emerging SSME trends and requirements, the MSCN program will initially add a *track* in Services Engineering, which we envision as a precursor to a new masters program. Students in the Services Engineering track of MSCN would take the new Services Management course (jointly taught with MBA faculty) as their required business course. They then would take three MBA courses: Management of Technology, Managing People in the High-Tech Environment, and Process Analysis and Design. The MSCN program also would launch two new technical courses: (1) Architecture and Design of IT Service Systems and (2) Design and Performance Evaluation of Network Services and Systems.

Currently the program offers a non-thesis and a thesis option, structured around a core set of courses, and three areas, namely, network design, network hardware and network software.

As the program evolves towards a new Master's in Networking and IT Services, we envision a new core, consisting of a service management course in addition to a performance evaluation course, and additional courses from three groups, namely, networking, information technology and business.

Overall, we intend to maintain a close link between the curriculum and the key skills required by industry, government and academia, in the emerging "service oriented" world. An important ingredient in our thinking is finding a balance between depth and breadth (the ongoing discussion about the so-called "T-model"), as well as a balance between science/engineering, business and even broader subjects – related to the similarly motivated "liberal arts" view of engineering and technology education.

The Research Initiative

Traditionally, businesses model and enact their processes largely independently of each other. Notwithstanding the shortcomings of traditional approaches (slow accommodation of external changes and potential suboptimality), an advantage is that they are easy to manage. A "services focus" addresses those shortcomings by enabling reconfiguration of processes, including outsourcing processes to specialized vendors. However, doing so introduces major challenges. When processes cross enterprise boundaries and are provisioned across multiple administrative domains, organizational modeling and project management become harder (COM) as well as computational modeling and provisioning of services and SLAs (COE). Our interdisciplinary research effort seeks to address these challenges in a uniquely cohesive manner.

Even though doctoral students will matriculate in one of the three colleges, we anticipate co-supervision by faculty in all colleges. We have identified over 15 specific research topics; we intend to request support for 18 doctoral students. More specifically, we propose to do research in the following broad areas:

A. Research on the technical aspect of services (led by faculty in COE)

The problems will center on dynamic representations and techniques necessary to support adjustable pricing and resource allocation suitable for service businesses: (i) Service Level Agreements (SLAs) for IT services, and, (ii) SLAs for network services. SLAs formalize requirements customers pose on the IT or network system that delivers the service. They are typically expressed in terms of quality of service (QoS) metrics such as performance, reliability, availability, security.

A.1 Network Services.

Simple SLAs have been proposed, researched and even implemented in the context of networks, at the network, not the business process level. The bundling of multiple services together, the abundance of Web-based new business opportunities create the need for offering entirely new, bandwidth-provisioned SLAs that extend beyond the customary "T1-leasing" type. Two such SLAs we will study are the following:

(SLA1): Point-to-multipoint bandwidth pipes to any destination. A user requests a bandwidth pipe of x Mbps. This, however, is a point-to-multipoint pipe, from the user's access point to virtually any point in the network. This service requirement is an enabler for e-commerce, and other applications in which the clients are geographically dispersed and access the server through multiple points.

(SLA2): Bandwidth pipes with "upgrades" and differential premiums. Consider a user who classifies his/her traffic into N classes (for example N=3 diffserv classes). The user purchases from the network x_i Mbps of bandwidth (with certain attributes, e.g., quality of service, level of security) and is willing to pay y_i premium for it, where $i=1,2,\ldots,N$ and $y_i>y_{i+1}$. If the user does not fully utilize bandwidth at a class with a high premium, the user wants traffic from a lower premium class or classes to be "upgraded". The "upgrade" can take different forms; for example, if only half of the class 1 bandwidth is presently used, the excess could be given to the second class in its entirety; or, it could be distributed to the remaining classes proportionately. This service requirement is suitable for enterprise-like users and Virtual Private Networks (VPNs), i.e., "volume" but cost-aware customers with traffic that can take advantage of bandwidth pipes with different sizes. An example application is distance education.

A.2 IT Services

Three major factors make SLAs in an IT service environment different from those in networks; they all give rise to new research topics. First, the complexity of the IT system offers the "service designer" plenty of design choices to satisfy an SLA. For example, such choices may include: the number of CPUs (servers in the server farm); the logical organization of the databases in the disk system; the organization of the Web caches; the physical implementation of the storage subsystem; the balancing of the request load to the server farm; the order in which requests are processed inside a server. Second, the service designer may have to rely on incomplete system feedback. For example, a Web portal may have to support a throughput guarantee "for 1,000 transactions per second", under the constraint of relying on server utilization measurements only. Third, IT SLAs are more "subjective" in nature. They often go beyond classic QoS metrics (used in networks) to include Quality of Experience, which would arise from business requirements, such as customer satisfaction.

B. Research on the business aspect of services (led by faculty in COM)

The research problems will center around two thematic areas: (i) how can organizations most effectively deliver services that meet customer needs and (ii) how organizations create service innovations.

B.1 Service effectiveness

Service Project Estimation. Estimating the time and level of effort for service projects is difficult and uncertain. As services become more customized and non-routine, traditional methods for estimation fall short. The objective of this research is to develop a predictive, contingent model that considers project technical characteristics as well as individual and group decision-making behaviors when developing estimates.

Services Supply Chain Assessment. This project will develop analytics to measure the effectiveness of the supply of resources to service engagements. The objectives will be to (A) Develop a thorough understanding of the most effective and appropriate measures of performance to enable superior management of services supply chains and (B) Create a comprehensive services supply chain current state map for use of technical subcontractors to capture existing activities and performance

B.2 Service Innovation

This research lies at the intersection of technology and marketing. It focuses on innovation processes and strategies and the role of technology as an enabler of decision-making. Two key issues are (A) analysis of the key drivers of success and failure in open source software development projects and (B) identification of the differentiators between product versus service innovation and the extent to which the same processes and best practices apply.

Conclusions

The new courses for the MBA and MSCN concentrations in services will be added between fall 2006 and fall 2007; the first graduates would be available in spring 2008. The Colleges of Engineering and Management also would be engaged in the following activities:

— Conduct basic and applied research relevant to services

— Support doctoral training in services

— Launch modules for executive education and lifelong learning

— Develop additional masters-level courses to enrich the curricula

— Create a joint masters degree program

Bringing Service Sciences into the Curriculum

Roberta S. Russell
Virginia Tech
Department of Business
Information Technology
rrussell@vt.edu
540-231-4532

Christopher W. Zobel
Virginia Tech
Department of Business
Information Technology
czobel@vt.edu
540-231-1856

ABSTRACT

This paper traces the development of Virginia Tech's Decision Support Systems and Operations Management majors, including plans to incorporate Service Sciences into a capstone seminar course and elective offering. Collaborative teaching between electrical engineering, computer science and business information technology as part of a Masters of Information Technology degree provides a basis for cross-functional cooperation in a service sciences initiative. The feasibility of creating a Center for Service Sciences, Quality and Innovation (SSQI) at the university is also discussed.

Current State Of Curriculum

Twenty odd years ago, the College of Business at Virginia Tech began to re-engineer its Management Science major into a more career-friendly high-tech major. Recognizing the impact of information technology (IT) on business success (and the marketability of students), but maintaining the importance of formal training in management science and operations research, the department decided to create two hybrid majors, (1) Decision Support Systems (DSS), and (2) Operations Management (OM). Both majors fulfilled stated needs from industry, and specifically from companies that typically hired our students.

The DSS major required students to take programming courses, as well as courses in data base design and systems analysis. In addition, they took several courses in mathematical modeling, artificial intelligence and decision analysis. The objective was to create a graduate literate in both computer applications and the quantitative modeling needed to help managers make intelligent decisions.

The DSS graduate would serve as a liason between the more technically oriented information technology (IT) department (composed primarily of computer science or engineering grads) and the "customer" department (composed primarily of business grads). Thus, from the beginning, the DSS major incorporated both science and service to the customer in its makeup. Later updates to the major included courses in networks and telecommunications, decision support system development and implementation, visual interface design, client/server systems, and object-oriented programming.

The Operations Management major also included a strong IT and mathematical modeling component. In addition, the major offered courses in quality and process improvement, project management, supply chain management, enterprise planning and control, and global operations. A service operations course, although on the books, has remained dormant for a number of years.

Several years ago, in a restructuring of the university, the Department of Hospitality and Tourism Management (HTM) joined the Pamplin College of Business, bringing with them a service orientation and several service courses, including an *Introduction to Services* course with approximately 500 students per year, and a Ph.D. level *Seminar in Services*. Unfortunately, we have largely neglected to integrate faculty expertise in services from HTM into our curriculum.

Revising the Curriculum

The curriculum in DSS and OM is revised on a regular basis as indicated by industry trends, employer/alumni input, and academic needs. As documented so succinctly by our colleagues at IBM, services account for over 75% of the economic activity in the U.S. and close to 90% of employment. As a natural evolution, all of our courses are shifting to a service emphasis in class examples, cases, and projects. However, we have found that a more formal inclusion of the service perspective is needed. Approaching services as a science appeals to the technical and quantitative orientation of both our DSS and OM majors. Including a service sciences module in our existing DSS seminar course and revising and promoting our service operations course appear to be the best alternatives for enhancing the coverage of services in our curriculum. The DSS seminar course is the capstone course for seniors and is designed to promote critical thinking on emerging concepts and polish the skills of our students as they enter the workforce. Teaching students how to maintain customer focus, approach their jobs with a service orientation, and apply science to service problems is an excellent way to conclude the DSS curriculum.

Service operations has not been a popular elective for our students because of a perceived lack of rigor. Services are erroneously viewed as:

— Less complex than manufacturing with little or no need for quantitative analysis;

— Not as high-tech as manufacturing with more emphasis on human interaction (i.e., soft);

— Containing too much variability to be efficiently managed;

— A post-purchase marketing afterthought;

— A sometimes unpleasant preface to getting real work done;

— Composed mainly of low-paying, long- hour, servitude-type jobs.

Re-orienting (and renaming) the course to promote *Service Quality and Innovation* would add both rigor and excitement to an increasingly important field of study. We also anticipate working with the HTM department to offer this elective to their students as a follow-up to their *Introduction to Services* course, or as a cross-listing.

A Model for Collaboration

A relatively new graduate degree at Virginia Tech can serve as a model for cross functional cooperation in Service Sciences. The Masters Degree in Information Technology is administered jointly by the Departments of Electrical and Computer Engineering, Computer Science, and Business Information Technology. Students take four core courses and select two courses in each of three modules. The three modules are chosen from the following six modules:

— Communication Systems,

— Networking,

— Computer Engineering,

— Software Development,

— Business Information Systems, and

— Decision Support Systems.

A reasonable proposal would be to add a seventh module, Service Sciences, which would include three courses, (1) Managing the Customer Relationship, (2) Process Analysis and Design, and (3) Service Innovation. Similar courses maybe considered as a concentration in our MBA program.

Towards a Center For Service Sciences, Quality And Innovation

The real measure of a new field of study is its body of research. The Center for Global Electronic Commerce at Virginia Tech has expressed interest in working in the area of service science. We welcome that collaboration and hope to attract new grants and contracts in the area of services. A long term goal for the authors, however, is to create a Center for Service Sciences, Quality and Innovation (SSQI) at Virginia Tech to foster research is such areas as knowledge management, customer relationship management, measuring and maintaining service quality, developing standards for outsourcing services, optimizing service delivery, balancing the voice of the customer with the voice of the business, developing cost structures for high-contact services, assuring security and privacy, and innovating service design.

The university has a successful Center for High Performance Manufacturing supported by industry. It is time for a similar commitment to services. We hope to gather ideas and input on similar programs in industry and other academic institutions.

Conclusion

Virginia Tech has a well-respected undergraduate program in Business Information Technology which includes majors in both Decision Support Systems and Operations Management. While the curriculum has been successful, it is time to upgrade the service content of existing courses and propose new courses in service sciences, at both the graduate and undergraduate level. These changes can be implemented in a relatively short period of time. Research is best supported through centers that can obtain funding from industry and government agencies. A proposed Center for Service Sciences, Quality and Innovation is a long-term goal for enhancing the study of service sciences within the university.

Strategy for Inserting SSME into the Undergraduate Experience at a Minority Serving Institution

Edward L. Jones
Florida A&M University
Tallahassee, Florida 32303
ejones@cis.famu.edu
850-599-3050

Jakita N. Owensby
IBM Almaden Research Center
San Jose, California 95120
owensby@ibm.us.com
408-927-3539

Clement S. Allen
Florida A&M University
Tallahassee, Florida 32303
allen@cis.famu.edu
850-412-7359

ABSTRACT

SSME reflects both paradigm and actual shifts in the world economy, and represents an opportunity to reassess the relevance of and instructional methods used in undergraduate academic programs in computer science and IT. This paper outlines a strategy being considered at a minority serving institution, where concerns for student recruitment, retention and career success are paramount. An incremental adoption approach is proposed that exploits existing opportunities to give students multiple exposures to services as end-users, software developers and designers, and business/system analysts.[1]

Introduction

The adoption of new paradigms is challenging. Things to overcome include organizational inertia, characterized by a commitment to "do things the way we always have done them." In many ways, industry and academia react to change in a similar way. Fortunately, conditions for organizational change are more favorable when organizations realize that survival may be at stake or that an unprecedented opportunity presents itself. Business challenges related to market share and survival parallel current challenges in academia such as declining enrollments, student retention, and the place of computer science in the new world order.

The Department of Computer and Information Sciences (CIS) at Florida A&M University (FAMU) serves nearly 300 undergraduate students in two academic programs, and 25 students in a graduate program in software engineering. The recent nationwide decline

---
1   This work was partially supported by NSF Minority Institutions Infrastructure Grant #0424556.

in enrollments has impacted our department, and has stimulated discussion of ways to increase retention of current students and to attract new students. A two-fold strategy is evolving where (1) academic tracks (2-3 courses) are being defined for key emerging specialty areas; and (2) student exposures to these emerging areas are spread across existing courses in the curriculum.

Services Science Management and Engineering (SSME) is a recent movement that recognizes the worldwide growth in the services sector overall. SSME recognizes the multidisciplinary skill set needed to innovate, implement and support services, and the variety of situations for which IT services are contained in an SSME solution.

This paper presents a strategy for inserting SSME into undergraduate experience. The approach is evolutionary since SSME is an evolving discipline. To date, most SSME academic programs are offered at the graduate level. It is our position that efforts at the undergraduate level are needed to create a pipeline of students who will study SSME at the graduate level.

Background and Related Work

The challenge of sustaining effective and relevant computer science curricula is well documented. During the process of preparing the ACM/IEEE Curricula 2001 report, several concerns surfaced that are relevant to the SSME movement [7]:

— Many institutions give insufficient consideration to the needs of industry, which employs most of the graduates in CS&E.

— New curricula should be developed that stress the interactions between computer science and other disciplines.

SSME shares many of the same motivations and challenges as the field of informatics. The School of Informatics at Indiana University describes informatics as a field of study that gives students the skills to apply information technology to another field, to understand the impact of technology on people, to develop new uses for technology, and to apply IT in the context of another field [1].

The Department of Informatics at the University of California at Irvine, gives this description of informatics [8]:

> *"Informatics is the interdisciplinary study of the design, application, use and impacts of information technology. It goes beyond technical design, to focus on the relationship between information system design and use in real-world settings. These investigations lead to new forms of system architecture, new approaches to system design and development,*

new means of information system implementation and deployment as well as new models of interaction between technology and social, cultural and organizational settings."

Informatics programs tend to require an application development project outside the area of computing. Some require students to declare a cognate area (also called a minor or concentration), in order to develop adequate expertise in a second discipline to which computing will be applied. In some instances a computing department may designate the cognate areas it offers to students from other disciplines. For example, the Princeton Computer Science Department offers the Undergraduate Certificate Program in Applications of Computing [6] to students in non-computing majors.

These efforts move in the direction of SSME, but do not, and probably can not, accomplish the broad and ambitious objectives of SSME. This is particularly true in the area of innovation outside the domain of computing. On the other hand, current computing programs represent a starting point for evolutionary process of promulgating SSME.

Statement of Positions

Feedback from our students recommends increasing the hands-on component of the undergraduate experience. We have found that student interest and performance are improved when there are frequent and timely connections made between concept and practice. Students need to know how to apply a particular topic or concept.

The undergraduate CIS curricula at Florida A&M University force students to gain some expertise in a subject matter outside of computing. Students in one curriculum must take courses in business (e.g., accounting, management, marketing, and economics), while students in the other curriculum take courses in science (Calculus II and III, numerical analysis, and physics).

The following statements represent the position the Department of Computer and Information Sciences is taking relative to SSME insertion into the undergraduate experience.

1. Certain aspects of SSME are sufficiently multi-disciplinary that a curriculum in SSME is best offered at the graduate level.

2. It is appropriate to begin the process of inserting SSME concepts and experiences at undergraduate level.

3. An appropriate goal for the insertion is to stimulate interest in and preparation for graduate study in SSME.

4. It is expected that insertion will lead to evolutionary curriculum changes.

A long desired goal may result from SSME insertion: implementation of cross-disciplinary courses between the CIS Department and the FAMU School of Business and Industry. This development will enable an effective treatment of SSME issues of services innovation based on economic and organizational factors.

Curriculum Evolution Strategy

The tenets of the SSME insertion strategy are based upon the approach previously proposed for increasing the exposure of students to software testing. In the paper "Integrating Software Testing into the CS Curriculum – Arsenic in Small Doses," Jones [2] espoused certain principles that are applied to the insertion of SSME into the student experience:

1. Every student should acquire a minimal exposure to SSME.

2. Multiple courses in the curriculum must provide SSME experiences that require students to learn new skills and to adapt previously learned skills to new situations.

3. Students should be afforded an opportunity for advanced study and experience in SSME.

4. Students should be able to participate in the implementation of an SSME product within the department and university infrastructure.

5. SSME should be practiced in full view of the students, i.e., teachers should employ SSME derived services in the delivery of courses.

6. SSME activities must be inserted into selected existing courses in a value-added manner that does not disrupt or compromise course content or flow.

7. Assistance must be provided for instructors who incorporate SSME experiences into their courses.

Representative SSME Experiences

The strategy for integrating SSME into the curriculum is to give students multiple exposures that span different aspects of the SSME process.

— *Use a service to complete a course assignment.* This can occur in any course, starting with freshmen courses.

— *Use a service as an executable specification.* In a programming course, have students infer requirements from a working version of the desired program.

— *Use a program grading service.* Implement a grading service that grades student assignments, such as [5].

— *Integrate a service into programming assignments.* Students develop applications that invoke services to complete an overall task.

— *Utilize software development tools implemented as services.* Analyze the specification, and generate a complete set of test cases based on the specification only [3, 4].

— *Export services to other universities.* Develop a community of collaborators that share in the development and deployment of services.

— *Evaluation of services.* Assign students the task of evaluating and ranking service offerings based upon student-developed and SSME criteria.

— *(Capstone) Implement the SSME lifecycle for a client/end-user.* Apply analysis, design and implementation skills to create a service based application.

A Model Elective Course

We propose offering an elective introductory SSME course to give an overview of the emerging discipline, and to provide a conceptual explanation for the isolated SSME experiences the students may have had in other courses. Ideally, this course should be inter-disciplinary. Initially, CIS and Business students should take the course. The emphasis should be on innovation and the business and organizational processes and decisions that affect the direction innovation takes. Case studies should be used to show the fundamentals of the innovation process, independent of the domain. Guest lecturers from IBM and other SSME institutions would be used to emphasize employment and graduate study opportunities. Finally, this course should be team taught by faculty from CIS and Business. Eventually, this course may become a first course in a formal SSME interdisciplinary academic track.

IBM and SSME Community Support

The CIS Department is participating in the Technology Transfer Project sponsored by the Executive Leadership Forum. Under the terms of this project, each university selects an IBM technology (currently in the public domain as open source software) to insert into the student experience. Our department has selected the Eclipse platform, which is the most popular Java development platform in use. One of the authors is spearheading the departmental effort to integrate Eclipse into the curriculum. To date, two capstone course and the application development technology course use Eclipse exclusively. Starting in the Fall 2006 term, Eclipse will be adopted for the CS1 and CS2 courses. Graduate courses and thesis projects are developing Eclipse plug-ins to customize the environment for course-specific objectives [4].

Conclusions

The CIS Department at Florida A&M University is positioned to be a leader in the SSME movement at minority serving institutions. A set of guiding principles has been presented to ensure that the SSME insertion effort adds value to all students without detracting from required curriculum elements. The objective of FAMU CIS involvement is to increase the attractiveness and relevance of our academic programs. Although the proposed SSME insertion is bounded, we believe that our participation will position our students to assume leadership roles in this emerging discipline.

References

[1]   "What is Informatics?" Indiana University at IUPUI Informatics Program website. http://informatics. iupui.edu/overview/what_is_informatics.php (June 20, 2006).

[2]   Jones, E.L. Integrating Testing into the Curriculum – Arsenic in Small Doses. *Proc. 32nd Technical Symposium on Computer Science Education*, 337-341.

[3]   Jones, E.L and Rembert, A.J. A Simulation Based Trainer for Software Reliability Modeling, *Proc. 12 International Symposium on Software Reliability Engineering* (ISSRE 2001), 160-165.

[4]   Kottayi, S.P. *Automated Generation of Boundary Test Sets*, M.S. Thesis, Florida A&M University, Tallahassee, FL, Spring 2006.

[5]   Nowicki, C.B. *An Extensible Framework for Online Testing and Certification*. M.S. Thesis, Florida A&M University, Tallahassee, FL, Summer 2005.

[6]   Princeton University Undergraduate Certificate Program in Applications of Computing. http://www. cs.princeton.edu/academics/ugradpgm/pac.php (June 28, 2006).

[7]   Tucker, Allen B. Strategic Directions in Computer Science Education, *ACM Computing Surveys* 28, 4 (December 1996), 836-845.

[8]   UC Irvine Informatics Program website http://www.ics.uci.edu/informatics/about/index.php (June 20, 2006).

Putting Requirements and Quality at the Core of Global Service Delivery: Current Efforts and Future Plans at Pace University

Olly Gotel
ogotel@pace.edu

Christelle Scharff
cscharff@pace.edu

Pace University
Ivan G. Seidenberg School of Computer
Science and Information Systems
New York, NY, USA

ABSTRACT

This paper outlines some initial steps we have taken at Pace University to prepare Computer Science students for working in a service-oriented business environment. In such an environment, we suggest that software procurement and development become tasks that revolve around articulating needs and finding a way to match these needs to available supply, wherever this supply may be sourced. The capability to act as either a client or a provider in this context thereby demands the mastery of a number of skills. Firstly, the ability to determine the changing services that are required and to describe these needs so as to support on-demand service acquisition. Secondly, the ability to develop, assure and assess the quality of component services as part of a larger global supply chain. Our Software Engineering teaching emphasizes the centrality of requirements engineering and quality processes, and designs student projects that provide experience in co-production via distributed global software development. We believe these skills are fundamental to supporting service determination and delivery.

Introduction

Over the past few years, the way in which we procure and develop software has been changing to leverage the economic advantage of global markets. To prepare students for this way of working, we have been making incremental changes to the Computer Science curriculum at Pace University, both at the undergraduate and graduate levels.

Our position has been that there are some prerequisite and enduring skills that need to be emphasized to fully realize the benefits of service-orientation and so enable on-demand business. These skills revolve around determining what customers need and specifying these needs in a service-oriented manner, along with the capacity to develop quality software to implement such services, assured to a sufficient level of quality and dependability. These skills pertain to the disciplines of requirements engineering, quality assurance and software testing. These are core skills that we advocate and promote at the graduate level in the curriculum of a specialist Masters degree in Software Design and Development.

Within this degree we offer a sequence of courses on Systems Requirements Engineering, Software Reliability and Quality Assurance, and Software Testing.

At the undergraduate level, we bring the essence of this graduate teaching into the capstone course on Software Engineering. This is a practical course that is centered on group project work. To give students requisite exposure to global working, we craft projects that enable students to experience multiple sides of the offshore outsourcing relationship. We have been working closely with the Institute of Technology of Cambodia and the University of Delhi to set up an innovative three-way partnership to achieve these objectives.

This paper outlines our efforts to date with the graduate courses and the integration of this knowledge into the project-based undergraduate teaching. It highlights both why and how we propose these efforts support the move towards service orientation. We further illustrate how we have been using IBM technology in these courses, leveraging the benefits of the IBM Academic Initiative, and also suggest how we hope to capitalize upon and contribute to the proposed Shared Software Infrastructure (SSI) initiative to further support our efforts.

Centrality of Requirements

The term 'service' has been defined as "a provider/client interaction that creates and captures value"[1]. 'Value' can be considered the quality that renders something desirable or worthwhile. Central to this definition is therefore an understanding of the stakeholders involved in an exchange and their respective needs. The area of Software Engineering that deals with these concerns is Requirements Engineering.

Our teaching in the area of Requirements Engineering focuses on stakeholder identification, needs elicitation and negotiation, and requirements description. Notably, the issue of who is a provider and who is a client is not always trivial; there is often a reciprocal element to consider if the engagement is to be mutually beneficial. Students therefore learn about the dependencies and social networks that underpin any complex software development project. In addition, it is rarely sufficient to write a monolithic requirement specification, so students learn the skills required to break down needs into interlocking and smaller component areas, within a framework that is supportive of change and integration. These skills are critical to the articulation and definition of services.

How the satisfaction of a requirement is sourced is increasingly immaterial. It may be outsourced to a software house, capability may be purchased off the shelf or a service may be requested dynamically over the Internet. Writing requirements in terms of services, and

---

1   http://www.research.ibm.com/ssme/services.shtml.

conversely the task of describing software components in terms of services, is a focal aspect of our requirements training.

Assuring and Assessing Quality

In a service-oriented world, one can select off the shelf services, on the fly, to satisfy dynamically changing requirements. The issue here becomes one of not only ensuring that the selected service does what is required, but also one of trust or dependability. The service will have to satisfy specified functional requirements within certain constraints, be these with respect to performance, reliability or security, etc. There may also be the need to check that the selected service does not do anything that is not required, particularly when integrated into a wider systems context. Students need to acquire the skills that are essential to both assess candidate services and to assure services when initially developed prior to deployment. We provide training in these fundamental skills through a series of courses on Software Quality Assurance and Software Testing.

Our Software Quality Assurance course focuses on the critical link between requirements and software quality, and considers the issue of testing at a systems and user acceptance level. Our Software Testing course covers developer-level testing, such as unit testing. All our testing-related courses revolve around test planning, test design and development, test execution, test reporting and test exit criteria. Inspired by the practices of the Agile Methodologies, our teaching emphasizes test-first, test-driven development and the close involvement of the client when considering software quality factors. The general ability to assess and assure quality of software is a skill critical to deploying and procuring dependable services.

Global Co-Production Experience

Since 2005, the focus of our undergraduate capstone Software Engineering course has been global software development. In 2005, teams of Pace University and Institute of Technology of Cambodia students worked together to develop software products for the Cambodian market [1]. We organized the student projects so that: (a) the Cambodian students acted as clients and end-users – they knew the problem the proposed system was to tackle, the environment it was to operate in and had the authority to accept the work of the providers (or not); and (b) the Pace University students acted as providers – it was their responsibility to 'capture' the requirements for the system, propose design options, develop the selected design and test the eventual system, while also handling requirements changes.

In 2006, this model was extended to include students from the University of Delhi. These students had considerable technical expertise in database design, so the concept of a lead contractor and third-party supplier was introduced. While the Cambodian students remained as clients, the provisioning of the solution was changed. The Pace University students subcontracted part of the system design and development to the students from India, while also managing the end-to-end contract.

The intention behind this effort was to provide students with a realistic co-production experience where software products get engineered by global partners with disparate skills and expertise. The US and Indian students obviously had to work closely together to develop a product for a Cambodian client. Such a project requires students to learn about the delineation of responsibilities and the management of changing expectations across supply chains. One of the important skills they must develop is learning how to elicit requirements from a distance and how to write these requirements in such a manner so as to validate understanding, support change, and facilitate distributed working and continuous integration. The Software Engineering course thereby becomes a wider learning experience where students find out about the processes and measurements involved in setting up, running and evaluating a service engagement. They discover the need for contracts and agreements, relationship management and softer communication skills. More significantly, they learn about different cultures, professional regulations and motivations, and develop skills to address business and technical issues in a service-based business environment.

Supporting Tools

Our graduate courses introduce students to some of the IBM product offerings in the requirements and testing areas. Specifically, Rational Requisite Pro is used to illustrate the importance of requirements description, requirements management and requirements validation. Our Software Testing courses introduce students to IBM Functional Tester to test GUI applications. Here we focus on the capabilities of automated functional testing and regression testing via Java scripting. Our courses also emphasize open source and open standards, with Eclipse/JUnit typically being used for unit testing.

The undergraduate capstone Software Engineering course introduces students to some of the IBM product offerings and open source technology supporting the Software Engineering process. Students are introduced to the Unified Modeling Language (UML) and use IBM Rational Modeler as a stand-alone application to model design options for realizing the software specification, thereby achieving a better understanding of how the system should behave and correspond to client needs. This also facilitates the communication between designers in India and developers in the US. The developed software is generally web-based Java applications with back-end databases implemented in MySQL. The Eclipse development environment is regularly used so that developers can take advantage of the wider support tools. Students use the JUnit plug-in for unit testing and CVS for code sharing, change and version management, as well as the externalization mechanism to internationalize the software — the software needs to be delivered in English and French for a Cambodian audience. Trac[2] is an open source wiki-based software solution for supply chain and project management. Clients use trac to report bugs and developers use trac to fix and manage bugs.

Future Plans

We have placed an emphasis on process issues over the past two years in order to determine the underlying skills that need to be established for students to move towards implementing and using service-enabling technology. Our strategy has been to introduce these core supporting concepts and technologies incrementally. We consistently rely on open source development environments and standards in our courses. Through the IBM Academic Initiative, we have been using IBM technology in our courses to support the different phases of the Software Engineering process. One of the limitations we have found has been the fact that the current offering for students includes only IBM Rational Modeler, IBM Rational Developer, IBM Application Websphere and IBM DB2 Personal Developer. This constrains students to use evaluation versions of IBM Rational Requisite Pro and IBM Rational Functional Tester.

One issue for smaller schools is the obvious cost incurred in installing, configuring and managing an end-to-end technical infrastructure for students to specify, design and build their software products within. To this end, Pace University has been participating in an initiative coordinated by IBM to promote a Shared Service Infrastructure (SSI) between schools. Over the next academic year, we hope to participate further in this initiative by determining the software and configuration requirements needed to support core courses such as ours, particularly as we build upon the enabling skills and move towards service-orientation. We view this as a crucial step towards overcoming some of the barriers to technology use in the classroom. Particular attention will be given to the configuration requirements to enable global distributed software development. The intention of the SSI initiative is also to share courseware. We hope to contribute experiences from our courses, in particular the studies from the global supply chain projects, to help put requirements and quality concerns at the heart of global service delivery training.

Our current challenge as Computer Science instructors is to provide students with opportunities and situations in which they can experience the multi-disciplinary nature of the computing field, integrating training in skills from traditional engineering, the social sciences and management. This implies the development of courses or Computer Science curricula that focus more on services and the alignment of business needs to technology – not only on teaching technology in isolation from real-world applications and working

2   http://www.edgewall.com/trac/.

contexts. We have begun to respond to these issues at the graduate and undergraduate levels, in particular with the global co-production experiment. We plan to collaborate further with IBM and the New York software industry to import (and then export) service-centered software development practices into our project-based courses.

Agile methodologies represent an advance in software processes, focusing on integrating people management, process and technology. They promote close working relationships with customers and end users to elicit and check requirements through a continual dialogue. As researchers, we are particularly interested in distributed agile software development if we are to fully realize the benefits of dynamic service provisioning.

Through our collaboration with IBM, we organized a seminar series for students and faculty in fall 2005 and spring 2006. In these seminars, students and faculty were introduced to the latest IBM strategies, research and technologies. The 2005 series paid particular attention to service-oriented architecture and web services as a precursor to the establishment of a graduate course on this topic. We believe that collaborations such as these are a good way to initiate new ideas and encourage curriculum changes that align with industrial needs.

References

[1]   Gotel O., Scharff S. and Seng. S. Preparing Computer Science Students for Global Software Development. *36th ASEE/IEEE Frontiers in Education Conference*, 2006 (to appear).

Rochester Institute of Technology— Service Management

James W Jacobs, Jr.
Faculty – Service Management
George Eastman Building Rm 4274
jwjism@rit.edu
585 475 6017

Guy Johnson
Executive Director, Center for Advancing the
Study of Cyberinfrastructure
102 Lomb Memorial Drive
Rochester, NY 14623
Guy.Johnson@rit.edu
585-475-2161

ABSTRACT

This paper addresses several issues related to Service Management education. Those issues are; the current state of service management education at our institution, the current state of service in organizations, a brief listing of our courseware themes, a brief rundown about current faculty research, project and grants and some examples of student research projects. Lastly, we have identified how collaboration around SSME would be beneficial.

Introduction

The Rochester Institute of Technology (RIT) Masters Degree in Service Management has existed for 16 years. With its initial roots in Hospitality and Service Management, the degree program has evolved today to be applicable to every imaginable business organization or service environment. Our most recent graduates are employed at the following; Verizon Dominicana, T-Com and T-Com Wireless, Banco Popular, Kompas, Microsoft, Marriott, the Coquille Indian Nation and other more general categories including multiple education organizations, tourism and food-related organizations, retail organizations, banks, health care facilities, non-profits, and independent consultants, among others. The masters program runs in the US at RIT and international locations in Croatia, Kosovo, and the Dominican Republic in a full time or executive format. We are entertaining many other international locations. Given the realities of today's changing and fast-paced business environment, we expect continued program growth over a long term.

The Current State of Service

While most organizational leadership regularly advertise their own versions of customer-focused beliefs and behavior, it would be our view that service performance(s) in many organizations would be rated average to below average, at best. One just needs to reflect about their personal experiences as an end-user customer or customer anywhere in a value chain to understand this. In the same light, there are significant and powerful examples whereby organizations understand and continuously seek to improve their service efforts. Over the long term, we see a huge need for all organizations to come to understand, develop, implement, evaluate and re-think their service beliefs, processes, and understanding of the customer. This need is necessitated by the following; the customers resulting experiences with the firm, new sources for understanding what customers value, customer activitism outside the realm of the firm, globalism and its effects, broad ranging availability and access to information, and the pace of new technological development and business practice(s) [1, 2]. Development of the capacity to learn and change is a real and long term need for all organizations. This need is significant as many common marketing, economic development, operations and other firm practices are in need of re-thinking in today's rapidly changing service environments.

Courseware Themes
The MS in Service Management with its highly flexible programming recognizes these needs above and has developed content themes to specifically address the new sets of skills and abilities required of today's and tomorrow's organization practitioners. These content themes, contained in core courses, include:

— Critical service system thinking and service system development.

— Service discovery, innovation and creativity.

— Service performance metrics for a new age.

— Learning to learn, changing our business paradigms.

— Scenarios, strategic process and decision making in service environments.

— Engineering service environments (in development).

— Human capital development.

— Building customer experiences and relationship development to obtain and retain customers.

— Service leadership.

In addition, several prominent options/electives are offered to full time graduate students including; human resource development, project management, information technology, health systems, and various business finance electives.

Research, projects and grants

Faculty teaching in the program are full-time or come from a variety of business organizations and from an equally large group of disciplines including; economics, engineering, system disciplines, information technology, health, and tourism. Sixty-percent of the faculty are adjuncts and employed at organizations external to RIT. Many faculty have ongoing research/projects or grant agendas, for example; health and nutrition major grant, economic impact study, multiple grants to construct information technology platform for the SUNY system, simulation development, tourism planning and development, and six-sigma training development and training deployment.

Student research projects cover all major content themes and are practically oriented. Two recent examples of their work are;

1. a major examination of an international telecom provider call center including analysis of the current system, development of new staging and processes in the system, the addition and analysis of training structure and implementation in the system, and the determination of the needs for and purchase of additional software and technology to enhance the call center total system. Their project recommendations have been implemented and the initial call center metrics demonstrate strong new performance.

2. In a second example, from a major course-based project (to be further explored and continued as a student research project), the owner/CEO of a software development company constructed a mind map of his service environment to indicate where major improvements to be offered to his clients (multiple banks) could be created. The project will initially will include the development of end-user action-communities and processes for these communities to collaborate about software/IT needs, to explore computer software and hardware implementation issues and problems and other changes in the system. At the front-end of the value chain, other action-communities will be developed to service the new end-user communities, explore best practices and benchmarks, and other practices both from within and external to the organization.

Action-Communities Within RIT

Within RIT, the Service Management program will embark to enhance its own class of action-communities, to collaborate with various partner departments and colleges at the university. This would also include other university and business connections. In the short term this includes connection with the Golisano College of Computing and Information Sciences (Cyberinfrastructure) and the College of Applied Science and Technology (Department of Engineering Technology and Packaging Science). This already includes cross-course utilization of courses in each others masters programs, the development of current and practical case studies and simulations, and the search for and implementation of innovative/creative new practices, processes, organizational structures, and planning, policy and implementation scenarios. In addition, a newly approved PhD program in the Golisano College focuses on domain-driven computing and graduate students pursuing this degree must establish expertise in a field outside of computing. SSME offers many opportunities for these students to achieve a terminal degree as the services industry modernizes.

Lastly, the Service Management program faculty has begun coordination with a university community partner above to design and implement a new Engineering Service Environments course and an enhanced service management concentration. The objectives of the course and concentration will be to;

1. Re-constitute a concentration that delivers basic service concepts and practices to our partnering department(s) and organizations. This will involve modifications to an existing certificate program.

2. Build a service engineering/service science course in cooperation with these partners. The partner(s) will design the goals of this course.

3. Identify various research agendas for selected faculty and students.

4. Invite external partners to participate in the development of the above.

Conclusion

We believe, as does IBM and others, that it is imperative for new-broad ranging work to continue in this evolving disciplinary focus. RIT's program in Service Management in collaboration with various interested partners can serve together to provide businesses and business partners with new and exciting methods to create organizational wealth and success. In the end, this success can establish and maintain a relationship of trust between customers and business organizations – a relationship founded in new business practices and beliefs and customer partnering

References

[1]   Lanning, M. J., (1998). *Delivering Profitable Value: A Revolutionary Framework to Accelerate Growth, Generate Wealth, and Rediscover the Heart of Business*. Great Britain; Perseus Publishing

[2]   Prahalad, C. K. & Ramaswamy, V., (2004). *The Future of Competition: Co-creating Unique Value with Customers*. Boston, Mass: Harvard Business School Publishing.

Getting Students Excited About Services: Providing a Context for Applying Their Newly Acquired Knowledge

Majid Iqbal
Project Scientist
IT Services Qualification Center
Carnegie Mellon University
Pittsburgh, PA 15213, USA
majidi@andrew.cmu.edu
+ 1 (412) 268-4631

ABSTRACT

Students make investments every semester when they spend their tuition credits, time, and limited opportunities on elective courses. Naturally, they expect reasonable returns in terms of the knowledge and skills they can gainfully employ immediately or in the near future. Their investments in general-purpose competencies such as information technology, software engineering, design, and management science are further augmented when provided with specific contexts for creativity and problem-solving. A graduate program at Carnegie Mellon University has been introducing students to a body of knowledge in service management by providing them with a layer of concepts, principles, and methods. Guest lectures from business executives and managers complement the instruction with practical insight, thereby removing any remaining causal ambiguity and also revealing new challenges and opportunities to be addressed.

Introduction

The knowledge of an organization can be stored in its people, processes, systems, tools, and technologies [1]. The individual members of an organization are an important store of tacit knowledge that can be transferred to other organizations when those individuals move, either temporarily or permanently [1]. Faculty and students can be reservoirs of the knowledge [1] created at universities through years of teaching and research. Such embedded knowledge can be effectively transferred to the industry, either through applied research or when faculty and students join the workforce [2]. Indeed, this form of knowledge transfer is found to have had a significant impact on the industrial performance of several sectors of the service economy [2] in the United States. A corresponding transfer occurs when individuals move from the industry to academia. This energizes the knowledge transfer to the industry in the form of a closed-loop system between academic research and education its impact on industrial performance. University graduates educated in the services can thus be an important factor by which service businesses can strengthen their organizational capabilities and competitive advantage. Collaboration between business managers and academics can lead to the definition of specific learning needs for organizational capabilities linked to competitive advantage [3]. Faculty and administrators of academic programs can then map those learning needs to specific courses to be taught at the graduate and undergraduate levels. The content and structure of existing or new courses can be adjusted to have the necessary impact on industrial performance through transferred knowledge when graduates of the program join or return to the work force. This approach, which has worked well at Carnegie Mellon, is illustrated below with the example of the graduate course *Managing Service Organizations* (Course Number 95-806).

Overview of Managing Service Organizations

Managing Service Organizations is an elective course at Carnegie Mellon that was introduced in the spring semester of 2003. It is part of a graduate-level concentration in service management. The concentration, jointly developed by the John H. Heinz III School of Public Policy & Management and the IT Services Qualification Center (ITSqc), presently includes courses on contract theory, negotiations, managing service organizations, sourcing management, capability improvement for service organizations, and IT program management [4]. The students for the concentration are mostly graduate students from the Master of Information Systems Management (MISM) program and the Master of Science in Information Technology (MSIT) program. The concentration also attracts a few students from software engineering and public policy programs. A number of students are full-time workers who are enrolled in part-time evening programs.

The course covers organizational capabilities, decisions, processes, systems, and methods that are useful for engineers and managers in service organizations. On the whole, the course provides a cognitive framework for students to think about problem-solving, innovation, efficiency, and effectiveness within the context of service organizations. Like most graduate courses, it requires them to engage in class discussions, work on exercises, write viewpoints, and conduct critical analyses of ideas and issues presented to them. The students are promised that at the end of the semester, given that they apply themselves well, they would develop a sense for services that would be useful in the industry and uncommon among their peers.

The First Shift is a Mind Shift

The very first step in teaching the course is preparing students with the fundamental concepts on services that act as receptacles for other knowledge. This is to ensure that the students have the absorptive capacity [5] to recognize specific behaviors, patterns, roles, relationships in service systems. Students get to question the widely accepted notions about the characteristics services such as intangibility, heterogeneity, inseparability, and perishability and then argue about whether or not those are generalizable [6]. In an early exercise students rapidly go through a large variety of randomly selected offerings, different from each other in some way or the other. Starting with a general notion of services as the production of change desired by customers [7], students identify the few commonly occurring patterns in which value is realized for customers [8]. They recognize that useful change in the customer's perception may be tangible or intangible, permanent or temporary, and may be manifested either their person or possessions [9].

The Second-Order Effects

Most of the students who take the course are committed to the study of information technologies and management science. Therefore, discussions throughout the course highlight the first- and second-order effects that students' knowledge in those areas can have on the performance of service organizations. By understanding the ways in which information technologies and management science may be used to enable or enhance the capabilities and resources for service management, students comes to appreciate the first-order effects. For example, in the case of managed IT services [10], students may learn that software that enables the virtualization of computer and storage systems would allow service managers to quickly adjust resource capacity to handle variations in the demand imposed by supported business processes. Virtualized resources could also provide a level of fault-tolerance by enabling the dynamic routing of demand from a failed resource to a replicated stand-by. Making this connection helps students to understand the potential first-order effect of their knowledge in software systems and architecture.

The epiphany for the students comes from understanding how the scalability and continuity of the service has an impact on, say, the performance of the customer's order fulfillment process or its customer care centre. That is when they understand the second-order effects of their knowledge in the context of services. Being able to make these connections can contribute to the learning experience by reducing causal ambiguity [5].

Three Molecular Bonds

An important aspect of this course is that it helps students appreciate the differences and similarities between consumer services and business services. Discussions focus on how the roles of customers and users differ between those two types. They consider issues such as user perceptions of service quality, the specification of needs, the selection of appropriate service levels, the nature of the relationship with service providers, and the ownership and control of service assets. As part of their case study exercises, students are required to examine the information flow, the interactions, roles, and the relationships that are in play between the customer and service provider organizations. The triangular prism shown in Figure 1 is provided to the students as a learning aid that facilitates their analyses, comparisons, and discussions across throughout the course.

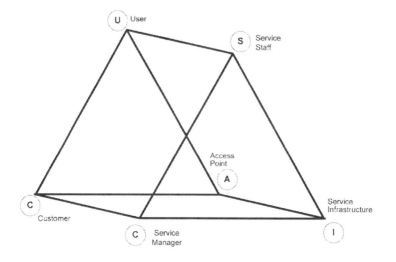

Figure 1 The prism as a learning aid

Using the prism in conjunction with other visualization techniques such as molecular models [11] and service blueprinting [12], students are able to get a good grasp of the fundamental principles and methods of service management. It is easier for students, for example, to analyze the contents and structure of a service level agreement (SLA), and comment on its likely effectiveness, once they have understood the relationships between the various actors, objects, performances, and measures described in such documents.

Four Cases of the Vicarious

The value of good case studies cannot be over-emphasized. Four case study discussions provide structural strength to the entire learning experience, each illustrating a different set of decisions that service organizations have to make. For example, once the students have learned how to use molecular models to visually depict services, they are asked to examine together the cases of Netflix [13] and Blockbuster [14]. They are directed to compare the considerably different structures of the two delivery models for film rental services and provide a critical analysis in terms of the similarities and the differences from several perspectives such as service recovery, delivery problems, and customer interactions. From this they appreciate the two major aspects of service design: what and how. Similarly, other cases studies either introduce new concepts or reinforce those already in play. A case study on UPS [15] has been useful to illustrate the concept of infrastructure services and how digital technologies can be used to automate and control service processes and interfaces. A case study on the Internal Revenue Service (IRS) [16] has been useful in illustrating the usefulness of customer-centric organizational designs and shared services in improving customer satisfaction while keeping control of costs. Finally, the case of Lion Financial Services [17] provides a useful context for discussions on the merits and demerits of certain capacity management strategies and the human factors in decisions to consolidate operations.

Five Plus Two Equals Fine

The mini (or half-semester) course combines five weeks of lectures and case studies with two weeks of assignments, field observations, and guest lectures by practitioners from the industry. The structure of the course ensures that the introduction of new concepts and principles is always within the reach of practical exercises that reinforce them. Feedback from students has shown that those exercises that closely mimic actual business activity are particularly helpful. A good example is the exercise in which students assume the role of external advisors and critically examine an SLA. An exercise, in which students observe customer behavior at self-service terminals and comment on their effectiveness, is another such example. Such role-based exercises are likely train students for future jobs or give them a lift in their present work environments.

Six Degrees of Freedom

The final opportunity for learning in the course comes actually in the form of a test. A closed-book exam with six essay-type questions requires students to focus on only the most fundamental concepts, ideas, and principles that arenas are expected to take away from the course. To help them prepare for the test, students are given a sample version of the test right from the beginning of the course and are encouraged to try the questions as the course progresses.

Each of the six questions on the final exam locates their level of understanding on an important aspect of service management. The questions are so designed that mere recall of facts and figures would not help formulate a good response. The questions place the students in different roles and situations in which they are encouraged to think freely. With six degrees of freedom, students are given an opportunity to express themselves in way that gives their instructor sufficient basis for evaluation. To score well on the test, students are advised that they should respond to all six questions knowing that only the best four of their responses will count towards their final grades.

Conclusions

To a good extent, existing knowledge from various academic fields when placed in the proper context can help create an exciting learning experience for students. To teach service management effectively it is useful to get students engaged and excited by informing them about additional potential for their capabilities. To get them engaged, it is necessary to supply them with certain basic concepts about services that are critical for their absorptive capacity throughout the course. With a few key concepts, students are able to identify interesting patterns and principles and begin to develop a sense for services. As they realize the power of having this sense that allows them to be creative and to solve problems, they can get very excited about the services industry and start liking the idea of a new science. Students like to know that other knowledge they have recently acquired can be put to use right away in fast growing sectors of the economy. However, the excitation will not occur if there is causal ambiguity between the knowledge they already have, that which they are about to acquire, and their value in the work place from combing both.

References

[1] Argote, L. & Ingram, P. Knowledge Transfer: A Basis for Competitive Advantage in Firms. Organizational Behavior and Human Decision Processes. Vol. 82, No. 1, pp. 150-169. 2000.

[2] National Academy of Engineering. *The Impact of Academic Research on Industrial Performance*. The National Academies Press, 2003.

[3] ITSqc. *Global Strategic Service Management Symposium*. [ITSqc Working Paper CMU-ITSQC-WP04-001a]. Carnegie Mellon University, Pittsburgh, PA, USA, 2004.

[4] Hefley, B. Educating an Innovative Services Science Workforce. Position paper for *Workshop on Education for Service Innovation*, National Science Foundation, US Department of Commerce, and IBM Research, Washington, D.C., April 18, 2006

[5] Szulanski, G. *Sticky Knowledge: Barriers to Knowing in the Firm*. Sage Publications, Thousand Oaks, CA, USA, 2003.

[6] Lovelock, C. & Gummesson, E. Whither Services Marketing? In Search of a New Paradigm and Fresh Perspectives. *Journal of Service Research*, Vol. 7, No. 1: 20-41. 2004.

[7] Hill, T. P. On goods and services. *Review of Income and Wealth*, 315-38, 1976.

[8] Rathmell, J. M. What Is Meant by Services? *Journal of Marketing*, Vol. 30, pp. 32-36, 1966.

[9] Lovelock, C. & Wirtz, J. Service Marketing: People, Technology, Strategy. Pearson Prentice Hall, Upper Saddle River, NJ, USA, 2004.

[10] Newing, R. Overview of Managed Services. Financial Times on FT.com. 2004. http://news.ft.com/cms/s/4090bdc4-000e-11d9-ad3100000e2511c8,dwp_uuid=59667ca8-fccb-11d8-ab9f00000e2511c8.html

[11] Shostack, L. G. How to Design a Service. *European Journal of Marketing*. Vol. 16, No.1: 49-63, 1984.

[12] Shostack, L. G. Designing Services that Deliver. *Harvard Business Review*. Vol. 62, No. 1: 133-139, 1984.

[13] Mayfield, E. S. Netflix.com, Inc. Harvard Business School Case No. 9-201-037, 2003.

[14] Hennessy, J. Blockbuster, Inc.: Casting a New Movie. Kellogg School of Management Case No. KEL066. Northwestern University, 2004.

[15] Ross, J., Draper, W., Kang, P., Schuler, S., Gozum, O., & Tolle, J. United Parcel Services: Business Transformation through Information Technology. [Sloan School of Management Working Paper No. 4399-03]. Massachusetts Institute of Technology, 2002.

[16] Edmondson, A. C. & Frei, F.X. Transformation at the IRS. Harvard Business School Case No. 9-603-010, 2002.

[17] Stanford Business School. Call Center Design for Lion Financial Services. Case No. OIT-29. Stanford University, 2003.

Educating Services Science Leaders to Think Holistically About Enterprises

Donna H. Rhodes
Massachusetts Institute of Technology
Engineering Systems Division
77 Massachusetts Avenue
Cambridge, MA 02139
rhodes@mit.edu

Deborah J. Nightingale [1]
Massachusetts Institute of Technology
Engineering Systems Division
77 Massachusetts Avenue
Cambridge, MA 02139
dnight@mit.edu

ABSTRACT

Modern enterprises are complex, highly integrated systems comprised of people, processes, and enabling technologies. A strategic business model defines the enterprise landscape and associated strategies for achieving the enterprise goals and mission. The elements of the enterprise exhibit multifaceted interdependencies and interrelationships which are dynamic in nature. The challenges inherent in these modern enterprises are driving an unprecedented demand for high end business services, where a *service* can be defined as a provider/client interaction that creates value. At the same time, availability of new technologies and the desire to be competitive in the marketplace are driving a focus on standardized *service offerings*. With this comes the critical need for many more skilled individuals who are able to lead and manage complex service projects; this need can only be fulfilled in a timely and effective manner through a partnership of service provider companies and academic institutions.

Introduction

A key challenge to services companies seeking such a partnership is to determine what type of academic unit might best provide the education aligned with the needs of a *services architect*. The skills of such professionals clearly span engineering, management science, social science, and humanities.

The MIT Engineering Systems Division (ESD) is a unique academic unit with a footprint that spans the various disciplines required for educating this new type of engineering leader. This interdisciplinary academic unit brings together departments from across MIT including the School of Engineering; School of Science; School of Humanities, Arts, and Social Sciences; and Sloan School of Management. ESD faculty, researchers, students, and strategic partners work together to understand, model, and predict the behavior of

---

1   The authors are equal contributors to this paper

technologically-enabled complex systems in order to help the engineering profession address contemporary critical issues and better serve the broad needs of society.

Within the last decade *engineering systems* has been evolving as an important new field of study that takes an integrative holistic view of large-scale, complex, technologically-enabled systems which have significant enterprise level interactions and socio-technical interfaces. One area of study in ESD focuses on understanding how to architect, integrate, manage and transform large-scale enterprises, taking into consideration the environment in which they are operating. ESD also places intensified focus on the interconnections of the product/service architecture and the enterprise (business) architecture.

Enterprise Science

The authors view the development of *enterprise science* as an important contribution within the overall field of *engineering systems* [3]. There is significant research ongoing at MIT and other leading universities across the globe that will serve to evolve this art and science, and more is needed. In particular, the Lean Aerospace Initiative (LAI)[2] research group at MIT has a significant research effort that uses real world enterprises as its laboratory, and codifies research results into 'products' usable by industry and government. Topics include enterprise architecting, enterprise integration, enterprise modeling, enterprise measurement, and enterprise change with a value focus. Two MIT graduate courses have been developed that draw heavily from the LAI research on enterprises and the engineering systems paradigm.

Enterprises have long been studied by management scientists and social scientists; however, this has largely been through taking one single view of the enterprise such as studying the organizational structure or the information technology architecture. At MIT, *enterprise architecting* takes a systems perspective, viewing the entire enterprise as a holistic system that can be understood by examining the enterprise through multiple perspectives which area elements of an overall integrated framework; these include strategy view, policy/regulatory view, people/organization view, process view, knowledge view, enabling information technology view, and the interrelationships between these views.

Enterprise Architecting

Current enterprise architecting practice is well established and has clear extensions from software/systems architecting practice [1]). The prevailing view tends to be information technology centric, and it works well for the simpler enterprises trying to align processes and technology with organizational structure. As the enterprise moves from simple orga-

---

2   The Lean Aerospace Initiative (LAI) is a large consortium of government, industry, and academia focused on enterprise value driven transformation. MIT is the academic research arm of the consortium, collaborating with other university partners through an extended education network. Information can be found at: http://lean.mit.edu

nization to a complex networked organization (an extended enterprise), the authors assert that an enriched view is needed. Further, we believe that this approach needs to be more highly integrated with strategy and culture, and requires some new lenses with which to view the enterprise. Additionally, understanding of the interactions of the views becomes of increased importance.

In enterprise architecting we are faced with an important consideration: How do you architect an enterprise that can most effectively produce its desired outcome? Today we can, at best, cite heuristics and emerging principles on how enterprises should be architected. MIT research in enterprise architecting is working toward transforming enterprise architecting from an art to a science, wherein enterprises can be predictability architected and engineered. There may possibly emerge common enterprise archetypes or patterns. Understanding these enterprise patterns will be essential to fully realize the vision of services providers to design and deliver offerings that are standardized business and infrastructure solutions.

Modern enterprises are highly complex and the management approaches applied are shifting. There are many aspects of an enterprise system that must be considered, including: political, cultural, legal, economic, environmental, technological, sociological, psychological, geographical, and temporal. As shown in the figure, any complex enterprise has multiple *stakeholders* that often involve many diverse perspectives.

While enterprise principles initially focused heavily on the client, more recent enterprise research has revealed that the critical success factor for today's enterprises is to *balance* the needs of *all* stakeholders. It is critical that these multiple stakeholder views and contributions to the enterprise be considered in its design to achieve desired performance objectives and deliver value.

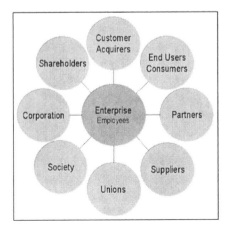

Figure 1. Multiple stakeholders of the enterprise

Maier [2] defines architecture as "the set of information that defines a system's value, cost, and risk sufficiently for the purposes of a system sponsor". Enterprise architecting provides the strategies and modeling approaches to ensure that adequate time is spent in developing the possible 'could be' states, and evaluating and selecting the best alternative given a set of desired properties and criteria for the future enterprise system. In the case of already established enterprises, enterprise architecting provides the approach for analyzing and understanding the 'as is' enterprise, and allows the various alternative changes and interventions to be analyzed. As enterprise complexity rises there are more possibilities to consider in designing an optimal enterprise, and so importance of architecting grows.

Through the emphasis on architecting, we look not just at the transition from an 'as is' to the 'to be' state, but also at the underlying decision analysis related to considering the various alternative 'could be' states of the new (or transforming) enterprise. Architecting enriches the thinking about the enterprise through a deeper exploration of each enterprise view, and more importantly at the interconnections and interrelationships between these views. Decisions are made about the alternatives in context of the business model, technology strategy, culture, purpose, and other factors.

Enterprise architecting is not a subject that is commonly found in academic units. Training that exists in the industry tends to have an IT dominant focus, and trains people skilled at using templates to describe aspects of an enterprise. Little education is available that develops the skill of thinking holistically about enterprises. The first course of its kind at MIT was developed by Nightingale in 1998. This course, "Integrating the Lean Enterprise", focuses on the practical aspects of managing and transforming enterprises using lean principles and practices and is positioned as an introductory level graduate class.

Enterprise Architecting Course

In the 2004, the authors developed a new advanced level graduate course, Enterprise Architecting. The students in the past classes have been active participants in shaping the research agenda, theory, and practice of a new type of enterprise architecting, and have produced many real world project reports. The authors believe that this course teaches essential subject matter and new ways of thinking for graduates who will be engaged in complex enterprise projects including those leading the design of standard service offerings and delivery/management of business services.

This advanced Enterprise Architecting course has been taught three times to date, the first as a doctoral seminar, and the second and third years as an advanced masters/doctoral course. The academic programs represented include MIT ESD masters and doctoral degree program; Systems Design and Management (SDM) Program; Leaders for Manufacturing Program (LFM) Program; Aerospace masters and doctoral degree programs; and Sloan

School of Management masters and doctoral program. Most students have at least several years of experience in industry or government, in a diverse set of fields. The learning objectives for this course include:

— Apply architectural thinking to enterprises to understand the "as-is" enterprise, explore and evaluate the "could-be" architectures; and select the "to-be" enterprise

— Understand how strategic drivers (business model, strategic focus, enterprise performance objectives, etc.) influence the enterprise architecture

— Articulate enterprise properties including the "ilities" (flexibility, scalability, agility, etc.) and make evaluative decisions related to these

— Describe the enterprise using different views (strategy, policy, organizational structure, processes, knowledge, product system, enabling technologies) that comprise an enterprise architecture and how these are interrelated

— Be familiar with enterprise architecture frameworks, models, and toolsets currently being applied in practice and research, and when these can add value in the process

— Understand how enterprise architecting is presently being applied in real world organizations and have insight into dimensions of enterprise architecting research

The course topics[3] include basic concepts in enterprise thinking, architectural thinking, and stakeholder/value thinking; a deep dive into the various views of the enterprise as well as their interrelationships; the architecting roadmap; and lectures on real enterprise cases and selected research. During the course students develop heuristics and participate in a team project to apply enterprise architecting to a real world enterprise. For a selected enterprise, student teams define enterprise boundaries, characterize the 'as is' architecture, conduct stakeholder and value analysis, articulate a future vision and desired behaviors, define candidate alternative 'to-be' architectures, apply trade-off evaluation to select a preferred 'to be' architecture, and outline a transformation plan.

Applicability to Services Science

This course is positioned to educate leaders to think in an integrative way about enterprises, as well as to provide experiential learning through the team project. The approach and methods of the course are applicable to different types of enterprises producing products and/or services. In context of the services industry, the authors envision it as applicable to three types of leadership roles:

---

3   The authors are presently writing a text, entitled *Architecting the Future Enterprise*, based on their course and associated research.

1. design of standard science-based service offerings to sell to multiple clients;

2. custom design of business services solutions for specific clients; and

3. deriving strategies for management of business services in the context of a changing enterprise environment.

For each of these three leadership roles, there is a need for a comprehensive and integrative understanding of the enterprise. In the first case, the architect must understand various enterprises to discern how a service offering couple be developed to suit the stakeholder needs, while accommodating variations from enterprise to enterprise. In the second leadership role, the architect needs to do deep analysis of the client enterprise, and the studies to find an optimal services solution. In the third type of leadership role, the ability to think with an enterprise frame of mind is critically important to understand the optimal strategies and changes required over the life of the services delivery contract.

Conclusion

There are many available courses in universities that are suitable for services science curriculum. However, most courses are designed to teach students about some individual focus area. The Enterprise Architecting course at MIT is one example of a course that teaches services science students to think holistically about the enterprise. We believe a course of this nature is essential for any services science education program.

References

[1]   Rechtin, E., *Systems Architecting of Organizations*, CRC Press, 2000
[2]   Maier, M. , Rechtin, E., *The Art of Systems Architecting, Second Edition*, CRC Press, 2000
[3]   Nightingale, D. and Rhodes, D. *Enterprise Systems Architecting*, MIT ESD Symposium, 2004

Services Research Collaborations: Beyond the Ivory Tower

Neeli Bendapudi, Ph. D.
Fisher College of Business,
The Ohio State University
556 Fisher Hall
Bendapudi_1@cob.osu.edu
614-292-2959

Mindy Stobart
Fisher College of Business,
The Ohio State University
306 Fisher Hall
Stobart_3@cob.osu.edu
614-292-9681

ABSTRACT

Academic institutions, businesses, societies, and governments all have a great deal to gain by investing in a better understanding of the science, management, and engineering aspects of services. However, instead of waiting for all the questions to be answered in the academic laboratory, services scholarship is best served in an iterative process that moves from the crucibles of academe to the portals of practice and vice versa. This paper describes three unique applications of this precept in The Ohio State University Fisher College of Business' Initiative for Managing Services. The contexts include projects for students, working with chiefs of police and superintendents, and a collaborative venture with a business to help public school principals.

Services Management at Fisher College

At the Fisher College of Business, The Ohio State University, the services journey is relatively recent. Under the leadership of Dean Joseph A. Alutto and the support of visionary businessman, William E. Arthur, a small group of academics came together in 2004 to address the needs of a services-dominant economy. The Initiative for Managing Services (IMS)[1] was the outcome. Ohio, like much of the traditionally industrial Middle America, faces the challenge of reinventing itself to be globally competitive in services. It was deemed unacceptable for OSU, as the flagship institution in the state, to move into the future without a formal structure and discipline around services in business education. IMS quickly rallied faculty across disciplines and a number of leading business organizations to promote the creation, dissemination, and application of best practices in service as well as interdisciplinary services research.

IMS activities are supported by a roster of ten charter partners: Alliance Data Systems, Cardinal Health, Convergys Corporation, Deloitte and Touche, Huntington Bancshares, Limited Brands, Nationwide, OSU Medical Center, Porter Wright, Morris and Arthur,

---

1 http://www.fisher.osu.edu/IMS

and Scott's LawnCare. True to its interdisciplinary charter, IMS benefits from the insights of faculty advisors in accounting, business strategy, finance, human resources, marketing, management, and operations. The business advisors are active participants in developing and encouraging town and gown interactions. We describe below our model of services and three applications.

A Model of Services Management

We propose the four pillars model of professional services. Managing services effectively requires attention to the four pillars of providers, partners, processes, and profitability. The first pillar of professional services is knowing how to manage oneself and others as service-providers. In a services-dominant world, a company's most important assets, its human and social capital, go home every night. Managing employees in a service organization requires leadership and understanding of the human resource management issues of recruiting, selecting, training, compensating, and rewarding service talent.

The second pillar of professional services is managing partnerships, with clients and other key parties in the services supply chain. This element of professional services requires a sound grasp of marketing principles, including an understanding of how other parties view the services firm, how to define a strong and compelling value proposition, how to communicate and deliver on the proposition, and finally, how to capture the value.

The third pillar of professional services is managing service processes to maximize both efficiency and customer satisfaction. In increasingly complex and tangled service relationships, the key to competitive differentiation may be simpler, easier-to-navigate service processes. Applying the principles of lean and six sigma process improvement methods requires more than mere duplication; it requires a deep understanding of the particular problems and potential of human-intensive service processes.

The final pillar on which a successful professional services firm rests is profitability. Service organizations struggle with clear allocation of overhead, optimal resource allocation and scheduling, and calculations of customer as well as service provider implications for revenue and profitability. Successful practitioners of services science must have a thorough understanding of accounting and financial principles.

We have used the four pillars model of professional services to educate our students and to inform our applications to business contexts. What follows next is an exposition of three practical applications of IMS services research.

Three Contexts Beyond the Ivory Tower

In the spirit of Fisher College's motto, "Where theory meets practice," IMS has applied the four pillars model and allied services principles in a variety of practical contexts. Three examples are discussed below.

Students as co-producers of their learning experience.

To better prepare our students for the rigors of a services environment, we have partnered with our charter companies to design innovative educational opportunities for Fisher College students. Associate Dean of Graduate Programs, Professor Karen Wruck, has supported the development of a services management track in our MBA program, whereby students develop a broad-based exposure to interdisciplinary approaches to services problems. This is a departure from, and, we believe, an improvement to, most programs with services degrees which emphasize say, a marketing, or an IT focus. To help students learn by doing, IMS has initiated a mini-internship program which allows first-year MBA students to work on specific projects in services companies as they complete their coursework. Thus, when the summer internship rolls around, our students have more to show for their first year than grades on courses. Our charter members help us plan the focus of these projects. Last year, students focused on best practices in gathering customer satisfaction information in service businesses. This year's batch will shift their focus to talent development in service firms.

Our honors undergraduate students, led by Associate Dean for Undergraduate Programs, Professor Rao Unnava, completed a project for one of our charter companies, Convergys. These projects allowed students to develop best practice recommendations for Convergys recruiting. The projects were enhanced by our students working with student teams in India, where Convergys has call center operations, to develop their recommendations. The experience brought home to our students the complexity of a global services operation, the realities of working across linguistic and cultural barriers in off-shore operations, and the difficulty of creating a transferable employment brand. Our students learned about professional services by acting as professional services consultants to a professional services company! These projects reflect our strong services philosophy that in education, as in so many other professional services, the customer is a co-producer of the services outcome [1].

Services we need but may wish we did not: Police chiefs and community relationships.

Services science is just as important in governmental agencies as it is in commercial organizations; indeed maybe more so. A unique program developed by the Ohio Chiefs of Police, in conjunction with a grant from the Department of Justice, gave us the opportunity to interact with and educate police chiefs and superintendents from across the country in the unique challenges of creating services partnerships with communities. A two-day workshop in Chicago in June 2006 was preceded by pre-reads of marketing material developed by IMS Associate Director, Mindy Stobart, in consultation with several faculty at the Fisher College of Business.

The police chiefs willingly tackled the challenges they face in ensuring public safety without being heavy-handed, the fine balance between ensuring the well-being of their officers and the rights of citizens, as well as the realities of competing for community and government support. The officers were intrigued by the idea that each of them was the living brand of the police department [2]. This concept reinforces the idea presented in a study done by George Mason University, which alluded to the importance of the public image of a law enforcement agency in relation to the agency's effectiveness [3]. A special focus on documenting the outcomes of police-supported projects, from D.A.R.E. (drug abuse resistance education) to community policing was an important example of bringing accountability to social services.

Services we want but may not be ready to co-produce: IMS project with School Principals.

A significant sector in public services is public education. It is impossible to read a local newspaper without some politician or pundit either deploring the state of our public schools or pontificating on pet policies. The reality, however, is that public schools today are being asked to do more and more with less and less. The only sustainable strategy is active engagement between schools, business leaders, and the broader community. The typical school principal must think and act as the CEO of a corporation with little of the formal training or resources available to practitioners of services science. In a bid to address and reverse this trend, IMS has co-sponsored a program for public school principals with our Franklin County Office of Educational Services. Drs. Bart Anderson and Ralph Johnson of the educational services community and IMS have identified business partners to coach school principals on the four pillars of professional services. This year, in May, the focus was on building partnerships by building strong brands.

IMS served as the resource for academic subject matter expertise as well as the clearinghouse for student involvement. A unique feature was the decision to choose a different corporate sponsor for each aspect of professional services. What better company to teach the fundamentals of branding than Limited Brands, home of Victoria's Secret and Bath and Body Works? Ed Gaydos, Limited Brand's community affairs officer made available several senior leaders of the company to coach school principals on branding, including the on-boarding process that is used by this successful retail giant. Each group of principals was paired with one business leader from Limited Brands and one student facilitator from the Fisher College. The feedback from the principals was extremely positive, especially regarding managing the evidence that the community sees [4]. Many confessed they had never really thought about the need for branding the services they provide or their particular school within a large district. An unexpected but highly gratifying outcome is the commitment by several business leaders and our graduate students to continue to support the cause of service excellence in "their" schools.

As these examples hopefully demonstrate, the Fisher College is committed to actively engaging with businesses, non-profits, and government entities to better prepare a cadre of graduates to tackle the challenges of services science, management, and engineering.

Conclusion

This paper has highlighted some of the ways in which a research center in a traditional academic setting can take a more active role in using service-learning methods[2] to propagate principles of services science in non-traditional venues. It is hoped that these examples will spur greater interaction among academe, business, and government for the benefit of the larger community.

References

[1] Bendapudi, Neeli and Robert P. Leone, "Psychological Implications of Customer Participation in Co-Production," *Journal of Marketing*; January 2003, Vol. 67 Issue 1, p14, 15p.
[2] Bendapudi, Neeli and Venkat Bendapudi, "Creating the Living Brand." *Harvard Business Review*; May 2005, Vol. 83 Issue 5, p124, 6p.
[3] Gallagher, Catherine, Maguire, Edward R., Mastrofski, Stephen D., and Reisig, Michael D. (2001) The Public Image of the Police, a report prepared for The International Association of Chiefs of Police.
[4] Berry, Leonard L. and Neeli Bendapudi, "Clueing in Customers," *Harvard Business Review*; February 2003, Vol.81 Issue 2, p100, 7p.

Progress Report of Efforts Towards a Research and Education Agenda for Services Science in the EU and Greece

Christos Nikolaou
CS Department,
Transformation Services Lab
University of Crete
Heraklion 71409
Crete, Greece
nikolau@csd.uoc.gr
+30 (2810) 393503

ABSTRACT

SSME is necessary to understand and predict trends in the emerging world service economy. Progress in determining an appropriate research agenda in Europe is reported. A new way for combining training and research is proposed. Ongoing, planned and proposed R&D activities at the University of Crete in Greece are reported.

Introduction

The global economy moves fast towards services today; the rate of change towards services was 191% in China for the last 25 years, and in most developed nations 70% of their economy is in services. This radical world economic transformation coupled with wave after wave of technological innovation especially in ICT, the globalization of labor markets and rising competition, force organizations (public and private, for profit and not-for-profit alike) to:

— Continuously transform business structures, processes, networks, alliances;

— Form alliances and networks with winning value propositions;

— Continuously strive to take advantage of frantically evolving technologies;

— Watch their back – for disruptive technologies that may destroy their market shares;

— Fully express and harness core competencies of people and organizations;

The magnitude of the stakes involved and the complexity of these challenges preclude any ad-hoc, empirical approach. A single discipline approach (for example, using computer science and engineering only) is also not effective.

Matching business strategy and objectives to business processes and these in turn to people and ICT infrastructures and components that compose services, all in an optimal (or at least efficient), observable and dynamically changeable way is a formidable multidisciplinary challenge. This is the challenge that SSME faces today.

The Current State of the Art

Awareness for the need of SSME arose in industry and in academia out of research in e-commerce and e-business, and more recently, in business process transformation. Many study programs, centers for research and research projects arose around the world, such as [1, 2, 3]. Departments offering interdisciplinary education in information systems and management are common today, but they are not focusing specifically on the rise of the service-oriented economy and the new social, economic, legal and engineering challenges that it poses. The SSME program offered at [4] is one of the first of its kind. A similar study direction was recently established at my university, and is described in this paper.

A New Research Agenda In the EU

In recent workshops, organized by "Networks of Excellence" (highly specialized research communities from industry and academia, focused on specific open research problems) and funded by the European Commission (IST/FET unit), there was increased awareness of the complex and dynamic nature of the emerging services economy and of the need for new scientific and engineering approaches to understand it and predict future trends. In addition the NESSI Technology Platform was created.

The ONCE-CS workshop on SoS [4]

ONCE-CS is the Complex Systems Network of Excellence, and the workshop that it organized examined services from the point of view of complexity. We concluded that "the grand challenge is the creation of computational theories that allow generation of models that help us understand and guide how services associating humans and information and communication technologies emerge, how they are helping the emergence, creation, or optimization of organizational structures, how these structures interact, evolve and adapt in order to better meet the needs and aspirations of people, business and wider society."

The Beyond-the-Horizon workshops [6]

This series of workshops was organized by ERCIM [8] to "provide input about IST-related emerging trends and strategic research areas that require support, through a well-organized, extensive and systematic consultation of the relevant research community throughout Europe, involving the main actors and experts in the related fields." The emergence of the service society and economy was noted in two of the "online communities" that were formed: intelligent and cognitive systems and software intensive systems.

The NESSI "Technology Platform" [7]

NESSI is "promoted by thirteen major European ICT corporations, totaling almost a million jobs and about 300 B€ revenues, … aims to provide a unified view for European research in Services Architectures and Software Infrastructures that will define technologies, strategies and deployment policies fostering new, open, industrial solutions and societal applications that enhance the safety, security and well-being of citizens." A Service Sciences working group was formed that is working on a research and educational agenda. Funding is provided partly by the European Commission.

Towards a New Education and Training Agenda

In addition to the more conventional, most likely interdisciplinary programs, that are being and will be developed, I believe that there is a need to generate opportunities for academia, industry and government to get together, so that they can discuss new problems that arise in real-world situations, explore best practices and individual case studies, nurture new service provider and client relationships and common projects, and allow the young generations of researchers and professionals to interact with each other, in a relaxed way, and with prominent members of our SSME community. Short courses or series of seminars of at most one to two weeks duration, such as summer schools, could serve that purpose. We will be organizing one, starting from the summer of 2007 in Crete, Greece.

The SSME Summer School at the University of Crete

The idea is simple: in a relaxed, vacation-style, away from the pressures of the office kind of environment, create a forum for educational and research activity on the Sciences of Services, in Europe.

Educational aspects of the Summer School are:

— Disseminate best practices and fundamental concepts on Services Science, Management and Engineering (SSME);

— Case studies of emergence of new services and of their survivability in various industry sectors;

— Leaders in the field (researchers, practitioners, business and political leaders) will be invited with keynote speakers, instructors (short one week courses), and panelists.

Research aspects of the Summer School are:

— Collocate conferences and workshops on SSME,

— Raise funds to pay attendance of graduate students from around the world,

— Host brainstorming workshops to set up SSME research agenda, in cooperation with EU-IST, NSF, others.

The audience for the Summer School is:

— Technical experts, decision makers, young professionals (attending different tracks of the summer school in general, although there may be plenary sessions with distinguished speakers and panelists)

— Customers, as the expectation is that the IT companies leading the SSME discipline creation, will use the summer school to meet, educate their customers (actual or potential):

— Young promising professionals can go through a more formal program (from a couple of weeks to one or two months) eventually coupled with graduation with a Master's Degree

— Executives can collocate strategy meetings with participation to panels, discussions with leaders in the field, etc.

— Researchers, academics, technical leaders, motivated to be exposed to "real world" problems, define new research agendas and problems.

— Students to learn, network, discover new problems, etc.

The local Organizers will be the Department of Computer Science of the University of Crete (leading research University in Greece) and the Institute of Computer Science (ICS) of FORTH (leading public research center in Greece, member of ERCIM). There will also be cooperation with the Department of Systems and Management, Faculty of Economics (leading school worldwide), U. of Tilburg, Netherlands.

Why in Crete
— Significantly strong research & academic infrastructure. In addition, ENISA (European Network and Information Security Agency) is based in Crete (FORTH buildings);

— Local research community has extensive experience in organizing big events & conferences: ECDL 98, HCI2003, iTrust2003, etc.

— Crete is a Mediterranean island with beautiful summer resorts, 3000 years of culture;

— Seed money to organize the first two summer schools (about 20-30K euros per year starting from 2007) is already available through University of Crete;

— Graduate program in computer science with strong orientation towards services and member of the IBM Academic Initiative;

— Strong network of cooperation with other universities around the world: joint graduate degree program with U. de Paris 6 (Orsay) and U. de Grenoble; summer program with U. of York, Canada; Cooperation with U. of Tilburg (Netherlands), Department of Systems and Management; plans for joint degrees with U. of Vienna, NCSU.

SSME at the University of Crete

We recently proceeded to a full re-organization of our e-commerce study orientation (now renamed to "science of services" orientation) of our graduate program. The courses that will be offered will cover the following topics; wireless networks and mobile computing systems, secure systems, cryptography, Internet systems and technologies, data and knowledge management on the WWW, process management systems, digital economy and e-commerce, advanced topics for e-business, introduction to economic theory for e-commerce, component-based programming, and SOA, CRM (Customer Relationship Management), Personalization and Data Mining. My department participates in the IBM Academic Initiative Program and uses several of the Websphere and Rational families of products.

In addition, my department recently established the Transformation Services Laboratory (TSL) to perform research, deliver services, train and educate on the subject of transforming organizations, so that they become more competitive and deliver better quality services. TSL is already active through a number of projects:

— Providing consulting services to a number of municipalities in Crete that are installing broadband and wireless networks, and facilitate the creation of broadband services.

— Participating in solution development efforts to transform government (e-passports).

— Conducting research, in cooperation with researchers at the IBM T.J. Watson Research Center in Hawthorne, NY, on value net modeling and analysis and service delivery models.

— Spearheading the creation of a Center for Business Transformation in Crete, with initial funding from EU, and with first mission to identify companies and public organizations that will be partners in transformation projects.

Government and SSME

Government has a crucial role to play; by establishing policies that ensure a stable transition to a service economy in which all citizens benefit, by funding R&D initiatives in that direction and by re-organizing its own services to improve their quality. On the other hand, inertia will have to be overcome, government employees have to be retrained and given incentives for doing so. At a recent conference of the Greek National Association of Townships and Municipalities our proposal was endorsed to create Regional Operations and Processes Transformation Centers that will take the responsibility, at the regional level, to promote best practices and innovation for the services provided for the citizens by municipalities.[1]

Conclusions

It is exciting to witness and participate in the development of a new discipline, SSME. The stakes involved and the challenges ahead force us to rethink many of our traditional activities as academics: how to teach and educate the young, how to conduct research with colleagues of different scientific background, how to form successful partnerships with both industry and government.

References

[1] Institute for eCommerce, Carnegie-Mellon University. http://euro.ecom.cmu.edu/indexoldsite.shtml/.
[2] Center for e-Business Technology (CEBT). http://www.cebt.re.kr/.
[3] Fisher Center for Information Technology and Marketplace Transformation (CITM), U. of California, Berkeley. http://groups.haas.berkeley.edu/citm/citmhome.htm/.
[4] News release – MBA Services Science Concentration, NC State College of Management. http://www.mgt.ncsu.edu/news/2006/mba_ssme.php/.
[5] ONCE-CS Portal: SOS Homepage. http://complexsystems.lri.fr/Portal/tikiindex.php?page=SOS+Homepage/.
[6] Beyond-the-Horizon. http://www.beyond-the-horizon.net/.
[7] NESSI – Networked European & Services Initiative. http://www.nessi-europe.com/.
[8] ERCIM – The European Research Consortium for Informatics and Mathematics. http://www.ercim.org/.

---

1 see http://kedke.ntua.gr/docs/KEDKE%20ICT%20C ONFERENCEconclusions08052006.doc

A Master Program in Services Engineering and Management at the University of Porto

J. Falcão e Cunha, Lia Patrício, Ana Camanho
Faculdade de Engenharia da Universidade do Porto
R. Dr. Roberto Frias
4200-465 Porto, Portugal
{jfcunha; lpatric; acamanho}@fe.up.pt
+351-22-508 2133

Raymond Fisk
University of New Orleans
2000 Lakeshore Drive
New Orleans, LA 70148-1566 USA
rfisk@uno.edu

ABSTRACT

The education of professional engineers has been mainly oriented towards the requirements of industry, although many graduates will start and end up working in service organizations. Services always involve interaction, either directly between people or using machines. Most services now require the use of technology, including self service machines, Internet and mobile equipments and may involve complex social and organizational issues. Although engineering programs have evolved in order to accommodate changes in the economy, new proposals must be taken into new graduate and postgraduate education.

This paper proposes MESG[1], a Master program in Services Engineering and Management compatible with the Bologna European framework. It is still a program to educate professional engineers, in the sense that graduates will be prepared to Conceive, Design, Implement and Operate (CDIO) complex value-added engineering systems. But MESG has a strong emphasis on: (i) understanding the innovative technologies now required for service provision, (ii) understanding the functional and the experience requirements of people using services, and (iii) management of the service CDIO process and understanding its value. Knowledge and experience about people and about business, in social-organizational environments, are important components in the advanced education of service engineers and managers.

Introduction

The services sector develops and implements systems that help businesses, governments and other organizations improve what they do, and innovate. Services currently account for over 70 percent of the USA, European and Japanese economies and are growing as organizations invent new business opportunities by building more efficient systems,

---

1   The paper will use original Portuguese acronyms and names in English. MESG: Mestrado em Engenharia de Serviços e Gestão. In the acronyms used, the initial "L" stands for Licenciatura and "M" for Mestrado. These are the names for Bachelor (BSc) and Master (MSc) Programs in Portuguese (Portugal).

streamlining business processes, in particular by embracing the Internet, mobile phones and other self service technologies.

The infusion of technology has deeply changed the service environment. People can now interact with businesses and other organizations through diverse forms of technology-facilitated contact. This environment creates new challenges for service providers and produces changes in the economy and society.

FEUP, Faculdade de Engenharia da Universidade do Porto (www.fe.up.pt), the School of Engineering of the University of Porto, has been involved for the past 20 years in courses involving science, engineering and management curricula, such as LEIG/MEIG, the Industrial Engineering and Management BSc/MSc, and LEIC/MEIC, the Computing Engineering and Informatics BSc/MSc. There are now about 1000 graduates from these programs, most of them working in service areas of the economy, in companies in Portugal and in many other countries.

Those companies value the education and training in basic engineering sciences and disciplines gained by students. They also value the more specific subjects and projects in information technology, quantitative methods and management science.

> *The best qualification for innovation is a basic training in Engineering. Engineers are taught that design matters, that most things are part of a system in which everything interacts, that their job is to worry about trade-offs, and that they must continually be measuring the robustness of the systems they set up. Such a frame of mind fosters innovation. It may be no coincidence that many of the greatest corporate leaders in America, Europe and Japan, past and present, trained first as engineers [1, p.77].*

Although all engineering graduates need to share some basic science curricula, mathematics and physics, and need technical expertise in some engineering disciplines (e.g.: civil, mechanical, chemical, electrical, materials or computing), more emphasis must be placed in the service systems, in understanding the way people interact with them, and in creativity focused on innovation.

The evolution of engineering programs at FEUP has been oriented by the CDIO™ initiative [2]², under the European Bologna framework, towards the education of professional engineers. Graduates from FEUP are increasingly assuming in their professional activities management responsibilities, and dealing with complex social and organizational issues. Therefore it is required that a professional service engineer will need to have education on management and other social sciences.

---

2   www.cdio.org

The CDIO Initiative

The CDIO initiative is an educational framework for helping to produce engineering programs adequate for the current environment. It aims at providing students with an education stressing engineering fundamentals set in the Context of Conceiving, Designing, Implementing and Operating real-world systems and products. The overall aspects that must be addressed in such education programs are: 1 – Technical knowledge and Reasoning; 2 – Personal and Professional Skills and Attributes; 3 – Interpersonal Skills: Teamwork and Communication; 4 – Conceiving, Designing, Implementing and Operating Systems in the Enterprise and Societal Context.

The CDIO framework is also useful in the process for professional accreditation of chartered engineering education by the certified institutional body in Portugal.[3]

European Bologna framework

Like most Schools in Europe, FEUP is evolving its degree structure in accordance with the Bologna Framework. Figure 1 shows on the left the degree model that will be followed at FEUP. Master degree will be granted after two years of full time successful study, on top of a Bachelor in Engineering Sciences.

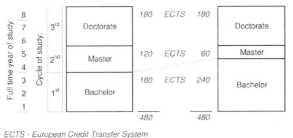

ECTS - European Credit Transfer System
60 ECTS correspond to one year full time of study

Figure 1. Two possible degree configurations under the Bologna European framework. FEUP is using the left scheme.

In the past, the initial engineering programs at FEUP used to last 5 years. The new programs, starting the next academic year, will still be aiming at providing an initial education of 5 years but in two steps: one 1st cycle of 3 years, with basic science and engineering courses, and a 2nd cycle to get advanced skills and knowledge about the specific area the student is aiming at for entering the profession.

---

3   Ordem dos Engenheiros: www.ordemengenheiros.pt

Professional Engineers

FEUP aims to educate professional engineers, in the following sense:

> *It can be considered that two distinct types of engineer are produced by the further and higher education systems of the various countries in the EU, and beyond. [We are] concerned with provision of the academic foundation knowledge and developing the corresponding skills that will lead our graduates to become 'professional' engineers. Professional engineers are those who are required to provide leadership, be innovative in their approach to engineering tasks and undertake design, research and critical investigations at the highest levels. For these engineers, a qualification at the 2nd cycle is the minimum level of attainment (a 3rd cycle qualification will be required in many cases). In such cases, the 1st cycle qualification is seen as an intermediate stage towards the 2nd cycle qualification [...] and not as an exit point from academic studies that would qualify for entry into the profession [3].*

This requires a high commitment and involvement of the faculty in research activities. All students graduating at the end of the 2nd cycle will be required to produce a Master Thesis, being involved in a research or similar internship project under supervision from FEUP.

Service Engineers and Managers

The authors have considerable experience of supervision of student internships and research work at the postgraduate level in cooperation with organizations, in particular with information system and marketing departments of banks, retail businesses or with government units. Such contacts emphasized the fundamental relevance of the following components in the education of service professionals:

— New technologies (i.e., ability to design, understand and evaluate innovative technologies and processes).

— New interaction modes or services (i.e., understand user and customer needs and be able to meet requirements and quality expectations).

— New business models (i.e., leadership and management capacity to meet stakeholder interests and the demand for organization flexibility, effectiveness and accountability). Service engineers and managers should be able to fully understand the science and technology required for providing technology based services to real people, in a way that generates value. This is in fact consistent with the required skills that a service scientist needs [5]: technology, business, social-organization.

Therefore, we propose to provide a Master in Services Engineering and Management that can be followed by any student with a good 1st cycle of studies in engineering sciences, with basic skills on mathematics, science, information and communication technologies, quantitative methods and social sciences (e.g.: databases, statistics, economics, operations research).

The following sections provide a short introduction to FEUP, its more relevant existing programs and resources, and its education environment. Then it will be shortly presented the characterization of research being conducted at FEUP. Finally it will be presented the design guidelines to be followed in setting up the master program and the general objectives and structure. This will include also a few ideas about ways IBM could be associated with this initiative.

Engineering Education at FEUP

FEUP is one of the largest and most prestigious research engineering schools in Portugal. It goes back to the Nautical School, set up in Porto in the 18th century, and has currently over 5000 students. Most of its lecturers and researchers have doctorates and are involved in projects in cooperation with other national and international organizations.

Although many of its graduates end up working in service areas of the economy, the graduates from LEIG/MEIG and LEIC/MEIC programs will most certainly do so.

The more Relevant Existing Programs

LEIG/MEIG, the Industrial Engineering and Management full time BSc/MSc is based on a sound science and mechanical engineering background and offers specializations in quantitative methods, information systems and operations management. Although it has an industrial orientation most of its graduates end up working in service organizations or departments, dealing with logistics, quality, marketing or information systems.

LEIC/MEIC, the Computing Engineering and Informatics full time BSc/MSc is based on a sound science and computer engineering background and offers specializations in information systems, software engineering and web engineering. Most of its graduates end up working in service organizations or departments, dealing with requirements engineering, user interface specification or project management.

Both programs were initially proposed with strong relations respectively to mechanical engineering and electrical engineering, due to the industrial economic environment in the North of Portugal. Both programs have been changing focus in recent years, evolving to address changes in environment needs, as manufacturing industries are no longer the main employers.

These programs have provided experience in education in technologies and management to engineering students. The MESG will bring together and improve such experiences and improve on an important component regarding services: understanding real people, users or customers. Social sciences, in particular psychology and sociology, and arts and humanities, will be very relevant in providing knowledge and skills on social and emotional aspects, usually absent in engineering education.

Science, Technology and Management in Engineering Programs

Most students at FEUP will have a first 3 year cycle of studies with a strong education in basic sciences and technology. Figure 2 shows our understanding of the relative position of Bachelor and Master Programs regarding science, technology and management (the MBA program of the University of Porto is pictured as a reference). Engineering Master Programs, MEIG and the proposed MESG, have similar management contents of MBA programs, in terms of ECTS, but maturity of students and focus of teaching are different.

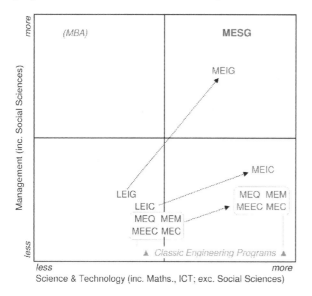

Figure 2. Management vs. Science & Technology emphasis of selected engineering programs at FEUP (based on authors' qualitative evaluation)

Environment and Resources Available

As it happens with similar institutions, FEUP education has been emphasizing for the past few years the student learning process. The CDIO initiative also stresses the importance of project based learning. In 2000 FEUP has moved into a new campus with excellent resources and environment, in particular for students. State-of-the-art Library, Computing and Communications resources are available all the time to students. Exchange programs with Europe, Brazil and the USA are available. Internships at external organizations before graduation have been available for many years, in particular for MEIG and MEIC students. Such

6 months full time internship project requires joint supervision by a faculty member. There is a requirement for a written final report that is presented and evaluated at a public event.

Students and faculty members are increasingly being involved in interdisciplinary projects involving different engineering skills, management and expertise from other schools of the University. Increasing use of Moodle, Luvit or WebCT eLearning platforms is also under way.

Service Research at FEUP

Service research in an Engineering School must involve science, engineering and management components. According to the Longman Dictionary of Contemporary English Online (www.ldoceonline.com):

Science: knowledge about the world, especially based on examining, testing, and proving facts.

Engineering: the work involved in designing and building roads, bridges, machines etc.

Management: the activity of controlling and organizing the work that a company or organization does.

Service: a particular type of help or work that is provided by a business to customers, but not one that involves producing goods.

Service can also be seen as "a deed, a performance, an effort" (Rathmell, 1966), cited in [4], or services are "value coproduction acts, promises, and relationships via sharing work, risk, information, assets, decisions, responsibility, and authority"[5].

Many research projects have been going on at FEUP in cooperation with external industrial and service organizations for example involving cooperation with banking, retail and government (e.g.: [6, 7, 8]). Such research has shown that human and social aspects are becoming more important, mainly due to the number and skills of people interacting with technology, and the social and organizational environment.

Some of the services research questions being addressed are therefore the following ones:

— How can technology be used to improve services, providing correct and suitable functions, and pleasurable experiences?

— What is the most appropriate way to improve services to people, in different situations in the society, by using a suitable mix of service interfaces?

— How to increase the value provided to the different stakeholders in a given business?

The approach followed at FEUP in master or doctoral research is the following: (i) identify a problem in a given context, (ii) study it from the theoretical point of view, considering the organization, user or stakeholders and social environment, (iii) propose a solution, (iv) build or define a prototype, and (v) evaluate it. Research projects are usually required to be in cooperation with external businesses or organizations.

Cooperation with IBM

IBM has been involved with FEUP in projects, mainly providing hardware and software systems, sometimes with very successful projects.[4] As it is happening in other parts of the world, IBM in Portugal has been moving into providing services to businesses, government and other organizations. For instance IBM offers data centre services to many companies and to government; in particular, the IRS submission service is hosted at an IBM service centre near Lisbon. IBM's direct and indirect support to projects at FEUP has resulted in several Master and Doctorate thesis. The authors also have established links concerning research projects with IBM UK usability services. Such cooperation has resulted in several theses and in the organization of seminars and workshops.

The MSEG Master Proposal

A formal proposal for the Master program in Services Engineering and Management has to comply with several regulations and frameworks at several levels: European, Portuguese, University of Porto, engineering school and engineering professional bodies. The more conceptual frameworks were summarized in previous sections, such as the Bologna framework, and the CDIO initiative. The curriculum proposed will emphasize 3 areas, summarized in Figure 3.

Figure 3. Three faces of Service relevant for MSEG.

---

4   For example, a Joint Study Agreement in 1991 with IBM has provided FEUP with software, hardware (RISC/6000 AIX workstations) and technical support for DSS research. From such cooperation resulted the GIST system and OPT www.opt. pt, a spin-off company. GIST is being used by the largest transport companies in Portugal for scheduling and daily rostering of buses and crews.

Some of the other relevant requirements for MSEG arise from common degree requirements. For instance, the program must include a final thesis project, resulting from a minimum effort of 42 ECTS, approximately 8 months of full time work.

Having all this in mind, we propose that the MESG program will have three curricular or scientific areas of interrelated study, and a final Project:

— ICT – Information and Communication Technologies.

— PSA – Psychology, Sociology and Arts.

— OMM – Operations, Management and Marketing.

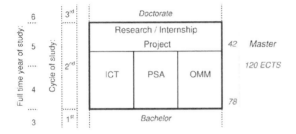

Figure 4. Main Components of the proposed MSEG.

Candidate disciplines, some possibly elective, could be the following:

— ICT: Mobile Technologies (hardware and software); Information Systems (process, planning and control), Human Computer Interaction, Internet Technologies (e.g.: XML, Ajax), Multimedia Technologies.

— PSA: Cognitive Sciences, Sociology in Organizations, Written and Oral Skills (humanities area), Persuasion Science.

— OMM: Services Marketing, Operations Reengineering, Investment and Finance, Multivariate Statistics, Management Science.

In parallel to each of these areas there could be a group project, with appropriate supervision, dealing with ICT (e.g.: defining and implementing a prototype of an innovative service), with PSA (e.g.: stage a play, theatre or advert, with multimedia video support; involve acting by members of the group), and with OMM (e.g.: prepare a business plan for the service proposed and set-up a company).

Detailed negotiation with stakeholders of this program must be conducted in order to refine and detail these preliminary ideas.

Conclusions

The western world is evolving towards a knowledge based society. Education of professional engineers has to take into account the evolution into a service economy. Solid understanding of mathematics, physics and technologies remains imperative, but more knowledge about people and about management seems to be also an important requirement for a larger group of graduates.

Service engineers will have to know how conceive, design, implement and operate the new service delivery processes, blending adequate technologies with the appropriate personal experiences, adding value in a competitive environment. Understanding how interaction between people and machines works, and considering real people's experience requirements, in particular the emotional ones, and understanding the social and organizational context of both producers and users, is playing an ever important role in service engineering education.

References

[1]   Michael Hammer: Re-Engineering the Corporation, Special Report on Business Innovation, *The Economist*, April 24, 2004.

[2]   Edward F. Crawley: The CDIO Syllabus – A Statement of Goals for Undergraduate Engineering Education, Massachusetts Institute of Technology, MIT CDIO Report #1, January 2001, 41 pp.

[3]   Imperial College London: Comments on the 2nd Version of the EUR-ACE Document "Standards and Procedures for the Accreditation of Engineering Programmes, 2005-10-31, 2 pp.

[4]   Ray Fisk, S. J. Grove, and J. John: *Interactive Services Marketing, 2nd Ed.*, Houghton Mifflin Co., Boston, 2004.

[5]   Jim Spohrer: Services Sciences, Management, and Engineering (SSME), A Next Frontier in Education and Innovation, IBM Research presentation, 2006.

[6]   Lia Patrício, Raymond Fisk, J. Falcão e Cunha: Improving Satisfaction with Bank Service Offerings: Measuring the Contribution of each Delivery Channels, *Managing Service Quality Journal*, Vol. 13, No. 6, 2003, 471-483.

[7]   Ana S. Camanho and R. G. Dyson: Cost efficiency, production and value-added models in the analysis of bank branch performance, *Journal of the Operational Research Society*, Vol. 56, No. 5, 483-494, 2005.

[8]   J. Falcão e Cunha, M. Leitão, J. Faria, A. Monteiro, M. Carravilla: A Methodology for Auditing e-Voting Processes and Systems used at the Elections for the Portuguese Parliament, 2nd Int. Workshop on Electronic Voting 2006 (www.e-voting.cc/2006), 2006.08.02-04, forthcoming in *Lecture Notes in Informatics*.

Engineering of Digital Services— A New Degree that Integrates Business Process and Information Engineering

Gianmario Motta
University of Pavia
Via Ferrata n.1 I-27100 Pavia (ITALY)
gianmario.motta@unipv.it
+39-335.611.7702

ABSTRACT

Major trends are orienting IT competences from traditional computer engineering toward engineering of IT enabled services. First, the growing share of services in IT expenditure that account over 50% in whatever country. Second, the growing volumes of service oriented business in most industries. Third, Service Oriented Architecture, that will enable to re-conceive service chains. To respond these emerging needs University of Pavia has launched from the next year a new syllabus for the fourth and fifth year of IT Engineering. Our graduate will be a designer of IT enabled services who knows how to analyze and design business service chains and to identify, customize and integrate appropriate IT modules. The specific service-orientation will be given by two classes on business process analysis and other two classes on enterprise systems design, while, last not least, two project works will provide students with hands-on experience.

Introduction

Services are the largest share in IT expenditure in whatever country. Italy (Figure 1) shows absolute figures much smaller than USA and even France, but a similar expenditure pattern, with the largest slice allocated to services. Roughly, professionals in IT services can be conservatively estimated between 100,000 and 200,000 with a yearly turnover ranging from 5,000 to 10,000 units (5%). These people are marginally in the software development and mainly in process and systems analysis; they work with multinational corporations such as IBM, Accenture or small local consultancies. Other needs have to be mentioned, such as engineers who work in Health Care, Utilities, Power, Communications, who are in charge of business process engineering and similar jobs.

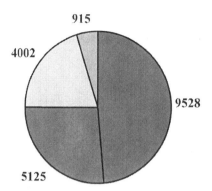

Figure 1 IT expenditure in Italy - Million € - year 2004 (source: www.aitech-assinform.it)

On the supply side, Italian universities in 2005 have been graduating about 3,000 engineers and computer specialists (five - years major). Of them, 490 Industrial Engineers have received a specific preparation on organizational and business process issues but they have only a first level understanding of IT engineering. On the other side, IT and Computer Science graduates, which have been less than 1,000, know well IT issues but they are only superficially aware of business process analysis and organizational issues. Finally, the vast majority of the 1.134 graduates on Economics and Business Administration have not received a deep preparation on the information requirements analysis and software implementation. Hence, with whatever math, the supply by universities is far from business demand. To fill the gap, corporations use in-house training and corporate academies, while universities and schools offer specialization and ad-hoc classes.

Our target is precisely this supply-demand gap and our objective is to prepare engineers who know enough on IT topics to design and implement a system and enough on organizational and process analysis to understand and analyze what their clients needs. Of course we are not alone in our strategy. Service Science [1] is a common target of many schools and universities in US and Europe. In the next section we sketch out our model of competences. In the following sections we comment our classes. Conclusions recap our positioning.

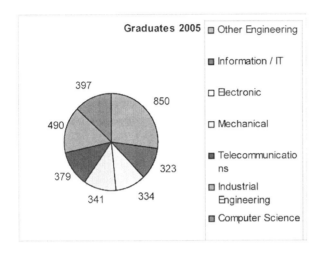

Figure 2 Graduates in IT Engineering and Computer Science, Italy, year 2005 (Italian Ministry of University, www.miru.it & statistics.miur.it)

The Competence Model

Our Major in Digital Services is for students who come from a three years Major on Information Engineering (or Computer Science). Therefore students have a good knowledge of the basics of Computer Science and Information and have already got one class, respectively, on Databases, Software Engineering and Information Systems. Therefore, you can work out a syllabus built on solid foundations.

In very simple terms, the core objective of the major is to put together three engineering competences, respectively Business Process Engineering, Information Technology Engineering, Information Engineering (Figure 3). The competence model encompasses family of methods and family of industry domains, here summarized in the three major domain classes of Industry, Services and Government. Let us shortly comment on methods.

The competence of Business Process Engineering should give the student a solid understanding of organizational theory and the ability of identifying and analyzing end to end business processes. To develop these competences we have planned two classes on processes and one class on organizational theory.

To build information engineering competences, we have classes on modeling techniques such as advanced software engineering and advanced databases and classes on enterprise systems (CRM, ERP and alike platforms) where students learn modules and functions to automate enterprise and build innovative digital services.

Finally, information technology engineering is developed by a series of classes on performances and networks.

However, a massive class program is ineffective without hands on. Therefore, not only most courses are built around a case study but we have two specific classes for project work. In these classes, placed in second and third semester, students organized in small groups will work out a prototype - typically a digital service developed in accordance with some organization.

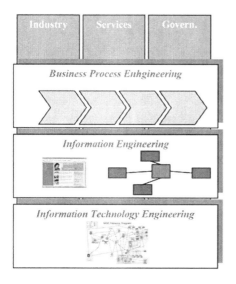

Figure 3 The competence model for digital services

Let us consider the question of competence on domains, that is the second dimension of Figure 3. In two semesters, we think there is no room to really develop a systematic competence on one or more industries. However, students will acquire a knowledge on a specific industry through their project works and by working on their final dissertation in the last semester. Also, we will teach industry process frameworks in the business process analysis classes by discussing industry models such as SCOR [2] and Telemanagement forum [3], that offers reference frameworks for Manufacturing and Telecommunications.

Finally, the graduate will get a twofold competence. The competence on designing IT enabled process and digital services is acquired by specific classes, while the industry competence is acquired by working on projects and it is based on the general background of organizational theory and alike matters. In short, the key abilities and knowledge will include:

— Analysis of business requirements of front-end, back-end and management control
   activities / processes of organizations;

— Design and implementation/customization of enterprise systems, based on modeling techniques of software engineering and data base & information engineering;

— Technology: design and implementation of service oriented architectures.

This competence model has been presented to and warmly received by managers in charge of university relations of major corporations as IBM, SAP, Telecom Italia and other companies and also of local industry associations. Therefore we think our graduates will easily find a good job.

The Syllabus: Overview

The syllabus has been developed by reshaping the existing syllabus of the "Laurea Specialistica" on IT / Information Engineering. The major is made of four semesters (Figure 4). Let us consider each semester individually.

SEM 1—Foundations	SEM 3—Analysis & Design
1. Numerical Methods	1. Business Analysis II
2. Multimedia Technologies and Systems	2. Enterprise Systems II
3. Enterprise Organization	3. Innovation Economics
4. Database (Advanced)	4. Computer Networks
5. SW Engineering	5. Project Work
6. Data Collection and Analysis Techniques	6. Elective on Business Topics
	(e.g. Innovation Management, Relational Marketing) or free choice
SEM 2—Analysis & Design	**SEM 4—Finalization**
1. Business Analysis I	1. Stages and certification on choice
2. Enterprise Systems I	(EUCIP Base / Elective Certification, Design Lab ccc.)
3. Processing Systems LS	2. Dissertation: typically a project or research work.
4. Project Work I	
5. Elective Class on Foundations (Optimization, Math)	
6. Elective on Management Information Systems or Artificial Intelligence	

Figure 4 Overview of the syllabus

The first semester has the objective to provide students with basic foundations and it includes classic information engineering topics as software engineering and databases and business topics such as organization theory. Additionally, numerical methods deals with computational algebra and data collection and analysis techniques gives a statistical and mathematical background for simulation and quantitative analysis.

Second and third semesters contain the core classes of the degree. Both semesters are dominated by three classes, namely Business Analysis, Enterprise Systems and Project Work. Let us consider specifically the Business Analysis class.

The Business Analysis Class

Business analysis is divided in two steps. Business Analysis I is on as-is analysis and develops a method to analyze processes in terms of process performance and process organizational configuration. Business Analysis II is on the to-be analysis in terms of requirements, software selection and business case.

In Business Analysis I, the analysis of business processes, considers the variables that defines the configuration of the process in a given organization. We use a systemic framework, that includes the process flow, the organization and work structure, the rewarding and control system, the competence of human resources and, last not least, the technology infrastructure. Students learn how to use this analysis checklist and related tools on a variety of case studies and define a diagnosis that addresses critical issues and opportunity changes (alike to the so called SWOT analysis). The framework is based on research framework born in the Nineties [10] and carried up to nowadays in MIT [8] and BPR/ BPM options [6].

Again in Business Analysis I, the analysis of process performance relies on a framework [7] that considers the key performances of cost, time and quality a process should deliver from the standpoints of the diverse process stakeholders, namely the management, who should ensure the economic viability, the customers who receive the output and the staff who work in the process. The students will learn the performance analysis and simulation techniques.

Business Analysis II focuses on the analysis of information requirements. The analysis uses UML and BPM techniques [9, 4, 5]. Students work out a report on the case study and propose a new flow for the digital service. The benefits of the project should be demonstrated by a cost-benefit analysis and the feasibility by a project plan. Students also present a draft of the IT architecture of the system that supports the process.

Business Analysis is not only theory. Students work in groups, with each individual owning a specific aspect of the analysis and design. To ensure an effective learning cycle, each topic goes trough a three-step cycle. Step 1 is lecturing and it has the objective to explain the conceptual foundations students will be using. Step 2 exemplifies how to use foundations on a simple case study. Step 3 is lab work, where students develop their own analysis and the teacher reviews the work. At the end of the class, students discuss their work and prove their command on the analysis tools they have studied.

Enterprise Systems

In the first semester students have learned background theory on web design (multimedia systems), software engineering and databases (inclusive of warehousing).

The class on enterprise systems has the objective of providing the students with a clear understanding of software application modules that support front end interactions (web and CRM systems) and back-end execution and service delivery (ERP and ad hoc systems). This includes the study of the overall architecture within the emerging frame of a service oriented architecture and the customization / implementation of sample functions.

Enterprise Systems I is on front end systems while Enterprise Systems II is on back-end systems. Both classes focus on operational, event-oriented systems. The design and development of Management Information Systems is in an elective class.

Conclusions

In the Italian landscape, our new degree is innovative. We are not aware of similar major in Engineering so far. It responds the challenge of a service oriented economy and it is a rather unique because of:

— Hands on: 6 classes with analysis and design activities (Business Analysis I & II, Enterprise Systems I & II, Project work I & II)

— Design Ability: the students learns how to assess existing process and systems design and how to design well formed processes and systems;

— Integrated Perspective: the classes bridge economic, organization and information engineering, including the innovation cycle, to which elective classes are oriented (Management of Innovation, Economics of Innovation)

Our wish is that a plenty of such degree will start in order to fill the gap between supply and demand in our service-oriented economy.

References

[1] Almaden http://www.almaden.ibm.com/
[2] SCOR www.supply-chain.org
[3] Telemanagement Forum www.tmforum.org
[4] Eriksson H-E., Penker M., *Business Modelling with UML: Business Patterns at Work*, Addison Wesley, 1999.
[5] Eriksson, E., Penker M., Lyons, B., and Fado D., *UML 2 toolkit*. Indianapolis, Ind.: Wiley Pub., 2004.
[6] Hammer M., "The Superefficient company", *Harvard Business Review*, September/October 2001, pp. 82-91.
[7] Longo, A., Motta, G. "Designing Processes for Sustainable Performances: A Model and a Method", *3rd International Conference on Business Process Management*, Nancy France, Nancy, France, 5 September 2005.
[8] Malone T.W., Crowston K., Herman G.A., *Organizing Business Knowledge (the MIT Process Handbook)*, MIT Press, Boston 2003.
[9] Scheer A. W., *ARIS - Business Process Modelling*, Berlin: Springer, 2000.
[10] Scott-Morton M (ed.) *The Corporation of the 1990s: Information Technology and Organizational Transformation*, New York: Oxford University Press, 1991.

SSME at Manchester: Bringing People, Business and Technology Together

Liping Zhao
University of Manchester
School of Informatics, Manchester, U.K.
liping.zhao@manchester.ac.uk

Linda Macaulay
University of Manchester
School of Informatics, Manchester, U.K.
linda.macaulay@manchester.ac.uk

ABSTRACT

IBM's Services, Sciences, Management, and Engineering (SSME) agenda proposes an emerging, multidisciplinary field that integrates a variety of technical and business fields under a general concept of "services". One important idea of the SSME agenda is innovative design in the 21st century. This paper presents our SSME related activities around innovative business and curriculum design. Our business design focuses on IBM's Patterns for e-business whereas our curriculum design aims at providing students with new skills. These two activities are cross-fertilized owing to our collaborations with IBM through IBM Faculty Awards and the Strategic Partner Programme. Future research depends on further collaborations and on the development of a critical mass of SSME researchers. The paper concludes with a description of beginnings of a UK network of researchers brought together by the authors.

Introduction

IBM's Services, Sciences, Management, and Engineering (SSME) agenda [10] proposes an emerging, multidisciplinary field that integrates a variety of technical and business fields under a general concept of "services". One important idea of the SSME agenda is innovative design in the 21st century. In his lecture at the University of Manchester, Wladawsky-Berger [26] put forward two cases of innovative design: business design and university curriculum design. The purpose of designing business is to identify its structure and components so that it can be integrated into a successful (and possibly global) enterprise; the purpose of designing university curriculum is to help students understand techniques for use in enabling such a business. Although the SSME framework is yet to be defined and developed, we believe that it builds on two foundations—systems theory and design theory—and three corner stones—people, business and technology.

This paper presents our SSME related activities around innovative business and curriculum design. Our business design is a research activity based on IBM's Patterns for e-business whereas our curriculum design focuses on providing students with new skills. These two activities are cross-fertilized owing to our collaborations with IBM.

Context

IBM Faculty Awards

In 2004, Jonathan Adams, a Distinguished Engineer at IBM, sponsored an IBM Global Faculty Award to the then two different universities, UMIST and VUM. The award was given to four academics, with Professor Linda Macaulay (Computation, UMIST) and Professor Brian Warboys (Computer Science, VUM) as Principal Investigators and Dr Peter Kawalek (Manchester Business School, UMIST) and Dr Liping Zhao (Computation, UMIST) as Co-investigators.

The original aim of the award was to bring together researchers of different schools and disciplines to explore IBM Patterns for e-business [1] from three dimensions: research, teaching and business. The actual effect of this award, however, was far more significant. First, the award brought together researchers from two universities during a time of change and in this respect the award facilitated an understanding of and respect for differing perspectives. Second, the award stimulated the development of a new MSc programme—MSc e-business Technology—which would bring IBM's Patterns to the attention of a new generation of graduate students. Finally, the award led to a deeper interest in patterns. Such an interest would later become a common core for our pattern-oriented SSME research under the Strategic Partner Programme between IBM and University of Manchester (UoM).

Following the success of the first IBM Faculty Award, Macaulay and Zhao were given a second IBM Faculty Award in 2005, to encourage them to explore the role of Patterns for e-business in supporting the emerging Services Sciences discipline through research and teaching.[1] This award has further strengthened the relationship between Informatics and IBM and helped to develop a new collaboration with Paul Verschueren, a Senior Consulting Architect at IBM and Chair of IBM Patterns Governance Board.

UoM-IBM Strategic Partner Programme

The UoM-IBM Strategic Partner Programme was launched in January 2006 to explore areas of overlapping strategic importance to both organizations across research, teaching and recruitment. Table 1 summarizes the UoM-IBM partner programme. Clearly, this programme accords with the SSME agenda.

---

1   http://www.research.ibm.com/ssme/workuniv.shtml

Table 1. The UoM-IBM Strategic Partner Programme.

Partners (UoM/IBM)	Programme
Linda Macaulay/ Jonathan Adams	Extend IBM Patterns in the area of Facilitated Collaboration and explore the SSME agenda
Liping Zhao / Paul Verschueren	Explore the role of patterns in the SSME agenda and develop techniques to support patterns
Bob Wood / Henry Law	Explore the role of the IT Architect and its future impact on teaching and research
Kung-Kiu Lau / Trevor Hopkins	Construct large software applications using components
Barbara Jones / Angelo Failla	Focus on developing new ICT skills in organizations that are undergoing rapid change and how employees apply that knowledge as new challenges arise
Alex May / Andy Heys	Develop bio-health informatics

Business Design Using Patterns

IBM is a leading business designer who has developed a large number of methods and technologies that support business design. Among these technologies are Component Business Modeling (CBM), Service Oriented Modeling and Architecture (SOMA), and Patterns for e-business (P4eb). CBM and SOMA are used to identify and describe the business processes whereas P4eb map these processes onto the architectural components of the software systems.

P4eb was identified from thousands of successful IBM application development projects by Adams and his colleagues at IBM [1]. These patterns give businesses a set of proven, reusable architectural components that can guide the design, development, implementation and extension of e-business applications.

P4eb are organized into a hierarchy. At the top level are four Business Patterns: Self-Service, Collaboration, Information Aggregation and Extended Enterprise. These four patterns represent four distinctive types of business interaction. Specifically, Self-Service describes the interaction between users and businesses; Collaboration captures the interaction between users; Information Aggregation represents the interaction between users and data; Extended Enterprise expresses the interaction between businesses. Each Business Pattern is specialized into a set of Application Patterns, which, in turn, are further divided into Runtime Patterns. An Application Pattern describes a logical design of the system whereas a Runtime Pattern suggests an implementation plan (product mapping) for the system. Business Patterns are supported by other patterns such as Integration Patterns, which are Access Integration, for the front-end system integration, and Application Integration, for the back-end system integration.

We are conducting research to enhance P4eb in the following areas:

— Extend the Collaboration pattern family with new patterns, such as facilitated collaboration patterns.

— Extend P4eb with business logic patterns. P4eb are the solutions to the architectural design of the business systems, but not the solutions for the business logic design of the applications. Although the business logic solutions can be provided by other approaches, such as CBM and SOMA, we are exploring a pattern-oriented approach to designing business logic and components.

— Develop methods and tools for pattern organization and selection. Although the top level of P4eb only has four Business Patterns, the number of patterns grows exponentially at the lower-levels. For example, there are about 100 Application Patterns and hundreds of Runtime Patterns. Methods and tools that support effective pattern organization and selection are therefore urgently needed.

We propose to use patterns to support business design in relation to SSME agenda for the following related reasons:

— Patterns are a universal design concept. Either in art or engineering, patterns represent geometric arrangements of parts that can be used over again. For example, patterns are used to design dresses, carpets, wallpapers, airplanes, buildings [2], and software [7], to name only a few. As a design concept, patterns preserve tried, tested experience and best practice. Patterns mean goodness and fit.

— Patterns are a recurring phenomenon. Thus we can speak of weather patterns, symptoms, DNA sequences, communication and control patterns, and behavioral patterns.

— Patterns are relationships between parts and wholes in natural as well as artificial systems [5]. Thus patterns capture fundamental organizing principles and structures in systems, such as the structures of molecules, society, and computer systems.

In addition, patterns give us an effective, common language for communication, so that we can say: "Let's use Self-Service for this business application", or "This is an Extended Enterprise problem." Patterns, as in the form of IBM P4eb, are organized as a hierarchy. By using such a hierarchy of patterns, we can decompose a problem space. For example, the Self-Service pattern can be decomposed into different Application Patterns which are then divided into different Runtime Patterns and so on. In this respect, patterns help us to reduce the design complexity.

SSME Course Design

According to Wladawsky-Berger [26], UoM is among 11 universities who have developed SSME courses. In particular, UoM has introduced a new Master of Science degree programme, termed as MSc e-business Technology, outlined as follows.

Today nearly every business involves some technology support. The Internet has become the gateway to most businesses. E-business is therefore a norm for business. This MSc programme equips the students with the skills in analysis, design and development of e-business application systems. Possible career paths for the students upon successful completion of the programme include e-business analysis and design, solutions development, and web service development and web site design.

Among other taught courses offered in this programme are *e-business* and *Patterns for e-business Applications*, which directly address the SSME agenda. The e-business course teaches the students the following components: (1) e-business infrastructure and strategy; (2) supply chain management and e-procurement; (3) customer relationship management; (4) e-marketing; (5) collaborative commerce; (6) case studies. The Patterns for e-business Applications course teaches the students the following components: (1) relationships between business requirements and e-business application architectures; (2) relationships between business drivers and technologies; (3) IBM's Patterns for e-business as solutions for e-business application system design; (4) relationships between business processes and IBM Patterns; (5) real world case studies.

These two courses are developed as a result of the two IBM Faculty Awards described above and team-taught by the four faculty: Macaulay is the academic instructor for the e-business course with Adams as the industrial instructor; Zhao is the academic instructor for Patterns for e-business course with Verschueren as the industrial instructor. The courses have attracted 80 students from the UK and abroad, and proved to be very successful and popular among the students. Students' performance and feedback have indicated that patterns provide an effective pedagogical tool to e-business application design and help the students to gain a better understanding of the relationship between business needs and technical solutions.

UK Network of Researchers in Services Sciences

In order to bring together researchers from a range of disciplines across the UK to develop a shared understanding and research agenda of SSME, Macaulay and Zhao are leading a UK Network of Researchers to develop a UK research agenda on SSME. The network, called SSMEnetUK,[2] is funded by the UK Engineering and Physical Sciences Research Council (EPSRC). The network currently has the founding members from 7 different UK universities and 5 companies (including, IBM, BT and HP). A number

---

2 http://www.ssmenetuk.org/index.asp

of grand challenges have been identified for the SSME agenda. For example, the NESSI (Networked European Software and Services Initiative) Working Group states that the SSME challenge is "to establish attainable expectations that services systems will function according to their specifications, at predicted costs, throughout their intended lifetimes" [15]. Associated with this challenge are the technical difficulties in developing services systems, due to their scale, integration, environment, communication problems. Other challenges include the semantic representation of people, technologies and organizations, as well as their capabilities, goals, rights and values, and the integration of information and knowledge from different artefacts and organizations [15].

This proposal, however, recognizes that dealing with service complexity is the ultimate challenge of the SSME agenda based on the following facts:

— Many of today's services require the cooperation of people, business and technologies in many different disciplines. Delivering and innovating services will involve understanding people's behaviour, the way they conduct businesses and the role of technologies in businesses.

— Services have become increasingly complex and dynamic owing to the cross-industry, cross-market, and cross-country business activities and collaborations.

— The Internet and IT technology have made it possible for companies to work together intensively and in new ways, to form complex supply chains and service networks. Technologies have become a crucial part of services and service innovation. It can be argued that technologies are the defining characteristic of modern services and the challenge of SSME is the complexity of *designing* and *innovating services* around technologies.

To address the above challenge, the objectives of SSMEnetUK are to facilitate the collaboration of research and education in service design and service innovation within and beyond EPSRC support. The founding members' expertise can be mapped onto this scope as follows.

1. *Service Design.* The purpose of designing services is to identify their structure and components so that they can be changed, managed and controlled [27]. Yet, service design is a challenge because today's services interact and integrate with other systems, including people, products, businesses, economics, social systems, political systems, and IT systems. Service design is therefore a highly complex activity. The proposed network will build on the strength and expertise of its founding members to identify the need for design methodologies, techniques and architectures for services. In particular, Bennett and Gold [3, 4, 8] are interested in service-oriented architecture whereas Zhao and Sampiao [6, 19, 20, 21] are looking into using the web service technology to support e-services; Hollins [9] is concerned with design

standards and regulations, while Macaulay and Zhao [27] advocate the pattern approach to business design. Van Moorsel is currently working on self-managing computing systems and services [23, 24, 25] so that services can be more efficiently and effectively operated, and better utilized by people and businesses. These efforts will be combined to address the service design challenge within the proposed network.

2. *Service Innovation.* Service innovation has become one of the success criteria in the modern economy [13, 16]. Since services depend critically on people working together and with technology to provide value for others, new skills are required for integrating business, people and technology. Skill innovation will therefore go hand in hand with service innovation. Two founding members, Miles and Jones [17, 11, 12, 13, 14] are experts in service innovation and skills. They stress the diversity of service activities and of related innovation processes, and have been characterizing different types of knowledge base and network organization. Fowler [22] is interested in Human Interaction with Services while Sako [18] takes a social science perspective on services. These efforts will be combined to address the service innovation challenge within the proposed network.

Conclusion

This paper has reported our SSME related research and teaching activities. Our research activity focuses on using patterns for business design whereas our teaching activity concentrates on designing new services courses for MSc students. The paper has also outlined our collaborations with IBM and highlighted the objectives of a UK academic network on SSME. We believe that the success of the SSME research agenda depends on a critical mass of researchers from different disciplines, who have a shared vision of the agenda and work together to make this vision a reality.

References

[1] J. Adams, S. Koushik, G. Vasudeva, and G. Galambos, *Patterns for e-business: A Strategy for Reuse,* IBM Press, 2001. Pattern descriptions also available at www.ibm.com/developerWorks/patterns

[2] C. Alexander, *The Timeless Way of Building,* New York: Oxford University Press, 1979.

[3] K.H. Bennett, M. Munro, N.E. Gold, P.J. Layzell, D. Budgen, P. Brereton, "An Architectural Model for Service-Based Software with Ultra Rapid Evolution", *Proceedings of the IEEE International Conference on Software Maintenance (ICSM) 2001,* 6-10 November 2001, Florence, Italy, pp. 292-300.

[4] K.H. Bennett, N.E. Gold, P.J. Layzell, F. Zhu, O.P. Brereton, D. Budgen, J. Keane, I. Kotsiopoulos, M. Turner, J. Xu, O. Almilaji, J.C. Chen, A. Owrak, "A Broker Architecture for Integrating Data Using a Web Services Environment," *Proceedings of the First International Conference on Service-Oriented Computing (IC-SOC),* Trento, Italy, 15-19 December 2003, pp. 409-422.

[5] F. Capra, *The Web of Life,* Flamingo. 1997.

[6] L. Eleyan, L. Mikhailov and L. Zhao, "Quality-of-Services in Web Services Architecture," *Ingénierie des Systèmes d'Information, Special Issue on Information Systems Quality,* vol. 9, no. 5-6, pp. 185-203, 2004.

[7] E. Gamma, R. Helm, R. Johson, and J. Vlissides, *Design Patterns.* Addison-Wesley, Reading, MA, 1996.

[8] N. Gold, "SOSoRNet: Service-Oriented Software Research Network," Case for Support, Proposal for EPSRC Grant.

[9] B. Holins, "About: Service Design", available at www.designcouncil.org.uk. 2006.

[10] P. Horn, "The New Discipline of Services Science," *Viewpoint, BusinessWeek online,* January 21st 2005.

[11] B. Jones and A.R. Miller, *Innovation Diffusion in the New Economy: the Tacit Component,* Routledge Advances in Management & Business Studies, 2006.

[12] B. Jones, J. Cullen and A.R. Miller, "European Movement Towards a Competency-based Skills Taxonomy and Personal Skills Profile," *Management of Technology,* T Khalil, L A Lefebre and R M Mason (eds), Pergamon - Elsevier Science, 2001.

[13] B. Jones and K. Hadjivassilou, "New Methods of Skill Definition and Accreditation", in *Identification, Evaluation and Recognition of Non-formal Learning: Agora V,* E Guggenheim (ed), CEDEFOP Panorama Series, Luxembourg, 2002.

[14] B. Jones, A. Failla and A.R. Miller, "Tacit knowledge in rapidly evolving organisational environments," *International Journal of Technology and Human Interaction,* (forthcoming Autumn 2006).

[15] M. Lyons, D. Pym, R. Taylor, J. Sairamesh, C. Schulze, L. Svobodova, "NESSI Working Group: Services Sciences & Systems Engineering," White paper, 2006.

[16] S Metcalfe and I. Miles (eds), *Innovation Systems in the Service Economy,* Dordrecht: Kluwer, 2000.

[17] I. Miles,"Knowledge Intensive Business Services: Prospects and policies" *Foresight* vol. 7 no. 6, pp 39-63.

[18] M. Sako, "Grand Challenges in Services," GCS Workshop Presentation, Said Business School. Oxford, 19 May 2006.

[19] P. Sampaio and H. Yong, "Unbundling and delivering CRM applications as e-Services: A case study in customer segmentation," to appear in *the International Journal of Services Technology and Management, Special Issue on e-Services Delivery,* 2006.

[20] P. Sampaio, "Business process design and implementation for customer segmentation e-services", *Proceedings of the IEEE International Conference on e-Technology, e-Commerce and e-Service,* Hong Kong. April 2005, pp 228-234.

[21] P. Sampaio and H. Yong, "Unbundling and Deploying CRM Applications as e-Services," *Proceedings of 5th Workshop in Enterprise Modelling and Information Systems Architectures, Current Research Topics and Future Perspectives,* Lecture Notes in Informatics, Klagenfurt, Carinthia, Austria, Oct 24-25, 2005, issue 75, pp 123-136.

[22] J. Van Helvert and C.J.H. Fowler, "Scenarios for Innovation (SUNA,". In I. Alexander & N Maiden (eds) *Scenarios and Use Cases Stories through the System Life-Cycle.* Wiley, 2004.

[23] A. van Moorsel, "Grid, Management and Self-Management," *The Computer Journal,* British Computer Society, Oxford University Press, UK, vol. 48, no. 3, pp. 325-332, 2005.

[24] A. van Moorsel, "Ten-Step Survival Guide for the Emerging Business Web," Invited paper accompanying keynote, in Lecture Notes in Computer Science, International Workshop on Web Services, E-Business, and the Semantic Web, pp. 1-11, Springer, LNCS 2512, 2002.

[25] A. van Moorsel. "Metrics for the Internet Age: Quality of Experience and Quality of Business," Hewlett Packard Laboratories, *Technical Report HPL-2001-179, 2001.*

[26] I.Wladawsky-Berger, "Innovation in the 21 Century," *The Irving Wladawsky-Berger Lecture at the University of Manchester,* 21 March, 2006. Available at www.cs.manchester.ac.uk

[27] L. Zhao, N. Mehandjiev and L. Macaulay, "Agent roles and patterns for supporting dynamic behavior of web service applications," *Workshop on Web Services and Agent-Based Engineering (WSABE), International Joint Conference on Autonomous Agents and Multi-Agent Systems (AAMAS'04)* New York, 2004.

A Research & Educational Framework for ICT/S Service Management

Guido Dedene
Universiteit Van Amsterdam
The Netherlands
Faculty of Economics and
Business Studies
PrimaVera Research Institute
&
Katholieke Universiteit Leuven
Belgium
Faculty of Economics and
Applied Economics
Decision Sciences & Information
Management Group (DSIM)

Monique Snoeck
Katholieke Universiteit Leuven
Belgium
Faculty of Economics and
Applied Economics
Decision Sciences & Information
Management Group (DSIM)

Rik Maes
Universiteit Van Amsterdam
The Netherlands
Faculty of Economics and
Business Studies
PrimaVera Research Institute

ABSTRACT

This paper explains how an extended Information Management framework can significantly help to enable ICT/S Services Management. Moreover it is shown how this framework is the basis for a new ICT/S Services Management course in the Information Management curriculum of K.U.Leuven.

Introduction

The recent literature reveals that Information and Communication Management remains a non-trivial task for many organizations [3]. The search for best practices in Business – ICT-Alignment and ICT governance is a good indication for the degree of mental dispersion in this respect [1]. The increasing maturity of ICT allows a better scaling and dissemination of the ICT/S (Information & Communication Technology & Systems) activities. The increasing use of (off-shore) outsourcing as a natural Business asset is a significant indicator for this. At the same time the gap between the "supply" side of ICT/S and the "demand" side for ICT/S is widening. No wide-spread accepted management frameworks are currently available to narrow this gap.

One approach consists of focusing on the "Services" aspects of the ICT/S activities. There are legion indicators for this. One of them is the emergence of Service-Oriented Architecture (SOA), a new way to unlock Information & Communication technologies.

Another is the increasing interest for services as a scientific management discipline, such as emphasized by IBM and ACM [6, 5]. This paper wants to explain how an extended Information Management framework can significantly help to enable ICT/S Services Management. Moreover it is shown how this framework is the basis for a new ICT/S Services Management course in the Information Management curriculum of K.U.Leuven.

An extended ICT/S Management Framework

One of the most cited models for representing the relationship between ICT and the Business is the model of Henderson and Venkatraman [2]. In this model the Business is opposed towards the Information Technology (IT) and the management of the Business and IT domains is considered from an external ("strategy") as well as an internal ("operations") point of view.

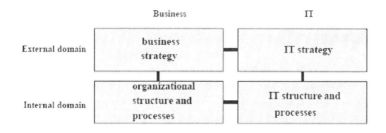

Figure 1. Previous view of ICT/S Management Framework

In repeated applications of this model in case studies, two fundamental flaws in the model became clear:

— The distinction between "Technology" and "Business" is too simplistic. Data can be seen as a technology issue, which is clearly different from information, which is data that gets a meaning in a particular context [4]. In turn, "Information" should not be confused with "Knowledge", which is turn is a consequence of the appropriate use of "Information" in Business Activities. So the dual distinction between Business and IT should be enriched into a triple of Business – Information/Communication and Technology.

— It is also somewhat naïve to assume that a "Strategy" (the analysis of the external factors) can straightforwardly be translated into "Operations" (internal actions). An intermediate "Structure" layer is needed to translate "Strategy" into "Operations" by means of models, which make use of structural concepts, such as objects, events and processes.

The result is an extended Information Management framework, which is a 3x3 framework (an "Enneahedron") in which each of the cells represents a valid subdomain of the ICT/S Management disciplines.

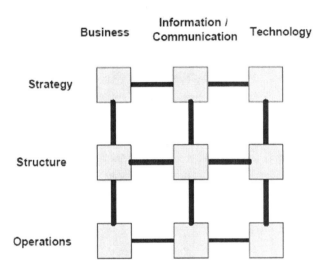

Figure 2. The IC Management Enneahedron

As a consequence, in this framework, Information Management concerns Strategy, Structure as well as Operations (the rows of the framework). Furthermore Information Management relates the Business and the Technology by giving a context-related meaning to Technology.

The major challenges in the proper understanding of this framework are in the new layer and the new column that is introduced. Very often, Information/Communication is confused with Technology, disregarding the proper value of giving a "meaning" to the technology, to transform it from a cost into a value factor. The columns make it also possible to distinguish *services* as a proper activity: ICT/S services are part of the middle column, and organizing ICT/S operations as a service discipline is precisely what contemporary frameworks, such as COBIT and ITIL prescribe. As such, the proposed management framework gives an appropriate position to ICT/S services in the context of ICT/S management. Such a position does not exist in the Henderson-Venkatraman framework.

The extended Information Management framework can be used as a roadmap for Chief Information Officers [3], but also as a ICT/S master plan guidance vehicle. It was successfully applied in various case studies to develop this type of ICT/S organizational master plans. The next paragraph will show how it can also be used as a didactical roadmap. The case study of one particular course is presented. The University of Amsterdam has a long-running Executive Master in Information Management which is based on the enneahedron for the overall Master education setup and content.

Case Study: ICT/S Service Management course outline

In the renewed Bachelor/Master curriculum of K.U.Leuven, a new master level course was introduced to increase the focus on managing ICT/S activities as services. In the previous curriculum three courses focused on IC Management aspects at the master level: a course on the Economics of Information Processing, a course on Software Management and a course on ICT Performance and Capacity Planning. The new course is not just a blending of the previous courses: it uses the IC Management Enneahedron as a fundamental guideline for the course content.

In particular, the rows of the framework are used to discuss the cost structures and the alignment aspects. The columns of the framework allow to focus on benefit and integration aspects. The diagonals of the framework permit a better discussion of outsourcing and governance aspects. This is the topical content structure of the new ICT/S Service Management course:

0. Introduction.
Motivation for the Information & Communication Management Enneahedron as a management framework and roadmap.

1. Review of relevant economic models.
Reminder of basis (micro-)economic models and financial techniques that are applicable throughout the course. All examples are ICT/S-based. A particular focus is given to modeling risk as well as quality aspects.

2. Cost structures for ICT/S operations.
Discussion of Cost Recovery of ICT/S operations. Activity Based Costing Service Oriented frameworks, illustrated with case studies. Alternative optimization models for "on demand" operations (incremental cost allocation, value-based costing).

3. ICT/S Strategy structures.
This chapter discusses the use of various scoring models, such as Benson/Parker Information Economics. Metrics for Business ICT-Alignment and ICT Governance practices. ICT/S Portfolio Models (revisited under ICT Infrastructures).

4. Cost Models for Systems Development.
COCOMO, Putnam, Function and Object Point models are critically discussed. Models for software maintenance, reuse models and system conversion models are presented. Outsourcing is discussed in a separate chapter !

5. Benefit Models for Business Process Integration.
Value Chain Integration Models (Forward versus Backward Integration & Customer Oriented Processes), E-Business & E-Hub Value Models, Business Process Discovery models. Transaction & Service Cost Analysis models.

6. Benefit Models for Technology Integration.
Critical discussion of Grosch' Law and Economies of Scale in Total Cost of Ownership (TCO) models for ICT/S. Investment/benefit models for on-demand ICT-infrastructures (using Weil/Broadbent ICT/S Portfolio models). Centralization/ Decrentralization management models. On-demand sizing models.

7. Information/Communication Benefit Models.
Ex/Post Ante Models for Information Decisions. Team Theory models and the value of Communication. Analytic models of Information as an economic asset (including Response Time versus Throughput models). Experience & Emotion based value indicators in Information/Communication. Benefits of digital communities of expertise.

8. ICT/S Service Outsourcing Models.
Models for various forms of outsourcing are presented. Outsourcing management models and contract structure aspects are discussed using the Mc Farlan framework.

9. ICT/S Ethics.
The official "Code of Ethics" for software and systems workers is discussed. The economics of Peer-to-Peer Networks (Open Source, Asset Sharing, etc...) is analyzed. Privacy, ownership, piracy and marketing issues are presented.

10. ICT/S Quality and Management Frameworks.
This final chapter discusses the relevance of frameworks such as COBIT/ITIL as well as quality frameworks such as the various CMM and ISO models.

Some appendices can present further techniques (such as ROI models, investment models, financing models and tax considerations). It is our belief that the presented chapters give a fairly broad coverage of the Service Management issues that are relevant. The backing of the IM Enneahedron makes the course content open ended and agile, which is particularly relevant for the fast evolving ICT/S sector.

Discussion

This paper presented the applicability of an extended Information Management Framework to ICT/S Services Management, in particular from an educational point of view. Further research can focus on improved analytical models as well as quantitative case studies. The course material that is presented here is a milestone in the academic integration of service science as a major Information Management issue.

References

[1]   Cumps B., Viaene S. & Dedene G., How to management your Information Systems Investments for better Business-IT Alignment, accepted for *IEEE IT Professional*, vol. 8, No. 5, 2006.

[2]   Henderson J.C. & Venkatraman N., Strategic Alignment: Leveraging Information Technology for Transforming Organizations, *IBM Systems Journal*, vol. 32, No. 1, 1993.

[3]   Maes R., *Information Management: a Roadmap*, PrimaVera Working Paper 2004-13, University of Amsterdam.

[4]   Maes R., Data and reality: a plea for management realism and data modesty, *Journal for Convergence*, vol. 7, No 1, 2006.

[5]   Maglio P. P., Srinivasan S., Kreulen J. & Spohrer J., Service systems, service scientists, SSME, and innovation, *Communications of the ACM*, Vol 49, No. 7, 2006

[6]   Spohrer J. & Riecken D., Services Science, *Communications of the ACM*, Vol 49, No. 7, 2006

Education and Research of Service Science and Technology in Tsinghua University

Jie Zhou, Qiaoge Liu, and Yanda Li
Research Center of Modern Services Science & Technology
Tsinghua University, Beijing 100084, China
jzhou@tsinghua.edu.cn

ABSTRACT

With the coming of services economic times in China, the importance of education and research of service science should be emphasized. As a new subject, both talents and research related to service science are challenging. In this topic, the effort of Research Center of Modern Services Science & Technology of Tsinghua University is reported, both in education and research.

1. Background

The maturity of modern services industries is a significant indicator for measuring the country's economic and social development. Under China government's 11th 5 year plan, "Modern Services Industries" is one major topic on the list that the government wants specifically to promote in the coming next 5 years or more. It will have profound impact on China's economic development and China's competitiveness in global market.

Research Center of Modern Services Science & Technology was established in Tsinghua University one year ago. It was defined to work for educating talents and researching based on merging the current disciplines and developing a multidisciplinary subject. It focuses on innovating and researching extensively and systematically. It has wide collaboration with IBM China Research Lab in research and education. It has also set up a very good relationship with government and enterprises through joint research projects, consulting and re-education programs.

2. Service Industry in China

China's service industry is developing with a high speed. As reported in the blue book entitled "Service Industry in China: Growth and Structure", the service industry has expanded rapidly over the past more than two decades. It shows that service industry's added value accounts for 34 percent of China's gross domestic product (GDP) in 2002, comparing with 21 percent in 1980.

However, the development of the service industry is not as fast as that of the manufacturing industry, and still has a large gap from the developed countries. So China makes great efforts to push forward reform and innovation of service. And education and research are the most important aspects to implement it for universities.

3. Education

Our center pays much attention to education of service science. The requirement for modern service talents in modern China was invested. Serial courses on the subject of service science were being carefully organized. Additional, we also invited many famous scholars and specialists on service science all over the world to give lectures to the faculty and students.

3.1. Survey of SSME Talents in China

To know the requirement of the society for talents for modern service industry and direct the development of the subject of service science, an investigation was launched by the Research Center among some government organizations and enterprises.

This is the first investigation about service talents in China, so the whole process has gained a lot of help of not only Tsinghua University but also many units in the society. 156 government units and 278 enterprises units attended this activity. And there are 434 valid questionnaires returned. The investigation covered widely, including 26 provinces and 4 municipalities, which ensures the universality of the investigation.

Basic data was obtained and analyzed deeply. The report shows that, modern service industries require lots of specific talents that grasp advanced specialized technology and management knowledge. These people can help increase the economic benefit of enterprises, strengthen the service ability of government organizations, and then push the continuous development of the country economy. While China is absence of such talented persons, it is especially urgent and important to cultivate such students.

The survey gives us a great help in establishing the development plan and teaching scheme for the subject of service science.

3.2. Curriculum

With the purpose of bringing up senior talented persons contributing to the development of Chinese modern service industry, we began to make a special teaching plan.

For service science is a multidisciplinary subject, it need the students to acquire information about engineering, technology, management and etc. The curriculum should fit such requirement, cultivate students with not only basic knowledge but also professional area, and exercise their ability to solve practical problems. By analyzing the position and characteristic of the Center, we decided that our basic principle of education in the Center is "based on information science and technology, and combined with management".

Based on some subjects in existence, we will cooperate with famous international colleges and notability international Industries, and open new courses.

Our research center began collaborating with IBM China Research Lab on a curriculum named "IT service" to graduate students in THU. This is the first course related with SSME with the aim of preparing knowledge for talents needed by modern service industry and introducing representative information technologies and methods that applied in governments, industries and persons. This course has obtained good effect and students showed great interest in the content.

We are also making two educational plans for undergraduate students and graduate students, respectively. Some basic curriculums, such as "Introduction of service science", will be opened next year to undergraduate students. The students, who major in "service science", will be encouraged to select some other curriculums opened in the management school.

4. Research and Innovation

The research center has strong competencies in many research areas. Leveraging the past experience in Complex System Modeling, System Engineering, Information Fusion, Data Mining, Business Process Modeling and Management and etc, the foundation of SSME, especially Services Sciences is to be explored.

4.1. Research on Service-oriented Data Analysis

The recent advances in hardware and software have enabled the capture of different measurements of data in a wide range of fields. These measurements are generated continuously and in a very high fluctuating data rates. Examples include traffic surveillance system, e-commerce sites, large retailers, telecommunications providers, ATM and credit card operation in large banks. Data in this form is called data stream. It brings challenges not only to storage and querying, but also to understanding or mining.

The ubiquitous presence of data streams in a number of practical domains has generated a lot of research in this area. Algorithms, systems and frameworks that address streaming challenges have been developed over the past few years. Some methods have been proposed for streaming data mining task such as classification, clustering, frequency counting and time series analysis etc. But few research results can meet the need of application-driven mining tasks. So study of novel algorithms for real tasks of data stream mining is a challenge and deserves extensive research.

4.2. Research on Service-oriented Business Process Modeling and Optimization

With business paradigms' steady transformation from product-centric to customer-centric, services have become the new viewpoints while most enterprises scan their internal business processes. The performance of business processes, strongly dependent with efficient operations of internal information systems, is an important problem to enterprises' managers.

To tackle this problem, the methodology of service-oriented business process modeling and optimization has been proposed. Based on the definition and exact description of business services and IT services, we can model and visualize the relationships/dependencies between business processes and IT infrastructure. Then business and IT experts can monitor the performance of IT infrastructure, evaluate and optimize the performance of business processes.

4.3. Research on SOA and Semantic Web based e-government Platform

The web is revolutionizing the way in which citizens interact with businesses and government agencies. As a part of an effort to improve government-citizen interactions, government agencies are providing a wide spectrum of online services. The main e-government challenge is to facilitate citizen-public administration interaction enabling seamless services delivery to citizen through the network.

Web services constitute a related technology that has recently emerged to deal with the glut of web applications, including e-government applications. The Semantic Web plays a crucial role in automatic delivery of customized e-government services. It extends the existing web by providing a framework for technologies that give meanings to data and applications for automatic processing. Ontologies, i.e., formal, explicit specifications of a shared conceptual space, are integral to the Semantic Web in facilitating knowledge sharing and reuse.

4.4. Research on Human Behavior Models in the Service Industry

One of the most important aspects in service is the involvement of people, human organizations, and their interaction throughout the service creation and delivery process. However, because of the inherent complexity of human and organizational behavior, many researches have focused on qualitative trends and simple mathematical models.

The stochastic and agent-based models for human and organizational behaviors in service industry are to be developed. In particular, how the presence of social interaction for individuals, and the competition or cooperation dynamics between human in a networked environment affects the economics in service industry. Through the development and application of stochastic and agent-based models for economic and social networks, we will gain new insights into the traditional and non-traditional human behaviors in a networked environment. We intend to formulate a general framework that can guide the development of models for use in the service industry.

5. Conclusion

Modern services industries will become main driven forces for sustainable economic development and main channels for new employment.

The Research Center of Modern Service Science & Technology in Tsinghua University will work widely and deeply in service science, and keep closely with the requirement of our society for seeking establishment of a healthy Service Ecosystem in China.

The Current State and Development Plan of Research and Education on SSME in Harbin Institute of Technology

Xiao-Fei Xu
xiaofei@hit.edu.cn

Zhong-Jie Wang
rainy@hit.edu.cn

Tong Mo
motong@hit.edu.cn

Research Centre of Intelligent Computing
for Enterprises (ICE)
Harbin Institute of Technology
P.O.Box 315,
No.92, West Dazhi Street
Harbin, P.R.China

.

ABSTRACT

In this paper, our understandings on services and SSME are presented, then current state and development plans for research and education on SSME in the Harbin Institute of Technology (HIT) are briefly introduced.

Introduction

The percent of service industry in GDP is increasing quickly in the recent 30 years. In some developed countries above 70%'s labor force are working for service industry, and in China the number is 35% in 2004 and will grow up year by year in the future. The era of service economy has arrived, and how to provide better services to customers has been the focus of various service providers, e.g., governments, enterprises, medical organizations, etc.

In our opinions, goals of a good service may be described as: "In the most proper time schedules, allocate the most proper resources (people and various resources), to provide the most proper services to customers to response to demands of customers in 'On Demand' style".

In order to realize such goals, researchers and practitioners of service must try their best to put forward total solutions on the following issues:

— How to rapidly and soundly describe and understand customer requirements?

— How to effectively design service behavior and schedule service process?

— How to allocate right resources for specific services?

— What kinds of IT supporting tools and platforms are required to assist people inter-act with customers and collect essential data to better accomplish their tasks?

— How to assess the quality of the service before and afterwards to further improve the design of this service?

Services Sciences, Management and Engineering (SSME, first presented by IBM in 2004) [1,2,3], a new inter-discipline, sounds to be a beautiful solutions to above issues, but it is far from mature and there are still a lot of work to do.

According to our understandings, SSME is composed by the following three aspects:

1. *Service Sciences.* Try to develop an adequate service model for the formal descriptions on service behaviors, capacities, process, consultants, customers, and the most important, relationships between them. Such model may again be used for precise and repeated verifying, reasoning, simulation, optimization and refactoring in a scientific way.

2. *Service Management.* Try to answer "how to design good services for customers" and "how to guide service providers to deal with effective and favorable services", etc.

3. *Service Engineering.* "Service" is not just only a set of abstract concepts and theories, but also need the corresponding methodology, technical platform and infrastructures to support the analysis, design, modeling, construction and runtime management during whole lifecycle of a service.

Current research on SSME are concerning the following five aspects:

— Traditional service management;

— Service models and modeling techniques;

— Architecture of supporting platform for service execution;

— Service specifications and standards, aiming at the normalization, standardization and completeness of service process, e.g., ITIL, IT Service CMM, etc;

— Service quality evaluation, e.g., Economic Value Added (EVA) and Balance ScoreCard (BSC) based approaches, SERVQUAL, etc.

In education field of SSME, IBM is now cooperating or negotiating with some renowned universities in the U.S, U.K and China to establish a new service science subject on SSME, to help college graduates get new skills and ability to "integrate across traditional disci-plinary areas to obtain globally effective solutions in a service business environment".

The Current State Of Research on SSME In HIT

SSME and Service Engineering

At present, SSME research in HIT focus on the issue of "how to perform the good services".

In our opinions, similar to a software system, a service ecosystem has its own *models* (for behavior and process), *architecture* (for relationships among multiple partners and resources) and *platform* (supporting service execution), etc, and its core is *Service Methodology*, to realize service description, design, optimization, execution and evaluation in the lifecycle of service system.

Our objective is to propose an integrated service methodology and rapid construction approach for service platform, including:

— Service concepts, description, scope, metrics, models and processes;

— Service engineering, including methodology and the support tools;

— Service oriented model driven architecture (SMDA);

— On Demand service systems as the run-time execution platform, based on SOA technology;

— Service value evaluation and the corresponding metrics.

All these research have the common goal to optimize efficiency and performance of service systems and rapidly response to frequent changes of customer demands.

Methodology of Service Engineering: SMDA

We call our methodology of service engineering as *Service oriented Model-Driven Architecture (SMDA)*. The architecture of SMDA is decomposed into Execution Model (SEM) and Service Platform four layers, i.e., *Service Requirement Model (SRM)*, *Service Capacity Model (SCM)*, *Service Execution Model (SEM)* and *Service Platform (SP)*, as shown in Figure 1.

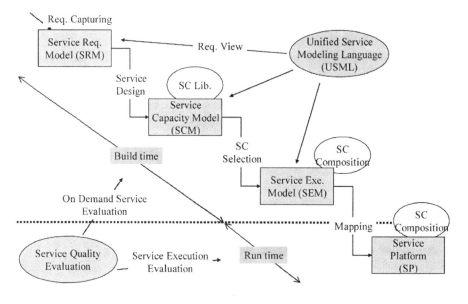

Figure 1. Service model driven architecture and platform

In SRM, customer requirements are formally described, i.e., "what and when to do". Then proper service process and behaviors are selected according to the specific SRM to form SCM, which answers "how to do". Following, concrete resources (i.e., people and infrastructure) are selected and composed together to form SEM, which answers "who to do". Finally SP is built according to SEM to support the collaboration and interoperability between multiple partners involving in the service execution process.

Some detailed research contents include:

Unified Service Modeling Language (USML)
We design a Unified Service Modeling Language (USML) as a tool to uniformly describe various models in different layers of SMDA. USML is based on the basic syntax of UML and extends UML to support unique features of services. Aiming at typical service patterns, standard model APIs and templates will be designed.

Service component based reuse
Various resources for services, e.g., people, supporting infrastructures, service processes, activities, knowledge and behaviors, are uniformly encapsulated into the form of reusable Service Component (SC) and be reused for SMDA modeling to realize rapid mapping between different layers of SMDA.

SFD and ODS based service evaluation

We import Service Function Deployment (SFD) technique to evaluation the quality of services, and the evaluation process is decomposed into three aspects: (1) "On demand Service (ODS)" oriented service model quality assessment; (2) Reusability and capacity oriented SC quality evaluation; (3) Execution efficiency and cost oriented service platform quality assessment.

SMDA oriented platform for collaborative IT consultation

SMDA will be applied in our IT consultation projects in recent future. As an example, Figure 2 shows the architecture of collaborative IT consultation service platform for the implementation of Enterprise Software and Applications (ESA, e.g., ERP, SCM, CRM). The platform is based on SOA.

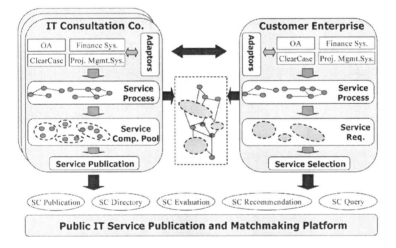

Figure 2. Architecture of SOA-based IT consultation platform

The Development Plan of Research and Education on SSME In HIT

Research work on SSME

Related research and development roadmaps have been specified with four successive phases In SSME research in HIT.

— Phase 1 (Theoretical and conceptual research) — Based on classical research on services, try to clarify the concepts, description, scope, and metrics of modern services and propose a multi-dimensional research framework, including a list of theoretical problems to be solved.

— Phase 2 (Methodology research) — By collecting requirements and analyzing some typical processes and behaviors of services based on our experiences in the implementation of IT services, try to present service models and the corresponding modeling methodology, i.e., SMDA.

— Phase 3 (Tools & platform research) — This phase includes architecture of service platform and support tools for constructing such platform, e.g., USML-based service modeling tool, service component library, service execution toolsets, etc.

— Phase 4 (Application) — After the development of such support tools, ESA consultation (as an IT service) will be adopted as practical cases to validate the theoretical and methodology research results.

Education on SSME: course development, division development, and discipline development

Based on the research on SSME and service engineering, in HIT we plan to open a new curriculum named "Introduction to SSME", in which SMDA-based service methodology will be added as a kernel chapter in this curriculum. This curriculum will be started in 2006.

In the next three years, a course series on SSME will also be opened in HIT, including service psychology, service behaviors, organization theory, strategic management, human capital management, managerial psychology, service marketing, etc.

In the next five years, a division of services will be set up in HIT, to train special talented students on SSME. This task looks a little rough, but some of outstanding researchers from School of Computer Science, School of Management and School of Humanities and Social Sciences in HIT have shown strong interests for such division. Several well-known experts on SSME will also be invited to HIT as visiting or guest professor in this division.

Conclusions

In conclusion, HIT has evolved in the research, development and education on SSME, especially on service engineering methodology and related work, e.g., SMDA, USML, etc. With close collaborations with IBM, R&D and education on SSME in HIT will surely gain rich achievements in the recent future.

References

[1]   IBM. Services Sciences, Management and Engineering. http://www.research.ibm.com/SSME/
[2]   Services Sciences, Management, and Engineering (SSME) - Course Materials. http://www.almaden.ibm.com/asr/SSME/coursemateri als/index.shtml
[3]   Paul Horn. The New Discipline of Service Science. *Business Week*, Jan.21, 2005.

SSME RESEARCH

Services Science Journey: Foundations, Progress, and Challenges

Mary Jo Bitner
PetSmart Chair in Services Leadership
Stephen W. Brown
Edward Carson Chair in Services Marketing
Michael Goul
Professor of Information Systems
Susan Urban
Professor of Computer Science and
Engineering

Arizona State University
Tempe, Arizona
Contact:
maryjo.bitner@asu.edu
480-965-6201

ABSTRACT

With the explosive growth of services in economies worldwide comes the growing recognition of a need for trans-disciplinary research, new business models, and innovative degree programs to propel innovation in services. This paper paints a picture of the history as well as new initiatives at Arizona State University that are aimed at addressing these needs. Building on over twenty years of research that is anchored in ASU's Center for Services Leadership in the W. P. Carey School of Business, we are currently embarking on a Services Science Initiative to enlarge our successes beyond the business disciplines and to engage a broader academic community. This paper shares our current vision of where we are headed as well as some of the challenges to overcome and resources needed to move forward. Authored by senior faculty across several disciplines, this paper symbolizes our conviction that cross-disciplinary efforts of this magnitude require the energy and commitment of senior faculty as well as partnerships with business and government.

The Services Science Journey Begins

The explosive growth of services in economies around the world has vast implications for business practice, academic knowledge creation, education, and government policy. Led by the visionary efforts of IBM, the academic pioneers, and some governments and governmental entities, there is a growing awareness of these implications and the need to focus on services innovation. For example, the Office for Economic Cooperation and Development (OECD) recently released a report in which it noted that government policy in developed countries has not been attuned to the service sector [1]. Along with the awareness of the need for service innovation, has come the discovery that research in service innovation requires cross-disciplinary work.

While the ultimate outcome is still unclear, this focus on service innovation may lead to the formation of a new discipline (e.g., "services science" or "services science, management and engineering"), or at the very least to greater cross-disciplinary collaboration to address educational as well as knowledge development needs. Failure to innovate effectively in services could doom individual companies in their efforts to compete and whole economies in their efforts to grow. The result of failure would be reduced opportunities and quality of life for individuals.

Within the business disciplines, Arizona State University (ASU), through its Center for Services Leadership, has been a leader for over twenty years in developing knowledge and educational programs for services management and marketing. To this end, we have led trans-disciplinary research across the business disciplines of operations, marketing, and human resources and with leading private sector, for-profit businesses. Today, we are embarked on a journey to replicate and enlarge these successes by expanding the scope of services leadership to become even more cross disciplinary—spanning the social sciences, engineering, and computer science—within our own institution and with alliance partners. Beyond the academic disciplines, we also envision greater involvement of governments, industry associations, private foundations, and non-profit entities to support service innovation research and education

This paper paints the picture of where we are on this journey, the challenges we and others will face, and some of the things we envision could be possible. It concludes with the type of help we believe is needed from government and the private sector if we are to keep moving forward. Note that this paper is coauthored by senior faculty from multiple disciplines. While it isn't easy, we firmly believe that this type of cooperation and leadership will be essential to move services science forward.

A Working Definition of Services Science

To facilitate our work, we have adopted the following working definition of services science:

Services Science is an emerging discipline that focuses on fundamental science, models, theories and applications to drive innovation, competition, and quality of life through service(s).

This definition suggests a focus on substantive outcomes (innovation, competition, and quality of life), grounded in rigorous research (science, models, theories and applications). The definition does not preclude any relevant discipline from participating, nor does it prescribe a particular type of research methodology.

Services Leadership Traditions in Business Schools and at ASU

There is a long tradition of services management and marketing research within business schools [2]. This work has focused on theory-based, yet practical issues of helping individual firms to be more competitive through focusing on service(s). Since the 1980s, models, frameworks, and empirical work have supported this focus. Since much of the work has emanated from the marketing discipline, there is a very strong customer-centric flavor to the research. There is much to be learned from this rich tradition and body of work that boasts contributions from academics around the world, is rooted in real issues of business, and spans multiple business disciplines.

At ASU, our services leadership efforts historically have been focused within the Center for Services Leadership (CSL) in the W. P. Carey School of Business.[1] Working with over forty leading businesses (including IBM, Marriott International, Hewlett-Packard, Charles Schwab, Southwest Airlines, Mayo Clinic, SAP and others), the CSL provides executive education and research to further science and services leadership in companies. The CSL's research faculty have published in the leading business journals, written a prominent services textbook used worldwide, and have received many national and international awards for their work in services science. The CSL also supports and provides guidance for our academic courses, degree programs, and student internships and projects in services leadership.

Services Science Initiative AT ASU

Currently, we are developing the next generation of services leadership for our campus. We are working across disciplines on a "Services Science Initiative" that will provide an umbrella for bringing together much of what is currently being done within the broad definition of services science on our campus. Ideally, the Initiative will also provide a forum and energy for new projects, degree programs, and funding. Faculty from the W. P. Carey School of Business, the Fulton School of Engineering, the School of Computing and Informatics, and the Prevention Research Center in Psychology are involved. In addition, the Initiative will provide a hub for inter-university alliances and business partnerships in services science.

Anchored in the CSL, the disciplines that are leading the Services Science Initiative are: services leadership, marketing, information systems, and computer science and informatics. We have also involved individual faculty from supply chain, health care, and psychology and envision including additional faculty from design, architecture and anthropology as we expand.

---

1   www.wpcarey.asu.edu/csl

Research Clusters

One of the challenges of cross-disciplinary research is how to motivate faculty and researchers to work across disciplines. The inherent semantic challenges, as well as incongruent incentive structures are barriers that keep many researchers from participating. It is hard work, and the rewards are not always clear. This is particularly true for younger faculty who are necessarily wedded to the promotion and reward structures of their disciplines. Dual appointments and shared rewards are partial answers.

Another complementary approach that we will use is to bring groups of faculty together around real-world, significant challenges that require investigators with different disciplinary backgrounds to learn enough about each other's perspectives (conceptually, methodologically and substantively) to work together to study and tackle those problems by relying on merged perspectives informed by the range of their disciplines. By identifying key challenges and organizing research clusters of faculty who are interested in applying their knowledge to solving these challenges, we hope to motivate the type of cross-disciplinary research collaboration needed to solve the problems, many of which have global implications. This type of collaboration can spawn innovative solutions that could have real impact on real problems.

Some of the research clusters we foresee developing within our Services Science Initiative include groups that would focus on: IT Services Solutions; Business Models for Services; Computing Models for Services; Healthcare Innovation; Technology and Service Delivery; Service Design; Customer Loyalty and Relationships. We already have individual faculty, and in some cases cross-disciplinary groups, working in all of these areas. We have begun to identify broader representations of faculty and industry partners within each of these challenge areas.

Services Science Degree Programs

There are a number of existing and proposed cross-disciplinary degree programs and specializations at ASU that fall within the broad definition of services science including:

— MBA Specialization in Strategic Marketing and Services Leadership (for over ten years)

— Shanghai MBA in Services Management (for Chinese executives, through the W. P. Carey School, beginning 2007)

— Technology, Science and Engineering MBA degree (for technology companies, offered through W. P. Carey School and Fulton School of Engineering)

— Undergraduate Dual Degree in Business and Engineering (proposed)

— Ph.D. Seminar in Services Leadership (in W. P. Carey School with anticipated cross-campus enrollment, beginning 2006)

In addition, a trans-disciplinary research effort known as *Collaborative Enterprise Services Ecosystems* (CESE) has been established, integrating research and education in computer science, industrial engineering, information systems, and services leadership in the study of the dynamic and self-adjusting behavior required for computing support of business-to-business and business-to-customer collaboration in a service-oriented environment. The CESE hopes to establish an interdisciplinary Ph.D. program with industry participation and support.

Executive Education in Services

In addition to formal degree programs for students, ASU offers a number of avenues for executive education in services leadership including two flagship annual programs: The Compete Through Service Symposium in November (annual for sixteen years), and the Services Leadership Institute in March (annual for twenty years). In addition, customized programs in services leadership and supply chain management are provided for individual companies.

Partnerships and Alliances

To be truly successful, we believe our Services Science Initiative must reach beyond our own limitations and academic borders to form alliances with private business, governments, and other universities.

Through the CSL we already have strong relationships with over forty business partners and a board of advisors made up of senior executives representing leading manufacturing and service companies. Each of these business partners recognizes the critical importance of services to their ability to innovate and compete in the future. We envision gradually expanding the number of partnerships as well as involving partners with faculty research clusters.

Beyond private business, we have alliances with individual services faculty and universities around the globe who have centers for services research and education. Most of these services science alliances are currently with business schools and business faculty. We envision expanding to include alliances with groups in the design sciences, computer science, and information systems.

Challenges for Developing a Crossdisciplinary Initiative

There is strong support at our university and many others for cross-disciplinary research and education programs. For example, ASU's President, Michael Crow, has made trans-disciplinary research and education a central platform of his vision for the "New American University." Over the past four years more than ten trans-disciplinary institutes or schools have been established including the International Institute for Sustainability, the School of Global Studies, The Biodesign Institute, the Institute for Computing and Information Science and Engineering, and the new School of Computing and Informatics. Some universities, like the University of Wisconsin at Madison, have placed paramount importance on trans-disciplinary work for a long time, while many others at least give it lip service.

Yet, there are many challenges and hurdles to overcome that sometimes get in the way of trans-disciplinary initiatives. Among those are inconsistencies in reward and incentive structures as noted earlier. We have become aware of this particular challenge as we combine efforts across business and engineering schools. While business faculty are asked more and more to generate revenue through research grants and other means, the tenure and promotion process in most business schools, including our own, is based to a large degree on publication of articles in premier journals. On the other hand, our engineering colleagues are strongly incented to raise dollars through large government grants and private funding, in addition to generating journal publications. These inconsistencies, while not insurmountable by any means, need to be acknowledged and dealt with in order for trans-disciplinary research partnerships to be successful.

Another big challenge is related to semantics. Each discipline has its own peculiar language. Often researchers in different disciplines find they are talking about the same thing but using different terms. While it may seem relatively inconsequential, these types of semantic and definitional discussions can sidetrack, or at least significantly slow, collaborative research progress.

Finally, there are funding and resource challenges. Trans-disciplinary efforts require funding across disciplines, yet traditional sources of funding tend to be discipline-specific. Thus, it is difficult to know where to look for funding of cross-disciplinary initiatives, and the outcome of proposals is uncertain. Further, to date there are few clearly identifiable sources of funding for services research, education, and innovation. Much of the research funding, particularly in the U.S., is tied to technology innovation and the hard sciences.

How Can Government, Industry, and Foundations Help?

There is significant enthusiasm and interest related to service innovation and services science building within the business and academic communities worldwide. We have shared insights with each other, published papers, held workshops, developed degree programs, and shared course syllabi and methods.

It appears we have reached a critical juncture where the enthusiasm and potential are high, and there is energy ready to move forward. To capitalize on the momentum, we need to find ways to significantly fund the next stages of services science. We need funding from government, private business, and foundations to catalyze these efforts and move them forward quickly. Other countries are doing this, and the U.S. should follow. Funding is needed for individual research programs as well as research enterprises and centers. Funding is needed to incentivize faculty and schools to become involved in cross-disciplinary research and educational offerings. Finally, funding is needed for advocacy work that will promote services science within governmental structures.

References

[1] Organization for Economic Cooperation and Development (2005), "Promoting Innovation in Services."

[2] Bitner, Mary Jo and Stephen W. Brown (2006), "The Evolution and Discovery of Services Science in Business Schools," *Communications of the ACM,* July, 73-78.

Service Supply Chain In The Department Of Defense: Opportunities And Challenges

Uday Apte, Geraldo Ferrer, Ira Lewis, Rene Rendon
Graduate School of Business and Public Policy
Naval Postgraduate School
555 Dyer Street
Monterey, CA 93943
umapte@nps.edu
(831)656-3598

ABSTRACT

In 2003, the Department of Defense (DoD) spent over $118B in purchasing services. In fact, in each of the last ten years, DOD has spent more dollars on services than on supplies, equipment and goods, which includes weapon systems and other military items. As DOD's services acquisition volume continues to increase in scope and dollars, the agency must provide greater attention to such issues as proper acquisition planning, adequate requirements definition, establishment of appropriate contracts, and proper contractor oversight. The unique characteristics of services and the increasing importance of services acquisition offer a significant opportunity for conducting research in the management of the service supply chain in DOD.

Introduction

DOD's services acquisition volume has continued to increase in scope and dollars in the past decade. Between FY 1999 to FY 2003, DoD's spending on services increased by 66%, and in FY 2003, the DoD spent over $118 billion or approximately 57% of total DoD's procurement dollars on services [13]. In recent years, DOD has spent more on services than on supplies, equipment and goods, even considering the high value of weapon systems and large military items [15]. These services belong to very broad set of activities ranging from grounds maintenance to space launch operations. The major categories include professional, administrative, and management support; construction, repair, and maintenance of facilities and equipment; information technology; research and development, and medical care.

As DOD's services acquisition volume continues to increase in scope and dollars, the agency must keep greater attention to proper acquisition planning, adequate requirements definition, sufficient price evaluation, and proper contractor oversight [11]. In many ways, these are the same issues affecting the acquisition of physical supplies and weapon systems. However, there are important differences between the production, acquisition and delivery of services and manufactured goods. For example, services cannot be inventoried, require customer contact and joint production, and have customer-specific inputs. Moreover, we observe intangibility in varying degrees, which makes it difficult to evaluate the quality and performance of a service operation [14]. The unique characteristics of services and the increasing importance of services acquisition offer a significant opportunity for conducting research in the management of the service supply chain in the Department of Defense.

The purpose of this research is therefore to conduct an initial exploratory analysis of DOD services acquisition so as to frame the totality of the DOD's services acquisition environment. Our research contributes to both the theory and practice of service acquisition in the Federal Government. Theoretical contributions include the development of a conceptual framework for understanding and analyzing the supply chain in services, based on rigorous literature in operations management, logistics, public policy, budgeting and microeconomics. We expect that the knowledge developed herein will lead to more effective and efficient management of the Department of Defense acquisition of services.

This exploratory research effort consists of a review of the service acquisition practices in the Department of Defense. It includes visits to a sample of DOD installations involved in the acquisition of services, with interviews of contracting officers, program managers, and other personnel at these installations.

The DOD installation visits were planned to cover a sample of Army, Navy, and Air Force installations. Thus far we have visited Travis AFB and the Presidio of Monterey with visits to the Naval bases in San Diego planned in the near future. These DOD installations have outsourced significant operation support services and provide an excellent source for analysis.

Service Characteristics

Service production differs from manufacturing in several ways. In many operations texts, the key issues that are identified include the intangibility of service output, the difficulty of portability, and complexity in the definition and measurement of services (for example, see [9]). To these we would also add the observation that services often involve joint production between the buyer and the supplier. These characteristics create certain differences in the production and marketing of services. For example, the joint production aspect means that the productive system is often not buffered from the customer.

The customer is often present and even participating in the production process, while simultaneously being a consumer. The resulting need for "customer contact" has been analyzed in the seminal work of Chase [4] to categorize different types of service firms and sectors.

Implications to Contacting

Intangibility of service outcomes makes it difficult to clearly describe and quantify services, and therefore to contract for services. Consider for example, the difficulty in writing a contact for an educational service involving academic lectures. How does one define a "pound of education" and how can one be sure when the contract is fulfilled satisfactorily. As Karmarkar and Pitbladdo [14] explain, this is the reason why in such cases we do not contract around quantities at all; rather we contract around process delivery. In general, the more information intensive the service is the more difficult it is to develop clear and meaningful contracts. This difficulty is somewhat reduced in services where physical objects play a dominant role.

Intangibility of outputs also makes it difficult to define and measure quality. For example, even for a simple custodial service such as cleaning, it is not easy to define the desired level of cleanliness. The levels of cleaning needed for an office is certainly different than for a hospital operating room. The desired time duration for maintaining a clean status can also be an important matter in writing a contract for cleaning service. As research in service quality has found, customers typically evaluate the quality of service based on the outcome of a service as well as the customer's experience with the process of service delivery. For example, in a dining facility, not only must the food be tasty but the manner in which the food is served must also be courteous, prompt and friendly. This means that the contracts for many services should not be based solely on outcomes but should include specifications on both the outcome and the customer's experience with the process.

Co-production requiring presence and participation of customers in the creation of many services is an important characteristic of services. For example, in an IT services such as software development, a customer's input in terms of desired specifications of a software system is critically important. For example, however competent the software developer may be, the developed software will not be satisfactory if the specifications do not accurately reflect the true needs of the customer. Hence, the contracts for services should ideally specify not only what the service provider should do but also what the customer should do. Otherwise, a satisfactory service outcome may not be realized.

Diversity of Services also makes it difficult and undesirable to use the same contract vehicles or procedures for different services. For example, given the differences in medical services versus custodial services, it is important that the contracts for these services are customized to suit the life cycle needs of individual services.

Finally, services are complex and may involve multi-stage processes. This makes it important yet challenging to write contracts that are flexible enough to cover all relevant scenarios and eventualities. Moreover, if such contract cannot be satisfactorily defined, it may be desirable to deliver certain services using internal resources as opposed to outsourcing them.

Services Acquisition Environment in the DOD

The DoD's procurement process is currently undergoing a transformation similar to the one experienced by private enterprises. This transformation is changing how the agency manages its procurement function, to include its people, processes, practices, and policies. Specifically, the procurement transformation is taking place in three major areas: "moving from buying goods to buying services, moving from a command and control relationship to a partnering relationship between the government and contractors, and moving from a paper-based procurement system to electronic procurement" [1] This research paper focuses primarily on the first transformation area: services acquisition.

The transformation from buying goods to buying services is considered the driving force behind the procurement revolution. Gansler [10] describes this transformation as a reflection of the changing role of the government from that of a "provider of goods" to that of a "manager of the providers of good and service…". In addition, the method of procuring services is also changing. Traditionally, through the Request for Proposal (RFP), the government would dictate what the contractor was to do and how to do it. Through the use of detailed specifications and requirements, the contractor was directed how to perform the contracted effort. The procurement transformation is changing how the RFP is being developed. RFPs are now being written to communicate the performance objectives or end-results of what the contracted effort needs to achieve, not how the work is to be done [5].

These two driving forces, the change in what the government is buying (services) and how the government is buying (performance-based contracts), is resulting in the government procuring solutions and knowledge, as opposed to specific supplies or standardized services [5].

Growth and Scope of DoD Service Contracts

In fiscal year 2004, federal government procurement spending totaled approximately $328 billion. Of that amount, approximately $99 billion was spent by the civilian agencies, with the remaining $228 billion spent by the Department of Defense [8]. Since FY 1999 DoD's spending on services has increased by 66%, to over $118 billion in FY 2003, approximately 57% of total procurement value.

Compared to other contract categories, the expenditure in services is the largest single spend category in the Federal Government. Figure 1 compares the procurement of services with the procurement of goods during the period between FY 1998 and FY 2002 in the Department of Defense [12].

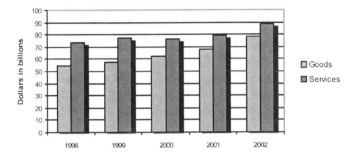

Figure 1: DoD's Contracts for Goods and Services

The DoD procures a variety of services in support of its mission. These services range from traditional commercial contracts such as IT support, custodial services, and grounds maintenance, as well as mission-related services such as aircraft and engine maintenance, and initial pilot training. Major categories of services procured by the DoD include Professional, Administrative, and Management Support, and Construction, Repair and Maintenance of Structure and Facilities.

We identified specific examples of these various services during recent visits at military installations in the central and northern California area. For example, at the Presidio of Monterey, an Army installation providing support services to the Defense Language Institute and the Ord Military Community, the Army contracts for base operations support, grounds maintenance, custodial services, and dining facilities services, among other contracts [3].

At Travis Air Force Base, a major Air Mobility Command (AMC) base, these same types of services are procured, as well as several mission-unique services such as transient alert services for the flight line operations, passenger screening for the airfield passenger terminal, and falconry services in support of the Bird Aircraft Strike Hazard (BASH) program. In addition, Travis AFB also provides contracting support to the David Grant Medical USAF Center. In this capacity, Travis AFB procures various medical services such as medical transcription, nurse services, blood testing, registered nurse staffing, and medical coding services [17].

Policies for Service Contracting in DoD

Compared with other federal agencies, the Department of Defense is often viewed as being particularly aggressive in complying with the Office of Management and Budget's Circular A-76, Performance of Commercial Activities. The circular directs that the "long-standing policy of the federal government has been to rely on the private sector for needed commercial activities." The circular also mandates that while actual performance of an activity may be outsourced, control remains with the government agency no matter what decision is ultimately made as a result of a competition between in-house and commercial providers [16].

Accompanying this growth in outsourcing activity has been a downsizing of the DOD civilian and military acquisition workforce, which is responsible for administering these contracts. Also, Congress has mandated a shift to Performance-Based Service Acquisition (PBSA). PBSA is intended to obtain higher levels of contractor performance at lower cost, and promote a partnership-oriented, long-term approach that allows the government – and the DoD in particular – to benefit from commercial best practices [2, 6, 7].

Outsourcing services on a large scale poses unique challenges for DOD. The department's employees, both those officially part of the "acquisition workforce" and those otherwise involved in the services acquisition process, are the focal point of any effort to increase the quantity and quality of outsourcing. Yet at the same time the numbers of those employees have been falling rapidly, it is not unreasonable to claim that, in many cases, the necessary numbers of staff or skills are not present to ensure the adequate monitoring of the increased scale.

Preliminary Observations and Conclusions

We want to underscore that this is an ongoing research project with several activities such as additional base visits and interviews of contracting personnel and customers yet to be completed. Hence, the observations and conclusions herein are preliminary and tentative, and should be viewed as such.

1. The Department of Defense's services acquisition volume has continued to increase in scope and dollars in the past decade. In terms of amount spent on services, four categories represent over 50% of total spending: (a) professional, administrative, and management support services, (b) construction, repair and maintenance of structure and facilities, (c) equipment maintenance, and (d) information technology services.

2. Presidio of Monterey (POM) has contracted maintenance of about 155 buildings and structures to Presidio Municipal Services Agency (PMSA), a consortium of the cities of Monterey and Seaside. The PMSA agreement has allowed the two cities to apply their expertise to routine municipal services, and the Army to focus on its military mission. Through this partnership and contract with PMSA, the POM has realized a 41% reduction in expenses when compared with previous base operation costs and private contracts. We recommend that DoD explore and evaluate the possibility of establishing such synergistic contractual relations with cities adjacent to other bases in supporting of their respective operations.

3. Proactive and frequent communications are essential for a successful services contract. We found a successful example of this at Travis AFB, where 60th CONS uses Business Requirement Advisory Groups (BRAGs) as the mechanism for conducting such communications. BRAGs are cross-functional teams representing the functional organizations as well as customers involved in the services contracts.

4. Our visits and interviews at Travis AFB, where the 60th Contract Squadron (CONS) is co-located with the 60th Air Mobility Wing (AMW), and at POM and NAS WI confirmed GAO's finding that "while the Army's and Navy's creation of centralized installation management agencies can potentially create efficiencies and improve the management of the facilities through streamlining and consolidation, implementation of these plans has so far met with mixed results in quality and level of support provided to activities and installations".

5. Given the unique characteristics of services, establishing service specifications, and measuring and monitoring the quality of delivered service is inherently more complex than that in manufactured goods. This factor combined with the continued growth in DOD's services acquisition volume means that it is critical to have on board a larger number of skilled contracting personnel to services acquisition. However, DoD's aggressive compliance with OMB's Circular A-76 has resulted in downsizing of the DOD's civilian and military acquisition workforce. Although this exploratory study is not yet completed, we believe that the above two trends clearly contradict each other. This could also mean that in DoD's outsourced services either the needs are not being fully satisfied, or the value for the money spent is not being realized.

6. Although the DOD acquires more services than goods, the management infrastructure for the acquisition of services is less developed than for the acquisition of products and systems. There is a less formal program management approach and life-cycle methodology for the acquisition of services. This results from the fact that the functional personnel currently managing the services programs are typically not provided the needed acquisition training. We recommend that this situation be changed through provision of formal training of services sciences to the service acquisition force.

References

[1]   Abramson, M. A., Harris, R. S. III: The Transformation of Government Procurement. In: Abramson, M. A., Harris, R. S. III (eds.). *The Procurement Revolution*. Rowman & Littlefield Publishers, Lanham, Maryland, 3-11 (2003).
[2]   Air Force Instruction: Acquisition: Performance Based Services Acquisition (PBSA). 63-124 (2005).
[3]   Auernig, M.: Director of Contracting, Presidio of Monterey (2006).
[4]   Chase, R.: The Customer Contact Approach to Services: Theoretical Bases and Practical Extensions. *Operations Research* 21(4), 698-705 (1981).

[5]   Denhardt, K. G.: The Procurement Partnership Model: Moving to a Team-Based Approach. In: Abramson, Mark A., Harris, Roland S. III (eds.). *The Procurement Revolution*. Rowman & Littlefield Publishers, Lanham, MD 59-86 (2003).

[6]   Department of Defense Office of the Inspector General: Acquisition: Contracts for Professional, Administrative and Management Support Services. (D-2005-015) (2003).

[7]   Federal Acquisition Council. F*ederal Acquisition Regulation—Part 37. Services Contracting.* Downloaded from http://farsite.hill.af.mil on March 27 (2006).

[8]   Federal Procurement Data System-Next Generation (FPDS-NG). Available at http://www.fpdsng.com/downloads/top_requests/total federal spending_by_dept.

[9]   Fitzsimmons, J. A., Fitzsimmons, M. J. *Service Management: Operations, Strategy, and Information Technology, 5th edition.* McGraw-Hill, NY (2006).

[10]   Gansler, J. S. A Vision of the Government as a World-Class Buyer: Major Procurement Issues for the Coming Decade. In: Abramson, Mark A., Harris, Roland S. III (eds.) *The Procurement Revolution.* Rowman & Littlefield Publishers, Lanham, Maryland, 13-57 (2003).

[11]   GAO. US Government Accountability Office. *Best Practices: Taking a Strategic Approach Could Improve DOD's Acquisition of Services.* (GAO-02-230) (2002).

[12]   GAO. US Government Accountability Office. *Contract Management: High Level Attention Needed to Transform DOD Services Acquisition.* (GAO-03-935) (2003).

[13]   GAO. US Government Accountability Office. *Contract Management: Opportunities to Improve Surveillance on Department of Defense Contracts.* (GAO-05-274) (2005).

[14]   Karmarkar, U. S., Pitbladdo, R. Service Markets and Competition. *Journal of Operations Management 12* (3-4), 397-411 (1995).

[15]   Levy, D. G., et al. *Base Realignment and Closure (BRAC) and Organizational Restructuring in the DoD: Implications for Education and Training and Infrastructure.* RAND, Santa Monica, CA, 36-50 (MG-153) (2004).

[16]   Office of Management and Budget, Executive Office of the President. *Performance of Commercial Activities.* (Circular No. A-76 (REVISED)) (2003).

[17]   US Air Force: 60th Contracting Squadron Mission Overview, Travis AFB (2006).

The Global Information Economy, Service Industrialization and the UCLA BIT Project

Uday S. Karmarkar
UCLA Anderson School of Management
110 Westwood Plaza, PO Box 951481, Los Angeles, CA 90095-1481
ukarmark@anderson.ucla.edu
www.anderson.ucla.edu/bit.xml

ABSTRACT

Most of the large economies in the world are already dominated by services. Developed countries are also close to becoming information economies; this is already true for the US and Korea. The confluence of these trends means that information services are the largest part of the US and other developed economies, with others close behind. This evolution is being accompanied by a revolution: the rapid industrialization of information services.

These developments have manifold consequences for the economy as a whole, as well as for productivity, trade, jobs, globalization and competition. At the sector level, many industries are undergoing massive changes in structure. There are also significant implications for management strategies and internal organizational structure for all firms.

The Business and Information Technologies (BIT) project at UCLA Anderson is a global effort to track and assess these changes through GNP studies, surveys of business practice, and studies of key industry sectors.

Introduction

Of the largest 25 economies in the world, all but one are dominated by services, in that services comprise more than 50% of the GDP. This is even true of countries like India, where although agriculture dominates employment (60%), services still comprise over 55% of the GDP. The sole exception is China, and it could be conjectured that this is a matter of reporting conventions. It seems that even if manufacturing or agriculture play large roles in an economy, no economy can really function without a large service sector. Today it is valuable to recognize another important trend: that from a material to an information economy. Apte and Nath [4] establish that the US in 1997 was already an information economy, with over 60% of GNP attributable to primary and secondary information sectors. Choi, Rhim and Park [18] following the same methodology, conclude that Korea in 2000, while having a relatively larger manufacturing sector than the US, was also effectively an information economy. Karmarkar [22] has noted that superimposing the two dichotomies of product-service and material-information (Figure 1) gives a useful perspective.

Information services, by 1997 already constituted the largest sector in the US private economy in terms of GNP. The arrows in Figure 1 show the direction of change over 30 years, that we expect to continue for two or three decades. However, note that in terms of employment, it is physical services (such as distribution, transportation, construction) that dominate the US job scene. The data for Korea show similar patterns. While we do not yet have the data for other countries, it is more than likely that this pattern holds for all developed economies. It also seems likely that developing economies will follow the same path, and probably at an accelerated rate. However, this picture is still to be filled out.

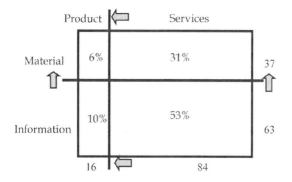

Figure 1: Distribution of GDP in the US economy [22] excluding government, agriculture and mining, based on data from Apte and Nath [4]. The information sector includes both primary and secondary information sectors

The movement towards economies dominated by information services is now accompanied by an "industrialization" of that sector [24]. This industrialization is fundamentally technology driven, and has some resemblance to the industrial revolution in manufacturing. This development has very significant implications for global trade and competition, for economies and national policy, for industry sectors, for firms and organizations, and for individual jobs and functions. In short, these changes are far reaching and broad as well as deep.

The Business and Information Technologies (BIT) project at UCLA Anderson School was created to study these changes at multiple levels of economic and business activity ranging from global and national, to sectors, firms, functions and jobs. The project has 16 research partners around the world as of June 2006, and this network will eventually grow to cover perhaps 20-25 countries. The purpose of this network is to understand the global shift to information economies, to track a new wave of service globalization and to compare development levels and business practices in different countries.

In the following section I first describe what we consider to be the most important research issues related to management in the emerging global information economy. These issues are the basis for the projects being conducted globally under the BIT umbrella.

Research Issues

The evolution of all major economies towards service has long been visible and for the developed economies it is very far along. But that towards information is less well studied and very much still in process. Establishing the extent of this evolution is one of the core activities of the BIT project. There are many other issues and trends that are important and are difficult to study. I describe some of these issues, progressing from a general and global level to the specific and operational. Not all are central to the project, but all underlie and inform our approach.

Production Issues

It is likely that productivity is a fundamental cause of the trends noted in Figure 1. The relatively low productivity growth in services has been long identified as a reason for the growth of services [9, 10]. Symmetrically, high productivity in sectors like manufacturing and agriculture plays a role in their relative decline. Another basic cause may be that there are some limits to the consumption of certain goods and services (satiation). Now a new factor in this equation is that productivity in services (and especially information services) is beginning to show growth [20, 21].

The 'Industrialization" of Information-intensive Services

The industrialization of manufacturing was driven by standardization coupled with efficient logistics. The standardization of end products was followed by standardization of components, processes, and capabilities. This enabled the creation of modular processes, and distributed supply chains which today have become global. In the information sector too, we see standardization (resulting in specifiability) of software products and information processes, coupled with modern information logistics. This industrialization at the "shop floor" level of processing and communication is now migrating upwards into transactional processes, business processes, and business structures [22]. This is visible as the increased modularization of processes and businesses, the creation of distributed information chains, and the restructuring of many information service sectors with a marked tendency towards de-integration of industry value chains. To carry the picture of de-integration and modularization to its extreme: it almost seems as though the efficient scale of production in the information economy of the future will be close to the level of the individual. While this is not quite true yet, it has large implications for industry structure, organizational design, and company scale in the future.

Globalization

An immediate consequence of industrialization is the globalization of data, information and knowledge intensive services (and production processes), coupled with the increased intensity of competition that comes from both standardization and globalization. We are reminded once more that the world is not flat. Or at least that while the playing field might be level in terms of capability and opportunity, the economic gradients on the field are extremely large, leading to large potential relocations of economic activity. However, in contrast tot he material world, information world is naturally more influenced by linguistic and cultural divisions, that determine its topography. This is particularly true of consumer markets, and less so of industrial information services and products [5, 24]. From a comparative perspective, the BIT studies from different countries reveal very different patterns in the use and implementation of new technologies [27]. For example, the US data shows a very substantial level of organizational change occurring in all companies because of new information technologies. However, in contrast, the data from Italy shows very little change (at least as yet). Rather, on-line technologies are being used more to reinforce existing external business relationships. There is a wealth of such comparative information emerging from the parallel country studies within BIT.

Sector Restructuring and Information Chains

Much of the attention in the early days of the appearance of modern on-line information technologies went to the B2C layer between firms and consumers. However, the BIT project takes the perspective of the end-to-end information production and delivery chain. While ecommerce developments have been very visible to all, a substantial degree of restructuring has occurred and continues to occur across entire information intensive sectors, down to the function, job and operation level. We have undertaken several studies on technology driven restructuring and the creation of information and service chains in sectors such as retail banking [17], mortgage banking [13], financial services [23], film and video distribution [12], RFID in supply and service chains [15], and health care delivery [1]. These studies have included cases studies [2, 7, 14, 15, 16, 18, 22] in addition to analyses of current and future information chain structures, and of issues related to technology management, strategy and policy.

These sector studies have verified and reinforced the concept of industrialization, and the consequences such as globalization, new competition, modularization, and the de-integration of chains. However, they have also revealed that in many sectors, change is occurring slowly due to a rational reluctance to undertake costly change and difficulties in orchestrating change, combined with defensive moves by incumbent firms who are threatened by new business models and chain structures.

The Economics of Information and Chain Services

We have leaned upon analogies with the manufacturing world when addressing industrialization, and the structure of information and service chains. However the analogies have their limits. In particular, the economics of information service processes are very different from those of material goods and services. At a very basic level, quantification of outputs is often a problem [25]. While it is tempting to think that information theory might provide a solution in the case of information chains, that turns out not to be the case. It is true that information logistics yields to technical analysis for purposes of analyzing transport, storage and processing capacity. However, production costs, productivity, process quality and customer value present difficult problems for services in general and information services in particular. Some of the issues that we have begun to address include quality management [3], intermediation in information chains [19], collaboration and joint production in services [11], and service competition [25].

Industrialization Strategies at the Company Level

From a management perspective, industrialization and globalization have led to a set of strategies at the firm level, that are intended to improve productivity in the monetary sense (i.e. monetized output/input or revenue/cost). This is not the same as true factor productivity and in fact, it can often involve lower productivity as is often true with off-shore production. However, it is a measure more directly related to the firm level objective of profit maximization.

The most basic issues are of course

— Standardization of services and products

— Modularization of processes down to an atomic level

— Implementation of on-line information logistics

More "macro" strategies are

— Automation

— Outsourcing

— Off-shoring

— Service and product re-design

— Process re-engineering and technology insertion

— Globalization of markets and providers

— Self service (more generally, operation shifting in the information chain.)

Except for the last, these strategies *mutatis mutandis* reflect to a substantial degree what occurred in manufacturing over many decades. The catch is that experience in implementing such strategies is still lacking in many service organizations as our cases studies show [13,15,17].

Organizational Change and the Company Structure

It is vital to note that the issues of industrialization and process change do not just apply at the industry and sector level. They are just as relevant to all information intensive processes within a firm. Clearly most managers and many employees in any firm are engaged in internal information and service processes. The modularization, de-integration, and restructuring occurring at the sector level is also occurring at the level of organizational departments, functions, and jobs. These effects are very visible in the case studies we have undertaken.

One of the most serious issues related to firm level changes, is the need for reconsidering the organizational structures of companies from the top down. It appears that the traditional functional organization of the executive suite is not well aligned to the needs of the internal and external work structures that are emerging. And of course, these organizational changes are the most difficult to make.

At a more detailed level, we are able to track changes that are occurring in the workplace across different industry sectors and different countries. We have begun to conduct these comparative analyses.

Company Strategies and Operational Management

There is a very large set of issues to be tackled at the level of management of the firm, ranging from strategy to operations. We are presently focusing on the issues of quality management, productivity, competitive strategy, the integrated treatment of operations and marketing, and the practical aspects of process engineering, outsourcing and off-shoring.

The Business and Information Technologies (BIT) Project

As stated earlier, the BIT Project was started at UCLA Anderson in 2004 as a global research network. The partners are the leading management research and educational institutions in their countries: IAE (Argentina), The Catholic University (Chile), Theseus/EDHEC (France), Humboldt University and ESMT (Germany), The University of Athens (Greece), IITB (India), SDA Bocconi (Italy), Politecnico di Torino (Italy), Korea University (Korea), The University of Auckland (New Zealand), ESAN (Peru), ISCTE (Portugal), IESE (Spain), The World Internet Institute (Sweden), The University of Lugano (Switzerland) and National Sun Yat Sen University (Taiwan). We continue to add new partners, with a goal of covering at least 20-25 countries.

As of 2006, six countries have conducted studies with the UCLA group having the longest history. We expect most groups to be active within a year.

The structure of the project is a federation, with each team operating independently but with an agreement to conduct certain common studies. The major common activity is a survey of business practice, where each partner uses exactly the same survey instrument, subject to translation to local languages. All participating teams also agree to share the data, with the UCLA team acting as the hub for data collection and transfer.

In addition, all country teams will conduct GDP analyses to track the evolution of their economies. At this point, three teams have undertaken this analysis. A major difficulty here is in the variability of data sources and definitions in each country. At the sector, issue and technology level, we do not expect complete commonality either in subject or method. Teams differ widely in their interests depending on their home countries. But certain sectors and issues (finance, business services, RFID/supply chains, ecommerce/ retail, security, telecommunications, media and publishing, health care) are clearly of universal interest, and we expect that most teams will examine these sectors in the future.

References

[1]   Andersen, M., F. Hasenberg, C. Inglesi, S. Lahooti, R. Simmons, "Impact of IT on Healthcare: The Development of a National Health Information Network", UCLA Anderson AMR Research Study for BIT, 2006.
[2]   Andersen, M., F. Hasenberg, C. Inglesi, S. Lahooti, R. Simmons, "MEDS Inc. in 2005: Wireless Capsule Endoscopy", UCLA Anderson AMR Research Case Study for BIT, 2006.
[3]   Apte, U., U.S. Karmarkar and R. Pitbladdo, "Quality Management in Services: Analysis and Applications," in Karmarkar, U.S., and P. Lederer, *The Practice of Quality Management*, Kluwer 1997.
[4]   Apte, U. and H. Nath, "Size, Structure and Growth of the US Information Economy," in Apte, U.M. and U.S. Karmarkar (eds.), *Managing in the Information Economy: Current Research Issues*, Springer, 2007.
[5]   Apte, U. and U. Karmarkar, "BPO and the Globalization of Information Intensive Services," in Apte, U.M. and U.S. Karmarkar (eds.), *Managing in the Information Economy: Current Research Issues*, Springer, 2007.
[6]   Apte, U. and C. Goh, "Applying Lean Manufacturing Principles to Information-Intensive Services," *International Journal of Service Technology and Management*. Fall 2004.
[7]   Bashyam, A. and U.S. Karmarkar, "Aspect Development Inc (A)", in J. De La Torre, Y. Doz and T. Devinney (eds.), *Managing the Global Corporation: Case Studies in Strategy and Management*, McGraw Hill, New York, 2000.
[8]   Bashyam, A. and U.S. Karmarkar, "Usage Volume and Value Segmentation in the Business Services," in Chakravarty A. and J. Eliashberg (Eds.), *Managing Business Interfaces: Marketing, Engineering, and Manufacturing Perspectives*, Kluwer Academic Publishers, 2004.
[9]   Baumol, W. J. Macroeconomics of unbalanced growth: the anatomy of urban crisis. *American Economic Review*, 57, 415-426, 1967.
[10] Baumol, W. J. Productivity policy and the service sector. In R. P. Inman (ed.) *Managing the Service Economy: Prospects and Problems*. Cambridge: Cambridge University Press, 1985.
[11] Carr, S., U. S. Karmarkar, "Joint Production and Collaboration in Services," UCLA Andersen Working Paper, presented at the MSOM Conference at USC, 2002 .
[12] Chang, J., K.-w. Chang, J. Chu, Y. Lee, Y. Zhao, "Technology Induced Change in FIlm/Television Distribution", in Karmarkar, U.S. and V. Mangal (eds.), T*he UCLA Business and Information Technologies (BIT) Global Project*, World Scientific Press, (Forthcoming 2006).

[13] Chaudhary, S., M. Green, R. Mahmoudi, V. Ting, "The Impact of New Information technology on the US Mortagage Industry", in Karmarkar U.S. and V. Mangal (eds.), *The UCLA Business and Information Technologies (BIT) Global Project*, World Scientific Press, (Forthcoming 2006).

[14] Chaudhary, S., M. Green, R. Mahmoudi, V. Ting,, "IndyMac Bank in 2004," UCLA Andersen AMR Research Case Study for BIT, 2005.

[15] Chaudhary, P., G. Huang, J. Sun, K. Takekura, D. Zu, "Technology in Supply and Service Chains: The RFID Adoption Decision", UCLA Anderson AMR Research Paper for BIT, 2005.

[16] Choi, D., "Wells Fargo and Electronic Banking"; *Technology and Operations Review*, 1996.

[17] Choi, D., U. S. Karmarkar, H. Rhim, "Service Technology Selection, Pricing, and Process Economics in Retail Banking Transactions", UCLA Anderson Working Paper, Submitted for publication, 2005.

[18] Choi, M., H. Rhim, K. Park, "New Business Models in the Information Economy: GDP and Case Studies in Korea", Korea University Working Paper. 2006 .

[19] Corbett, C., U.S. Karmarkar, "Optimal Pricing Strategies for an Information Intermediary", UCLA Anderson Working Paper 2002.

[20] Jorgenson, D. W. "Information Technology and the U.S. Economy." *American Economic Review* no.91, (March): 1-32 (2001)

[21] Jorgenson, D. W., and K. J. Stiroh. "Raising the Speed Limit: U.S. Economic Growth in the InformationAge." *Brookings Papers on Economic Activity*, no. 1: 125-211, 2001.

[22] Karmarkar, U. S., "Service Industrialization and the Global Information Economy", presentation at multiple seminars and conferences, 2002 – 2006.

[23] Karmarkar, U. S., "Financial Service Networks: Access, Cost Structure and Competition", in Melnick, E., P. Nayyar, M. Pinedo, and S. Seshadri (Eds.), *Creating Value in Financial Services*, Kluwer 2000.

[24] Karmarkar, U. S., "Will You Survive the Services Revolution?", *Harvard Business Review*, June 2004.

[25] Karmarkar, U. S., R. Pitbladdo. "Service Markets and Competition." *Journal of Operations Management* 3, 397-411, 1995.

[26] Karmarkar, U. S. and U. M. Apte, eds., *Managing in the Information Economy: Current Research Issues*. New York: Springer, 2007.

[27] Karmarkar, U.S.,Vandana Mangal, (eds.), with contributions by Alfredo Biffi, Anna Canato, Atanu Ghosh, Uday Karmarkar, Andreina Mandelli, VandanaMangal, Paolo Neirotti, Kwangtae Park, Cinzia Parolini, Emilio Paolucci, Hosun Rhim, Sandra Sieber, Josep Valor, *The UCLA Business and Information Technologies (BIT) Global Project*, World Scientific Press, (Forthcoming 2006).

Data Support Design for Services Science Modeling

Terry P. Harrison
Dept. of Supply Chain and Information Systems
Penn State University
459 Business Building
University Park, PA 16802
USA
tharrison@psu.edu

Seán McGarraghy
Management Information Systems
University College Dublin
Belfield
Dublin 4
Ireland
sean.mcgarraghy@ucd.ie

ABSTRACT

The emerging area of "Services Science" is centered on the principles of understanding of how to organize, model, implement and execute supply chains which are heavily based on human capital. A key aspect of this work has been identifying and developing concepts from traditional manufacturing-oriented supply chains and applying them to supply chains where the primary deliverable is a service. A fundamental and necessary part of any services supply chain implementation is the availability of a detailed, flexible and extensive database of human resource attributes. Given the greater variability and uncertainty of service operations, data modeling with stochastic elements is especially critical.

We describe our work to define and implement an architecture to provide access to a wide variety of data resources in support of services science modeling. Our approach is especially oriented towards a flexible and extensible use of data, so that new sources of data may be added to support future modeling and business needs.

Motivation

Many kinds of data are needed to create a high fidelity representation of a supply chain. When the supply chain contains a large human-resource-based component, there may be additional needs to represent data in a stochastic fashion. Some examples of the kinds of data needed to support services science modeling include, but are not restricted to

— Bill of Resources to allow the formation of project teams based on demand for skills over project time line (matching of supply to demand for skills).

— Relationship among skills: closeness or affinity, along with distributions of costs in time/money to train up from one skill to another. This allows for approximate matching of skills.

— The ability to abstract a successful project team profile into a template, to allow for development of standard offerings from first-of-a-kind projects.

— Distributions of hiring/training/attrition rates.

The initial phase of this work is a proof of concept. We wish to allow for a rich architecture that is as "future-proof" as possible and retain the possibility of enhancing the model to (for example) deal with stochastic information or unforeseen attributes/emerging concepts (provide dummy handles or stub methods).

Architecture

The key architectural design principle for the organization and manipulation of data to support the modeling and analysis of a services science data engine is the concept of a "class". Borrowing from the Java programming language, a class is a description of the various kinds of data and methods for manipulating an object, where for our purposes we define five types of elemental or *base* objects or classes. These are:

1. Person

2. Organization

3. Skill

4. Project

5. Subgroup

The first four classes are defined in the traditional sense. That is, the *person* class contains data about an individual; the *organization* class about the firm, etc. The last class, *subgroup*, allows for the extension of any of the other four classes, along with the ability to define other kinds of data objects.

These ideas are implemented in the *services science data engine* (SSDE). Conceptually the SSDE is a meta-database. It links together existing databases, such as a Skills Inventory database, via a custom designed query language to support data needs for service science applications that cannot be supported via traditional means.

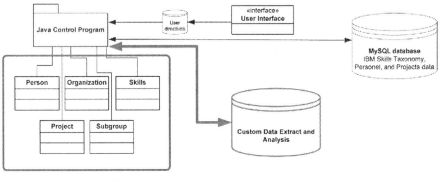

Extensible Base Classes

Figure 1. Services Science data architecture.

Figure 1 is a schematic representation of the SSDE. The key components are:

1. A *user interface* that permits a series of queries in the SSDE language. Representative examples of queries are found below.

2. A *Java control program* that takes the SSDE queries as input and provides the results of the queries as output. The control program implements the SSDE base classes and extensions. It also provides the logic for "techniques / algorithms / heuristics for rolling up or down from low-level (individuals) to aggregated objects", for example, in forming (sub)groups with summary attributes.

3. A *collection of standard databases*, such as the Skill Inventory database and others, which are accessed from the Java control program via SQL queries.

The core function of the SSDE is to provide a single point of access for providing data to support services science modeling efforts. This support includes two fundamental kinds of capabilities:

1. The ability to query multiple, distinct, and possibly distributed databases

2. The ability to aggregate, disaggregate, and further refine and analyze elemental data to create meta-data.

The following questions are representative examples of the kinds of data and information support.

Organizational

1. What are the groups within the organization?

2. What individuals are within a given group?

3. What are the hierarchical relationships between subgroups in the group?

4. What groups and subgroups does as individual belong to?

5. How are groups and subgroups defined by geography?

6. For a given engagement, what groups provide the necessary skill sets and are also "closest"?

Skill Sets

1. What are the major skill sets in the organization?

2. What are the minor skill sets within a major skill set?

3. What major/minor skill sets are found within a group?

4. What is the transition path from one skill set to another?

5. What skill sets are available in a geography, in what quantities?

6. What skill sets can substitute for others?

7. What is the expected turnover for a skill set within a geography over a given time period?

Projects

1. What are the engagement categories?

2. What are the actual engagements within an engagement category over a given period?

3. What skill sets, and by what amounts, are required for a given engagement?

4. What is the revenue associated with phases of a project over time?

Persons

1. What skills does a person have?

2. What options exist to add a particular skill to a person?

3. What is the probability that this person will leave within the next year?

4. What is the cost/hour for this person?

5. What is the revenue/hour for this person in each of their qualified skill sets?

6. How long would it take and how much would it cost to train a particular C++ programmer to become a Java programmer?

Conclusions

Services science offers an important new area of research that presents significant challenges which span a variety of disciplines—-organizational behavior, supply chain management, operations research and information systems, to name a few. Underlying the theory and practice in service science is a fundamental and necessary requirement of data from disparate and heterogeneous sources. Old data must be organized in new ways and new data is also necessary, especially to model the stochastic aspects of human resource supply chains.

We have described an extensible framework to defining and implementing a services science data engine. Follow on work will focus on defining additional data needs to support new models and constructs. We also envision a Service Science Modeling Language with an underlying XML structure to provide the organizing principle for long term services science data modeling.

Process and Services Fusion Impact Assessment: SSME Findings from Industry Collaboration and the Need for Competency Centers

Haluk Demirkan [1]
Department of Information Systems
W.P. Carey School of Business
ASU Tempe, AZ 85287- 4606 USA
haluk.demirkan@asu.edu
Phone: 1-(480) 965-9067

Michael Goul
Department of Information Systems
W.P. Carey School of Business
ASU Tempe, AZ 85287- 4606 USA
michael.goul@asu.edu
Phone: 1-(480) 965-5482

ABSTRACT

Properly applied, services science, management and engineering (SSME) approaches - coupled with service oriented architectures (SOA) - are intended to support enterprise agility, but one of today's most pervasive challenges deals with where and how organizations can start such a journey. So, how should a company begin assessing the real impacts of these paradigm shifts, and how could a company benefit from them if planning started today? We established an enterprise-directed, integrated exploration approach, "Process and Services Fusion Impact Assessment" (P&SFIA), for creating an organizational roadmap to realize visions of how to deliver reliable, scalable enterprise processes built upon SOA. From our collaborations with two local Fortune 100 organizations, we found that a chronology of eight lessons learned, a conceptual model and a generic reuse approach are relevant to viable P&SFIA. We propose that "Process & Services Fusion Competency Centers" be supported to advance SSME/SOA understanding.

Introduction

A "Service Oriented Enterprise" (SOE) is an enterprise that implements and exposes its business processes through a Service Oriented Architecture (SOA) and that provides frameworks for managing its business processes across an SOA landscape [1]. SOE builds on current conceptualizations of SOA with an eye towards the extended enterprise and the potential advantages of leveraging SOA in a value chain context. In reference to the Services Science, Management and Engineering (SSME) extended enterprise framework, an SOE reference model is already advancing through an OASIS standards process. Based on the Federated Enterprise Reference Architecture (FERA), the ebSOA TC vision statement reflects the necessity of aligning business and technology vantage points [3]. This is consistent with SSME, specifically the "Continual Business Optimization" and "Business Standards for the Extended Enterprise" tracks of the Architecture of On Demand Business

Summit [4]. The Value Chain Group [7] has also recently advanced the Value Chain Operations Reference (VCOR) model in alignment with FERA and ebSOA. VCOR's value proposition provides for: 1) Common semantics across the value chain, 2) Common KPIs across the value chain, 3) Visualization of the performance(s) of the total value chain or parts thereof, and 4) Capabilities for corporations to translate business strategy into value chain strategy.

To aid organizations in developing SOE strategies consistent with FERA and ebSOA, we have established a "Process and Services Fusion Impact Assessment" (P&SFIA) approach that has been reliably used in organizations in the Phoenix metropolitan area. Two specific applications of the approach have been at Fortune 100 enterprises [1, 5, 6]. Based on these experiences, we posit that:

1. SOE strategy cannot be based on business process management solutions alone,

2. SOE strategy cannot be based on SOA solutions alone,

3. SOE strategy necessarily fuses processes and services perspectives which likely requires a jolt or shock to enterprise stakeholders through a formalized impact assessment,

4. Pattern reuse at the 'business process to services' and 'services to computing infrastructure' transformations must be taken into account in developing a viable strategy,

5. Eight chronological phases, a conceptual modeling approach and a generic reuse approach are applicable to P&SFIA, and

6. Process and Services Fusion Competency Centers (which can serve as a clearing house for industry use cases standardized to FERA-based ebSOA and VCOR) can be used to support research (which can be leveraged to augment both industry SSME strategic planning and SSME education that aligns business and technology vantage points).

Process And Services Fusion Impact Assessment

P&SFIA cannot be done by an IT Department alone; it must be part of a larger scale enterprise change agenda, which increases the complexity of the change process - and the need for success. P&SFIA is not a one-time event; rather, it is the beginning of a journey. In addition, that journey is as much about people and reuse as it is about processes and services. From the perspective of people, it is important that stakeholders visualize, through a conceptual modeling tool, actual use cases relevant to their enterprise ecosystem that illustrate interdependencies between processes and services. It is also necessary to show that these interdependencies are dynamic and reflective of an emerging marketplace with the increasing commoditization of infrastructure (utility or on-demand computing), services (the software-as-a-service model) - and even the predicted commoditization of business processes themselves [2]. Our position is that agility is gained by facilitating changes to the enterprise ecosystem in only predicted ways that can be rapidly planned for and accommodated.

In short, our ontology-based conceptual model takes practical use cases and maps their business process activities to service structures (SOA) with individual services mapped to infrastructure (hereafter SOI). These mappings or transformation points represent opportunities for reuse, i.e., many business process activities may share the same service structure patterns, and frequent executions of service structure patterns may be cached for rapid virtualized infrastructure provisioning. This reuse of patterns at both transformation points can be characterized as a process of **D**iscovery of relevant patterns, **I**nstantiation or population of the pattern with instance specifics, **S**coring of instantiated patterns, **C**horeography selection, **O**rchestration or execution and then 'Bang' or '!' which we refer to as the DISCO! model (Figure 1) [1].

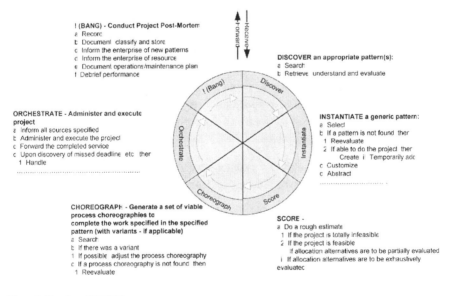

Figure 1: Overview of DISCO!

The P&SFIA Chronology

P&SFIA is a focused discovery process beginning with a review and evaluation of organizations' strategies, current organizational structures, and architecture and information management methodologies. The intent of P&SFIA is to map strategy to workable solutions. In the end, a critical mass of SOE initiatives is defined by forging a consensus of key stakeholders to an agenda that is tailored to the enterprise's strategy. That agenda is enriched with new common perspectives and culture regarding reuse strategies, an understanding of the importance of semantics and ontology, an appreciation of upcoming commoditization trends, and a new transparency to ecosystem interdependencies. It should be noted that the outcomes are not necessarily technology acquisitions; rather, outcomes are linked to integrating people, processes, systems and inter-organizational capabilities. A viable P&SFIA chronology consists of 4 major phases, as depicted in Figure 2.

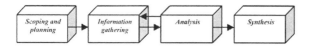

Figure 2: Overview of P&SFIA Process (Adapted from [1])

In the following section, we discuss the lessons learned from our experiences by applying P&SFIA at two Fortune 100 companies.

P&SFIA Process Lessons Learned

With our two case studies, P&SFIA opened a gateway for the organizations to realize new visions of how to deliver reliable, scalable enterprise processes built upon the premise of the SOE. An SOE perspective moves beyond an IT perspective to SOA as processes and services are fused throughout the enterprise and beyond. Transitioning to an SOE should be just that, a transition – a slow adaptation, not a big bang. From our studies at these two organizations, a chronology of lessons learned for viable P&SFIA are:

1. Convince business process and IT stakeholders they are players in a complex services ecosystem with under-addressed interdependencies.

2. Begin by examining the existing culture for aligning strategy, business and IT with an eye towards how that culture will need to change.

3. For business process owners, component developers, infrastructure managers, etc., establish a baseline of current pattern template reuse and lessons learned.

4. Conduct a detailed examination of both simple and complex use cases for representation in a P&SFIA SOE conceptual model.

5. Examine current 'business process' to 'infrastructure resource sourced' transformations with an eye towards identifying surprising bottlenecks to agility, surprising failures in stakeholder coordination, and do this in the context of bringing transparency to business and IT perspectives.

6. Brainstorm new roles using a P&SFIA-based process framework to surface transformation ideas and action items, to lead, specify, design, develop, deliver and manage interoperable and flexible services, as well as organizing an effective design "reuse factory".

7. Repeat the process considering both transitory and long-term inter- and intra-orgnizational alliances and services ecosystem interdependencies; reinforce stakeholders' dual roles as both customer and provider depending upon business process context.

8. Iterate 1-7, to build sufficient critical mass to realize an SOE action agenda [1].

Conclusion

Services computing can provide the agility many enterprises have been looking for, but only if considered as part of a more holistic enterprise perspective and agenda. SOE increases productivity, reduces development cycle time, provides an environment for reusability, flexibility and adaptability and multichannel/multi-constituency support. The foundations for SOE can be found in current applications of SOA, business process and workflow, computing resource virtualization, business semantics, service level agreements, increasing standardization and other areas of applied research.

One overriding lesson from this research is that SOE is about people, the ways that they engage with computing to execute processes, and it is about the semantics that put people and machines together in new ways. It's about executable semantics and preparing for commoditization of processes, services and computing horsepower. These paradigm shifts – services science, management and engineering and SOA - are not about a specific technology or a product, they represent a major cultural change for organizations. A transdisciplinary education program needs to be developed by utilizing organizational sociology, law, services marketing, business strategy and operations, accounting and finance, information technology, industrial and computer engineering to provide the knowledge necessary for this culture change.

Process and Services Fusion Competency Centers can serve as clearing houses for industry use cases to analyze SSME research issues and allow students to investigate application challenges and globalization issues that cannot easily be replicated in typical university laboratory settings.

References

[1]   Brown, G., Demirkan, H., Goul, M. and M. Mitchell. Process & Services Fusion Impact Assessment at American Express and Intel. working paper submitted to Society of Information Management 2006 Paper Awards Competition (SIM 2006).

[2]   Davenport, T. The Coming Commoditization of Processes. *Harvard Business Review*, June 2005.

[3]   ebSOA TC, 2006. http://www.oasisopen.org/committees/documents.php?wg_abb rev=ebsoa)

[4]   IBM. Architecture of On Demand Business Summit. 2006. http://domino.research.ibm.com/comm/www_ fs.nsf/pages/index.html

[5]   Keith, M., H. Demirkan, M. Goul, J. Nichols and M. Mitchell. Contextualizing Knowledge Management Readiness to Support Change Management Strategies. *Proc. HICSS 2006.*

[6]   Keith, M., H. Demirkan, and M. Goul. Coordination Network Analysis: A Research Framework for Studying the Organizational Impacts of Service-Orientation in Business Intelligence. Working Paper, Submitted to HICSS 2007.

[7]   Value Chain Group 2006. http://www.value-chain.org/

iLab.1: A University-Industry Collaboration to Enhance Health Plan Services

Jeffrey A. Lasky
Golisano College of Computing and
Information Sciences
Rochester Institute of Technology
Rochester, NY 14623
Jeffrey.Lasky@rit.edu
+1.585.475.2284

Michael Cardillo
Excellus Health Plan, Inc.
165 Court Street
Rochester, NY 14647
Michael.Cardillo@excellus.com
+1.585.238.4299

ABSTRACT

There is an urgent need to transform all elements of the U.S. health care services system. Concerns about increasing costs and questions about quality have moved the health care system to center stage on the nation's agenda.

Within this system, health plans are a critical component. They provide insurance financing for health care services, and participate in efforts to increase health care quality and reduce health care costs. iLab.1, the Information Laboratory for Health Plans, is a new collaboration between Rochester Institute of Technology and Excellus Health Plan, Inc. The Lab's programs and activities seek to enhance health plan services by developing system architectures, processes, and tools for increasing the availability, exchange, and sharing of health care and health services information. Increased information availability is considered to be a necessary condition for moving the transformation forward. [1]

Introduction

Health plans are a critical component of the U.S. health care system. Health plans provide insurance financing for health care services, and develop programs aimed at increasing health care quality and reducing health care costs. As with the entirety of the health care service system, health plans are embedded in vast, complex, and disparate information ecologies. Unrealized value to patients, in the forms of improved health outcomes and lower health costs, are locked within these inefficiently used socio-information ecologies. Hence, integration of these information ecologies to increase information availability, and to support discovery of new and more efficient means to deliver health care services, is receiving urgent and considerable attention from both the private and public sectors.

---

1   Thanks to Bruno Nardone and Claude Yusto, both at IBM, for sharing their thoughts about the benefits and challenges associated with improving the delivery of disease and medical management services.

Regional Health Information Organizations (RHIOs) are one reflection of the imperative to increase the availability of health care information [1]. RHIOs seek to improve health care delivery by providing an infrastructure for creating and accessing comprehensive patient health records in electronic form. Specialized health care advising services are another response to the call for increased availability of health care information. These service organizations have entered the marketplace to provide patients, referring providers, and health plans with quality-rated physician undecorated recommendations for treatment of serious and complex medical problems, together with expected treatment costs. In the long run, RHIOs, patient advising services, and other health care information availability models will help shape the coming transformation of the health care system.

By virtue of their claims processing and reimbursement roles, health plans receive patient information, at differing levels of detail, from providers, pharmacies, and laboratories. Hence, health plans are in a unique position to comprehensively assess the effectiveness and efficiency of health care services, to coordinate health care services, and to offer health and medical guidance. For many years, health plans have offered disease, medical, and care management programs to increase the effectiveness of ongoing interventions in serious and chronic care cases. Care for chronic conditions receives special attention because quality of life issues are present, and the level of care costs is disproportionate to the size of the impacted populations [2]. Going forward, as health literacy among the population increases, and the population ages, there likely will be pressures to expand the number and scope of these information-intensive medical management programs. Some predict that medical management and related activities eventually will supplant financing as the primary role of health plans [8].

IT provides critical information processing services to health plan operations and to health care services. The importance of IT will be pervasive in all 21st century service systems [7, 12]. Due to the centrality of health plans in the health care service system, the efficiency of health plan operations impacts all system stakeholders. Health plan IT systems need to be open to providers, pharmacies, laboratories, plan sponsors, and others with a need to know. While openness brings special requirements for system reliability, robustness, performance, security, and usability, openness also enables new opportunities for interoperability and thus for new information channels.

iLab.1: Information Laboratory for Health Plans

Given the dynamics of the health care services industry, a vision of increased information availability suggests opportunities for innovations in health plan services. In turn, more advanced information systems may be needed to enable and support these innovations, and more attention will need to be placed on designing effective communications with health plan members. In collaborative settings, the university community can offer health plans academic perspectives on the potential advantages, disadvantages, and impacts of emerging information technologies, critical analysis of entrenched organizational thinking, share research findings about health communications, and perhaps offer new insights into challenging issues.

However, compared to health care providers, health plans have received less attention from the academic community. To address this state of affairs, Rochester Institute of Technology (RIT) and Excellus Health Plan, Inc. (EHP) have developed iLab.1, the Information Laboratory for Health Plans. iLab.1 is focused on optimizing the use of information to support health plan operations, and on realizing stakeholder value from increasing the availability of health care information. It is hoped that iLab.1 will stimulate the creation of additional focused iLabs at RIT and at other universities, both for the health care services industry and for other information-intensive service industries. Work and findings across information-intensive service domains may yield contributions to the broader Services Science discipline.

Founding organizations
Golisano College of Computing & Information Sciences at RIT
The Golisano College of Computing and Information Sciences at RIT includes the departments of Computer Science, Information Technology, Networking, Security, and Systems Administration, and Software Engineering. One hundred full-time faculty offer 2,600 full-time equivalent students abroad spectrum of degree programs. Students have access to exceptionally well-equipped general-purpose and special purpose computing laboratories. As a graduation requirement, all undergraduate students in the college complete 30 to 40 weeks of paid, full-time cooperative education work.

The College offers a broad spectrum of degree programs. As of Fall 2007, the College expects to be offering 18 degree-granting programs: seven undergraduate programs, 10 masters level programs, and a Ph.D. program. The programs cover the disciplines and fields of computer science, information technology, software engineering, security and information assurance, networking and systems administration, game design and development, human-computer interaction, learning and knowledge management systems, medical informatics, and software development and management.

Excellus Health Plan, Inc.
Excellus Health Plan, Inc. (EHP) is a regional health insurance company headquartered in Rochester NY. The company's revenues are approximately $5 Billion per year. Two million individuals are covered by the company's issued health insurance policies. EHP is the result of 1998-2002 merger and acquisition activity that combined BlueCross BlueShield of Rochester with three central New York BlueCross BlueShield health plans, and one western New York independent health plan.

The College and EHP enjoy a close and successful working relationship. In 2002, the two organizations established a cooperative education program to place students in EHP'sIT Division. Since that time, nearly 60 RIT undergraduate students have satisfied at least 50% of their co-op requirement in the CCIS/EHP co-op program. The authors co-manage the co-op program, and the university-based author is on site at EHP one day a week as a Professor-in-Residence [4].

Health Plan Services

At health plans, mission critical operations and customer-facing services are labor and information-intensive. Such service properties point to iLab.1 target work areas. Although information in the broadest sense is the Lab's focus, the systems engineering discipline's end-to-end total systems perspective will be the over arching framework for the Lab's investigations and R&D work [9, 11].

Claims processing and customer service are the primary touch points for most health plan members. Claims processing is a health plan's primary service, and claims processing volumes are considerable. For example, EHP processes an average of 100,000 claims per day, and each claim may have more than one line item. As is the case at other insurance companies, significant numbers of claims cannot be completely processed by software without review and decision-making by claims analysts. Manual intervention is costly, may delay claims to a point where service level agreement penalties or regulatory fines are imposed, and can lead to customer dissatisfaction. Here, service improvements will result from reducing the number of claim processing exceptions and reducing the human time required for exception processing.

Health plan members and other stakeholders expect rapid and accurate responses to their inquiries. Health plan companies maintain sizeable customer service call centers, and these centers receive very high volumes of inquiries, on the order of several millions to tens of millions per year. This is the case even though a large percentage of inquiries are self-served via touch-tone telephone or Web access. Initial and follow-up customer service representative (CSR) training is challenging, both for the CSR staff and the training staff. Typically, newly hired CSRs have no prior health plan experience, and must master volumes of detailed information. The health plan business is subject to constant change. Terms and conditions of health plan contracts may change annually, and the health plan business environment is controlled by a myriad of state and federal regulatory mandates. CSR work in a health plan environment is demanding, and well-structured and easily accessible information is essential to rapid and accurate CSR work.

From time to time, spikes occur in call center volumes. Typically, these spikes are driven by changes to an existing benefit or by the availability of a new benefit. Medicare Schedule D is a recent example of the later. Maintaining high levels of call center service is a complex undertaking, and involves matters of information and knowledge management, training, performance support tools, and resource allocation and scheduling plan optimization.

Relatively few health plan members consume medical and disease management services, but these services address high-cost health conditions. Here, care planning and coordination, and patient monitoring are primary service characteristics. Medical management staffs need timely notifications when patients seek unplanned interventions, including emergency treatments. In practice, this sometimes is not the case, since the arrival of a claim is typically the notification event. Time delays can occur between a medical intervention, the submission of a claim by the provider orthe member, and notification to the medical management staff. Greater integration between provider and health plan systems, and development of event capture and event processing extensions to middleware have potential to address notification and information availability concerns [6]. Patient compliance with care plans is a critical success factor. Here, the behavioral sciences can inform and help to evaluate care plan design [5].

The design and ultimate effectiveness of health communications is another critical factor in enhancing and optimizing health care services. The field of health communications rests both on communications theory and on information science. Hence, health communications addresses a broad range of communications matters, from communication design to effectiveness evaluation. For example, see [3] for an analysis of a communication program designed to inform employees about changes in a prescription drug benefit plan.

Summary and Conclusions

There is an urgent need to transform the U.S. health care services system. We believe that increased availability of health services information, together with system architectures and standards that facilitate information sharing and exchange, are necessary conditions for the transformation moving forward. While our thoughts are health plan centric, information availability is global to the health care system.

Given the complementary academic and business interests in seeing the development of a services science discipline, it seemed natural and sensible to embed a sustained effort in a ongoing services system. A successful and ongoing collaboration between the parties suggested health care services as an attractive services domain. The result is iLab.1, an Information Laboratory for Health Plans. Although the capabilities and interests of the College of Computing and Information Sciences faculty and students are sufficiently broad for initial work, over time we envision inviting faculty and students from other RIT colleges and colleagues from other universities to participate in the Lab.

In this paper, we identified a number of disciplines that are related to the strategic goal of increasing the availability of health care and health services information. Although the list is already surprisingly long, we suspect that other disciplines will surprise as to their relevance. For example, the explosive growth and pervasive presence of computer-based games already has reached out to the health care system. Although game design and development is a new academic discipline, the use of games for non-entertainment purposes has spawned a Serious Games sub-discipline [10], which includes Games for Health as a specialized application area.

References

[1]   Center for Health Transformation. (2005). Accelerating transformation through health information technology. <http://www.healthtransformation.net/content/events/special_events/1865.cfm>

[2]   Hoffman, C., Rice, D. P., and Sung, H. Y. (1996).Persons with chronic conditions: Their prevalence andcosts. *JAMA, 276*, 1473-1479.

[3]   Feldman, R., Abraham, J., Davis, L., and Carlin, Caroline. (2005). Consumer knowledge of the impact of a change in prescription drug benefit design. *Disease Management & Health Outcomes 13*(6), 413-420.

[4]   Lasky, J. A. and Cardillo, M. (2004). Designing a cooperative education program to support an IT strategic plan. *Proc. 5th Conference on Information Technology Education,* 106-110. Available from ACM Digital Library.

[5]   Linden, A. and Roberts, N. (2006). Disease management intervention II: What else is in the black box? *Disease Management 9*(2), 73-85.

[6]   Luckham, D. (2002). *The Power of Events*. Addison-Wesley, Boston MA.

[7]   Maglio, P., Srinivasan, S., Kreulen, J. T., and Spohrer, J.(2006). Services systems, service scientists, SSME, and innovation. *Comm. ACM, 49*(7), 81-85.

[8]   Porter, M. E. and Teisberg, E. O. (2006). *Redefining Health Care: Creating Value-Based Competition on Results*. Harvard Business School Press, Boston MA.

[9]   Rust, R. T. and Miu, C. (2006). What academic research tells us about service. *Comm. ACM, 49*(7), 49-54.

[10] The Serious Games Initiative. An overview is at <www.seriousgames.org/about2.html>; the site includes a link to Games for Health.

[11] Tien, J. and Berg, D. (2003). A case for service systems engineering. *J. Systems Science and Systems Engineering 12*(1), 13-38.

[12] Zysman, J. (2006). The algorithmic revolution: The fourth service transformation. *Comm. ACM 49*(7), 48.

SSME: How to Solve It

Shiu-Kai Chin
L.C. Smith College of Engineering &
Computer Science
Syracuse University
Syracuse, New York 13244
skchin@syr.edu

Alex Wilkinson
School of Information Studies
Syracuse University
Syracuse, New York 13244
ACWilkin@syr.edu

James S. Royer
L.C. Smith College of Engineering &
Computer Science
Syracuse University
Syracuse, New York 13244
royer@ecs.syr.edu

ABSTRACT

The challenge of delivering services that are reliable, secure, and trustworthy in a timely and cost effective manner is a key to global competitiveness. To meet this challenge, Service Science, Management, and Engineering (SSME) needs rigorous, mathematically-based underpinnings in support of conceptual and computational tools for modeling services in a composable fashion. Such tools should lead to rapid and accurate design, verification, validation, and deployment. As services, by their very nature, cross boundaries between a wide range of organizations and individuals, this development must involve principles, methods, and tools from engineering, information studies, management, law, etc.

"How to Solve It"

At the core of Polya's famous book, *How to Solve It* [7], are four commonsense steps he sets out for problem solving.

1. *Understanding the problem:* What is the unknown? What is the data? What is the condition? . . .

2. *Devising a plan:* What is the connection between the data and unknown? What are subproblems? Have you seen similar problems before? . . .

3. *Carrying out the plan:* Can you check each step? . . .

4. *Looking back:* Can you check the final result? Can you do it differently? . . .

Polya's steps certainly apply when solving a particular SSME problem. But they also apply to the issue of crafting a methodology for specifying, analyzing, and solving SSME problems. In this paper, we consider a certain class of SSME problems, sketch our ideas on understanding the problems and devising a plan for solving them (steps 1 and 2), and conclude with a few comments on executing the plan and judging its success (steps 3 and 4).

Understanding Service Problems

We shall focus on the following questions:

— How can the real-world needs motivating a service be specified?

— What is the "glue" that enables services to be combined in ways that yield predictable results?

— What are the building blocks for creating larger services and that lend themselves to predictable behavior?

— How can services be mathematically modeled, and what useful information can be extracted from these models?

— How can we check that a given service has the predicted outcomes and fits the original needs?

We believe these are crucial questions, the answers to which will lead to critical capabilities when answered. To address these questions requires expertise drawn from the disciplines of management, information studies, engineering, computer science, law, etc. Success will ultimately depend on the ability to deliver value-added business services using innovative and trustworthy technology.

In this paper we shall take the view that:

Integrating Services ≈ Composition of Large Programs and Applications

From this perspective, services themselves resemble large programs that are specific to a business application operating in an observable business environment. To understand such a service requires insight about the programs composition and its interaction with an organizational context.

A broader view of services is that they are solutions to business or organizational problems where software plays a key role, but so does the organization itself. In this more general setting, the issues of needs, glue, building blocks, model, and verification are still vital, but they apply both to the service *and* to the organization, adding an extra dimension of complexity. Following Polya's advice,[1] we restrict ourselves to a narrower view. While not ignoring the human organization, we forebear analyzing it *per se* and more modestly examine how a service behaves when it interacts with an organization and its members.

We are not done "understanding the problem" yet. New services will be developed, deployed, and judged in an emerging computational and business milieu with some stark differences from the preceding era. Below we discuss a few of these changes and how they influence the task of crafting an SSME methodology.

Software evolution and services

Some trends in the architecture and technology of software can shed light on the problem of composing services. The web is emerging as the new services platform and the new generation of web applications suggest potential frameworks for developing and delivering services. Of particular interest is the notion of a *mash-up*, i.e., a website or web application that combines content and code from multiple, usually public, sources to create something completely new. In regard to mash-up and services, we note the following observations which are certainly not original to the authors:

— No one knows how to mash-up services, i.e., decompose and recompose existing services into new services.

— As part of understanding the mash-up problem, one should think about programs that combine programs to create new programs where programs are services.

— In particular, the "spreadsheet" model is an attractive example of a program-producing-program that provides an intuitive framework through which non-programmers can create new applications.

There is much underlying and developed theory in the area of declarative programming languages and semantics dealing with *higher-order functions* (functions that take functions as inputs and return functions as outputs) that apply to program composition and verification.

With the spreadsheet paradigm in mind, consider the scenario where a user specifies that a column of numbers is to be summed up. What is going on from the standpoint of higher-order functions is the user is specifying that a *list* of numbers, say [1, 2] is to be operated upon by a function, in this case addition, +, which has an associated identity or

---

1   "If there is a problem you can't solve, then there is an easier problem you can't solve: find it." – G. Polya

base element 0 (recall that x + 0 = x). We can define a "glue" function named *foldr* that takes three arguments:

(i) a mathematical function *f,*

 (ii) a base or identity element *b,* and

(iii) a list of arguments (possibly empty).

The definition follows where [] is the empty list, *x : xs* is a list where *x* is the first element of the list and *xs* is the remainder of the list, and : is the list constructor, which takes as its left argument an element and its right argument a list and returns a list. The first definition describes what value *foldr* returns when applied to an empty list []. The second definition is recursive and describes what *foldr* returns when applied to a non-empty list *x: xs*, where the first element is *x* and the remainder of the list is *xs.*

$$
\begin{aligned}
foldr\ f\ b\ [\ ] &= b \\
foldr\ f\ b\ (x : xs) &= f\ x\ (foldr\ f\ b)\ xs
\end{aligned}
$$

Recall that the user wanted to sum a list of numbers, say [1, 2]. This works out as follows:

$$
\begin{aligned}
foldr\ +\ 0\ [1,2] &\rightsquigarrow 1 + (foldr\ +\ 0\ [2]) \\
&\rightsquigarrow 1 + (2 + (foldr\ +\ 0\ [\ ])) \\
&\rightsquigarrow 1 + (2 + 0) \rightsquigarrow 3
\end{aligned}
$$

The utility of a "glue" function such as *foldr* can be seen by considering that the user could just as easily have wanted to take the *product* of all the numbers in a column, say [1, 2, 3]. In this case we can reuse the "glue" function *foldr* as follows:

$$
\begin{aligned}
foldr\ \times\ 1\ [1,2,3] &\rightsquigarrow 1 \times (foldr\ \times\ 1\ [2,3]) \\
&\rightsquigarrow 1 \times (2 \times (foldr\ \times\ 1\ [3])) \\
&\rightsquigarrow 1 \times (2 \times (3 \times (foldr\ \times\ 1\ [\ ]))) \\
&\rightsquigarrow 1 \times (2 \times (3 \times 1)) \rightsquigarrow 6
\end{aligned}
$$

The point of this bit of mathematics is this: *behind the glossy user interface of spreadsheets are higher-order "glue" functions that make everything work.* Our view is that a large degree of mathematical sophistication is required "behind the scenes" to provide non-technical users the ease and reliability they desire. We believe that when looking for models of services, we need to pay attention to the creation of useful "glue" functions or programs that will predictably combine programs to produce new and verifiable services.[2]

Systems evolution and services

Some trends in systems architecture can also shed light on the problem of composing services. The outlines of how some aspects of hardware and systems will change in the next 10 or so years are fairly clear:

— Performance gains will come from process and processor concurrency rather than by faster processor-clock speeds.

— Application programs will be *virtualized*. That is, the execution environment for applications will be virtual machines downloaded by users. This addresses current issues with security and differing versions of software that cause application programs to fail.

— Systems will emphasize specific applications and be modular. Platforms will tend to be application specific rather than general purpose.

These observations speak to the need for mathematically based models and methods (e.g., process algebras, modal logic, and model checkers) that account for concurrency and composition. This is particularly the case for concurrent programming, which is notoriously difficult to get right.

The use of virtualization [8] to guarantee consistent runtime environments and security has performance implications. Briefly, in order to avoid a significant degradation in performance while guaranteeing secure process isolation and sharing, so-called *innocuous instructions* (instructions with no security risk) must be executed directly by hardware while all other instructions are trapped by the supervisor program. When similar applications are grouped together, presumably a larger percentage of innocuous instructions will be shared by all service programs, making direct hardware execution feasible and thereby preserving performance.

The above discussion illustrates that in order to answer performance questions about services (an important quality of service consideration), security and computer architecture must be taken into consideration from the start.

---

2   A spectacular example of the sort of glue discussed here is Google's MapReduce programming model [4]. It has considerable sophistication under its hood, but it also permits non-expert users to simply program highly-parallel computations over huge (> 1 terabyte) data sets. Google's own indexing of the web is now done via MapReduce.

Verification evolution and services

Recent trends in verification technology are, we believe, also germane to the problem of composing services. Formal methods for checking or verifying designs are an established, multibillion-dollar part of hardware design. They are beginning to be practically applied to software. For instance:

> "[S]oftware verification has been the Holy Grail of computer science for many decades, but now in some key areas, for example, driver verification, we're building tools that can do actual proof about the software and how it works in order to guarantee the reliability." Bill Gates, keynote address at the Windows Hardware Engineering Conference, 18 April 2002.

Gates is referring to Microsoft's Static Driver Verifier (SDV) tool [2, 1]. SDV takes a developer's source code for a Windows driver, automatically builds (and iteratively refines) a formal model of the the driver, and uses this model to check whether the driver fails to satisfy around 90 safety properties. For each fault found, SDV reports a trace that violates the pertinent safety property. Since 85% of Windows XP crashes are caused by driver errors [11], tools like SDV potentially can make a considerable impact on Microsoft's core products. Prompted by successes such as SDV and by recent improvements in a range of tools and approaches, there is now an international grand challenge in verified software [5, 6]. Software verification is still very much a research topic, but one primed for growth over the next decade. We believe that as verification technology improves, some degree of verification will inevitably become a standard requirement in software contracts.

A key domain for SSME is sourcing agreements, wherein one company identifies support functions or business processes that it will contract another company to perform on its behalf. The stakes are high, with opportunities both for lucrative success and spectacular failure. Which functions or processes a company ought to outsource is a topic of much discussion [3, 9], but even more challenging is the task of implementing such arrangements. Can services be outsourced in a verifiable manner that instills justifiable confidence for all parties and assures objective standards of performance? We believe recent advances in software and system verification offer promising leads for rigorous research on this question.

A Start at a Plan

Below, we propose two key elements of a plan for academics to assist other professionals in crafting an SSME methodology.

First, small multi-disciplinary teams need to study SSME problems. Services, by their very nature cross boundaries between a wide range of organizations and individuals. Thus, fully understanding an SSME problem will involve principles, methods, and tools drawn from engineering, information studies, management, law, etc. The hard part will be in making sure that people on different sides of a boundary agree on what the problems are, what the solutions should be, and how to judge the success of the proposed solutions.

Second, the academics need hard data in the form of case studies. Case studies of projects completed, projects in process, and projects not attempted because they were deemed infeasible. Without this sort of data, academics cannot hope to understand the next level of useful detail on SSME.

As an example of what we mean here, we consider a published case study carried out by IBM's China Research Laboratory (CRL) in Beijing [13] to assess the strengths and weaknesses of a particular SSME methodology being developed by IBM: Model-Driven Business Transformation (MDBT). We first outline some of the key points of MDBT.

Model-Driven Business Transformation. The *model-driven* part of MDBT comes from the fact that both the business-process and IT components are organized around high-level formal-descriptions/models: a *business view* and an *IT view*. The business view gives a top-level description of the whole endeavor and is developed in concert by the client and consultants. The business view can fairly directly be translated into a Petri-net formalism which can be property checked standard concurrency-related properties. The IT view job is to lay out the bones of the IT components of the project. The IT view can be property checked and refined; can form the basis for a rough prototype, and can also be the basis for specifications for subcontractors. The *transformation* part of MDBT comes from the fact that the business view is semi-automatically translated into the IT view. During development, the business view will inevitability change. When it does, the transformational part also helps limit the damage to the work that has been done so-far in filling out the IT view.

The case study. The study [13] was a modern-day version of a classic office-automation project for Bank SinoPac, an international bank headquartered in Taiwan. The business view was pieced together from interviews of Bank SinoPac personnel and "debugged" to form a coherent business process. (The Petri-Net formalism turned out to be too weak to test for non-trivial conflicts in the business view [13].) There were seven major requirement changes after the Bank SinoPac signed-off on the original specifications. The transformational aspects of MDBT did their job of limiting the impact of these changes and aiding the customer and IBM to quickly workout the details and effects of these changes. The project came in on-time, on-budget, and with the costumer satisfied. They estimated that compared with conventional approaches to the problem, their approach was 30% more efficient.

What the study suggests. The study, while sparse on technical details, suggests many questions, each of which could be the basis of an interesting academic project. For example:

— What support is needed to develop and debug a new business process from scratch?

— The business-view model is more like a program than a specification. How can one co-develop a crisp statement of the problem that the final business view solves?

— How can issues such as access control, security, and compliance with statutes be worked into verifiable business views?[3]

— Can business-view to IT-view translation be automated? How can one check that the two views are consistent?

4 Judging Success

How can we check our final result? A methodology is not a mathematical construction nor proof, which were Polya's concerns. Neither is it expressed, typically, with the syntactical rigor of a computer programming language. If the objective is a verifiable methodology for decomposing and recomposing services, then academic research must, we believe, develop new tools to ascertain whether the objective has been met.

Indirectly, we could assess the methodology by measuring its outcomes, much as one would evaluate a manufacturing process or government program by measuring its products or observable results. Does the methodology generate services which in turn have customers who are satisfied, have high value, and are profitable [10]? These are customer-oriented measures of service quality and financial value. Taking a broader view, we suggest that indirect measures of a methodology's outcomes should encompass two perspectives and three dimensions. The two perspectives are those of customers (*Am I getting good service?*) and suppliers (*Is my organization delivering service effectively and efficiently?*). The three dimensions are intrinsic quality (*Is it good, correct, predictable?*), economic value (*Is it admirable, distinctive, profitable?*), and generative capacity (*Can I get the right amount, on time?*).

Indirect measures, although highly informative, merely say that the black box of methodology spits out something good. We believe it should be possible to do more—to check inside the box itself. A methodology should be amenable to formal specification, else it is not truly reliable and reproducible. We have in mind an engineered, mathematical model that goes beyond expressive diagrams of the sort commonly used to describe business processes. Like the "glue" that invisibly gives a spreadsheet its power, formal specification of a methodology will, ultimately, enable proof (or disproof) of a solution to the problem of service composition.

---

3   See [12] for an example of something along these lines.

References

[1] Thomas Ball, Ella Bounimova, Byron Cook, Vladimir Levin, Jakob Lichtenberg, Con McGarvey, Bohus Ondrusek, Sriram K. Rajamani, and Abdullah Ustuner, Thorough static analysis of device drivers, *Proceedings of the First EuroSys Conference*, 2006, in press.

[2] Thomas Ball and Sriram K. Rajamani, Automatically validating temporal safety properties of interfaces, *SPIN 2001: Workshop on Model Checking of Software*, Springer LNCS 2057, 2001, pp. 103–122.

[3] N.G. Carr, The end of corporate computing, *MIT Sloan Management Review 46* (2005), 66–73.

[4] Jeffrey Dean and Sanjay Ghemawat, MapReduce: Simplified data processing on large clusters, *6th Symposium on Operating Systems Design and Implementation*, 2005, pp. 137–150.

[5] Tony Hoare, Jajadev Misra, and M. Shankar, *The IFIP working conference on verified software: Theories, tools, experiments*, IFIP Conference Report, 2005, available as http://vstte.ethz.ch/report.html.

[6] Cliff Jones, Peter O'Hearn, and Jim Woodcock, Verified software: A grand challenge, *IEEE Computer* (2006), 93–95.

[7] G. Polya, *How to solve it, 2nd ed.*, Princeton University Press, 1957.

[8] Gerald Popek and Robert Goldberg, Formal requirements for virtualizable third generation architectures, *Communications of the ACM 17* (1974), 412–421.

[9] M.E. Porter, Strategy and the internet, *Harvard Business Review* (March 2001), 1–19.

[10] Roland T. Rust and Carol Miu, What academic research tells us about service, *Communications of the ACM 49* (2006), 49–54.

[11] M. M. Swift, B. N. Bershad, and H. M. Levy, Improving the reliability of commodity operating systems, *SOSP 03: Symposium on Operating System Principles*, 2003, pp. 207–222.

[12] Kaijun Tan, Jason Crampton, and Carl A. Gunter, The consistency of task-based authorization constraints in workflow systems, *Proceedings of 17th IEEE Computer Security Foundations Workshop*, 2004, pp. 155–171.

[13] J. Zhu, Z. Tian, T. Li, W. Sun, S. Ye, W. Ding, C. C. Wang, G. Wu, L. Weng, S. Huang, B. Liu, and D. Chou, Model-driven business process integration and management: A case study with the Bank SinoPac regional service platform, *IBM Journal of Research and Development 48* (2004), 646–669.

Models, Contexts, and Value Chains for Services Sciences

William B. Rouse
Tennenbaum Institute
Georgia Institute of Technology
Atlanta, GA 30332-0205 USA
www.ti.gatech.edu

ABSTRACT

This paper explores the nature of service phenomena, the processes underlying these phenomena, and how these processes create value. This exploration begins with an initial model of service processes and then progressively adds various contextual elements to elaborate the notion of a service value chain. This exploration provides the basis for an overarching hypothesis about services.

Introduction

The notion of Services Sciences, Management, and Engineering has many implications. Some are quite straightforward. For example, services management has received much attention for many years, e.g., [8]. The engineering of service systems also has been extensively addressed, for instance for supply chain services [1].

In contrast, there does not appear to be a common understanding of the sciences of services. On the one hand, there are studies of service systems by the behavioral and social sciences – e.g., economics, psychology, sociology, and anthropology. In these cases, services are the objects of study. Phenomena of interest include, for instance, customer satisfaction, server motivation, and the functioning of server teams.

On the other hand, one might expect services science to denote a unique branch of science along the lines of astrophysics or biochemistry. For this to be a reasonable view, there would need to be a rough consensus on the nature of the phenomena of interest, salient hypotheses regarding the underlying nature of these phenomena, and acceptable methods and tools for addressing these hypotheses.

To this end, this paper explores the nature of service phenomena, the processes underlying these phenomena, and how these processes create value. This exploration begins with an initial model of service processes and then progressively adds various contextual elements to elaborate the notion of a service value chain. This then provides a basis for contrasting products and services as a basis for suggesting an overarching hypothesis about services.

Initial Model

An initial model of the nature of service processes is shown in Figure 1. Customers, human or otherwise, queue for service processing. Service is good if there is a high probability of being satisfied (P), short time to wait and receive the service (W), and low cost of providing the service (C). In this model, services consume capacity which is represented as the time required to provide processing. There is no context in this model, just time spent waiting and being processed.

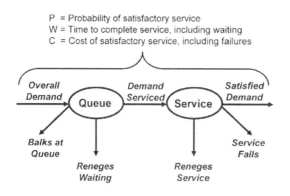

Figure 1. An Initial Model of Service Processes

The process in Figure 1 is optimized by determining the allocation of resources that value of P, W, and C that maximizes the value provided across stakeholders, e.g., customers and providers. Such optimization is a traditional operations research endeavor.

Service Context

Figure 2 summarizes a variety of types of services, in broad categories of service delivery and service management. This range of services is often enabled by products and systems such as buildings, equipment, and vehicles. These enablers are, in turn, enabled, by tools and materials. From the perspective of Figure 2, much of the economy is associated with services and the distinction between products and services becomes less meaningful. Vargo and Lusch [9] make a similar argument.

Considering the range of contexts in Figure 2, it is clear that the measures of P, W, and C may not capture key differences between, for example, trucking and health care. Additional service characteristics, say X, differ across domains. Further, we have to allow for nonlinear relationships between these characteristics and customer utility, i.e., more of something is not always better. Thus, our optimization criterion now becomes U = U (P, W, C, X). We also have to consider the differing utility functions of key stakeholders which leads to important tradeoffs across stakeholders.

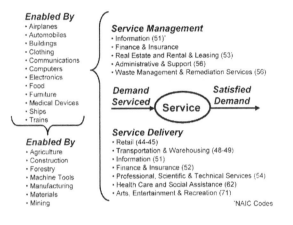

Figure 2. Types of Services and Enablers

Service Value Chain

Figure 3 addresses the question of value – the benefits customers receive when they purchase services, or products. While there may be exceptions, value is not synonymous within owning the rights to a product or a service transaction. Value relates to the benefits of these rights. Thus, people buy products and services but they want comfort, entertainment, nourishment, etc. [4]. Products and services are, for the most part, enablers rather than ends in themselves.

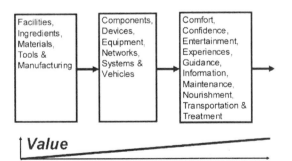

Figure 3. The Nature of Value – Enablers vs. Benefits

Value is shown as increasing along the value chain because the end value from business to consumer drives the overall value proposition. Wonderful composite materials may enable a highly fuel-efficient aircraft, but the success of these investments depends on passengers being willing to fly on the airplane. The marketplace determines which inventions become innovations, providing sustainable value to customers [5].

Business-To-Business

Figure 4 broadens our evolving model to consider services that enable products and services. Business-to-business (B-B) services represent a major portion of the service economy. In supporting other businesses' products and services, these B-B service providers enable B-C value. Examples range from facility management services, to customer service call centers, to strategy consulting for the executive team.

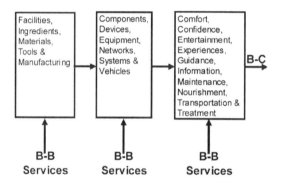

Figure 4. Business to Business Services Enable Business to Customer Value

Table 1 depicts a range of B-B services, ranging from strategy and design, to execution and operations [6]. There is a wealth of ways that B-B providers enable downstream B-C value creation, via service endeavors ranging from business process improvement to enterprise transformation [7]. This table reflects a wealth of business opportunities and activities. Virtually anything and everything can be outsourced [2]. Consequently, a company's only asset may its relationships with its customers. In this case, they own the B-C business and employ B-B services for everything else.

Table 1. Illustrative Business-to-Business Services

Enterprise Level	Strategy	Operations
Purpose	Vision of Enterprise Transformation	Assessment of Change Implications
Objectives	Goals, Strategies & High Level Plans	Financial Planning & Monitoring
Functions	Work & Workflow Process Design	Work & Workflow Process Support
Tasks	Job/Task Design & Assessment	Management of Task Performance
Activities	Outsourcing Planning & Design	Performance of Work Activities

An Example

The apparent linearity of this process can be dispelled by the simple example in Figure 5. The value stream of interest here culminates with a consumer accessing web-based health information. This is clearly a service transaction, perhaps enabled by advertising.

However, this consumer is using a software product, his or her browser. This product would be of no use (for the value transaction of interest) without additional products, namely other software products and information products. Yet, these two enabling products were enabled by other services for software development and research. These services, in turn, depended on computer and medical hardware that were created via engineering services that resided in facilities and employed equipment.

All of the above was pursued in an environment of maintenance, transportation, human resources, education, and so on. So, is the value delivered to the consumer best described as a service or a product? The answer, obviously, is not as simple as has often been articulated.

Figure 5. Services Enable Products & Products Enable Services

A related example is Porter and Teisberg's elaboration of the health care delivery value chain ([3], p. 204). Beyond this general framework, they also provide specific examples for chronic kidney disease (p. 403), stroke (p. 407), and breast cancer (p. 409). These value chains are laced with services enabled by information, products and other services. While the consumer receives a service – health care – the value chain is enabled by many things that we do not usually think of as services.

Conclusions

Value is maximized by optimizing P, W, C, and X relative to the expectations of customers and other stakeholders. Value is enhanced by tangible things that enable optimizing P, W, C, and X. Tangible things are, in turn, enabled by facilities, ingredients, materials, and so on.

Value chains are typically an amalgam of services and products enabling each other. The driving B-C value aspirations are typically enabled by a plethora of B-B services. Overall, the distinction between products and services becomes fuzzy. Ultimately, almost everything we used to think of as ends are now primarily means.

The foregoing discussion of models, contexts, and value chains, suggests an overarching hypothesis that services sciences should address. The hypothesis is as follows:

The nature and extent of B-C service value drives and determines B-B service value, as well as the value of products and other value enablers.

The pursuit of this hypothesis should be a primary element of the services sciences research agenda.

References

[1]   Belman, D., & White, C.C. (2005). *Trucking in the age of information*. New York: Alfred P. Sloan Foundation.
[2]   Friedman, T. (2005). *The world is flat: A brief history of the twenty-first century*. New York: Farrar, Straus and Giroux.
[3]   Porter, M.E., & Teisberg, E.O. (2006). *Redefining health care: Creating value-based competition on results*. Boston, MA: Harvard Business School Press.
[4]   Rouse, W.B. (1991). *Design for success: A human-centered approach to designing successful products and systems*. New York: Wiley.
[5]   Rouse, W.B. (1992). *Strategies for innovation: Creating successful products, systems, and organizations*. New York: Wiley.
[6]   Rouse, W.B. (2001). *Essential challenges of strategic management*. New York: Wiley.
[7]   Rouse, W.B. (Ed.).(2006). *Enterprise transformation: Understanding and enabling fundamental change*. New York: Wiley.
[8]   Schneider, B., & Bowen, D. E. (1995). *Winning the service game*. Boston: Harvard Business School Press.
[9]   Vargo, S.L., & Lusch, R.F. (2004). The four service marketing myths. *Journal of Service Research, 6* (4), 325-335.

Complexity and the Services Science Agenda

Yasmin Merali
Warwick Business School
The University of Warwick
Coventry CV4 7AL
UK
Yasmin.Merali@warwick.ac.uk
+44 (0)24 7652 2456

ABSTRACT

The services science agenda is essentially a trans-disciplinary one, borne of the network economy. Promises and expectations for technology to deliver flexibility, customisation and responsiveness of service provision within this context give rise to a number of challenges for the IT profession. However, profound challenges also exist with regard to the requisite capabilities for strategising, organising and managing the transformation of organisations so that they are able to effectively leverage emergent technological capabilities for viable, sustainable futures in the network economy. Delivering the Services Science value proposition rests on the co-evolution of requisite business intelligence, business transformation and technological capabilities.

This paper takes the view that the challenges and opportunities inherent in the dynamics of the network economy *are different in kind* from those that we have met in the past, and may necessitate a paradigm shift for researchers, practitioners and educators. It sets out the case for drawing on Complexity Science to conceptualise the research and human resource development agenda for addressing the challenges that confront us.

Introduction

The Internet has given rise to an increasingly inter-connected world. The dynamic of emerging (information and technological, social, organizational, economic and political) networks confronts institutions, societies, and nations with unprecedented complexity *and* new choices and challenges for modes of existence, organization, competition, collaboration and survival.

The increased connectivity and access to an increased variety and volume of information afforded by emerging technologies constitute greater informational complexity [8]. Increased global connectivity and speed of communication effectively contract the spatio-temporal separation of world events – informational changes in one locality can very quickly be transmitted globally, influencing social, political and economic decisions in geographically remote places.

Promises and expectations for technology to deliver flexibility, customisation and responsiveness of service provision within this context give rise to a number of challenges. The speed of change (in socio-economic contexts and in technological innovation) and the complexity of organisation and integration are implicated in the rise of these challenges.

Arguably the advent of the internet and related technologies has resulted in a profound change in

— the way that business and society *are* organised, and

— the *potential* that exists for organising differently.

The design, delivery and leveraging of service architectures that are responsive to changes in the socio-economic and business "context of use" for services entails working across traditional boundaries. The call for collaboration and intimate partnership relationships between service providers and their clients, between academics and practitioners, and between academics from different disciplines has been voiced from a number of different platforms. The realisation of such collaboration in practice is critical for accelerating the iterative cycles of theory development, testing and practical application that are necessary for realising the Services Science value proposition.

This paper takes the view that the challenges and opportunities inherent in the dynamics of the network economy are *different in kind* from those that we have met in the past, and that they necessitate a paradigm shift for researchers, practitioners and educators. It contends that Complexity Science offers the requisite conceptual foundation for supporting the development of a coherent framework to serve the conceptual and practical demands of the network economy.

The next sections present some thoughts on the features and direction that would be desirable in a collaborative Services Science research and human resource development agenda.

Features for a Research and Human Resource Development Agenda

In the managerial discourse [2, 4, 7, 17, 21, 22], the Internet-enabled world is associated with the emergence of the "information economy" (or "information society") characterised by increased complexity, dynamism, uncertainty and discontinuity in the competitive context. In academe and in practice the boundaries between technological, organisational and economic capabilities and disciplines are becoming less distinct. In the Services Science space, both, academic and pragmatic concerns are driving the quest for conceptual and practical frameworks and tools for trans-disciplinary, inter-organisational enterprise.

The Services Science community has the potential to orchestrate a coherent agenda for research and practice across the entire spectrum, ranging from trans-disciplinary, fundamental research on epistemological and ontological aspects, through to the implementation of service architectures that are responsive to changes in the socio-economic and business "context of use" in dynamic environments.

Intellectual Foundations and Methodology for Services Science as Situated in Complex Dynamic Socially Situated Systems

The importance of the Human Sciences in the Services Science space is prominent in the discourse around technology-enabled innovation. However there is a danger that in the current climate the importance of the "hard" sciences may be downplayed. It is thus important to define a robust intellectual framework to underpin the current and future development of Services Science as a coherent discipline addressing the social, economic and technological aspects of the Services Science value proposition.

Complexity Science [1, 10, 15, 17, 18, 19] is an important contender as the basis for the development of such a framework. Its concepts and modelling techniques [3, 6, 13, 16] have been used to characterise and explicate complex systems' behaviour across the Natural and Social Sciences, and to address phenomena (like adaptation, transformation, evolution, robustness) that are common across the disciplines, and that are salient features of the discourse on organisational dynamics in the Services Science space.

The Network Form of Organising

Network thinking offers a powerful device for dealing with both, the structure, and the dynamics of complex systems. The network form of organising and its manifestation in complex adaptive systems (CAS) embodying emergence and self-organisation are amongst the fundamental Complexity Science concepts that are useful in developing a conceptual infrastructure for the Services Science discipline [9, 14, 20].

At the most fundamental level the emerging technological developments that are implicated in Services Science have the potential to increase

— connectivity (between people, applications and devices)

— capacity for distributed storage and processing of data

— reach and range of information transmission

— rate (speed and volume) of information transmission.

The exploitation of these capabilities has given rise to the emergence of new network forms of organisation embodying complex, distributed network structures, with processes, information and expertise being shared across organisational and national boundaries. The challenge of achieving the requisite "fit" between the dynamism of the "use context" and IT-based delivery architecture and implementations is at the heart of many of the contemporary debates and discussions about Services Science.

The increase in the number of components to be integrated across diverse technological platforms and business systems demands complex architectures. Greater connectivity and access to an increased variety and volume of information constitute greater informational complexity [8], creating the need for more powerful semantic, algorithmic, and computational capabilities [19].

At a more profound level, the deployment of the technological capabilities has the potential to generate an increasing dependence on *representations* of reality and a decreasing capacity for experiential or *embodied* participation in interactions with the world. This has resulted in a shift

— from social networks [5, 11] to cyber-social networks

— from the social construction of the world to the informational construction of multiple worlds, and

— from consideration of issues of discontinuity in the world over a time line to consideration of discontinuity of contemporaneous parallel worlds [18].

This suggests the need to move from the traditional goal-oriented *alignment* perspectives of business and technological architectures to a new perspective that accommodates the *integration* of business, social, information and technological networks. The information network is both technologically and socially constructed and mediated, and it is the information network that is accessible as the meta-level representational device for the integrated network (note that "representation" here is used in the sense of semiotic representation rather than representation as a type, i.e. one member of a class of object that is representative of the class) [18].

The business level flexibility and agility that Services Science aspires to deliver is predicated on information networks and the exploitation of the network form of organising in the integrated complex, multi-dimensional network of networks outlined above.

Complexity Science provides the conceptual scaffolding for dealing with the inherent complexity and the dynamic nature of this emergent integrated network.

Concepts from Complexity Science: Complex Adaptive Systems, Emergence and Self-organisation

Systems thinking is at the heart of the Information Systems discipline, and the complexity of systems has traditionally been addressed using modularisation based on the top-down decomposition of the system into its constituting components and their inter-relationships. Complexity Science challenges the traditional bounded top-down approach of definition and introduces the concept of *emergence* of higher-level behaviours from the interactions of its components with each other and with the environment.

The network form of organising is the signature of complex systems. The concepts and tools of Complexity Science furnish us with useful abstractions for articulating the network phenomenology for the trans-disciplinary Services Science agenda.

The concept of Complex Adaptive Systems (CAS) incorporates the key characteristics that the management literature highlights for the viable organizational forms in the information economy: CAS are non-linear, open, dynamical systems that adapt and evolve in the process of interacting with their environments. They embody self-organisation and emergence[1] and have the potential (capacity) for adaptation and transformation.

For example, the characterisation of biological systems as CAS is often invoked both as a powerful metaphor, and an analogy, for organisations in dynamic contexts. Its potency derives from its articulation of concepts and mechanisms that can deliver the requisite balance between persistent form, and responsiveness and flexibility in dynamic contexts.

Biological systems typically comprise of large numbers of functional, and frequently multifunctional, sets of elements interacting selectively and nonlinearly to produce coherent rather than complex behaviours. This set of characteristics closely matches the characteristics that are of interest in the holistic evolution of Services Science, which IS characterised by multiple, diverse, interacting stakeholders and components, and where the notion of "the system" embraces the technological, social and organisational dimensions of the services *architecture-in-use* in the socio-economic context. Moreover, advances in molecular biology provide a very strong evidence base for understanding the relationship between network topology, complex network dynamics and emergent properties [12]. Biological networks may thus provide a useful analogy for the development of models for exploring the Services Science space with its echnological, social and economic dimensions.

For example, one feature that invites the engagement of organisational theorists and technologists alike, is the network topology and mechanism for maintaining the coher-

---

1 The interactions at lower levels of the system display self-organising behaviour (they evolve towards order rather than disorder), and the system is characterised by emergence (new properties appear at each level in the hierarchy). The interactions at lower levels of the system display self-organising behaviour (they evolve towards order rather than disorder), and the system is characterised by emergence (new properties appear at each level in the hierarchy). The self-organising networks are maintained by importing energy

ence of local and global behaviours and allowing robustness and flexibility in the face of environmental perturbations. A conceptually and pragmatically important challenge is that of determining and delivering *requisite* flexibility, control and diversity in complex *dynamic* contexts. The molecular biology models suggest that the mechanism for balancing plasticity with robustness is one that combines scale-free network topologies [4, 22] (with spatio-temporal variation in hub connectivity) with a mechanism of modularisation for dynamic co-ordination and control. These are exciting concepts for exploration with respect to dynamical distributed systems in the Services Science context, and the modelling tools of Complexity Science offer the means of carrying out such exploration through simulation

These examples merely serve to illustrate the utility of the CAS concept, and the potential for Services Science to tap into existing work in disciplines outside of those traditionally associated with computing. At the more general level, in the Services Science context, Complexity Science enables us to extend the current concern with structure and process to

— include a more focused treatment of the dynamics and mechanisms underpinning the changes of state in the context of use, and to

— design systems that are capable of anticipating and supporting the contingent requirements of the dynamic context of use.

Implications for Human Resource Development for Services Science
Recent debates amongst educators and practitioners have speculated on the makings of a suitable curriculum for the delivery of graduates for recruitment into the Services Science profession. Many of these discussions have resulted in a polarisation of

— those who believe that we should be developing generalists who have an understanding of business, IT, civil society, organisational change management and who have the requisite interpersonal skills to deal with IT and non-IT colleagues and clients, and

— those who believe we need to continue to develop specialists (in IT, Business, Human Sciences etc.) who have the capacity to learn "on the job" (and through mentoring, continuous development and training) how to interact with other professions and clients.

The pro-generalists fear that the specialist education will turn out graduates with mono-vision. The pro-specialists fear that the generalist education will sacrifice depth for breadth and turn out graduates who lack any profound understanding of any of the core disciplines that constitute services science.

With regard to the specialists *versus* generalists debate, the position of this paper is that we should continue to develop specialists BUT with the following caveats:

That the specialist programme of study

— equips the student to recognise the multi-dimensional character of real-world situations, and to appreciate the complementarity and relevance of expertise form diverse disciplines in addressing these situations,

— enables the student to understand and achieve the sense of mastery over a domain of study,

— equips the student with a robust foundation in the "home discipline" on which to continue to develop further education and training, and

— develops the student's capacity to be a self-propelled learner.

That the curriculum delivery entails the development of

— information skills –i.e. the ability to understand, interrogate and develop informational representations of real and virtual entities and relationships; recognise patterns in these representations,

— abstraction skills –i.e. be able to develop abstract concepts from specific instances of experiential and representational information,

— analytic, synthesising and articulation skills[2], and

— communication skills – both face-to-face and through the use of diverse media

These skills can be acquired in any discipline. The question is not one of what subject is taught, but of how it is taught.

This paper also advocates that Services Science educational agenda should be concerned not only with educating those that will be employed in the Services Science profession, but also with educating those who will be the "users" and clients of the capabilities offered through Services Science professionals and institutions. Educators have a role in the development and provision of programmes for continued education and life-long learning.

---

2   The importance of network thinking and the capacity to recognise and deal with requisite contingent complexity in the Services Science implies a paradigm shift, particularly for the disciplines that have traditionally dealt with complexity using purely reductive approaches sustained by heroic assumptions for simplification.

Conclusions

The Services Science community is confronted with challenges and opportunities inherent in the dynamics of the network economy that are *different in kind* from those of the past, and that necessitate a paradigm shift for researchers, practitioners and educators.

Progress in this area entails the development of robust theoretical foundations. The travail is a trans-disciplinary, trans-boundary one and necessitates collaboration and intimate partnership relationships between service providers and their clients, and between academics and practitioners and between academics from different disciplines. Practitioners are at the coal face, confronting and dealing with the challenges of the network economy. The practitioner-academic partnership is thus critical for accelerating the theory development-testing cycle for Services Science.

Complexity Science offers the requisite conceptual foundation for supporting the development of a coherent framework to support the conceptual and practical needs of Services Science in the network economy.

In particular the contribution of Complexity Science in explicating the network dynamics that underpin complex adaptive systems, and the power of its modelling techniques, are profoundly useful in developing the theoretical basis for Services Science.

With regard to human resources development the position of this paper is that we should continue to deliver specialist graduates, BUT with specific skills that will enable them to be

— effective conceptualisers of complex systems

— life-long learners

For sustainability, it is imperative that the Services Science educational agenda engages not only with educating those who will be employed in the Services Science profession, but also with educating the future "users" and clients of the capabilities offered through Services Science professionals and institutions.

References

[1] Anderson, P. (1999) "Complexity Theory and Organization Science", *Organization Studies, 10* (3), 216-232.
[2] Axelrod, R. and Cohen, M. (1999) *Harnessing Complexity: Organizational Implications of a Scientific Frontier*. Free Press, New York.
[3] Axtell, R, (2000) "Why Agents? On the Varied Motivations for Agent Computing in the Social Sciences." Center on Social and Economic Dynamics Working Paper No. 17, November 2000, The Brookings Institution, Washington.
[4] Barabasi, A. (2002) *Linked: The New Science of Networks*. Perseus Publishing, Massachusetts.
[5] Burt, R. S. (1992). *Structural holes: The social structure of competition*. Harvard University Press, Cambridge, MA.

[6]   Carley, K. (1995) "Computational and mathematical organization theory: Perspective and directions" *Comput. Math Organ Theory 1* (1) 39-56.
[7]   Castells, M. (1996) *The Rise of the Network Society*, Blackwell Publishers, Oxford.
[8]   Chaitin, G. (1990) *Information, Randomness, and Incompleteness*. World Scientific Co. Singapore.
[9]   Chesbrough (2005) Towards a new science of services. *Harvard Business Review*.
[10] Gell-Mann, M. (1994) *The Quark and the Jaguar*. Little, Brown and Company.
[11] Granovetter, M. (1985) "Economic action and social structure: the problem of embeddedness." *American Journal of Sociology, 91,* 481-510
[12] Han, J. et al (2004). "Evidence for dynamically organized modularity in the yeast protein–protein interaction network" *Nature, 430,* 88-93
[13] Holland, J. (1998) *Emergence: from chaos to order*. Oxford University Press, Oxford.
[14] Karmarkar, U. (2004). "Will you Survive the Services Revolution?", *Harvard Business Review*.
[15] Kauffman, S. (1993). *The Origins of Order: Self-Organization and Selection in Evolution*. Oxford University Press, New York.
[16] Lomi. A. and Larson, E. (eds.) (2001). *Dynamics of Organizations: Computational Modelling and Organizational Theories*. MIT Press, Menlo Park, California.
[17] Merali, Y. (2006) "Complexity and Information Systems: The Emergent Domain" *Journal of Information Technology Special Issue on Complexity and Information Systems, 21,* 216-228
[18] Merali Y. (2004). Complexity and information systems. In: Mingers J, Willcocks L, eds. *Social theory and philosophy of information systems*. London: Wiley; 2004. p. 407-446.
[19] Merali, Y. (2005). Complexity Science and Conceptualisation in the Internet Enabled World, *Proc. European Group of Social Studies Colloquium*, 2005.
[20] Rust, R. (2004). A call for a wider range of services research. *J. of Service Research*.
[21] Shapiro, C; and Varian, H. (1999). *Information Rules: A Strategic Guide to the Network Economy*. Harvard Business School Press.
[22] Watts, D.J. (2003). *Six Degrees: Small Worlds and the Groundbreaking Science of Networks*. Norton, New York.

Service Science, Management, Engineering and eOrganisations

Christof Weinhardt
Universität Karlsruhe (TH)
weinhardt@iism.uni-karlsruhe.de

Anupriya Ankolekar
Universität Karlsruhe (TH)
ankolekar@aifb.uni-karlsruhe.de

Rudi Studer
Universität Karlsruhe (TH)
studer@aifb.uni-karlsruhe.de

Nenad Stojanovic
FZI Research Center Information Technology
nstojano@fzi.de

Carsten Holtmann
FZI Research Center Information Technology
holtmann@fzi.de

Björn Schnizler
Universität Karlsruhe (TH)
schnizler@iism.uni-karlsruhe.de

ABSTRACT

Due to its long and rich background in product engineering, continental Europe and Germany especially can emerge as a strong force in service engineering. In particular, because much of the methods toolkit currently applied in service design and engineering builds upon traditional engineering methods. SSME only will be successful in the future if both areas are closely intertwined in interdisciplinary institutions, teams, and projects. In this paper, we present the institutions, projects and educational structures in place at our institution, KIT in Karlsruhe, Germany, for services research.

Services Science and Engineering

While the Anglo-Saxon countries are known for their well-developed services sector, continental Europe has traditionally focussed on designing and developing top-quality industrial products. However, there is reason to believe that Europe, especially Germany, can emerge as a strong force in the area of service engineering.

i.   Product engineering, and engineering in general, has always been a core research focus at most German universities. Since, a substantial number of existing (and future) services are and will continue to be closely related to physical products, service engineering for such kinds of services is a natural extension of product engineering.

ii. Interdisciplinary work and education, as required for service engineering, is well established in German universities and research institutions, as the technology region Karlsruhe successfully illustrates. They have also been successful at transferring research knowledge into the industrial engineering of physical products.

iii. Despite the relative emphasis on physical products, Germany already ranks second in global service quality [1]. Thus German industry is already able to deliver high quality products and services, in particular, because of the well-developed engineering culture in companies as well as at universities.

Here, we have focussed on Germany, but much of the above also holds for other European countries. As Germany is well-known for the quality of its products, other European countries are also leaders in various aspects of engineering. For example, France and Italy are well-known for their product design and Scandinavia for its work in product quality and security.

Due to its long and rich background in product engineering, continental Europe and Germany especially can emerge as a strong force in service engineering. In particular, because much of the methods toolkit currently applied in service design and engineering builds upon traditional engineering methods. SSME only will be successful in the future if both areas are closely intertwined in interdisciplinary institutions, teams, and projects. In this paper, we present the institutions, projects and educational structures in place at our institution, KIT in Karlsruhe, Germany, for services research.

Services Research In Karlsruhe

KIT (Karlsruhe Institute of Technology), one of Europe's largest research institutions is the result of the integration of the Universität Karlsruhe (TH) and the Forschungszentrum Karlsruhe (FZK), two well-known institutions combining world-class research in the area of engineering and international interdisciplinary cooperation. With 8.000 employees and a yearly turnover of about € 600 million, KIT competes with global research institutions. Research in KIT is focussed on natural and engineering sciences, as well as on interdisciplinary work with additional sciences, such as economics, sociology and law.

One of KIT's five major research areas is 'Information, Communication and Organisation' with the subfield 'Organisation and Services Engineering'. An important cadre for this research field is the scientific alliance 'eOrganisation', under whose auspices the new Karlsruhe 'Centre of eOrganisation and Service Sciences' is going to be established. A critical success factor for SSME – and simultaneously the core task for the multiple institutes involved – is understanding the nature and the embedding of services in innovative forms of organisations and networks.

In order to transfer goal-oriented fundamental research into practical application, know-how transfer between industry and research has to be accompanied by a mutual knowledge exchange process. Thus, requirements from industry have to be fed back into research, focussing on problems that are critical for improving the competitiveness of individuals and enterprises in society. Several institutions in Karlsruhe, are involved in transferring research and technology into industry, such as, e.g., the FZI Research Centre for Information Technology in the area of innovative information technology.

Services Science – Interdisciplinary Research

The vision of the scientific alliance eOrganisation is that eOrganisations will play a central role in the future of any area of society. eOrganisations are organisations, where tasks, competencies and/or responsibilities are (at least) partly delegated by human beings to technical units that perform their actions through electronic media. These units are a means to provide services for humans, but they themselves may consist of services coupled by possibly complex relationships. In order to realize eOrganisations, research on three closely related levels is required:

— the *service-driven applications* level (with corresponding knowledge of the domain and its economic models),

— the level of flexible, adaptive *services*, *components* and *models* (with high degrees of freedom with respect to their application possibilities), and

— the stable, highly-scalable, foundational level of the technical infrastructure and regulatory conditions – referred to as a *service substrate*.

The research vision is to drive services science by basic and applied research in and between all of these levels. This allows for enhanced and distributed service scenarios with autonomous, partly technical, units that share common targets but may also have potentially conflicting goals. The main concern is to enable eOrganisations to handle technical, economic and sociological challenges in spontaneous coordination and collaboration.

Related research in Karlsruhe is mainly based on a long experience in and a vast knowledge of the fields of coordination mechanisms, incentive engineering and semantic technologies, to name just a few of the technologies needed in the area. As a vivid and successful example for service engineering research, we present "computer aided market engineering", one field in Karlsruhe that exceptionally integrates those competencies [2].

Computer Aided Market Engineering

Deviating from a purely economic view, where markets are primarily conceived of as abstract mechanisms, we treat the existence of an electronic market as a result of a structured engineering process and the use of electronic markets as a complex service. The process of consciously designing markets as services, called "market engineering", is obviously an interdisciplinary challenge: it involves designing the market structure by providing methods and tools for all design steps, from initial economic and legal design ideas to technical implementation, testing and roll-out, as well as redesign during runtime. The integrated computer-aided market engineering (CAME) workbench, meet2trade, strives to automate and support these procedures, from the design of the market mechanism and complementary services, to the implementation[3, 4, 5].

CAME is a SSME approach and the meet2trade workbench showcases an integrated outcome of service sciences, management and engineering. CAME and meet2trade have already been applied in several well-recognized research projects:

i.   *EFIT* (Federal Ministry for Education and Research (BMBF), 2002-2006): development of a generic market workbench,

ii. *STOCCER* (BMBF, 2005-2007): international forecasting market for the soccer World Cup 2006,

iii. *SESAM* (BMBF, 2004-2007): design and development of distributed and spontaneous electricity markets, and

iv. *SORMA* (EU, 2006-2009): design and development of a platform for dynamic trading of ICT resources.[1]

Additional SSME Research in Karlsruhe

Service Ecosystem (SE): Services ecosystems, like ecosystems in nature, are networks of co-existing elements that depend on each other for survival. The dynamic changes in business environments require efficient approaches for service integration of multiple systems. Research on SE and enabling technologies has been performed in the scope of the project Digital Business Ecosystems (EU, 2003-2006) and will likely be continued in QUAERO (BMWI, 2007-2012).

Strategic Service Management/Planning (SSM): Our initiative sees SSM as an approach for acquisition, representation, analysis and validation of organizational strategic knowledge. SSM enables not only the vertical information integration needed for boosting innovations, but also a simplified interaction and automatic negotiation between business part-

---

1   See also http://www.iw.uni-karlsruhe.de/ DesktopDefault.aspx/tabID/38/lang/enbeen

ners. This research has been performed in the scope of the SAKE project (EU, 2006-2009) that aims to develop methods for the formalization of strategic knowledge.

Service Innovation (SI): SI is a multidisciplinary approach for managing the whole innovation cycle, from generating ideas to assessing them economically. It represents a lengthy, interactive and social process embedded in the legal, economic and social environment, QUAERO (BMWI, 2007-2012) will fund cooperative work in this area with additional German experts.

Change Management in Services (CM): CM stands for an integrated approach for discovering, implementing and propagating changes in complex systems. CM serves as a mechanism to close the loop in the usage of a service, i.e. to support its self-adaptivity. This research is performed mainly in the scope of the following projects: (i) OntoGov (EU, 2003-2006), aiming at developing methods and tools for managing changes in law and regulation, (ii) FIT (EU, 2006-2009), for developing methods and tools to customize existing eGovernment services to user preferences by learning from usage.

Educating Knowledge Workers

The Universität Karlsruhe (TH) in KIT offers several different study programs, which address a wide area of SSME-related topics.

The first pillar of the programs are the bachelor and master programs on 'Industrial Engineering and Management', 'Computer Science, and 'Information Engineering and Management'. Each of the programs has just received the top position in several university rankings once again. Within the programs, the strengths of the technical university come into play: the high experience in different kinds of engineering disciplines on a well-founded mathematical basis is combined with computer science, economics, and operational management. The courses on 'Industrial Engineering and Management' and 'Computer Science' integrate traditional engineering methodologies with economics, management and informatics. Complementary to this, the 'Information Engineering and Management' program focuses on an interdisciplinary view on computer science, economics, strategic and operational management, and law. The goal of this program is to organize the usage of information as an economic good and competition success factor. In particular, the program teaches students how to (i) analyze and manage internal information services in companies, (ii) establish and evaluate complex information systems, and (iii) facilitate efficient and effective user interaction with information services. The program's graduates qualify as service scientists and engineers.

To expand the existing programs towards a more holistic view on eOrganisation and service engineering, there will be two new industry-sponsored professorships. These professorships will be dedicated to research and teaching in these new fields. Furthermore, a new cross-faculty study program on 'Service Sciences and Engineering' has already been requested at the regional authority.[2]

To complement the bachelor and master programs, an international and interdisciplinary PhD program on 'Information Management and Market Engineering' is the second pillar of the SSME-related study program. This graduate school addresses topics from an interdisciplinary point-of-view, comprising computer science, law, operational research, economics, and business administration. The purpose of the school is to investigate interdisciplinary and problem-oriented approaches to all aspects of electronic markets and services, with special emphasis on the role and power of information.

Finally, the third pillar is the Hector School of Engineering and Management, an executive master program. The school provides technological, management, and leadership training, working closely with leading German companies. A closer cooperation with the executive master program at the Carnegie Mellon's Tepper School of Business in Pittsburgh is planned to strengthen the international study program on SSME-related topics.

In the Year 2020 ...

... our economies will have changed significantly. Currently novel phenomena will have made their way to everyday life. The amount and role of services – be they between humans, between human and technical units or only among technical units – will have increased tremendously. IT-based service design, provision, delivery, monitoring and improvement will be a necessity and SSME will have to cope with the methodological, technological and social challenges of this.

The success of SSME critically depends on how we can create and transfer new knowledge from science to industry and vice versa. And of course, although the ways we manage our knowledge will be different in the future, it will be crucial to educate people of all ages lifelong by applying new teaching and learning approaches.

Scientific institutions depend on the support of the industry: on the one hand, industry has to support the identification of business-critical problems; on the other hand, the industry will have to provide necessary technical infrastructures and financial support for research and education. Joining forces in research and knowledge exchange centers will be the way to cope with challenges while realizing synergies for all parties.

---

2   In Germany study programs have to be requested by the universities' president and approved by the responsible ministry. The program is now in permission phase.

Conclusions

SSME arises from the integration and interaction of the core disciplines of engineering, economics, management and cultural sciences, sociology, and law. Therefore, the future and success of SSME crucially depends on an integrated and interdisciplinary effort. Integrating different and complementary methodologies will enable us to further develop innovative solutions. New ways of designing and running businesses will shape the future. SSME will have to anticipate them to cope with the challenges of an IT-based services age.

KIT, the Karlsruhe Institute of Technology, has already set up organizational structures to address these challenges. Due to its solid foundation in engineering sciences, KIT, among many European institutions, is uniquely positioned to contribute to SSME.

References

[1]   IMPULS (2004): Interview with R. Berger and J. Weihen, Partner for Innovation, 12/2004, p. 9.
[2]   Ch. Weinhardt, D. Neumann, C. Holtmann (2006), "Computer-Aided Market Engineering – A Service Engineering Approach". *Communications of the ACM, 49/7*, p. 79.
[3]   B. Schnizler, D. Neumann, D. Veit, Ch. Weinhardt (2006), "Trading Grid Services - A Multi-attribute Combinatorial Approach". *European Journal of Operational Research*, forthcoming
[4]   S. Lamparter, A. Ankolekar, D. Oberle, R. Studer, Ch. Weinhardt (2006), A Policy Framework for Trading Configurable Goods and Services in Open Electronic Markets. *Proceedings of the 8th Int. Conference on Electronic Commerce (ICEC'06).* Fredericton, New Brunswick, Canada, August 2006.
[5]   S. Lamparter, A. Ankolekar, R. Studer, Ch. Weinhardt (2006), "Towards a Policy Framework for Open Electronic Markets". Thomas Dreier, Rudi Studer and Christof Weinhardt, *Information Management and Market Engineering, Volume 4 of Studies on eOrganisation and Market Engineering*, pp. 11-28. Karlsruhe, 2006.

Towards Customer Centric Physical and Virtual Environment – Platform for Services

Suvi Nenonen
Research Manager, PhD
Helsinki University of Technology
Construction Economics and Management
Tammasaarenkatu 3
Helsinki, Finland
suvi.nenonen@tkk.fi
+358 50 5985342

Jukka Puhto
Research Manager
Helsinki University of Technology
Construction Economics and Management
Tammasaarenkatu 3
Helsinki, Finland
jukka.puhto@tkk.fi
+358 50 5680031

ABSTRACT

The development of ICT facilitates the worldwide service industry. Society is changing from industrial structures to dynamic value networks, and this has an impact on the activities and structures of private and public sector organizations. Organizations have both virtual and physical action environments. The question is how these action environments and services can support the core business. The traditional way of organizing processes and facilities have changed. Service science is indeed needed. This paper describes how a multidisciplinary research group from the Helsinki University of Technology functions in order to face the challenges of service science.

Introduction

Information and communications technology (ICT) is a key driver in changing society and industry. ICT companies account for around ten percent of all businesses in Finland and for more than half of the country's research and development activities. Innovation and R&D have a huge meaning for companies in the information and communications sector. Finland has attained a pioneering position as a developer of ICT and is also a leading ICT applier. In telecommunications the fastest growth is in activities related to mobility and broadband, while basic telephony continues to diminish. The service provision sector, too, is expected to grow rapidly [1].

But there are two important issues to work further:

1. Firstly as Paul Horn says: " there's a shortage of skills at the intersection of business and IT. As companies build more efficient IT systems, streamline operations, and embrace the Internet through wholesales changes in business processes, a huge opportunity exists. Nonetheless, little or no focused efforts are preparing people for this new environment or to even to thoroughly understand it" [2].

2. Secondly ICT sector offers us a virtual environment. It should be approached hand in hand with the physical environment. Both these are the means for interaction [3].

These two cornerstones are essential for services science, which would merge technology with an understanding of business processes and organization, a combination of recognizing a company's pain points and the tools that can be applied to correct them. To thrive in this environment, an IT-services expert will need to understand how that capability can be delivered in an efficient and profitable way, how the services should be designed, and how to measure their effectiveness [2].

Physical And Virtual Work Environment – Platform Supported By Services

New work and business cultures, along with ICT-driven working methods, have become a fundamental development trend for increasing productivity and for making profitable business. The success of individuals and the work community is based on effective knowledge management and the long-term increase of professional expertise.

To improve Finland's competitiveness and productivity the Information Society Council suggests that developing work culture is chosen as the priority target. In this the focus areas are:

1. Work community's culture of working together;

2. Efficient utilization of ICT and know-how that influences productivity;

3. Work processes and process methods; and

4. Innovativeness, self-renewal and the capacity of organizations and their management to foresee.

The former challenges presented by Markkula can be supported both by virtual and physical work environments and services [4]. The Japanese philosopher Nishida has identified the Ba concept as a physical, spiritual and virtual meeting place. At the same time Nonaka has, with his colleagues, examined the meaning of the meeting place (Ba) and found that Ba enables the discovery, sharing, refining and reproduction of something new [5].

The Finnish researcher Katariina Raij [6, 7] has identified the orientations of knowledge as orientations of the specialist, processes, client and researcher. These together formed the original framework of a Well Life Center as a meeting place for welfare specialists, welfare production and development processes, welfare clients and welfare researchers as one example in practice [6, 7]. Nenonen has investigated different office solutions in the context of knowledge sharing processes [8]. Likewise, service solutions are important and Tuomela presents a model of Network Service Solutions in his dissertation [9].

FSR-Group

A service is a provider/client interaction that creates and captures value. The construction and real estate industry is on its way to apply more service orientation to its core business processes. Customer centric thinking is influencing little by little the operational, tactical and strategic levels in organisations, which traditionally have been building orientated instead of user focused.

It is a justified fact, that provider and client coordinate their work (co-production) and in the process, both create and capture value (transformation). Services typically require an assessment, during which provider and client come to understand one another's capabilities and goals. Such understanding poses a challenge in technically orientated businesses, even though its value is significant. The challenge is in modeling this– not only from one perspective but from multidisciplinary perspective.

Because the huge challenges in the field of customer-orientated real estate industry, a new research group "Facility Services Research (FSR)" was founded in the Laboratory of Construction Economics and Management (CEM) in Helsinki University of Technology at the beginning of the new millennium. It operates in close collaboration with the facility service industry as well as with other research units in Finland and abroad.

This research group specializes in the research of the customer orientated construction and facility service businesses within four focus areas:

1. Facility services management,

2. Construction management,

3. Life-cycle technologies and management, and

4. Workplace management.

Within these four focus areas, CEM Facility Services Research addresses three as important perceived dimensions: Procurement, Customer Relationship Management and Performance Measurement.

1. Procurement — In a long-lasting business relationship a contract works as the basis for co-operation. However, the target of procurement is not to make contracts but to achieve a satisfactory co-operation by using contracts. A contract works not only as a means of financial exchange but also as a tool in business process control, value production, risk management and communications.

2. Customer Relationship Management — Customer Relationship Management refers to the management of vertical business relationships between suppliers and customers. This area also includes other aspects of the relationship such as the networking of service providers to generate a more extensive service selection, or the feedback process for continuous improvement and customer driven product design.

3. Performance Measurement — Performance measurement research projects aim at developing state-of-the-art methods for measuring performance in both construction and real estate industries. The research service covers all major performance measurement needs during the life cycle of facilities.

The research group pursues the further development of the domestic construction and facility industry as well as the international competitiveness of the companies in this business sector.

As stated, facility services management is one of key research areas. Within this area our research focuses on service procurement, organizational buying behavior, inter-organizational relationships, performance management and service contracting.

In the construction management research area, the research interests cover the different phases of the construction process. The focus is on procurement and contracting, customer relationship and performance measurement. The construction process must become an integrated process to deliver quality, value for money and satisfaction for all participants. The process itself must be designed to achieve these goals.

The life cycle technologies and management research team focuses on the construction, real estate as well as the service industries. It studies the short and long term impacts of technical systems both in companies and more widely in society. The research introduces new scientific concepts and models and tests them in practice in co-operation with companies and other organizations. The research covers all major aspects of life cycle performance including the economic, environmental and social dimensions. The research team has long tradition both in developing life cycle assessment methods and design tools, as well as in presenting life cycle-based business models. During the last years there has also been a focus on the sustainability management of companies.

Workplace Management research and development focus on the connection between the work environment and an organization's performance. The focal areas are the physical, social, and virtual workplace, the productive use of the workplace for knowledge work, and the development of workplace management services in real estate businesses.

The research projects are constantly including industry partners to ensure that the results and solutions produced can be accepted by and are useful for all parties involved in service creation. Besides research CEM Facility Service Research is acting as forerunner in developing bachelor, master and postgraduate curriculums in educational institutions. The competencies for future professionals are developed from an academic perspective, but beyond that in close dialogue with company representatives.

Conclusions

The intention to develop service science grows from the changes, which the ICT development has brought with it. The success factor for service science lies in its multidisciplinary approach. The development of services as an industry and profession are essential for future development. New knowledge is created quickly when significant links and bridges are built over the traditional discipline borders. CEM Facilities Services Research Group is one institution in Finland working towards this direction. The starting point is the physical work environment but it ends up to questions around services and virtual environments. The national success in ICT industry in Finland is one driver towards the service science direction. But as important is the international network and knowledge sharing globally.

References

[1]   Nordgern, K. (2006). Large, Challenging Projects in Information and Communications Technology. In *ICT Cluster Finland: Review 2006*, p.20.

[2]   Horn, P. (2005). The New Discipline Of Services Science, *BusinessWeek Online*, January 21, 2005, http://www.businessweek.com/technology/content/jan2005/tc20050121_8020.htm, accessed 15.6.2006.

[3]   Fruchter, R., (2005). "Degrees of Engagement in Interactive Workspaces," *International Journal of AI & Society* No. 19, pp. 22-33.

[4]   Markkula, M. (2006) Super Productivity in Working Life. In *ICT Cluster Finland Review: 2006*. http://www.tieke.fi accessed 15.6.2006.

[5]   Nonaka I., Reinmoller P. & Sennoo, D. (2000) Integrated IT Systems to Capitalize on Market Knowledge. In G. von Krogh, I. Nonaka & T. Nishiguchi (Eds.) *Knowledge Creation: a Source of Value*, Macmillan Press.

[6]   Raij, K. (2000). *Toward a Profession: Clinical learning in a hospital environment as described by student nurses*, Helsinki University Department of Education. Research report 166. Academic dissertation.

[7]   Raij, K. (2003). Producing knowledge as a goal of the University of Applied Sciences, in: Kotila, H. (Ed.) *University of Applied Science Pedagogics*. Helsinki. Edita.

[8]   Nenonen, S. (2005). *The Nature of the Workplace for Knowledge Creation*. Turku Polytechnic. Research Reports 19. Turku.

[9]   Tuomela , A. (2005). *Network Service Organisation - Interaction in Workplace Networks*. Helsinki University of Technology Construction Economics and Management A Research Reports 4.

Constructing Service Machines—
Global Sourcing of Knowledge-Intensive Services

Professor Paul Lillrank
Helsinki University of Technology
P.O.Box 5500, 02015
TKK Finland
paul.lillrank@tkk.fi
+358 500 703 848

Olli Tolkki
Helsinki University of Technology
P.O.Box 5500, 02015
TKK Finland
olli.tolkki@tkk.fi
+358 400 339 195

ABSTRACT

Outsourcing highlights the need for explication and conceptualization of the relationship between the parties involved. Within the Service Sciences, Management and Engineering –framework service production systems can be studied as Service Machines. The machine –metaphor focuses research on the contractual constructions that link together various productive resources and capabilities and their evolution over contract generations. Essential attributes of the Service Machine are the tenacity of its incentive structure and the amount of friction created by transaction costs and administration.

This paper outlines a research project on the management of the sourcing of knowledge intensive services. The leading partner in the project will be Helsinki University of Technology, and the project will join together eight academic institutions in Finland, India, USA and Estonia.

Introduction

The focus of our study is sourcing of services and business processes. These are of various competence and complexity levels, ranging from routine (inbound voice help desks, payroll administration) to non-routine and knowledge intensive operations (teleradiology, equity analysis, network maintenance). The issues to be explored are:

— The mechanisms of post-selection contracting, i.e. the construction of contractual relations and their evolution through various stages.

— The service industry related drivers and inhibitors of sourcing, such as the impact of volume, the economics of repetition, and the contractual management of non-routine processes in open business systems.

— Development of business relationships in the context of on-, near-, and off-shore outsourcing.

The classical "make or buy" question, the trade-off between specialization benefits and transaction costs, defines the boundaries of a firm [1]. For the past few decades the answer has increasingly been "buy". Specialization benefits have been accentuated by product and process complexity, time criticality, and factor cost differences between regions [2, 3]. Simultaneously transaction costs have been alleviated by information and communication technology together with increasing competence in contracting. Consequently, sourcing expands from on-shore to off-shore, incorporates both products and services, and develops from subcontracting to partnerships. This leads to complex service production arrangements, which here are called "Service Machines".

Global sourcing, especially off-shore outsourcing, has created both anxiety and euphoria. Particularly the rise of India as a major supplier of business process outsourcing (BPO) has attracted attention [4]. However, the phenomenon itself has been little researched. There is an abundance of how-to manuals, but the academic literature is rather thin. Consequently, the terminology is confusing. Here the following definitions are used [5]:

— Sourcing = the strategic decisions about which resources an organization produces internally or acquires from outside, and how the outside relations are to be found, structured, and managed

— Purchasing = all activities that result in an invoice

— Procurement = the operational level formulation of contracts and the management of relevant logistic flows

— Outsourcing = transforming an existing operation or function to an outside producer

The scope of sourcing can vary from local to global. On-shore sourcing refers to activities within the same national economy; near-shore to the same economic region (e.g. the EU), and off-shore to more distant locations. Outsourcing is an organizational transformation process that includes steps, such as vendor selection, contracting, and the management of the business relationship [5, 6].

Objectives

1) Create modeling tools for contract systems and their evolution

Sourcing appears to follow a general economic logic similar to the development of the wealth of nations. The initial stage is based on low factor cost, typically off-shore labor arbitrage. As volumes and experience accumulates, focus shifts to quality and productivity enhancement, and ultimately to product and process innovations [7].

Indian BPOs are increasingly reengineering their customers' processes before start of operation. The next stage, which is already emerging, focuses on innovation. This includes co-evolution between customers and vendors. This kind of cooperation enables developments that neither party could have achieved independently. The co-evolution phase will likely imply an increasingly two-way traffic between partners, spill-over effects, and have a significant impact on the way customers run their business. In the long run it is crucially important for the outsourcing company to understand the logic and co-evolutionary development of the business to be able to control the relationship and maintain the competitive advantage it has gained by outsourcing.

The assumption is that rapid growth, deregulation, abundant resource supply, high volume, technical advances, and attractive business opportunities create self-reinforcing virtuous circles in India and therefore a platform from which the next generation of big management ideas will emerge. Sourcing has several spill-over effects to the Indian economy which may help the Indian companies to enter western markets.

The primary objective of this research will be to explore these patterns and mechanisms as well as their evolution, build models, and thereby improve the understanding and management of sourcing and its potential to both sides and their economic environments.

2) Explore the impact of volume, scope and nature of repetition on service system design

The Finnish service sector is proportionally smaller and to some extent underdeveloped compared within OECD [8]. The primary constraints are small size of market, low population density, long distances, and a large public service sector. On the other hand, many Finnish service providers have a high level of technology and a good brand value internationally. To overcome the constraints and benefit from the strengths, a deeper understanding of service business models is required. In this light, the question of volume is important. The Finnish market may be of suitable, even ideal size for managing, say, health care systems. However, following evolutionary theories of organizational development, it can be argued that service innovation will happen in high-volume high growth environments, simply because there are more combinations (mutants), tougher competition (natural selection), and strong incentives (survival of the fittest). In this light it is essential to build research and practice links to high-volume high growth business environments, and explore the scalability of various Service Machine designs [9].

3) Build working relations between Europe and India in academia and business.

India is one of the fastest growing economies of the world, with a huge potential and a growing impact on the world. In contrast to many other rapidly developing regions, India is already a rather stabile democracy and has a long business tradition. Further, through its strong links with the Anglo-Saxon world, many of the cultural, linguistic and intellectual barriers encountered elsewhere in Asia are less prominent in India. For these reasons this study is conducted in close cooperation with Indian partners.

Theoretical And Methodological Approaches

Service sourcing as bundles/networks/structures of contracts

This research draws on and contributes to the emerging field of Service Science, particularly Service Engineering. The approach can be illustrated with the following metaphor.

> *In services, the equivalent to a machine is a system of contracts. Various competences and resources are brought together through a set of defined, measurable, and legally enforceable contracts. The service system includes elements, such as revenue models, forecasts, costing, pricing, service level and volume-based adjusting mechanisms, quality metrics, scheduling, staffing, and human resources management. A schematic view of the service system of an Indian inbound voice call center is given in Figure 1.*

> *In services, the equivalent of machine tenacity is the incentive system. The incentives built in the metrics of the revenue model and compensation schemes should support both organizational and individual objectives. Poorly constructed incentive systems may lead to malfunction, sub-optimization, and breakdown of the system.*

> *In services, the equivalents of friction are the transaction and administrative costs.*

Consequently, the core task is to study the nature and evolution of contracts. In general, contracting can be assumed to evolve from crude capacity or transaction-based models towards more finely adjusted multi-factor models, as in Figure 1, and further towards outcome, incentive, mutual benefit and other models.

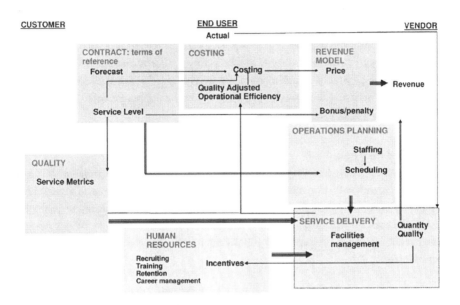

Figure 1. A schematic view of the business system of an Indian inbound voice call center

As sourcing applications move from routine, and thereby easily measurable business processes towards knowledge intensive business services (KIBS) including non-routine processes, risk-taking, and creative elements, the need for more sophisticated contractual arrangements is essential. The core issue thus is performance measurement.

The impact of volume in services

Benefits of service outsourcing have primarily been focused on factor costs, typically off-shore labor arbitrage. However, simultaneously with increasing factor costs in India and elsewhere, new and different benefits emerge.

In manufacturing it is generally known that volume has a significant impact on costs through the economics of scale and scope, and on efficiency through the learning curve. These effects depend on identical repetition, the ratio of fixed to variable costs, synergies, and the capability to learn. In services, these conditions are not always present. Therefore the effects of volume and the possibility of scalability are problematic, which is illustrated by the difficult debate on optimal unit size in health care.

The effects of volume, the nature of repetition, synergies between different offerings, and the learning curve therefore need to be carefully studied. This is of importance to Finland, since the domestic markets may, in some types of services, not support the volumes needed for service innovations.

Transaction costs and total cost of ownership

It is generally acknowledged that outsourcing carries significant transaction costs, including vendor selection, contracting, and monitoring [10]. These are accentuated in services, where the immaterial nature of output makes quality assurance and control problematic. The initial costs of establishing a relation are by and large unavoidable. However, the design of the contractual framework has an impact on the ongoing transaction costs, and therefore needs to be considered.

Culture and management

The impact of national cultures on management has been widely debated since the establishment of Japanese off-shore manufacturing plants in the 1980s. The rapid globalization of manufacturing has downplayed the importance of national management styles and cultural constraints. The effect of national cultures can, to an extent, be boiled down to differences in regulative environments and the nature of contractual relations, particularly labor markets.

Services, however, are typically more labor intensive than manufacturing. Therefore it can be assumed that services are more dependent on national cultures. Building on the culture and management debate, however, we assume that research should start from the business models and contractual arrangements, which eventually may have to be adjusted and amended with cultural considerations.

The Structure of Research

This research will include the following parts.

1. Descriptive and analytical research on the sourcing

2. Phenomena, classifications, conceptualizations, and modeling of the current state of outsourcing. This phase will be primarily desk research on the existing body of knowledge, detailed discussions with cooperating companies, interviews with selected players, and the application of relevant economic and administrative theory.

3. Explorative research on the emerging new relations and patterns. The core will be modeling of the evolution of contracting, including business models, revenue models, risk management, costing, and pricing. The interactions between contracting, operations management, quality management, and human resource management will be studied. Explanations for the evolution of contracting will be sought from various historical, economic, and social factors. Involvement from the corporate partners will be expected in finding appropriate case study locations.

4. Action research in evolving cooperative arrangements between Finnish and Indian players.

5. Parts 2 and 3 will be developed together with corporate partners in the following manner.

    a. Business Process Outsourcing (BPO), i.e. back-office operations of increasing complexity, in the realm of IBM's operations in New Delhi, India and Finland;

    b. Telecommunications service outsourcing, in the context of Nokia's service center in Chennai.

    c. Teleradiology in the context of planned Finnish-Indian venture in Kolkata, involving Suomen Terveystutkimus Oy and its owner (SITRA), and Indian partners.

6. A part of the field work in India will be outsourced to International Management Institute, a business school located in Delhi. The Finnish-Indian research team, together with corporate partners and cooperating universities, will arrange bi-annual workshops.

7. Reporting will be done in the form of dissertations, academic journal articles and a practitioner-oriented book. Research findings will be turned into practical consulting product in cooperation with Laatusuhde Suomi Oy.

Research Partners

The chief investigator will be Helsinki University of Technology (HUT), BIT Research Centre. The leading Indian partner will be International Management Institute (IMI) in Delhi. Professor Alok Chakrabarti, of New Jersey Institute of Technology, will be visiting faculty at these both institutions during the research.

Cooperating academic institutions in Finland will be University of Tampere, School of Business, Asian Management Academy (AMA) and Research Unit for Urban and Developmental Studies (Sente). Cooperating Indian institutions will be Indian Institute of Health Management Research (IIHMR), Jaipur and Indian Institute of Management (IIM), Kolkata. Other cooperating academic institutions will be The Technical University of Tallin (TTU) and Science, Management and Engineering (SSME) Center of Information Technology Research in the Interest of Society (CITRIS) of Berkeley (University of California)

Corporate partners will be IBM Finland, Nokia Networks, Suomen Terveystutkimus Oy and Laatusuhde Suomi Oy.

References

[1]   Williamson, Oliver E. *The Economic Institutions of Capitalism - Firms, Markets, Relational Contracting.* The Free Press, New York, 1985.

[2]   Birou, L. M., & Fawcett, S. E. (1993). International purchasing: Benefits, requirements, and challenges. *International Journal of Purchasing & Materials Management, 29*(2), 93.

[3]   Nellore, R., Chanaron, J. -., & Eric Soderquist, K. E. (2001). Lean supply and price-based global sourcing -the interconnection. *European Journal of Purchasing and Supply Management, 7*(2)101-110.

[4]   *The Economist* (2006), May 4th.

[5]   Trent, R. J., & Monczka, R. M. (2003). International purchasing and global sourcing —what are the differences? *Journal of Supply Chain Management: A Global Review of Purchasing & Supply, 39*(4), 26.

[6]   Trent, R. J., & Monczka, R. M. (2002). Pursuing competitive advantage through integrated global sourcing. *Academy of Management Executive, 16*(2).

[7]   Porter, M.E., (1990) *The Competitive Advantage of Nations.* The Free Press, New York.

[8]   *OECD Economic Surveys – Finland* (2004). OECD, Paris.

[9]   Nelson R.R. & Winter S.G. (1982) *Evolutionary Theory of Economic Change,* Harvard University Press

[10] Greaver M.F. (1999). *Strategic Outsourcing,* AMACOM, New York.

Service Engineering of Call Centers: Research, Teaching, and Practice

Sergey Zeltyn
Postdoctoral Fellow
Industrial Engineering and Management
Technion, Haifa, 32000, Israel
zeltyn@ie.technion.ac.il
(972) 4-8292333

Avishai Mandelbaum
Professor
Industrial Engineering and Management
Technion, Haifa, 32000, Israel
avim@tx.technion.ac.il
(972) 4-8294504

ABSTRACT

A course on Service Engineering has been taught at the Technion for over ten years [19]. Some unique aspects of the course are the incorporation of state-of-the-art research and real-world data in lectures, recitations and homework. Currently, the application focus of the course is telephone call centers, which constitute an explosively-growing branch of the service industry. Indeed, due to their practical importance and the diversity of their operational problems, call centers provide numerous challenges to Service Sciences, Engineering and Management.

In this contribution, we discuss significant research directions in the field of Service Engineering of Call Centers. The role of measurements and data collection at the individual-call level is emphasized. We describe software tools and databases that have been developed at the Technion in order to analyze operational performance of call centers and facilitate their statistical analysis. This prepares the ground for a survey of our "Service Engineering" course, with which we conclude.

Introduction

Service Engineering is a newly emerging scientific discipline [11, 17, 19, 20]. As we perceive it, it caters to operational service-challenges that arise in our postindustrial society. To this end, researchers in the area develop scientifically-based engineering principles and tools, often culminating in software, which support the design and management of service operations. Moreover, a multi-disciplinary approach is called for in order to balance service quality, efficiency and profitability from the likely conflicting perspectives of customers, service-providers, managers and society. In our research, and clearly biased by our scientific roots, we focus on methodologies from Operations Research and Statistics.

In this note, we are concerned with Call Centers. These are service organizations for customers who seek service via the phone. Due to advances in Information and Communication Technology, the number, size and scope of call centers, as well as the number of people who are employed there or use them as customers, grows explosively. Indeed, some estimate that, in the U.S. alone, the call center industry employs several million agents which, in fact, outnumbers agriculture.

The call center environment gives rise to numerous managerial challenges that differ in their nature and time-scale. For example, training and hiring problems should be solved on a yearly and/or monthly scale, staffing and scheduling is typically treated on a weekly/daily basis and Skill-Based Routing (SBR) decisions – matching of customers with telephone agents - should be exercised in real time. In the first part of this note, we discuss some central research directions, active and desirable, that can help to address these challenges.

In the second part, we describe a course on Service Engineering that has been taught at the Faculty of Industrial Engineering and Management, Technion, Israel. This is a compulsory course that is attended by over 120 students per year. Its goal is to provide students with knowledge and skills necessary for their future professional activities, accounting for the fact that they are likely to be employed in service enterprises that constitute the major part of the modern economy. Our experience has been that call centers provide an excellent motivational and training field for service-engineering methods; and that call-center real data, blended into lectures and homework assignments, perfectly complements active learning of these methods. There exists a publicly available Internet site of our "Service Engineering" course [19], and its materials have been used for research and teaching worldwide, both in academia and industry.

Operational Models in Call Centers: Research Survey and Practical Challenges

We focus on operational applications of Service Engineering methods in call centers. We do not discuss strategic problems, such as the development of new services or long-term workforce management. The reader is referred to [7] for a comprehensive survey of the state of research on telephone call centers.

Data Collection - a Prerequisite for Scientific Research

We strongly believe that systematic measurements and data collection are prerequisites for the analysis and management of any service system. In addition, detailed transaction-based measurements provide information that is inaccessible via aggregated (e.g. interval-based) summaries. Call centers are no exception.

Specifically, large call centers generate vast amounts of data. A detailed history of each call that enters the system can, in theory, be reconstructed via the Automatic Call Distributor (ACD) and Interactive Voice Response Units (IVR). However, call centers have not typically stored or analyzed this data, using instead the ACD reports that summarize performance over certain time intervals (say, 30 minutes). We advocate the change of this approach and emphasize the practical and research advantages of call-by-call data analysis. In [4] we applied our approach in a comprehensive analysis of a small Israeli call center and continuing research on larger call centers is currently underway.

DATA-MOCCA - database of call-by-call measurements

Call center data is processed by vendor-specific programs, in formats that are not amenable to operational analysis. DATA-MOCCA (DATA MOdel for Call Center Analysis) [21] has been developed to address these shortcoming. It is a universal model for call center data that, together with a graphical user interface, enables real-time statistical analysis at second-to-month resolutions. Currently, DATA-MOCCA covers call-by-call data of two large call centers, a U.S. bank and an Israeli cellular-phone company, over periods of 2-3 years each. (For example, the U.S. bank data has close to 120 million calls, out of which about 40 million were served by agents and the rest by a VRU – Voice Response Unit.) The raw data for DATA-MOCCA is dumped by commercial routing and call recording systems. Transforming it into our universal format takes a significant data-cleaning effort. This effort has been partially funded by the IBM Academic Fellows program, with the ultimate goal being the creation of a data-repository that is publicly accessible via the Internet, and which draws data from industries such as Financial, Telecommunication, Healthcare, Hospitality, etc. Till then, researchers and practitioners can ask the author (AM) for the data and its accompanying software.

Forecasting Arrival Rate

The standard model of call arrivals to a call center has been the time-inhomogeneous Poisson process, which accommodates both predictable and stochastic demand variability. Statistical analysis [4, 7] shows that this model provides a very good approximation to reality. However, prediction of future arrival rates, being a crucial first step for staffing decisions, turns out to be a complicated statistical task.

Two research directions are important in this regard. First, *time series* prediction techniques should be enhanced. Different methods could be appropriate for predictions that are performed weeks-ahead, days-ahead or hours-ahead. In addition, a specific call center often has unique features for its call arrivals (e.g. monthly bills sent by a cellular-phone company imply surges of incoming calls following billing cycles). Taking these features into account would significantly improve prediction accuracy.

Second, in certain circumstances one should accept the fact that there exist significant uncertainty and temporal correlation in the arrival-rates themselves. Appropriately, models with *random correlated arrival rates* must be employed, in contrast to the classical queueing models where the arrival rate is assumed known (deterministic).

Service Time: Definition and Modeling

The service time in call centers is typically defined as the time that an agent spends handling a call. It must include the talk time between an agent and a customer, as well as times on hold, after-call work, etc. If λ denotes the arrival rate per time-unit and E[S] is the mean service time, their product R=$\lambda\cdot$ E[S] is called the *offered load*. It is the basic quantity needed for staffing decisions, as discussed below. (λ is assumed here constant for simplicity; later we address time-varying rates.) The most widely used parametric model of service times is the *exponential* distribution. However, the *lognormal* distribution seems to provide an excellent fit for the call centers that we have analyzed recently [1]. Since models with exponential service times are much more tractable analytically than their alternatives, and since even seconds of service durations could have significant economic impact, the effect of the service distribution on performance of queueing systems should be carefully studied (see [23]).

Impatience and Abandonment

Until recently, most call centers used the classical M/M/n queueing model, also called *Erlang-C*, in their staffing. Erlang-C assumes Poisson arrivals at a constant rate λ, exponentially distributed service times with a rate μ, and n independent statistically-identical agents. However, Erlang-C does not acknowledge customers' abandonment and consequently can depict a distorted picture of a call center's operation [8, 15]. For example, even a minor abandonment rate in a heavily-loaded system can improve waiting times of those who do not abandon by orders of magnitude. This improved operational performance must be traded off against customers' frustration and lost business due to abandonment. Nowadays, an increasing number of call centers incorporate customers' abandonment in their staffing/scheduling software and performance goals.

The Erlang-A (Palm) Model

The theoretically simplest and practically most feasible way to account for customers' impatience is the following: in addition to the Erlang-C assumptions described above, suppose that each arriving caller is equipped with an exponentially distributed patience time. Customers abandon when their required waiting exceeds their patience. This model, first introduced by Palm [18], will be denoted by M/M/n+M and referred to as Erlang-A (A for Abandonment). See [15] for a recent summary and [6] for software that enables calculations and staffing according to Erlang-A.

Operational Regimes

A central challenge in the design and management of a service operation in general, and of a call center in particular, is to achieve a desired balance between *operational efficiency* and *service quality*. Here we consider the staffing aspects of this problem, namely having the right number of agents in place. "The right number" means, first of all, not too many, thus avoiding overstaffing. This is a crucial consideration since personnel costs typically constitute about 70% of the costs of running a call center. "The right number", however, also means not too few, thus avoiding understaffing and consequent costs associated with poor service quality. We now present two approaches to the staffing problem, both within the framework of Erlang-A.

Quality and Efficiency Driven (QED) Regime

This operational regime is governed by the so-called *Square Root Staffing Rule*:

$$n \approx R + \beta \sqrt{R}, \qquad -\infty < \beta < \infty;$$

where $R = \lambda \cdot E[S]$ is the offered load defined above and β is a Quality-of-Service (QoS) parameter. This rule was first used by Erlang (at the Copenhagen Telephone Company) close to 100 years ago. However, a formal QED analysis for various queueing systems appeared much later. The pioneering work is [9] that analyzed Erlang-C (β then must be positive); Erlang-A was considered in [8].

It turns out that if the number of servers n is not small, QED staffing enables high levels of *both* Efficiency (utilization of agents, say, around 90-95%) and service Quality (say, 50% of the customers are served immediately upon calling, average wait is 5-10 seconds, and abandonment rates are 1-3%). The QED regime arises also as economically optimal when minimizing the sum of staffing costs and waiting costs [3].

Efficiency-Driven (ED) Regime

Another common operational regime is characterized via the staffing rule $n \approx R - \gamma R$, *(0<γ<1)*. In this case, virtually all customers are delayed prior to being served and, approximately, the fraction abandoning is γ. The ED regime is to be used if efficiency concerns dominate those of service quality; for example, this is common practice in not-for-profit environments.

Stationary vs. Time-Dependency

A standard approach to staffing decisions in call centers is to break the day of work into short time-intervals (usually 15 or 30 minutes), assume that the Poisson arrival rate is constant over these intervals and apply stationary queueing models (e.g. Erlang-A) in order to determine how many servers are needed during each interval. Although this approach seems adequate for many call centers, it cannot capture the performance of highly time-varying systems. In the latter case, one should resort to models with time-dependent arrival rates. See [5] for an adaptation of the square-root staffing rule to time-varying arrival rates.

Staff Scheduling and Agents Assignment

As mentioned, staffing problems are typically solved by using steady-state models over short time intervals, separately. In practice, however, individual service agents are typically assigned to shifts (say, 8 hours including breaks) where the duration and location of breaks is constrained by trade-union agreements. This setting gives rise to two separate problems. First, one should determine the timing of shifts and the number of agents working during each shift, while satisfying also the staffing requirements considered above. This problem is typically solved by Integer Programming. Second, individual agents must be assigned to shifts. Here the complexity of the problem renders it analytically intractable and, hence, one resorts to heuristic techniques. (One could also attempt "shift bidding", where the employees themselves state their preferences and are then assigned to shifts according to their ranking, taking into account priorities – for example seniority – and systems constraints.)

Skills-Based Routing (SBR)

SBR technology enables the differentiation of many types of customers/calls and many skills of agents. Segmenting customers is a marketing task, while agent segmentation is human-resource-management. The need for type-skill matching suggests new types of operational challenges. For example, at the real-time level, one should manage the so-called agent selection and call selection problems, choosing to which free agent should an arriving call be routed, if any, and which waiting call should be attended by an agent who becomes idle, if any. In addition, multi type/skill environments significantly complicate the staffing and scheduling problems discussed above. SBR in the ED regime is relatively tractable [2, 13]. However, QED SBR is the subject of intense research [1]. Readers are referred to [7] and [22] for more details.

Human Behavior

One of the most challenging aspects in the modeling of call centers is the incorporation of human factors, for both customers and agents. This opens up a vast agenda for multi-disciplinary research, involving psychology, marketing, operations research and statistics. Below we present two relevant examples from our studies on call centers.

Short Service Times

Figure 1 shows the empirical distribution of service times in a call center of an Israeli bank during July, 1999. We observe a peak of very short service times: more than 7% of the calls were shorter than 10 seconds. These short calls were due to certain agents who were taking "rest breaks" by hanging up on customers. At the end of October, the problem was discovered and corrected. Figure 2 reflects the data of December, 1999: no peak is observed and, moreover, the lognormal distribution provides an excellent approximation to the empirical data.

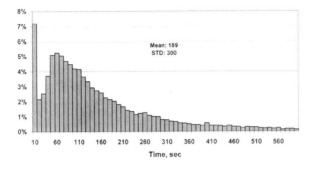

Figure 1. Histogram of service times in an Israeli call center, July 1999.

The problem of agents "abandoning" their calls can arise when short service durations (or many calls per shift) are a prime performance objective. The problem becomes immediately apparent from a histogram in Figure 1, based on call-by-call data. However, it can be hardly discovered through the prevalent standard of reporting only half-hour averages.

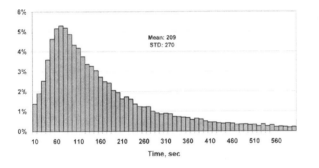

Figure 2. Histogram of service times in an Israeli call center, December 1999.

Psychology of Customer's Impatience

Figure 3 presents empirical hazard rates of patience times for Regular and Priority customers in an Israeli call center. The value of the hazard rate at time t is proportional to the likelihood to abandon during a short time interval after t seconds of wait, given that the customer already waited t seconds. (See [7] for detailed explanations.)

Figure 3 provides one with two important observations. First, priority customers turn out to be more patient than regular customers. This could be the reflection of a more urgent need on the part of priority customers; or could be an evidence of their higher level of trust that they will be served soon after arrival. Second, both functions have peaks of abandonment around 10-15 and 60 seconds, which turns out to reflect two announcements to customers: upon joining the queue and for those who have waited one minute, respectively. The announcements inform customers on their relative position in the tele-queue. This phenomenon gives rise to important questions. Do, in fact, announcements encourage abandonment, which could be in contrast to their original goal? Do they, on the other hand, provide customers with an opportunity to take a rational decision concerning abandonment which could decrease frustration and, probably, overall abandonment? (In principle, announcements could imply larger immediate abandonment but smaller abandonment during the periods between announcements.)

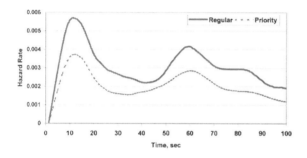

Figure 3. Empirical hazard rates of patience time in an Israeli call center.

Integration of theoretical, field and laboratory studies is needed in order to answer these questions, as well as many similar ones. See [16] for an example of a psychological study that is based on laboratory experiments.

Operational Models and Customer Relationship (Revenue) Management (CRM)

CRM automatic systems promise to enable companies to better track and understand the service experience of their customers, and then analyze its effect on the long-term relationship with the company (e.g. purchasing behavior, amenability to cross-selling). The interaction of our operational models with CRM could, hopefully, manifest itself in the ability to answer questions such as: "How a change in the service process (e.g. adding an agent for answering calls) affects company revenues?"

The "Service Engineering" Course at the Technion

Many of the issues discussed above are taught, or at least addressed, at the Technion's "Service Engineering" (ServEng) course [19]. The course has been taught for over ten years at the Faculty of Industrial Engineering and Management (IE&M). It started as a seminar for graduate students and has gradually developed into the present undergraduate compulsory course, taught almost each semester and attended by over 120 students yearly.

Its site [19] contains course materials (lecture notes/slides, recitations, homework), related research papers, slides of seminars, software and databases.

Teaching Goals

Although the service industry generates more than 70% of the GNP of many developed countries, prior to ServEng IE&M students had been exposed mainly to methods and techniques inspired by manufacturing applications. (This situation is likely to prevail among IE departments.) ServEng aims at filling this gap by providing students with appropriate models and tools for design, operation and analysis of service systems. Examples from various service sectors are presented at lectures and recitations, with the call center industry being the central application area.

Course Syllabus

The course has four general parts: 1. *Prerequisites*: measurements and models; 2. *Building Blocks*: demand, services, (im)patience; 3. *Models*: deterministic (Fluid) and stochastic - mainly queueing models, both conventional (Markovian) and approximations; 4. *Applications*: design, ED/QD/QED workforce-management and skills-based routing. The course's teaching philosophy was inspired by the book by Hall [10], which serves as a recommended textbook.

Measurements, at the level of individual service transactions, are prerequisites for design, analysis and management of service systems. After a ServEng Introduction, we survey transactional measurement systems in face-to-face, telephone, internet and transportation systems. These measurements immediately give rise to deterministic (fluid/flow) models of a service station, which capture average behavior and enables relatively simply yet far-reaching analysis – for example, capacity (bottleneck) analysis. Then we proceed with an introduction to Modeling, using Dynamic Stochastic PERT models as a modeling framework that captures operational congestion, due to resource constraints and synchronization gaps.

The next segment is dedicated to three building blocks of a basic service-model. First we study *service demand*, emphasizing the importance of reliable forecasting techniques. (For example, arrivals of incoming calls to a call center are typically Poisson or Poisson-related.) Then we analyze the *service process*, describing models for service durations. (For example, service durations in call centers "are" log-normally distributed [4].) We end with *customers' impatience* and its manifestation – the abandonment phenomena, which is important in call centers and other services (e.g. Internet and even Emergency Rooms).

The building blocks are now fused into basic queueing models where customers are i.i.d. and servers are i.i.d. A central role is played by Markovian Queues, emphasizing the applicability of the Erlang-A queue [15]. Then we discuss design principles (pooling to exploit economies of scale) and present operational workforce management techniques (staffing and scheduling), including staffing in the QED and ED operational regimes. We conclude the course with models that acknowledge customers differentiation (priorities) and servers heterogeneity/skills (SBR). An optional last lecture surveys queueing networks as models of multi-stage service systems.

Data-Based Teaching

ServEng students are trained with real-data and software. Early generations of the course used one-month tellers' data from a bank in Israel [14], in support of recitations and homework. Later, we added one-year call center data from another small bank [4]. The tellers' data has been since used in recitations while the telephone data in homework. DATA-MOCCA [21] currently serves in examples, lecture presentations and few homework assignments. As mentioned, we are in the process of making DATA-MOCCA publicly accessible and, then, we shall be able to incorporate it much more actively in the course.

The main software tool that students use is 4CallCenters [6]. This package, based on [8], allows them to solve staffing problems, using various queueing techniques that are inspired by call centers but are applicable more broadly (for example, to nurse staffing).

Our Service Engineering course is an ongoing R&D process. We already mentioned the incorporation of DATA-MOCCA. We are also planning to enrich near-future versions of the course with examples and techniques from health care and hospital operations management.

Conclusion

In this contribution, we surveyed possible applications of SSME in call centers and described the Technion's Service Engineering course. We believe that only such integration of data-based research, teaching and practice can provide the service industry with the necessary engineering tools as well as qualified specialists that are capable and trained to apply these tools.

We emphasize the need for multi-disciplinary approach to the Service Engineering problems [7, 12]. For example, in order to understand and exploit the phenomenon of customers' abandonment in call centers, as described above, one should use Statistics and Operations Research to measure and model impatience, Psychology to understand and interpret customers' behavior, and Marketing to assess the economical impact of abandonment. We hope that such cooperation between academic and industry researchers, from various branches of science, will provide solutions to the numerous challenges that arise in the Service Industry.

References

[1] Atar R. (2005) A diffusion model of scheduling control in queueing system with many servers. *Annals of Applied Probability*, 15(1B), 820-852.

[2] Bassamboo A., Harrison J.M. and Zeevi A. (2006) Design and control of a large call center: Asymptotic analysis of an LP-based method. *Operations Research, 54*, 419-435.

[3] Borst S., Mandelbaum A., and Reiman M. (2004). Dimensioning large call centers. *Operations Research, 52*(1), 17-34.

[4] Brown L.D., Gans N., Mandelbaum A., Sakov A., Shen H., Zeltyn S. and Zhao L. (2002). Statistical analysis of a telephone call center: A queueing science perspective. *Journal of the American Statistical Association (JASA), 100*(469), 36-50.

[5] Feldman Z., Mandelbaum A., Massey W. and Whitt W. (2005) Staffing of time-varying queues to achieve time-stable performance. Submitted to Management Science. Available at http://iew3.technion. ac.il/serveng/References/references.

[6] 4CallCenters Software (2005). Available at http://iew3.technion.ac.il/serveng/4CallCenters/Downloads. htm.

[7] Gans N., Koole G. and Mandelbaum A. (2003). Telephone call centers: a tutorial and literature review. Invited review paper, *Manufacturing and Service Operations Management, 5*(2), 79-141.

[8] Garnett O., Mandelbaum A. and Reiman M. (2002). Designing a telephone call-center with impatient customers. *Manufacturing and Service Operations Management, 4*, 208-227.

[9] Halfin S. and Whitt W. (1981). Heavy-traffic limits for queues with many exponential servers. *Operations Research, 29*, 567-588.

[10] Hall R.W. (1991) *Queueing Methods for Services and Manufacturing,* Prentice-Hall.

[11] IBM Research site. Service Sciences, Management and Engineering, http://www.research.ibm.com/ssme/

[12] Mandelbaum A. (2006). Call Centers. Research Bibliography with Abstracts. Version 7. Available at http://iew3.technion.ac.il/serveng/References/references.

[13] Mandelbaum A. and Stolyar A. (2004) Scheduling flexible servers with convex delay costs: Heavy-traffic optimality of the generalized cμ-rule. *Operations Research, 52*(6), 836-855.

[14] Mandelbaum A. and Zeltyn S. (1998) Estimating characteristics of queueing networks using transactional data. *Queueing Systems: Theory and Applications (QUESTA), 29*, 75-127.

[15] Mandelbaum A. and Zeltyn S. (2005) Service engineering in action: the Palm/Erlang-A queue, with applications to call centers. Invited chapter to IAO book project. Available at http://iew3.technion.ac.il/ serveng/References/references.

[16] Munichor N. and Rafaeli A. (2006) Numbers or apologies? Customer reactions to tele-waiting time fillers. To appear in the *Journal of Applied Psychology*. Available at http://iew3.technion.ac.il/Home/Users/ anatr/JAP-Tele-wait-FINAL.pdf.

[17] National Science Foundation. Service Enterprise Engineering (SEE) program. Available at http://nsf.gov/ funding/pgm_summ.jsp?pims_id=13343&org=NSF&more=Y.

[18] Palm C. (1957). Research on telephone traffic carried by full availability groups. *Tele*, Vol. 1, 107 pp.

[19] "Service Engineering" course website, Technion, http://iew3.technion.ac.il/serveng.

[20] Service research at the Fraunhofer Institute for Industrial Engineering. Available at http://www.management.iao.fhg.de/English/Overview.pdf.

[21] Trofimov V., Feigin P., Mandelbaum A. and Ishay E. (2005) DATA-MOCCA: Data Model for Call Center Analysis. Technical Report, Technion. Available at http://iew3.technion.ac.il/serveng/References/ references.

[22] Wallace R.B. and Whitt W. (2005) A staffing algorithm for call centers with skill-based routing. *Manufacturing and Service Operation Management, 7*, 276-294.

[23] Whitt W. (2005). Engineering solution of a basic call-center model. *Management Science, 51*(2), 221-235.

Innovation in Services: From Service Concepts to Service Experiences

Brian Fynes
University College Dublin
Ireland
Brian.fynes@ucd.ie
+ 353 1 7168841

Ann Marie Lally
University College Dublin
Ireland
amlally@wit.ie

ABSTRACT

Identifying the nature of service experiences is recognised as being of primary importance in the shaping of an enhanced competitive position for industry; however service managers often have difficulty articulating the true nature of their service concept. The definition of service concept is a fundamental part of the strategic advantage seeking processes of service design, service development and service innovation. In response to the competitive imperative for improved product/service development, this paper will develop a conceptual model of the components of service experience and the process by which the service concept can be articulated.

Introduction

The term New Product Development originated in the manufacturing sector but has more recently come to represent any improvement or alteration to product or service attributes and so is often used interchangeably in discussing service development. Booz, Allen & Hamilton [2] and Lovelock [11] categorised product and service developments as encompassing a myriad of activities from major innovations and new to the world products to lesser magnitude changes in style and repositioning activities. The process of produce/service development has been dealt with by a number of eminent service operations researchers and a number of models have been developed which map the sequence of activities from the setting of strategic objectives, through idea/concept development, service design, development, testing and implementation. A common component of most all of these models is the stage of service concept development. Menor, Tatikoda & Sampson [13] identify that new product development researchers have defined 2 macro-stages within the overall product development process; the fuzzy front end and the execution orientated back end. Khurana & Rosenthal [10] define the "fuzzy front-end" of the process as the portion of the development effort that consists of the activities involved in determining what service concept should be developed, this includes activities such as strategic positioning, idea generation and concept development /refinement. The definition of service concept is a fundamental part of the strategic advantage seeking processes of service design, service development and service innovation; however many practitioners have difficulty articulating the true nature of their service concept. In response to the competitive imperative for improved service innovation, this paper will seek to clarify the components of service concepts and the make clear the process by which the service concepts can be articulated.

The Service Concept

Identifying the nature of service experiences is recognised as being of primary importance in the shaping of an enhanced competitive position for industry; however service managers often have difficulty articulating the true nature of their service concept [6]. The definition of service concept is a fundamental part of the strategic advantage seeking processes of service design, service development and service innovation [16].

As services are driven to become more experiential and therefore increasingly intangible, the articulation of service concept invariably becomes more difficult but also more necessary [1]. Definitions of service concept are of value to service managers in understanding what a service concept should be, but many do not go far enough in assisting practitioners in the arduous task of actually defining their individual service concept.

In reviewing the existing definitions of service concept, a number of core themes emerged from the varied definitions. The concept of value is at the centre of a number of service concept definitions and the service concept is seen by many as a means for the service provider to identify the value being delivered to customers and the value expected by customers from the organization. The term value is commonly used in association with monetary worth, however Ziethaml and Bitner [17] define value is a individualized customer perception based on a composite judgements of a number of product/service attributes such as perceived quality, perceived costs; monetary or personal and other high level abstractions, intrinsic and extrinsic attributes such as prestige, accessibility and performance.

The service concept has also commonly been defined in terms of the service package; Collier [5] coins the phrase "Customer Benefit Package" whereas Goldstein et al [7] see it as the mix of physical and non-physical components that combine to create the service. Marketing theorists [12, 17] have sought to identify the sub-components of the service package using the numerous P-models which encompasses the elements of the service product – product, process, place, physical evidence, people, productivity plus additional marketing elements of price and promotion.

The need to incorporate customer requirements into the definition of service concept is directly identified by Khurana & Rosenthal [10] and Goldstein et. al. [7]. The need to articulate how customer needs are to be satisfied is dealt with through the inclusion of the service process [12] and the form and functions of the service operation [9, 4]. The need to balance the attainment of a holistic picture of the service with the desire to break the service concept into components for operational ease of articulation remains a fundamental area of discourse. Practitioners that focus too heavily on the development of a mental picture often have difficulty in translating their picture into operational deliverables whereas those that concentrate too heavily on the sub-components often fail to develop a unifying picture of the whole. Given that many practitioners have difficulty articulating the true nature of their service concept the author postulates that breaking the service concept into its constituent components would encourage practitioners to partake in what is commonly seen as a difficult and fuzzy process [10] and although there remains a risk that a holistic picture may not be developed, this risk is lower in magnitude to the scenario where service practitioners fail to develop of a service concept due to the perceived difficulty of the process. In Figure 1, we propose a conceptual model of the components of a service concept based on the common themes identified in the review of existing service concept literature.

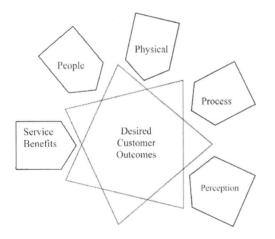

Figure 1 Conceptual Model of Service Concept Components

From Service Concept To Experience Concept

Experiences create added value by engaging and connecting with customers in a personal and memorable way [6] and progress the economic value of the organisations' market proposition via increased differentiation and premium pricing opportunities. Carbone & Haeckel [3] define experiences as the aggregate and cumulative customer perception created during the process of learning about, acquiring and using a product or service. Other key characteristics of experiences that emerge from the literature are that experiences require active participation by the consumer [14], involve the acquisition of knowledge and sensations [8], and create emotional connections that are revealed over time rather than merely at the moment of delivery [15].

Efforts to deliver experiential components to customers must be incorporated into service design deliberately [14] and from the outset. The incorporation of experiential components into service design would therefore require the development of service experience concept. Since experiences are a progression from services, an experience concept would include the core service elements, proposed in Figure 1, but would also require some additional experience-specific components. A proposed model for a service experience concept is outlined in Figure 2.

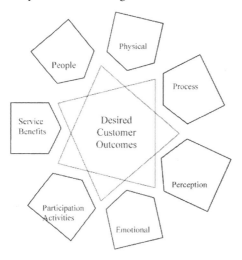

Figure 2 Conceptual Model of Service Experience Concept Components

Process of Concept Articulation

Methodologies for service development borrow heavily from manufacturing orientated product development strategies and although there exist considerable differences in the attributes of product and services, the methodological approach advocated is broadly similar. A proposed model of the stages of concept articulation outlined above are represented in Figure 3.

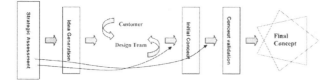

Figure 3 : Stages of Service Experience Concept Development

Conclusion and Future Research

The literature on service development along with industry reports stressing the importance of improved service experience design, give credence to the need for the improved articulation of a service experience concept as part of the service development process. This paper has sought to integrate and build upon prior contributions in order to propose a preliminary model of the components of a service experience concept and offers a methodological framework for service experience articulation. It is envisaged that the proposed models will be tested with a number of service providers.

References

[1]   Bitran, G. & Pedrosa, L. (1998). "A structured Product Development Perspective for Service Operations", *European Management Journal*, Vol. 16 No. 2 pp. 169-89.

[2]   Booz, Allen and Hamilton (1982). *New Product Management for the 1980's*. Booz, Hamilton and Allen; New York: NY.

[3]   Carbone, L. P., & Haeckel, S. H., (1994). "Engineering Customer Experiences" *Marketing Management*, Vol. 3 Issue 3, pp. 8 – 19.

[4]   Clark, G., Johnston, R., and Shulver, M., (2000). "Exploiting the service Concept for Service design and Development" in Fitzsimmons, J. A. & Fitzsimmons M. J., (Eds.), *New Service Development: Creating Memorable Experiences*, Sage: Thousand Oaks, pp. 71 – 91.

[5]   Collier, D. A., (1994). *The Service/Quality Solution: Using Service Management to gain Competitive Advantage*, Irwin, New York: NY.

[6]   Fitzsimmons, J. A. & Fitzsimmons M. J., (2004). *Service Management: Operations, Strategy and Information Technology*, McGraw-Hill: London.

[7]   Goldstein, S. M., Johnston, R., Duffy, J. & Rao, J., (2002). "The Service Concept: The missing Link in Service Design Research" *Journal of Operations Management*, Vol. 20 pp. 121-34.

[8]   Gupta, S. and Vajic, M., (2000). "The Contextual and Dialectical Nature of Experiences" in Fitzsimmons, J. A. & Fitzsimmons M. J., (Eds.), *New Service Development: Creating Memorable Experiences*, Sage: Thousand Oaks CA, pp. 33 –51.

[9]   Johnston, R. & Clark, G., (2001). *Service Operations Management*, Prentice Hall: England

[10]   Khurana, A. & Rosenthal, S. R. (1997). "Integrating the Fuzzy Front End of New Product Development" *Sloan Management Review*, Vol. 38 (2) winter.

[11]   Lovelock, C. H. (1984) "Developing and implementing new Services" in George, W.R. and Marshall, C. E. (eds.), *Developing New Services*, American Marketing Association, Chicago:IL pp 44-64.

[12]   Lovelock, C.H. & Wright, L., (1999). *Principles of Service Management and Marketing*, Prentice Hall, Englewood Cliffs: NJ.

[13]   Menor, L. J., Tatikoda, M. V., & Sampson, S. E., (2002). "New service Development: Areas for exploitation and exploration" *Journal of Operations Management*, Vol. 20, pp. 135-57.

[14]   Pine, J. B. II, & Gilmore, J. H., (1998). "Welcome to the Experience Economy", *Harvard Business Review*, July- August, pp. 97 – 105.

[15]   Pullman, M. E., & Gross, M. A., (2003). "Welcome to your experience: Where you can check out anytime you'd like, but you can never leave" *Journal of Business and Management*, Vol. 9 No. 3, pp. 215 – 232.

[16]   Stuart, F. I., & Tax, S. (1997). Towards an Integrative approach to designing service experiences; lessons learned from the theatre, *Journal of Operations Management*, Vol. 22 pp 609 – 627.

[17]   Ziethaml, V. and Bitner, M. J., (1996). *Services Marketing*, McGraw Hill, New York: NY.

Service Beyond—Enabling Technologies to Boost Service Business

Pentti Vähä, Anne Tolman
VTT Technical Research Centre of Finland
P.O. Box 1100
90571 Oulu, Finland
Phone +358 20 722 111

Paula Savioja, Piritta Lampila, Sonja Kangas
VTT Technical Research Centre of Finland
P.O. Box 1000
02044 VTT, Finland
Phone +358 20 722 111

ABSTRACT

A major trend currently shaping the field and profoundly influencing the practices of services marketing is the information technology (ICT). It is also radically changing how services are delivered by enabling both customers and employees to get and provide better, more efficient customized services. Therefore, it is highly important to recognise generic service concepts valid across business area boundaries and which utilise state-of-the-art ICT technologies. For emphasising innovativeness and business potential beside the technology, VTT launched a five years *Service Beyond* theme programme in 2005. In this paper we introduce this approach with some examples from the selected focus areas.

Introduction

Transfer from manufacturing community towards service oriented one is going on, and today services represent about 70 percent of Finnish GDP and work places. Main growth of employment and economy is expected to come from services. In addition to growth and revenues services can bring savings in different business sectors; e.g. health care, maintenance, construction. Traditionally, service encounters were viewed as person-to-person interactions. Technology is also being deployed to enhance the performance of the front line employee in interacting with the customer and it is also allowing introduction of entirely new service innovations. Thus far, VTT's main focus has been on the development and application of technology, but nowadays also technology based business and innovation research are emphasised. Hence, for boosting the service business, VTT launched a five years *Service Beyond* theme programme in 2005. The programme was suggested and strongly supported by the industry.

Based on VTT's competencies and know-how the focus areas for the theme programme were defined to be 1) Services for citizens - Wellbeing and quality of life, 2) Industrial services - Enhanced human technology interaction for mobile workers and 3) Services for living - Living in buildings. Reasoning for services for citizens focus area is the health care costs being over 10 billion € a year. Although ICT expenditure is rather low, 1-2 percent of total health care, its yearly growth is expected to accelerate. Health care is also facing challenges and is forced to look for new solutions for improving operations in order to offer better services to citizens. It is also the biggest service sector in the world. In the industrial sector, machinery and equipment manufacturing industry accounts for close to 60 billion € and 10 percent of the national assets. Regarding to industrial services usage of ICT among mobile workers is emerging; still paper documents are widely used. Usability of today's terminals is defective, natural way to interact is not supported and multi channel features not exploited. Potential savings can be gained with the aid of improved communication and updated information. In the living sector, facilities and building sector account for about 400 billion € and 70 percent of the national assets. Facilities management services is one of the fastest growing service sectors having 17 billion € turnover with about 200 000 employers. According to statistics, turnover growth in service business speeded up to 7.8 percent on the last quarter being in average 6.4 percent in 2005 without trade [6].

Conceptual Foundation

Major trend currently shaping the field, changing services deliveries and profoundly influencing the practices of services marketing is the ICT. In the product centric industry this has lead to enlarging the offering from products towards services. The change process from goods-dominant firms is prevalent when shifting their position on the good-service continuum [4]. It is quite obvious that ICT is essentially used in the service sector. Tertiary production activities are therefore unquestionably among those witch use information processing tools the most [3].

In addition to the ICT there are also other important issues related to service delivery. According to Neu and Brown [4] the organizational performance depends on the proper alignment among three sets of variables: environment, strategy, and factors of organization design. Strategy must align with factors of organization design, and both sets of internal factors must be designed to fit conditions in the external environment. In addition, successful service development depends on the degree to which existing organizational resources provide sources of competitive advantage in the new product market. Furthermore, they [4] contend that, given market conditions, technology can and should play an instrumental role in establishing a competitive advantage.

Our viewpoint in developing ICT based services is in finding and elaborating concepts having business potential. Focus is on modelling and innovation of service concepts and implementation of service systems with enabling ICT. VTT's trump card is strong competence in technology and know-how in several application domains. Therefore, we emphasised formulation of end user requirements in collaboration with industry. Service solutions shall be based on standard, open and interoperable components and interfaces, and development of generic ICT-based solutions applicable to wide range of business areas is important. We also adopted a flexible and agile method in the development of services. Flexibility means a mechanism for sensing the market for getting feedback from the customers to capture customer needs and alternative technical solutions as the project progresses and to integrate that knowledge into the evolving product design. The idea is to use internal staff and partners in cooperation to provide the test bed [2]. Agility means ability to rethink and innovate and to adapt quickly to changing circumstances. There is an increasing demand from industry to get rapidly from idea to products although requirements at start of project are vague and technology develops rapidly. Services offered to mobile Internet users must respond to consumer needs and be introduced into the marketplace ahead of the competition.

Case Studies

Three case studies from the three application areas are shortly described.

Exergame (exercise + game) project focuses on the growing demand for digital wellness products and interactive, playful ways to provide health related information. The scientific aim of the project is to accumulate a general view of playful wellness services internationally by studying innovative ways to give positive feedback and motivate people to take care of their wellbeing as well as create playful, inspiring solutions to support this challenge. Therefore, both qualitative as well as quantitative methods were utilized. We created future scenarios (2010) with the support of a steering group consisting of wellness and game software developers, wrist top manufacturers and leading sport associations. Also use cases of exergames focusing on mobile or wireless sportive games combining gaming with physical exercise were created. The four elaborated scenarios were analyzed in a consumer study (N=1489) in January 2006 focusing on four age groups: 13-18, 19-30, 31-65 and 66-76 year olds. According to this study, half of the young people participating in the survey had tried sportive games (51%), and every tenth of them had a game at home (9%). Adults have tried sportive games less than young people (21%). The attitude towards sportive gaming is positively neutral. Of the participants in the survey, young people were more interested in sportive games than adults. Although it is often felt that playing computer games reduces physical exercise among young people, the study did not establish any connection between physical exercise and playing games.

Based on the consumer study two exergame concepts called 'Figuremeter' and 'Fitness Adventure' were selected for implementations. The idea in this case study is to use internal staff and cooperation partners as well as to apply agility in the development of these concepts.

Plamos –project (Plant Model Services for Mobile Process Engineer from Industrial services) aims at developing new work tools and tool concepts for "mobile maintenance workers". With mobile workers we mean people who work for a service company and carry out the maintenance work at a client's facility. The facility might be e.g. a paper mill, a power plant, or a large building with heating, plumbing and air-conditioning –systems. The objective is to identify the user needs for work tools within such a novel work practice. The need rises from the current trends in industrial maintenance and process operation: the production processes are becoming more and more complex and at the same time lesser personnel is expected to maintain and operate the production. In addition maintenance is usually outsourced. This might lead into a situation in which the maintenance workers are not as familiar with the production process and equipment they are taking care of as they used to be. Hence we need more information about the work of mobile maintenance personnel in order to understand the user needs that have merged in the new business situation.

Top-down and bottom-up methods were used. The overall framework used was core-task analysis developed at VTT to analyse complex work [5]. Core-task analysis aims at identifying the core-task of a particular activity i.e. the objectives of the activity and the functions that have to be fulfilled. Top-down approach to core-task analysis was carried out in an industrial support forum where participants were experts in the field of maintenance work. The work aimed at identifying the various, often conflicting objectives of maintenance activity. In addition the means to reach the objectives were identified along with the different stakeholders related to maintenance. As a bottom-up method 14 maintenance workers were interviewed. The interviews were semi structured thematic interviews. The themes and part of the questions had been predefined. The themes were constructed with the aid of activity system model of Engeström [1]. The model of activity system connects the object of work, the objectives of the activity, and the work tools in a way which aids in eliciting the user needs for new technology.

As a result of the end-user study the research group came up with a tool concept in which many kinds of information is combined and presented in one device. The information that is needed in maintenance work is broad in scope. It varies from dynamic process information (e.g. parameter values) to information on spare parts and maintenance procedures. Currently all this information is available in different plant systems, but for the mobile workers it is essential that they can have access to all the information independent of their physical location. Thus the information must be combined to be usable.

In Facma –project (Mobile Facility management services from Services for living.) a market study was carried out among the companies involved in services for facilities management (FM) sector either as service providers or clients. The consensus result among the companies was that the companies recognize their need for upgrading their activities (either as service providers or clients), but feel the development of mobile supporting systems as outsider to their core business and even more outside of their capabilities. Currently the enabling technology for upgrading the FM related services is in relatively mature stage, but the value chains lack the business intelligence for sharing even the identified benefits. Furthermore many benefits remain unidentified. The professional aspects are at demand, domestic applications are currently of lesser interest but have very high future potential. The reason for optimism is the new generations which are more accustomed for mobility in services and are becoming a market force. Another driver for home based services is the growing portion of elderly in need of personal care and housekeeping services to promote independent living [7].

An example of an identified mobile FM service is an electronic key-lock service with market analysis for access rights control to various premises. In this concept the physical keys are replaced with phones having JAVA enabled secure chip covers and a server for customer data base management. When entering the room, the RFID reader checks access rights to the room at a given time instant and give opening commands to the electric lock. Authentication of the user is done by using secret keys. Updates of user profiles (expiry date/ access rights) can be done over the air. Such electronic key-lock services can be used for instance to allow customized access to exhibitions, performances, sport halls etc. Further applications may be created within many types of professional services such as maintenance personnel access.

Conclusions

Our aim has been to conceive and introduce new service concepts from the three focus areas by taking the advantage of the latest ICT in service delivery. In elaborating concepts we have done market research, invited customers to our workshops or done interviews with persons involved in services, either those who offer or those who deliver services. In workshops we were able to initiate the discussion by demonstrating some service ideas with the aid of the latest ICT. As a result of workshops and end-user study we have been able to come up with a preliminary service concept elaborated by small test groups. Two playful concepts based on market research focusing on playful ways to provide health related information are under development in Exergame. Plamos resulted in a tool concept where many kinds of information is combined and presented in one device needed in maintenance work. Facma identified mobile FM service for access rights control to various premises by replacing physical keys with phones. These preliminary concepts are further developed incrementally together with end-users.

References

[1]   Engeström, Y. Activity theory and individual and social transformation. In Y. Engeström & R. Miettinen & R.-L. Punamäki (Eds.), *Perspectives in Activity Theory* (pp. 19-38). Cambridge: Cambridge University Press.

[2]   Iansiti, M., MacCormic, A. Developing products on internet time. *Harvard Business Review*, September – October 1997, pp. 108 – 117.

[3]   Meyronin, B. ICT: the creation of value and differentiation in services. *Managing Service Quality*, Volume 14, No. 2/3, 2004, pp. 216 – 225.

[4]   Neu, W. A., Brown, S. W. Forming Successful Business-to-Business service in Goods-Dominant Firms. *Journal of Service Research*, Volume 8, No. 1, August 2005. pp. 3-17.

[5]   Norros, L. *Acting under uncertainty. The core-task analysis in ecological study of work*. VTT Publications, ISBN 951-38-6410-3; 951-38-6411-1

[6]   Statistics Finland, Statistic releases, March 16, 2005, www.tilastokeskus.fi/

[7]   Tolman, A., Möttönen, V., Tulla, K. Mobility in Facility Services. *Proc. of Changing user demands on buildings, needs for life cycle planning and management*. Edited by Haugen, T. I., Moum, A., Bröchner, J. Trondheim international symposium CIB W70, June 12-14, 2006. Norwegian University of Science and Technology. Trondheim June 1996. ISBN 82-7551-031-7. pp 559 – 56.

Bringing Service Design to Service Sciences, Management and Engineering

Stefan Holmlid
Human-Centered Systems
IDA Linköpings universitet
581 83 Linköping
Sweden
steho@ida.liu.se

Shelley Evenson
Carnegie Mellon University
School of Design MMC 110
Pittsburgh, Pennsylvania 15232
evenson@cmu.edu

ABSTRACT

Service design is defined as applying design methods and principles to the design of services. Service design is complimentary to conventional service development approaches and as such should become a contributor to Services Sciences, Management and Engineering (SSME). Two examples of the unique contribution of methods that Service Design offers are described.

Introduction

Service design is often described as the outside-in perspective on service development [14]. More precisely, service design is concerned with systematically applying design methods and principles to the design of services. Just as Industrial Management and Engineering depends on Industrial Design, the service industry needs to develop, integrate and appropriate design as a central competence.

What is Service design?

Service design is often described as the outside-in perspective on service development [14]. More precisely, service design is concerned with systematically applying design methodology and principles to the design of services. Service design as a field has a history almost as old as Interaction Design [7, 15, 14]. It began in earnest in the 90's and was positioned relative to industrial design. Service design from our perspective assumes the customer/user as the starting point or lens into a specific service and through the use of creative, human-centered and user-participatory methods models how the service can be performed. At the same time, service design integrates the possibilities and means to perform a service with the desired qualities, within the economic and strategic intent of an organization. Thus, in service design, collaborators "visualize, express and choreograph what other people can't see, envisage solutions that do not yet exist, observe and interpret needs and behaviors and transform them into possible service futures, and express and evaluate, in the language of experiences, the quality of design" [18].

As a discipline it should not be viewed in isolation, but as complementary to service development, management, operations and marketing [6, 14, 5].

Service design activities appear throughout a service development process (see e.g. [5, 9, 17]). In our approach to designing for service innovation we integrate these activities across a service development process that includes exploratory, generative, and evaluative research that spans the entire design process—from discovery to release [8]. The process differs from conventional approaches (see [2, 3, 11, 22]) in that instead of starting by defining strategy—we start with exploratory or immersive research to lead to opportunities for innovation in strategy. Another difference is that, service design as a design discipline (see e.g., [14, 16]), is not singularly focused on designing processes—though process analysis is one dimension of our approach to designing for service. Service design contributes to service development in areas such as user orientation, contextualization, and design as a strategic instrument [5, 12, 20, 4, 10].

The human-centered approach to designing for service innovation draws on a variety of methods and ultimately depicts through enactment and prototyping how the service can be performed, and with what qualities [18]. Service design in this sense, aims to create services that are useful, usable, desirable, efficient and effective.

Bringing Design to Service

In the text that follows we describe two high-level categories of methods that can contribute to the advancement of SSME and drawn from our experience in service design and innovation.

Human-centered methods

In other design traditions, such as architecture, and interaction design, human-centered methodology has been a central part of research and practice since the 1980's (see e.g. [10]). Our approach to service design builds on this practice as we strive to involve customers in all stages of the design process.

A human-centered approach begins with the person; with her goals, what she does, what she wants to achieve, what she experiences. An important attribute of human-centered methodology is that the overall process is iterative. That is, we frequently evaluate service design solutions and ideas with the customers and other stakeholders, and their input during these meetings heavily influences everything from incremental changes to breakthrough innovations. Two particularly useful methods for centering on the person are documenting the customer journey and using genre as a lens for exploring expectations.

Documenting customer journeys

To get an understanding of the service experience it is crucial to "walk in the customer's shoes"—to understand and experience the customer journey—just the way a user would. There are a variety of techniques for documenting the journey such as process mapping, shadowing, and video ethnography, but what is most important is to understand all the activities and constraints involved, and to chart out options that might be needed to be tried later. Gathering quotes from actual customers about their service experience is one way to highlight problems, opportunities and what people value with a service. For example, in a museum where a lot of the visitors are children, one should walk through the museum at the height of a child. When designing a parking service, one needs to experience the signage to get to the facility as well as the parking meter, or when going through the process of purchasing a book online, understanding delivery at the door can be as important to the experiences as the electronic shopping cart.

Using genres as a lens to expectations

Understanding the role that people's expectations play in approaching a service is an important topic in service research [21]. Working with genres as a framework for design is a powerful technique [13]. Simplified, a genre can be described as an implicit contract between producer and consumer, directing both the production process and the expectations of the consumer. For example, in the US there are several genres in health care delivery, from local clinics to large medical conglomerates. Explicitly exploring what evidence communicates what attributes within and across the genre helps in setting expectations at the service encounter. When we can identify clear genres and the components that differentiate between genres and sub-genres, it provides a base-line and a model of expectations and efficiency in service design.

Modeling, prototyping and enacting methods

Visualizations or models, prototyping, and enactments are crucial to successful service design. Modeling, prototyping and enacting are closely related to activities in service development, such as documenting the environment or servicescape [1], blueprinting [19], and defining touchpoints [21]. Modeling, prototyping and enacting in service design draws on the broader arts (such as Drama) as well as communication, industrial and interaction design.

Modeling stakeholders

In the service design process, stakeholders are modeled in two ways. First, at the abstract level a mapping or diagram of all stakeholders and their influence is created in order to understand the relationships between providers, partners, users and peripheral influencers to the service. Secondly, using this mapping and based real-world observation, personas are created to capture and communicate different goal-oriented customer categories and to maintain a deep connection the activities of the service. The personas are then used to drive scenarios.

Modeling activities—the role of scenarios

Modeling what happens, how people act, in what order things happen and coordination of backstage and front-stage activities can be done through scenarios. Story-boards are created as a narration, often in the form of comic strips, to describe the activities of a particular stakeholder (or persona) in the service process. In the generative stages of the design process, enabling users to illustrate, narrate and choreograph their ideal scenario, highlights solutions and design objectives and often leads to service innovation. When expressing their ideal scenario in this way, people embed the value they want from a service, at the same time they express how it will fit it into their activities, lifestyle, and fulfill their goals.

Prototyping

Prototyping in service encompasses the experience as well as the touchpoints. Prototypes can range from rough sketches of "moments of truth" [5], to full scale brick and mortar facilities. Creating cultural probes can also be effective in capturing a wider array of concerns from customers. For example, with a technology probe a customer provided with a white box to achieve her goals. In doing so she inscribes the service concept and behavior in the white box, and distinguishes between parts of the service concept that she believes can be performed through technology and parts that may need a human touchpoint.

Enacting

Working with dramaturgic methods allows designers and users to enact or perform service experiences before they have been established in an organization. By doing that, anomalies and alternative solutions can be found.

Letting users look at, try out and act out different suggestions for a solution provides input on details as well as overall design decisions. Artifacts used in the enactment are prototypes that invite comments from the participants. Artifacts used in enactments are often designed to deliberately provoke users, in order to assess specific aspects of design alternatives.

Conclusion

Based on the description of Service Design as a design discipline, it seems to be well fitted to drive and support the development of SSME. Service design is human-centered and participatory by nature; it brings unique methods and perspectives to service innovation as illustrated by the two examples explained above. The service design practitioner's focus on the entire range from useful to effective, as well as a vision to drive the development of technology that creates value together with people; make it invaluable in the advancement of SSME.

References

[1] Bitner, M. J., Servicescapes: The impact of physical surroundings on customers and employees. *Journal of Marketing, 55*(jan):10-25.

[2] Booz, A., Hamilton. *New Product Management for the 1980s*. New York: Booz Allen & Hamilton, Inc. (1982)

[3] Bowers, M. R. *New Product Development in Service Industries*. Doctoral dissertation, Texas A&M University. (1985)

[4] Bruce, M., Bessant, J. *Design in business: Strategic innovation through design*. Design Council, UK. (2002)

[5] Edvardsson, B., Gustafsson, A., Johnson, M., D., Sandén, B. *New service development and innovation in the new economy*. Lund: Studentlitteratur. (2000)

[6] Edvardsson, B., Gustafsson, A., Roos, I. Service portraits in service research: a critical review. *International Journal of Service Industry Management 16*(1):107-121. (2005)

[7] Erlhoff, M., Mager, B., Manzini, E. *Dienstleistung braucht Design, Professioneller Produkt-und Markenauftritt für Serviceanbieter*. Herausgeber: Hermann Luchterhand Verlag GmbH. (1997).

[8] Evenson, S. Designing for Service. *Proceedings of DPPI 2005*, Eindhoven.

[9] Grönroos, C. *Service management and marketing: Managing the moments of truth in service competition*. Lexington Books: New York. (1990)

[10] Holmlid, S. Interaction design and service design: A comparison of design disciplines. Submitted to NordiCHI. (2006)

[11] Khurana, A., Rosenthal, Stephen R. Integrating the fuzzy front end of new product development. *IEEE Engineering Management Review, 25*(4,):35-49. (1997)

[12] Kristensson, P., Gustafsson, A. and Archer, T. "Harnessing the Creative Potential among Users", *Journal of Product Innovation Management, 21* (1) 4-14. (2004)

[13] Lundberg, J. *Shaping online news: Genre perspectives on interaction design*. Linköping Studies in Science and Technology Dissertation No. 918. Linköping, Sweden: Linköpings universitet.

[14] Mager, B. *Service design: A review*. KISD, Köln. (2004)

[15] Manzini, E., Il Design dei Servizi. La progettazione del prodotto-servizio, in *"Design Management"*, n° 7, Giugno, (1993)

[16] Moritz, S. (2005). *Service design: Practical access to an evolving field*. MSc thesis, KISD.

[17] Scheuing, E., Johnson, E. A proposed model for new service development. *The Journal of Service Marketing, 3*(2):25-34. (1989)

[18] Service Design Network. *Service design network manifesto*. Unpublished. (2005).

[19] Shostack, L. Designing Services That Deliver," *Harvard Business Review*, January-February, 133-9. (1984)

[20] SVID. Design ladder, available at http://www.svid.se/wlt/7FFF9336-1086-4965-8C4F0CD72E90700B. wlt

[21] Zeithaml, V. A., Parasuraman, A., Berry, L. L. *Delivering Service Quality: Balancing Customer Perceptions and Expectations*. The Free Press, 1990.

[22] Zeithaml, V. A., Bitner, M. J., and Gremler, D. *Services Marketing: Integrating Customer Focus Across the Firm, 4th edition*, New York: McGraw-Hill, 2006.

Research and Education of SSME in Japanese Universities

Hideaki Takagi
Graduate School of Systems and Information Engineering
University of Tsukuba
1-1-1 Tennoudai, Tsukuba-shi, Ibaraki 305-8573 Japan
E-mail: takagi@sk.tsukuba.ac.jp
Phone: +81-29-853-5003 Fax: +81-29-853-5070

ABSTRACT

We first comment on how services are viewed in Japan. We then discuss roles of universities in advancing research and education of SSME as well as in promoting the innovation in services. We present, as examples from the University of Tsukuba, a new line of research on customer-centric business innovation and a university-originated venture company for health care service. We also describe education programs on SSME in two Japanese universities. Finally, we make some recommendations on the SSME class in graduate and professional programs. [1]

Introduction

Like in other advanced countries, more than 60% of working population is now involved in service industry in Japan, and this ratio will increase further. However, the productivity of service industry is said to be not as high as that of manufacturing industry, which was a major driving force of the remarkable economic growth during the 1980s. Therefore, it should be evident that the innovation in service industry would lead to the productivity enhancement in the whole industry, which is mandatory for the sustainable prosperity in the 21st century. This is particularly true in Japan, where the total population has already started to decrease.

On the other hand, the Third Five-Year Basic Plan for Science and Technology for 2006-2010, recently announced by the Japanese Government, identifies four major areas (life science, information and communication, environment, nano-technology and materials) and four other areas (energy, manufacturing, social infrastructure, frontier sciences) for the concentration of national R&D investment [1]. A brief paragraph follows which

---

1 I would like to thank Dr. Kazuyoshi Hidaka of IBM Japan and Professor Akio Kameoka of JAIST for stimulating our research and education of SSME. I am also grateful to my colleague: Masato Koda, Ryo Sato, Yuichiro Kanazawa, Hideo Suzuki, Shinichiro Watanabe, Makoto Mizuno, and Fumiyo Kondo for the discussions made in the course of starting a research project on service sciences at the University of Tsukuba.

refers to the need of innovation in service by combining the knowledge of human, social, and natural sciences.

Many foreign tourists feel that the service in Japanese hotels is superb. Japanese car dealers and electric appliances stores provide long-term "after service." However, these are instances of service improvements by each company for their own business. Dr. Tadahiko Abe of Fujistu Research Institute points out that the foundation of scientific research on services is weak in Japan [2]. He mentions the following reasons:

— The service is not considered in terms of business functions; it is viewed as personal spirit, attitude, and sometimes merely self-sacrifice for lowering the price of products.

— Invention/improvement in business processes is often kept and inherited as personal wisdom. It is not subject to formalization, modulation, standardization, or documentation.

— Open discussion is rare among private (often competing) companies on research results and business practice.

— Universities do not have many faculty members who have working and management experience in industry, IT skill, and insights into human mind and behavior.

Nevertheless, or rather in order to overcome these difficulties, it is important to initiate research on SSME in Japan. It is my strong belief that universities and industries can collaborate toward this direction.

Contribution to Research of SSME

In this section, we address the contribution to the research of SSME from the academic side. We mention scientific study of service management, applications of mathematical and statistical sciences, and a new research project on customer-centric business process innovation started at the University of Tsukuba.

Scientific Study of Service Management

Complete manuals are available for handing customers uniformly in fast-food restaurants, hotels, and call centers. So far, researchers and consultants of service management have collected a number of good-practice instances in service, and they provide useful guidance. However, the engineering approach may not have been exploited enough due to the inherent difference of service from the agricultural and manufacturing production. Many engineering techniques have been developed for decision making (scientists' invasion). They may be applicable to the service management as well.

Application of mathematical sciences

Various techniques of operations research have been applied to the evaluation and design of service systems so far. They should remain useful as scientific approach in the framework of SSME. To name a few, they are:

— Mathematical programming for optimal design of systems subject to complex restrictions, such as airline crew and sports game scheduling.

— Queuing theory for capacity planning and quality evaluation of service systems.

— Graph theory for representation of relationships among entities, and network flow theory for transportation, distribution, and communication networks, manufacturing process, etc. Petri nets may be used for describing protocols of service.

— Stochastic processes, in particular, Markov processes and Markov decision processes, for macroscopic modeling and design of time-dependent probabilistic processes.

— Discrete-event simulation of complex systems for which mathematical analysis is difficult.

Application of statistical sciences

Statistical methods are essential in service science. In the traditional sense, theoretical models must be verified against real data. Items and targets of questionnaire must be planned based on statistical analysis. An example of more advanced statistical modeling is the structural equation modeling (SEM) based on the simultaneous demand-and-supply equation model in econometrics. It can be used in organizational behavior, in marketing, and in many other fields of service sciences.

Data mining now represents an indispensable tool for assisting intelligent rule finding as well as decision making in the highly complex business environment. It has a significant advantage over conventional hypothesis-based data analysis. The technique of knowledge discovery has become possible by capitalizing on the machine learning (AI), statistical analysis, operations research, and database research along with the advancement in information processing technology.

Research project at the University of Tsukuba

At the University of Tsukuba, a number of faculty members in management sciences have been conducted extensive research on service quality evaluation, system optimization, business process management, marketing, customer management, consumer behavior, organizational behavior, and so on. However, these efforts have been separate. Getting an idea of SSME, a group has been formed by combining individual projects into a collaborative research project on service sciences. Rather than pursuing a wide scope from the start, we have decided to focus on the customer-centric business innovation as one of key subjects in SSME. We plan to study the following items in the forthcoming three years:

— *Customer-centric business innovation model:* We study the method of service innovation management with the example of e-market place. We also apply the data mining method to the customer relationship management.

— *Quantitative methods for understanding customers:* We first classify various measures of customer characterization such as customer satisfaction/delight, royalty, and lifetime value in the service industry. Sorting the survey data by the American customer satisfactions index, we construct a scoring model of these measures.

— *Customer-oriented marketing models:* We develop a quantitative method for estimating the consumer's behavior by testing if they buy cars only based on the price tag or based on the total cost of ownership. We also study a model of campaign engine by the field experiment on marketing promotion using mobile media such as cell phones and PDA.

— *Customer-oriented employee management:* We examine if there is positive relationship between the company's sales and the customer-orientated attitude of its employees.

Innovation by Collaboration of Industry and University

Innovation is possible through technology transfer from academia to industry or suggestions of problems from industry to academia. In this section we tell one such successful story in the service area. We also urge university researchers to change their mind on research for innovation.

Innovation in the health care service: A venture company with university origin

Tsukuba Wellness Research, Inc. (TWR) was founded in July 2002 based on the research results by Dr. Shinya Kuno at the University of Tsukuba [3]. On the concept of "Making Japan healthier," his business includes giving local communities and health insurance associations reliable consultation on health promoting systems, developing and providing tailor-made physical exercise programs based on scientific evidence (the "e-wellness system"), and training the staff for planning and organizing health promotion activities. It prevents the elderly people from lifestyle-related diseases and the bedridden stage. Medical electronics companies took part. Profits have been made from the first year, and they have already cooperated with more than 20 local communities all over Japan, with more than 3,000 people participating in the program. For example, a regional health care system is developed in collaboration with Chiba prefecture government. The accomplishment of

TWR has been cited as a forefront case in some national policies such as the "Strategy for the Creation of New Industry" and "Frontier Strategy for Health."

How universities can contribute to service innovation

University researchers used to search existing literature such as academic journals when they tried to initiate new research. For the study of SSME, however, they should turn to the industry and society at large for the research subject. The purpose of research is the innovation and the resulting value creation in the target organization, not writing papers on theoretical findings. Such collaboration with people outside academia has been unpopular as it is not appreciated much as academic achievements in Japanese universities. In order to make innovation happen, university people should share the prospects and problems of research with industry people normally. No innovation will be possible if both sides just sit in their own comfortable armchair.

Education of SSME in Japan

Not many universities in Japan seem to provide classes on service management, let alone the service sciences. Below we give two examples of educational programs on SSME in Japan.

JAIST: MOT Course

In the Management of Technology (MOT) course at the Japan Advanced Institute of Science and Technology, Professor Akio Kameoka teaches a class on Service Sciences for students with job experience. According to their brochure [4], the service science constitutes a key element in the education of next-generation MOT. Students learn basic concepts of services along with related theories, and they study how innovative services have contributed to making the companies more competitive.

University of Tsukuba: MBA Program

In Master's Program in Business Administration (MBA) and Public Policy (MPP) at the University of Tsukuba, we have just started a short-term class named "Science of Services: Theory and Practice" in the Fall Quarter of 2006. This program educates professionally minded students with non-math background. The class consists of five weeks of lectures as follows:

Week 1: Introduction to Service Sciences; Paradigm shift in society, industry and R&D.

Week 2: Service innovation based on information and communication technology.

Week 3: Quantitative planning and evaluation of the quality of service (queuing theory).

Week 4: Resource optimization in service: applications of mathematical programming and network flow theory.

Week 5: Innovation in heath care service; School education as service.

Referring to the queuing theory, we do not elaborate on the stochastic process as we do in the operations research class. Instead, we explain Little's theorem as a generic system principle, and the trade-off on the evaluation of service quality between the operator's viewpoint and the user's viewpoint. We may present the application of mathematical programming to the scheduling of sports games such as soccer and baseball, which is usually formulated as optimization problems subject to many restrictions. Basic algorithms and applications of network flow theory will also be taught.

Recommendation for SSME education in the universities

The SSME is a comprehensive subject to be understood by integrating knowledge of several academic areas along with practical business examples. Therefore I think it is appropriate to teach SSME in the graduate and professional school for those students who have finished solid undergraduate education in specific areas and possibly have job experience.

Education of SSME in graduate level may cover:

— Increasing significance of services in the industry of the 21st century.

— Potential of mathematical approach to service management for non-math oriented students.

— Application of methodologies available from mathematical and statistical sciences for math-oriented students.

— Term projects in addition to lectures.

— Internship in industry if possible.

Advanced mathematics is not necessary. However, as a preliminary of scientific study of services, working knowledge of calculus, linear algebra, and statistics are mandatory as well as practical skill in information processing.

Conclusion

It is our common understanding that the scientific approach to services is very important as a means to enhance the productivity in service industry for the sustainable development in the 21st century. However, we are still in the process of exploring research directions in governments, industries, and universities. The research and education in the universities are complementary to the efforts in industries where each company develops innovative methods individually tailored to their own business areas. Interactions by both parties should result in fruitful progress in SSME.

References

[1] http://www.mext.go.jp/a_menu/kagaku/kihon/06032816/001/001.pdf (in Japanese).
[2] Tadahiko Abe, "What is Service Science?" *Economic Review*, Vol.10, No.2, pp.10-26, April 2006, Fujitsu Research Institute (in Japanese).
[3] http://www.twr.jp/ (in Japanese).
[4] http://www.jaist.ac.jp/ks/mot/panfu.htm (in Japanese).

Service Science–A Japanese Perspective: Pitfalls and Opportunities

Toshiaki Kurokawa[1]
CSK Fellow, CSK Holdings Corporation, Affiliate Fellow, Science and Technology Foresight Center, National Institute for Science and Technology Policy (NISTEP), Ministry of Education, Culture, Sports, Science and Technology (MEX), and Project Manager of Exploratory Software Project, Information-Technology Promotion Agency, Japan (IPA)
CSK Aoyama Bldg., 2-26-1 Minami-Aoyama, Minato-ku Tokyo 107-0062 JAPAN
kurokawa@mlab.csk.com
Tel. +81-3-6438-3541

ABSTRACT

Service Science, Management and Engineering (SSME) has become a hot issue in Science and Engineering Communities in Japan; however, there are discrepancies on what is and how to do SSME. Typical example can be found that those who claim practitioners in SSME in Japan are not in Science and Engineering community but in Management of Enterprises and of Technology. I will point out some pitfalls in SSME in Japan, and explore how to avoid them and also try to depict a few unique opportunities in SSME in Japan. The pitfalls discussed are: lack of clear goals of SSME, lack of leading figures of SSME, lack of focused customer of SSME, lack of agreed government role in SSME, and the obscure relationship between innovation and SSME. Traditional Japanese superb service and ecosystem are listed in unique opportunities.

Introduction

Service Science, Management and Engineering (SSME) has become a hot issue in Science and Engineering Communities in Japan [1, 2, 3], although those who claim to be practitioners of SSME in Japan are mostly in Management of Enterprise and of Technology. This is a typical picture of discrepancy and show a pitfall on "Service Science in Japan."

In this paper, I will point out some pitfalls in SSME in Japan that may hinder or may even do harm on the proper development of SSME. Then I will explore how to avoid these pitfalls and also try to depict a few unique opportunities in Japan.

---

1   Disclaimer: Views expressed in this article is the author's personal account and does not reflect any organization's positions that the author is or was engaged with.

Pitfalls of SSME in Japan

In any new discipline, there will be, and should be, pitfalls. SSME is no exception, and we need not regret about the situation. What we need to do is to see straight these pitfalls and understand them so that we can avoid them for further development of SSME. Let us discuss the following pitfalls:

Goals of SSME

In general, goals of a branch of science can be diversified depending on the individual who commit the science. However, too broad diversion is observed in the goals of SSME in Japan.

For example, Ministry of Economy, Trade and Industry (METI) set up a committee for SSME in fiscal year 2006, whose main target is an innovation of traditional service industry with IT employment.

An officer at Ministry of Education, Culture, Sports, Science and Technology (MEX) expressed his view that if SSME is just for traditional service sector (or so-called third group Industry), it would be nothing for science. A quite opposite view against METI's.

In a symposium on SSME in 2005, a voice in floor expressed that the most concern in SSME is the traditional Japanese view that the service is free of charge. His concern is that no science/technology can be developed if the material is free of charge, and no cost is claimed to get.

An editor of *IPSJ Magazine* expressed that the word "Service Science" is great but the content is obscure[4]. He thinks "Service Science, Management and Engineering (SSME)" is more concrete and explaining some, but he still wonders if this is new discipline or not.

An editor of another science journal thinks that SSME is another new fraction of Computer Science/Engineering. People are trying to put new labels on their profession for some reason.

We definitely need some agreed-upon goals of SSME. Established and shared goals for SSME will help people to understand SSME better and participate and cooperate in the development of SSME.

Who Drives SSME

In my understanding, science and engineering field is no different from the field of sports and arts in the sense that the advances are achieved by the individual people, not the system nor machinery.

I have had an interesting experience that most people in any discipline seem to get inspired by the word "Service Science," and thinks that there are some opportunities he/she can contribute.

On the other hand, I have not met any scientist in Japan who declares that SSME is his/her very discipline. Most people think that SSME relates their own field, but it does not replace/overtake all of their profession.

In a way, "Service is Everywhere, Service is for Everyone" in Japan. But the science for everyone might be a science for nobody. We need a dedicated professional who drives this field.

From this viewpoint, it is an interesting idea to define "Service Scientist" to understand what is SSME [5]. However, we need further work on what these experts do (and what they do not do.)

Also, we may need a great person in this field as a role model for what a service scientist will achieve. A kind of mythical person that will attract young people to join the new field.

Normally when we talk about scientific discipline, we try to name concrete, tangible results of knowledge that represent what the discipline is. However, in SSME where people matter, we need the human touch, and some interesting anecdotes may work for that purpose.

Customers of SSME

It may not be a common approach to define customers for scientific discipline. However, customers are very important components in SSME, and it is also valuable to consider who get benefits from the pursuit of this discipline.

Unfortunately, answers to "who are the customers of SSME?" are also widely diversified as goals of SSME that we have discussed.

For example, Service Section of METI thinks the primary customer of SSME is the Japanese Service Industry. It is also interesting to note that METI has a concern that the performance improvement may result in lay-offs or less employment in Service Industry.

Science and Technology Council members under Cabinet seem to think that SSME brings innovation. So, the customer should be among science and technology community. In accord to this line of thought, some Japanese electronic companies have established a SSME group.

An Information-related Service Provider thinks that SSME is a next sales focus, but have no result yet. One of the reasons why they make investment on SSME seems to be the fact that IBM who boasts itself as a service company is promoting SSME.

MOT and MBA course in Japanese Universities now provide SSME as an option. However, it is not yet clear about what kinds of students need to take this course, and what kind of companies or departments of companies to employ the graduates who complete the SSME course.

If "service is everywhere and for everyone," customers for SSME might be everyone, and come to nobody as we discussed in *Who drives SSME*. However, even though it is true that "service" is everywhere and for everyone, we need to identify the customers of SSME, or who benefit most in the pursuit of SSME, because "service" is always boiled down to the concern of customers.

If we can agree upon the goal of SSME, we can deduce the customer of SSME as well. Or vice versa, the customer can tell the goal of SSME. We need to identify the customer of SSME.

Role of Government in SSME promotion

I have talked diversification, however, there seems to be no discrepancy about the Japanese government's need to promote SSME. No objection. Unfortunately, there are discrepancies about what kind of role the government should play. A clear discrepancy is observed between METI who promotes SSME for Service Sector and MEX who promotes SSME for Innovation in Science and Technology. Even though both ministries think that Government need to help SSME promotion, approaches, directions and customers (industry or community) are different.

One may tend to think that let they do whatever they like as long as they promote SSME anyway. However, this attitude has a negative implication that may end up future confusion on what is SSME, goals of SSME and even who are the professionals of SSME. For example, just think of the development of university/college courses for SSME under government promotion. Current METI and MEX approaches are quite different on courses: one for school of commerce and one for science/engineering schools.

Another confusion may come to the R&D effort for SSME. Traditionally, service sector in Japan do not invest much on R&D, and this SSME promotion may open their executives eyes up on R&D expense, however, it may not be easy thing to manage, not to say how to perform.

Other roles that the government can play would be to deprive any barriers or regulations that hinder the promotion of SSME. I have not heard any of this kind so far, however, the pursuit of SSME may bring this opportunity in the future.

Also, one possibility that has once been discussed in 2005 symposium for SSME is that the government's operation is one of the application area of SSME. Japanese governments, local or central, does not have a good reputation of their service, which is a sharp contrast to the private companies who usually enjoys the good reputation of their services.

Historically speaking, governments have played an important role for new scientific disciplines in Japan. This will be true in SSME, and for that, we need to think the proper role of government in Japan for SSME promotion.

Innovation and SSME

"Innovation" has been an accompanying word for SSME. There is nothing wrong that SSME provides innovation. The problem with innovation and SSME is the ambiguity what it means and the false expectation that SSME is a magic for innovation.

As you see, the very word "innovation" may mean different things for different people. Unfortunately, "innovation" has become an overworked word, and may even end up to mean something/anything good for you. We know that there are lots of ways to bring innovation. And we also know that there is no easy way to achieve valuable innovation.

As a scientific discipline, SSME may bring some components for innovation. On the other hand, some innovation will help pursuit SSME and bring SSME to reach the new stage. But the innovation itself is essentially a different beast from SSME. As a scientific discipline, SSME should be pursued even if it does not bring any innovation.

Avoiding Pitfalls

I have suggested solutions to avoid these pitfalls in the preceding section, but let me reemphasize some of them here.

Grand Challenge

We need to establish the Grand Challenge, the great questions in SSME. This may not stop the diversification itself, but makes people to work together, and inspires people to join the field.

Great Leaders

I believe the very driving force for a scientific discipline is the person and his/her dedication and commitment which bring the fruitful results and provide roll-model for the followers. We need to find a Japanese hero/heroine in SSME.

Open Discussion

It is necessary to discuss openly on these pitfalls. It is more important especially when we want to deal with difficult pitfalls such as government roles, target customers, and the relation with innovation, since there will not be a simple and easy solution. The open discussion here definitely include international interactions as well

Unique Opportunities in Japan

Even though I have listed pitfalls, I also see that there are some unique opportunities in SSME in Japan.

Traditional Superb Service

Japan has a good tradition of "Superb Service," which has been appreciated from wide audience. We may find out the key component of this kind of high-quality of service in the pursuit of SSME.

Service Ecosystem

Yasutomi [6] presents his view that the Goal-Plan-Achieve scheme does not work in today's complex world, and instead the ecosystem scheme should be established and handled. He seems to be inspired by Gregory Bateson's ecological viewpoint. This kind of ecosystem viewpoint is also with Japanese tradition, and gives powerful positions for studying service in nowadays complicated world.

Conclusions

I have discussed some pitfalls in SSME promotion in Japan. They may hinder the development of SSME, and may confuse people who want to contribute SSME. To avoid these pitfalls, it is necessary to establish the challenge or shared goal for SSME. Well-known leaders will give role-model and tangible example to do SSME. And the open discussion about SSME is indispensable for any aspects such as the role of government. It is also noted that Japan may have some unique opportunities in the course of SSME development such as its traditional superb service and ecosystem for SSME.

References

[1]   Hidaka, K. Trends in Service Science in Japan and Abroad. *Science & Technology Trends – Quarterly Review*, NISTEP (MEX), No.19, April 2006, 35-47

[2]   Mizuta, H. (ed.) Special issues on Emergence of Service Science: Service Science, Management and Engineering (SSME). *IPSJ Magazine*, Inf. Proc. Soc. of Japan, May 2006.

[3]   Kurokawa, T. From Computer Science to Service Science?. *Kagaku (Science)*, Iwanami Shoten, August 2006.

[4]   Editor's Column, *IPSJ Magazine*, IPS of Japan, May 2006.

[5]   Spohrer, J., Maglio, P. P., Kreulen, J. T. and Srnivasan, S. Becoming a Service Scientist. *IPSJ Magazine*, Inf. Proc. Soc. of Japan, May 2006.

[6]   Yasutomi, A. *Live in Complexity: soft controls*. Iwanami-Shoten, June 2006.

Services Science Empowers Next Generation MOT—Just-in-Time Innovation Management by Service Layer Integrated Strategic Roadmapping

Akio Kameoka
Senior Research Professor
MOT
Knowledge Science
Japan Advanced Institute of Technology
JAPAN

Visiting Professor
Ritsumeikann University
Hosodaigaku (University of Air) Broadcasting University
Seisaku-Kenkyu University (GRIPS)

Affiliate Fellow
NISTEP (National Institute of Science and Technology Policy)
kameoka@jaist.ac.jp

ABSTRACT

Advanced management of technology moves its focus to the higher value added services innovations by integrating more sophisticated service functions to the conventional products and systems. This paper provides a scheme for the newly emerging "service science" expected to support services innovations and derives practical methodology to integrate new services.

A Definition of "Service"

The concept of "service" is not yet well defined and not widely accepted, but here is broadly, defined as "a supporting activity to help an individual or organization to achieve its objective". Accordingly, it includes physical supporting functions, psychological supporting functions, intellectual supporting functions, spiritual supporting functions, as well as technological supporting functions provided through products. Valuating products and systems with their added services improves customer satisfaction and the total customer value should be considered as the summation of the products/system value, added services value, and individual user added value.

Multi-layered Roadmap/Roadmapping

Advanced strategic roadmap/roadmapping here developed for future next generation innovation management introduces a new independent layer of "service" between the service and product layers, which involves a new concept of function that link products with their supporting services. The service sides have to clarify "requiring functions" and product sides have to clarify "supplying functions" to fill the gaps between the service and product layers. These require/supply functional analysis-by-synthesis iterations provide a creative roadmapping process, in the future goal setting and inter-relational scenario development. This expansion from products to services is critically important for the Japanese manufacturing companies.

Strategic Goal of Next-generation MOT: Challenge to "Just-in-Time Innovation"

Future MOT faces various challenges as follows. It has to bring in new fields of management domain including science driven innovations, science and technology fusions, advanced technologies convergence for example NBIC (Nano-technology, Bio-technology, IT technologies and Cognitive sciences), and technology-service convergence, which have very different factors from the past and conventional innovation process. Consequently, the new methodology for the next generation innovation management should integrate those various aspects so as to achieve comprehensive understanding of the emerging technologies and their social and business impacts. Such an integrated strategic planning and dynamic innovation management of technology is to be focused on "Just-in-Time Innovation" by expanding its scope of integration domain from manufacturing to the total process of innovation, and the time horizon to see the future, by developing an advanced technology roadmapping methodology that fits to the demand of corporate practices. At the same time, the next generation innovation model should be considered from global point of views, including international collaboration, global alliances, and competition depending on the "Symbiotic Competitiveness" for the 21st century, proposed by Professor Hiroshi Inose.

Research & Education in Service Economics & Management at China Center for Service Sector Research (CCSSR)

Jiangfan Li
China Center for Service Sector Research (CCSSR)
Sun Yat-sen University
135 Xingang Road West, Guangzhou 510275
China
Tel/Fax: +8620 8403 8476
E-mail: drljf@163.com
URL: http://mns.sysu.edu.cn/ccssr/new/show.asp?id=831

ABSTRACT

This paper presents the background of the China Center for Service Sector Research (CCSSR). The prior and current research topics and activities of the CCSSR at both the national and provincial level are described, as well as its educational activities. Since its establishment in 2001, the CCSSR at Sun Yat-sen University has made many contributions to research and education in the service economy within China. Research efforts and publications have been recognized at the national and international level.

Background of China Center for Service Sector Research (CCSSR)

China Center for Service Sector Research (CCSSR)of Sun Yat-sen University was established in 2001 as the first tertiary industry research institute in China. It specializes in research focused on the service sector and is a leader in service economy research in China.

The main research orientations of CCSSR are:

1. the theory and practice of service sector economics;

2. strategic planning for development of service industry in provinces, cities, counties, towns and districts;

3. service economy analysis and development planning;

4. management of service business operations.

The research addresses such service industries as transportation, warehousing and post, information transmission, computer service and software, wholesale and retail industry, hoteling and catering, financial industry, real estate industry, leasehold, business service, scientific research, technical service and geological prospecting, water conservancy, environment and public facilities, community service and other service industries, education, health, social security and social welfare industries, culture, sports, entertainment, public management and social organization, and international organizations.

The CCSSR research team currently has 27 special researchers and 35 PhD and PhD students now. The director and chief researcher is Professor Jiangfan Li. Dr. Guanlin Li, Associate Professor Wangcheng Yang, and Dr. Meiyun Li are assistant directors of CCSSR.

CCSSR Research Program

For the period from China's Seventh Five-year Plan to the Ninth Five-year Plan National Research Program, CCSSR research team has been actively involved in national-level research on:

— service sector development strategy and policy in China (1993-1996),

— current situations and strategies for service sector development in China (1997-2000), and

— the internal structure of the service sector and China's policy for developing service sector (1998-2001).

More recent national research topics have addressed:

— reform strategies and policies for monopolies in tertiary industry in China (2002-2004),

— industrial structural changes and front edge questions in the service economy (2005-2007),

— the education industry and education service product theory (2002-2005),

— non-profit organization operational mechanisms and management (2001-2005), and

— the role and function of the sports industry in the development of China's economy (2004-2005).

CCSSR has also long been involved in a strong province-level research program. Key areas of this research program in Guangdong Province include tertiary industry economics (1986-1988), tertiary industry management studies (1992-1996), the adjustment and improvement of tertiary industry structures in China (1997-2000), the development and management of tertiary industry in the Pearl River Delta Region (1992-1995), operational research on the tertiary industry economy (1993-1996), and comparative research on the development trends within tertiary industry, both domestically and abroad (1997-2000). More recent research topics in the province-level research program have focused on the leadership role of Guangdong Province in realizing modernization and change in tertiary industry (2002-2003); monopoly industrial reform (2004-2005); industrial correlations, effects, and development strategies in the service sector in Guangdong province (2002-2005); the growth of tertiary industry and new trends for service management (2005-2006); Guangdong's policies for service sector growth (2003), improvements in the business environment to support service sector development and speed its further growth (2005-2006); and the information revolution in the service sector (2005).

CCSSR has accomplished a number of significant research achievements throughout the years. Professor Jiangfan Li's book, Tertiary Industrial Economics, which as first published by the Guangdong People's Press in 1990, won the Sun Yefang Award for Economic Science Works in 1991. This award is the highest academic award for economics in China. Another key result of CCSSR's research efforts was the publication of the Analysis on China's Tertiary Industrial Economics by the Guangdong People's Press in 2004. Another book resulting from CCSSR's research efforts, sponsored by the National Social Science Fund, is Research on China's Service Sector Development. This book was published by the People's Press in 2005; it was recognized for its achievement in the 985 Project by Sun Yat-sen University.

Two major research programs funded by the National Social Science Fund have been undertaken by the CCSSR. The first of these research programs, Monopoly in China's tertiary industry - Research on Reform Strategies and Policies, was launched in 2002 and finished in 2004. The second program, tertiary industry changes and front edge problems in service economy, launched in 2005 and is planned to be completed in 2007.

Several CCSSR research efforts have received major recognition in the assessment opinions of experts. These efforts were

— Current situation and strategy for developing tertiary industry in China (2001),

— Internal structure of tertiary industry and research on China's policy to promote tertiary industry growth (1998-2001), and

— Research on strategy and policy for developing tertiary industry in China (1996).

Future research plans at CCSSR continue research on the service economy, service management, e-commerce, and logistics management. A project on service science research on computer network construction is being sponsored by IBM. It is planned to address these key research fields and topics:

— Communication Service: research on service charges and the geographical distribution of phone calls originated.

— Business Service: branch locations, customer volume analysis, making pricing strategies, organizing supplies, and work assignment.

— Banking Service: improvement of business flow, development of new services, establishment of service rules, and arrangement of human resources.

— Medical treatment service: medical treatment establishment equipment, and optimization of the flow of clinic operations.

— Transportation Service: location of stations, reservation system, price policy analysis, anticipation of traffic flow, setting up service routs and timetable, and the allocation of vehicles and staffs.

PhD and Postgraduate Education at CCSSR

Post-doctoral/PhD/Postgraduate students at CCSSR, Sun Yat-sen University, Enroll in majors in either Enterprise Management: Service sector economy and management, or in Industrial Organization and Management: Service sector economy and management. Doctoral papers have been completed on these topics (shown along with the student):

— The rise of service sector in China (Zuolei Wei)

— The development of service productivity in China (Naihua Gu)

— Regional development of service sector in China (Xia Hu)

— Leisure service and the development of related industry (Qianlong Qing)

— Integration and development of service sectors (Meiyun Li)

— Service resources outsourcing and development of the service sector (Fei Chen)

— Research on the development of producer service (Doudou Bi)

— Comparative research on service sector's international competitiveness (Yunlong Kong)

— Information economy and service sector development (Jinghua Xu)

— Operations and management of non-profit organizations (Wangcheng Yang)

— Mechanism and development of manufacturing services (Jiguo Liu)

Key courses taught in these programs include Tertiary Industrial Economics and Service Management. Additional training plans will focus on the development of eight new courses, each with 15 hours. These courses and major topics are:

— Service Strategy Planning: analyzing environmental factors during strategy making by service companies, types of strategies and how to choose among them, and strategic planning and implementation for service organizations.

— Service Quality Management: the definition and main factors of service quality, SERVQUAL - the tools for measuring service quality, controlling services at all processes, and service guarantees and remedies.

— Service Organization Management: planning a service organization orientated by quality service and customer satisfaction, and the establishment of its team, evaluation of the organization by using the method of Balanced Scorecard, and setting up key performances standards.

— Designing and Improving Service Business Flow: main factors and major types of service delivery system, structural module for service processes, and general means for designing a service delivery system.

— Management of Service Outsourcing: reasons for outsourced services, setting up outsourcing strategies, analysis on outsource gains and risks, analysis on costs and performances, management of service providers, and negotiations and contracts.

— Simulation of Service System and Analysis on Service Policy: steps and methods for the development and usage of computer simulation system, how to forecast service demands change patterns using the simulation system, and evaluation of the feasibility of specific service rules and policies changes.

— Management of Non-profit Organization: types of non-profit organizations, characteristic and operation steps for the management of non-profit organizations, and comparison among Chinese and foreign counties in regard to non-profit organization management.

— Strategic Planning for Service Industry and Macro-policy Analysis: trend, structure change pattern and regional distribution characteristics as in the development of service industry, development strategies for service sector, and the regulations and policies for promoting service sector growth.

Conclusion

Since its establishment in 2001, the China Center for Service Sector Research (CCSSR) at Sun Yat-sen University has made many contributions to research and education in the service economy within China. Research efforts and publications have been recognized at the national and international level. Its faculty and students have greatly contributed to an enhanced understanding of service sector economics and the development and management of service sector enterprises in the region and across China.

CONCLUSION

Entreprenuership

Carl Schramm
President
Ewing Marion Kauffman Foundation
4801 Rockhill Road
Kansas City, Missouri 64110

I'm sure you all realize that this is an important conference, focussing on defining Service Science, Management, and Engineering (SSME), related educational activities, and SSME research, which is no doubt why you came, but I want to give you a little context of why I think it might also be historic.

There are moments in our history when events happen that have long-term consequences. One such event occurred in the 1920s, when the Rockefeller Foundation, which had an interest in eradicating disease, conceived of the discipline of molecular biology. As a result, our discipline of molecular biology is not the invention of academics and university people, but rather of an outside force pushing the academic community to address a vital issue. You might also think of Vannevar Bush's 1945 paper on science and the frontier of science as a voice from outside the academy because he was actually pushing all universities in the direction of high science, while also laying a popular groundwork for its support in the economy. Yet another example is the Rockefeller Foundation inventing the concept of American research groups and essentially pulling our American research universities into the future.

It is in this context that we might think about today's events because, in a sense, we have an industrial force pushing against universities, or pulling universities forward, into thinking about an unmet need in society, and articulating what might be done about it.

I want to present to you a larger context in which this might be considered: the transition of our economy away from a model that most of us carry in our heads toward the model that actually exists. And if I've done my job well you'll view this discourse in a different light.

I want to suggest to you that this economic transformation is enormous. I'm going to sketch it out very quickly and then I want to get into the implications of it. I want to discuss both the old economy we left behind and the new economy we live in now.

Much of the information I'm discussing today is found in a book called *Good Capitalism, Bad Capitalism*, which I coauthored with Will Baumol and Bob Litan [1]. The book describes the transformation of the American economy from the early post-War years to the present. In the postwar conception of the U.S. economy, there were three actors: big government, big business, and big unions. This conception came into being as a conceptual innovation of John Kenneth Galbraith because it promised one thing that everybody wanted out of the economy — predictability. In the 20th century the wild economy of Weimar Germany, followed by a worldwide depression, helped produce what we knew to be fascism — we made that connection quickly. We also knew that having a predictable economy was critical to fighting fascism and the perils of World War II, so we strived to maintain predictable economic growth.

This was set in place after the war because we had another war just beginning — the Cold War — which required predictability on the economic front. All through the 1960s and 1970s economists preached the virtues of predictability and we actually thought of ourselves as being almost as smart as physicists: by juggling interest rates and so forth we could make the economy work as planned.

Now, for an admissible epistemological moment with quality engineers: Consider an engineering department when electricity was being invented, or the computer was being invented, and what the dialogue might have been like. Academics were challenged by an outside invention.

Economics doesn't proceed that way. An economist proceeds much like a civil engineer: He makes a step when theory fails. So when a building collapses or a bridge falls down or a plane falls out of the sky, then big things happen. In the 1970s, the bottom fell out of the U.S. economy. Economists didn't see inflation coming and when it arrived they didn't know what to do about it. One thing we knew to be a mistake was that economists had constructed a bureaucratic plan for the future. John Kenneth Galbraith wrote that among other things, big firms would be responsible for innovation and creativity and invention. Galbraith, along with Peter Drucker, wrote that the age of the entrepreneur was over.

Someone asked me earlier why economists don't know much about entrepreneurship. And the answer is they willed themselves not to know anything about entrepreneurship. The last person to really write about it was Joseph Schumpeter in 1942. And in the decades after, our graduate schools produced tens of thousands of Ph.D. economists. They all studied macro theory, or micro theory that explained firm decisions. Yet nobody studied how firms came to be. Nobody studied the moment when a firm starts, and nobody cared a whit about entrepreneurs.

It was really one economist who resurrected our interest in entrepreneurship — Will Baumol, and it's been only in the last three or four years that a critical mass of economists have come together in support of studying entrepreneurship, largely because of the sponsorship provided by the Kauffman Foundation. The section on entrepreneurship at the American Economic Association is one year old. The decision of *The Journal of Economic*

Literature to include entrepreneurship as a legitimate category of literature is just four months old. This is the state of economic theory around this question. The preeminent issue for the longest time was predictability and there was no room for entrepreneurship in that model.

As we entered the 1980s, the Japanese emerged again as a threat — but this time an economic threat. The first invasion force was cars — smaller, lighter, more fuel efficient cars that responded to U.S. market demands the Big Three automakers didn't see (or refused to acknowledge). This was followed by a Japanese effort to buy U.S. real estate. They went after big names, things synonymous with American culture — Rockefeller Center, the Pebble Beach golf course. Our economy was in a catatonic state, and a sense of dread — a feeling that U.S. economic leadership might be a thing of the past — began to creep through the culture.

While the Japanese economy's eclipsing of the U.S. economy was a vivid manifestation of our economic worries, those worries were rooted in much more fundamental issues. Our companies were not growing. Our economy was stalled. We had hyperinflation that was without precedent in the 20th century: the Consumer Price Index was rising at 13 percent; health care costs were rising at almost 12 percent; the prime interest rate was 20 percent. Many people today don't remember this — and many of the workers entering the workforce today didn't live through it. I like to believe that the terrible economic times are like surgery — we lose our capacity to remember the pain.

But why is this episode of teetering on the brink of economic peril just two decades ago now confined largely to history books? Because we avoided bad decisions and benefited from a bit of political and economic serendipity.

The United States almost made a terrible mistake in the 1980s. This is the error of bureaucratic capitalism, and we almost made it permanent by using Japan as our economic model and establishing centrally planned industrial policy in Washington. John Kenneth Galbraith and other notable economists were recommending it at the time. And in light of Japan's apparent success in the 1980s, many people were ready to head down that path.

But we didn't succumb to the temptation of central planning, and the economy recovered. How it recovered is a result of a series of actions, some of which were accidental. We almost didn't have an entrepreneurial moment. But there were a number of reasons why we did. We didn't fall prey to temptation posed by central planning. Corporate America underwent a restructuring, which was very significant but also very painful. We clarified intellectual property law. We passed ERISA in 1974, which vested pensions and made our work force totally mobile. A later change to the same act of Congress permitted pension funds to invest in the nation's venture capital industry. We abrogated the Bretton Woods agreement. The invention of junk bonds helped to take our big companies apart and extract untapped value. All of these measures fundamentally led to the erosion of bureaucratic capitalism and the creation of entrepreneurial capitalism.

This is the economy we're in today. It is far from the bureaucratic model of capitalism that reigned from the end of the war to the early 1980s. Predictability has been replaced by change — and change at a faster velocity than ever before. Today's economy is, to put it simply, messy — and yet the fruits are undeniable.

As wrenching as the change was early on — and still is for many Americans — young people have experienced the velocity of change (helped along by ubiquitous technological advances) and are embracing it fully. We've heard already in this conference that kids are all innovative. At lesser universities students see starting businesses as being in their career path. And we need universities — not at the Ph.D. level or the master's level, but at the bachelor's level — to encourage this entrepreneurial inclination and give students the training to put it into action.

As often happens, the customer runs ahead of the supplier, and if that was ever the case look at the non-responsiveness of universities to many of the issues discussed at this conference. Isn't it curious that 70 percent of our GDP is being produced in the service industry, and yet we can't look back through the last 15 years of the Harvard Business Review and see this coming? Where are the people in the eminent business world, or the departments of sociology, or the economists that were telling us about the nature of this shift?

Economists, of which I'm one, are really a dunderheaded group because our vocabulary was beginning to tell us that people are more important than money. Gary Becker won his Nobel Prize in 1992 for a 1962 essay in which he said human capital is more important than financial capital. He looked at differential growth rates from country to country and found that growth is higher in places where they have more college graduates. This doesn't sound today like a groundbreaking discovery. But it highlights how slow economists have been to leave behind the bureaucratic economic model dominated by the iron triangle — big firms, big unions, big government — and embrace an entrepreneurial form of capitalism that sees growth rooted in individual enterprise.

Much of the nervousness about entrepreneurial capitalism is rooted in the messiness of the system. Nothing's predictable about it. Look at the actors. Unions used to be of great consequence. Nearly 35 percent of the industrial labor force in the United States was unionized. Today, less than 12 percent of the total labor force in the United States is unionized, and well over half of that is in the public sector. Essentially there is no union, no central organizing body workers can rely on to bargain over their labor requirements. Another telling statistic: More than half of the net jobs created this year in the United States are in firms that are less than five years old. This equates to hundreds of thousands of jobs created not by the large firms of old, but by new upstarts.

As these small firms take center stage, they're challenging the old giants. And we are seeing extraordinary productivity gains in our largest firms. Of course, productivity gains mean many fewer people work there, and that's another indicator of the messy and unpredictable nature of entrepreneurial capitalism.

Finally, I'll point to the changing concept of worker longevity and career trajectory. When I left college in 1968 the Bureau of Labor Statistics accurately foretold that I would have four employers before I retired. Today, I have a son who is 21 and will graduate next year from college and the Bureau of Labor Statistics suggests that he will have four employers before he is 30. And at least one of those employers is likely to either be himself or a firm that is less than five years old. Whereas once upon a time workers looking for stability would have been cautious about working for a new company, today it is viewed as an exciting opportunity for workers looking to grow and prosper.

Now I want to move very quickly through the actors in this new economic model — to have a sense of their relative importance, which is even harder to forecast — and then I want to talk about the implications of this model. Entrepreneurial capitalism features two new actors that weren't part of the old system. One set of actors consists of the start-up firms I just discussed. Today, they're home to many entrepreneurs, but in 1980 they were written out of the drama totally. If a student had gone to see a counselor or a professor in a fine business school in the 1980s and said, "I really want to start a business, I want to be an entrepreneur," he would have gotten very little help. In fact, he probably would have been discouraged from pursuing the whole venture.

I had a similar experience when I was in my 40s. I had already started three businesses and sold them, and I was on my tractor mowing the grass one Saturday afternoon – trained as an economist –when it dawned on me. I said, "My God, I'm an entrepreneur." How could that be? I was supposed to be on the academic track in a university and the switch got thrown and I told the people at the university, "I don't want to be here anymore, I want to start a business (or restart a business)," and they said, "Well you can't do both. Do you want to run a business or do you want to be a professor?"

That may not be the way the conversation goes at every school, but at many — and especially ten or twenty years ago — it was quite common. The academic community to this day sees entrepreneurial activity as something to be discouraged rather than encouraged and taught.

The number of young people who want to be entrepreneurs – who see entrepreneurship in their career path – is growing. And the same is true throughout the workforce. I make the case that the last recessions in the United States came to an end because many of the people who lost their jobs, including a lot of engineers, were already thinking about starting their own ventures. And because the new economy is much more conducive to taking that risk, when they lost their jobs they decided to move forward. Many have been successful, some have failed, but the economy allows those who fail to pick up and start again with another venture and put it out in the market and push the economy forward. The same thing will happen in the next recession, because it is even easier to start a new business, in part because of what we're talking about today. We're fabricating a conceptual scaffold and we're legitimating this process.

The other set of actors in this new economy are companies like IBM that are having a public discourse about openness. Today, we're thinking about the right size and scale of this company. We're thinking about the right mix of platform and we can conceive of buying a little company or starting little companies – asking some of our senior executives to move out of our mall and into a little strip mall with a business and figuring out what this means.

Government remains a player in the entrepreneurial economy, but I would suggest it has really become less relevant for a variety of reasons. Yet it has played a critical role through the SBIRs and the dedicated amounts of venture money in all the major executive departments, the funding of NIH, and over time the funding of universities. These actions are part of government's most essential contribution – the channeling of society's resources into science. Four percent of our GDP goes into research. Thank you, Vannevar Bush – one person, one report, phenomenal consequences.

And, of course, universities made important contributions to developing the new economy by churning out educated people – particularly through the National Defense Education Act, which helped many students (including me) attain degrees in math and sciences. But narrow mindsets at universities have prevented them from playing a more central role in this economic transformation.

These are the players who have helped shape the entrepreneurial economy. And I'd now like to discuss the implications of this transformation – what all this unpredictability means for our economy and our nation. There are four implications I'll highlight.

The first is that this new platform has allowed what I call continuous innovation, and this is a fundamental cultural shift in our thinking. The scaffolding of our minds has to be reordered. Many of us who grew up in the United States or Europe were taught the traditional Western Civilization timeline of progress: there was the Greco-Roman moment and then the dark ages came and the lights went out; and then Leonardo came along and we turned on Florence and the Renaissance happened; and after that, we had to wait until the Enlightenment and the Industrial Revolution, and then we had the American Industrial Revolution. It was all steel and railroads, and then suddenly there was electricity and telephones and underwater cable. Then the depression began, and then we had airplanes and commercial jets.

We still operate with the view that we're going along like this, even though the cycle of these technological leaps forward is becoming shorter. And right now, we're still experiencing some of the shock of 1999 when we did some stupid stuff – unwise investment decisions might be a kinder way to put it. I think history would suggest to us that we were caught up in a bit of overwrought excitement – irrational exuberance, some have called it. A lot of people lost a lot of money but that's how capitalism works. Some people lose money as they invent the future for other people to make money. This is what's known as the "first versus fourth entrant" advantage.

This constant process of innovation – of success giving way to failure giving way to success – is of great importance in understanding this transformation culture. It is why kids at any given moment in college don't say, "Well now I'll go out there and get in on the Internet, or cable television, or telecommunication." They sit in their dorm room and they think of the next advance. I don't have to list them all, but just think in your own personal technological life what you have today and what you didn't have not so long ago.

The second implication I want to talk about is how this bears on the question of what a firm looks like. Once upon a time IBM brought us up here and they could drive us from plant to plant, showing us all the products -- here's the huge plant, it's all air conditioned, it's a clean room, there's a loading dock, they put the products on and drive them away. Today, you're likely to hear somebody suggest that maybe we should just give the products away so that we can sell the service that connects to them. And suddenly the whole company looks different. When you sell the service that connects to the product, IBM is in this delicious position of having employees at Microsoft who are on the payroll but have never been in an IBM physical surrounding.

In this scenario, what exactly is the firm? How big will the firm be? What is the velocity of the firm?

Seventy-five percent of the Fortune 100 companies in the last 25 years do not exist in that stratum anymore because of corporate dynamism. Firms are changing size and shape, experiencing success and failure, at a much greater velocity. And if the company is changing that fast, as an investor you want to know; and as somebody who is going to take a job you want to know; and as somebody who is going to get bonuses based on whether or not you successfully sell to this firm, you want to know.

I suggest that the key to this is three factors that we basically don't understand, yet everybody knows them: people, technology (which determines the velocity of the continuous innovation cycle), and – of greatest consequence – how the financial market works. Historically huge firms existed because of the drive for predictability. The broker told his customers they'd be better off investing in General Electric because they know how to balance risk between ice boxes and jet engines. But in this age information is free, so why do I have to buy into a vision predicated on balancing risk in an industrial portfolio?

The third implication of the transformation to entrepreneurial capitalism is the creation of new institutional forms. Anytime there is a radical transformation like this, new institutions arise. We've seen it before. Foundations were formed and business schools launched to accommodate the new realities of capitalism early in the last century. More recently, we saw the rise of venture capital, which certainly had a central role in our current economic transformation. And I would suggest that the conduct of research is giving shape to new institutional forms today, which takes me to the fourth issue, namely, what role do universities play in the future?

Most university people would see this as a self-evident question. Universities are the future, they'd say. We teach the next generation. We do all the fundamental research. And one of the great conceits of a lot of universities is that they live in the future. But consider: When IBM called around two years ago and asked, "What do you know about service sciences?", the prevalent attitude was, "Oh, we know everything, we'll solve that problem and we'll start teaching kids about it." And this was followed by, "So what's the theory that we would teach?"

The issue here is are universities going to move fast enough – are they going to be flexible enough to absorb the new realities of the entrepreneurial economy? Can they meet the demand for teaching innovation in their classrooms and spurring innovation in their laboratories? The evidence so far says they can't. At the Kauffman Foundation, we have U.S. firms that report to us continuously that they spend more in Chinese universities on basic research than they do in the United States. That's a reality. How did it happen? It may be that the transformation of all these organizations hasn't happened. Universities haven't been re-institutionalized to respond to the demands of the new economy. Since they are not market actors, they have yet to undergo the overhaul that occurred in American businesses starting in the 1970s.

Now I'll finish with one thought. I want to go back to why economists missed the switch, and why universities haven't responded fast enough, and why engineers, particularly academic engineers, sometimes have to operate as the holy pagan by reading the signals of outside invention – the innovation taking place outside their research centers.

A theme that runs through *Good Capitalism, Bad Capitalism* is this idea that you should never bet against America. Our universities may not be responsive enough. The business schools may still teach the old economy. But we are very resilient at inventing the institutions we need to proceed. When AT&T, once the largest corporation in the world, went out of business, there was no discussion about it in *The Wall Street Journal*. There was reporting, of course, but not much fretting. That happens in America; it can't happen in Europe. If you excavate behind the equivalent of AT&T in Europe, they are likely to have some participation with outside shareholders, but there's a big family with very close ties to the government. It doesn't get caught up in market turmoil or changing market demands. It's not going to go out of business. There's little motivation to make the company better. This is fundamentally a cultural premise that is dampening and disquieting to most creative people in Europe, which is one of the main reasons why so many European entrepreneurs come to the United States to realize their ambitions.

We have to begin to think differently – and the way we think in America is one of our strong suits. We teach kids to think deductively and inductively. But the fact that we're here talking about service and sciences, I would suggest, is another example of an old fashioned American trait that was described as uniquely American by Charles Peirce. We are doing abductive reasoning. We are coming into the middle of a problem and towing up and towing down to make the rationale for how this works. This is detective reasoning. This in many ways is the genius that won't let all these other institutions stall – that will keep prodding, pushing, pulling to get the other institutions in proper shape.

The real genius of entrepreneurial capitalism is it permits enormous freedom to individuals. It gives them money, it resolves their mistakes, it encourages failure and learning from failure, it lets people go at it again, it permits enormous freedom of movement in society, it permits people to say really dumb things that may prove ten years down the line to be the smartest ideas ever uttered.

This event is probably a signal of a changing moment in our business culture and social culture and intellectual culture – and even in democratic culture. Don't forget that this freedom is in many ways deeper set and unique to the way America works. It is one of the reasons people come here, one of the reasons people watch us so carefully from the outside. This economic transformation we're examining exists as a symbiotic event which freed democratic capitalism. It cannot exist in another economic form. Economists may not know what they have, but we sure know that entrepreneurship is a stable fixture of our economy and vital to our future.

References

[1] Baumol, W. J., Lithan, R. E., & Schramm, C. J. *Good Capitalism, Bad Capitalism, and the Economics of Growth and Prosperity*. New Haven: Yale University Press, 2007.

Author Index